Miracle
MEN

Miracle
MEN

Hershiser, Gibson, and the Improbable 1988 Dodgers

Josh Suchon

TRIUMPH
BOOKS

Library of Congress Cataloging-in-Publication Data

Suchon, Josh, 1973–
  Miracle men : Hershiser, Gibson, and the improbable 1988 Dodgers / Josh Suchon.
     pages cm
  Includes bibliographical references and index.
  ISBN 978-1-60078-806-2
  1. Los Angeles Dodgers (Baseball team) 2. World Series (Baseball) (1988) 3. Hershiser, Orel. 4. Gibson, Kirk. I. Title.
  GV875.L6S838 2013
  796.357'640979494—dc23
                          2012048945

This book is available in quantity at special discounts for your group or organization. For further information, contact:

Triumph Books LLC
814 North Franklin Street
Chicago, Illinois 60610
Phone: (312) 337-0747
www.triumphbooks.com

Printed in U.S.A.
ISBN: 978-1-60078-806-2
Design by Patricia Frey
All photos courtesy of AP Images unless otherwise indicated

To my father, Frank Suchon

Contents

Foreword

The first time Josh Suchon approached me about writing a book on the 1988 Los Angeles Dodgers was Opening Day of the 2011 season. I said to him, "Think you've got a unique perspective?"

Josh detailed our famous exchange after Game 5 of the World Series in his introduction and how our lives have kept crossing since that day. Now here I am, writing the foreword to his book. Go figure, huh?

When we discussed possible topics, the word "legacy" kept coming up. On the 25th anniversary of that season, I thought I'd share with you what I think are some of the legacies of the 1988 Dodgers.

The biggest legacy of the 1988 Dodgers can be found in Chapter 19. It's all the people from that team who stayed in baseball. You have successful major league managers, coaches, broadcasters, and front-office executives. It's not limited to the major leagues, either. Some are coaching in the minor leagues or at colleges.

That illustrates the whole team's passion for the game, and the players' intelligence for the game. We loved the game. We loved playing. We loved competing. We loved studying the game. We played the game with a kid's enthusiasm and energy. To this day, we can't get enough of the game. We want to teach others and share our knowledge, the way it was passed down to us.

The legacy of Kirk Gibson's home run in Game 1 of the 1988 World Series is the guts he brought to our ballclub.

It started with the eye black that Jesse Orosco put on his hat in spring training. Gibson taught us it was cool to hustle, cool to care, that we would play every game with intensity, and that's what our team did all year. Then you fast-forward to his last at-bat of his year, when he should have never been up there, but he was, and he hit that home run.

Those were the bookends of the season. Everything between those two events is emblematic of the persona that Gibby made part of the Dodgers' culture.

The legacy of the 1988 Dodgers isn't just limited to the players. It's also the legacy of what a championship team does to a fan base and how it carries through the rest of their lives.

I can't tell you how many times people approach me, practically every day, and share with me their memories of that season. They tell me about watching a game at Dodger Stadium with their parents, or listening to Vin Scully on the radio in their backyard, or watching a game on television with their friends.

Since it was 25 years ago, we're talking about people who were kids at the time and are now adults. They're in their thirties or forties and now they take their kids to Dodger Stadium. They'll introduce their kids to me. They will tell their children about watching me pitch, or watching Gibby hit, or watching Saxy run the bases, or watching Tommy hug his players.

The feeling that Dodgers fans experienced in 1988 can never be taken away. Those memories are important. It's the lifeblood of being a fan.

Josh's book will enhance your memories. He's going to put a new spin on that season. He's going to tell you facts that you never knew and provide details that you had long forgotten.

Truth be told, this book is going to remind me of a lot of things that I'd forgotten about myself. It might be hard to believe, but there are a lot of things I don't remember about 1988. I pitched 18 years in the major leagues. They all start blending together after a while.

What I remember most from 1988 are the highlights that have been shown— over and over—like the final out of the scoreless streak, Mickey Hatcher's sprint around the bases after his home run, and Gibby's dramatic home run. But I couldn't tell you, in order, the opponents I faced during that streak. I was too focused on the next pitch, the next game, the next challenge for our team.

The last time I watched any of the games from the 1988 season was probably 12–13 years ago when I watched them with my son, Jordan, and those were the playoff games. I don't even know where those tapes are now. Yes, they are VHS tapes. That's how long ago it was. Those tapes are probably not in very good condition.

I've always lived my life in the present tense or in the future. Every day, I think I have something new to learn and accomplish. That's the attitude of our whole team. These are not guys who live in the past. That's why they keep accomplishing things.

That's why I've put some of the items from that season up for auction. My copy of that famous scouting report—that Dennis Eckersley would throw a 3–2 backdoor slider to left-handers, along with my handwritten notes on the A's hitters—was sold at an auction. Keith Olbermann bought it, in fact. We also had the baseball from the final out of the 59 scoreless innings streak auctioned off. Those items mean more to others than they do to me.

It's not that I don't care. I'm incredibly proud of what we accomplished. We weren't the best team on paper. But we consistently got timely clutch performances from everybody on that roster, we executed, and we played like the best team.

I still have some of the major awards: the Cy Young, the World Series ring, the Most Valuable Player trophies from the National League Championship Series and World Series, and the Sportsman of the Year award from *Sports Illustrated*. I'll keep those in my possession until I die, and then my kids can decide what to do with them. I just don't want to leave my kids with thousands of souvenirs one day.

The legacy of the scoreless innings streak might grow with each year, but I hope somebody breaks it. Some people might be surprised to hear that. But I truly do. Records are meant to be broken. I want another pitcher to experience what I was able to experience. I had my experience. It was an out-of-body experience. I'll be so happy for that pitcher. I'll be able to relive that moment with him, know exactly what he's feeling, and share a bond with him.

That's what Don Drysdale did with me. He was always so warm to me. He'd come down into the locker room to do an interview, and I'd always figure out a way to make him stay around a little longer. I would listen to him and hang on his every word, trying to get some information from him or some encouragement from him.

The longer the scoreless streak continued, I noticed that Don avoided me. I can't remember exactly when it started. It was probably around 30 innings or so. It was almost like a no-hitter was going on for weeks and weeks. Don didn't want to bring it up, or jinx me, or put pressure on me. My teammates were the same.

When I broke Drysdale's record, his smile was big and genuine. I knew he was happy for me. I hope that one day I can share that moment with the pitcher who breaks my record.

The final legacy of the 1988 Dodgers is a frustrating one, as Dodgers fans are well aware, since it's the last time the franchise won a world championship. I'm sure all of us former Dodgers are pulling for that day to happen again—and soon. We had a dream season in 1988. We made great friendships that will always exist. We have great memories of that year, and this book will rekindle many more memories.

We'd like to see the current generation of Dodgers players, coaches, and executives bring another World Series to Los Angeles, spray each other with champagne, hug each other, raise a trophy above their heads, taste the fruits of victory, and celebrate that moment with the fans.

Who knows, maybe when that day happens, a teenage kid will be in the stands watching—and 25 years later he'll write a book to chronicle that season, too.

—Orel Hershiser, September 2012

Acknowledgments

This book is dedicated to my dad, Frank Suchon, and I want to start by thanking him. My childhood laid the groundwork for my career as a writer and broadcaster. That wouldn't be possible without my dad. He took me to hundreds of games at the Oakland Coliseum and Candlestick Park.

We flew to Arizona during my freshman and sophomore years of high school, including 1988, for a week of spring training games. In 1990, we did a father-son baseball trip before my senior year to experience Wrigley Field, the old Comiskey Park, Tiger Stadium, the National Baseball Hall of Fame, the old Yankee Stadium, and Fenway Park.

Dad patiently drove me to baseball card shops and shows, waited as I got autographs, paid for tons of photos to get developed that I took with my camera, coached most of my Little League baseball teams, taught me how to keep score, and encouraged me to pursue my passion for baseball. He also left me at the Coliseum one fateful night, which triggered my unique relationship with Orel Hershiser and the inspiration for this book.

My partners in crime at the Coliseum in those teenage years were Foothill High classmates Corey Kell, Joe Pereira, Chris Poulson, Jim Putt, and Todd Strong. If it wasn't for Kell, I'd never know that Hershiser told me to grab a bat.

I'm grateful to everybody who was so generous with their time and sharing their memories with me for this book. That list includes: Dave Anderson, Don

Baylor, Tim Belcher, Brett Butler, Fred Claire, Ned Colletti, Steve Dilbeck, Alfredo Griffin, Ken Gurnick, Paul Gutierrez, Ron Hassey, Mickey Hatcher, Orel Hershiser, Jaime Jarrin, Mike Krukow, Tim Leary, Mike Marshall, Gary Miller, Mitch Poole, Steve Sax, Mike Scioscia, Vin Scully, John Shelby, Franklin Stubbs, Fernando Valenzuela, Steve Vucinich, Fred Wallin, Bob Welch, Tracy Woodson, and Toby Zwidek.

Claire was one of my first interviews, and the book wouldn't be the same without his candid reflections on how that team was built. The same goes for Belcher, Hatcher, Shelby, Leary, and Sax (whose energy is still contagious). When Scully thanks you for talking to him about 1988 and says he's eager to read your book, well... that's just pure goose bumps.

Then there's Hershiser. Honestly, I hated him as a kid. I didn't want to like him as an adult. But it's impossible not to like him. The magnitude of what Hershiser did in 1988 has been somewhat forgotten, perhaps because Kirk Gibson's home run is so unforgettable. I hope this book does justice to Hershiser's mind-boggling accomplishments that year.

Current Dodgers employees Cindy Adler, Yvonne Carrasco, Jon Chapper, Garrett Joe Jarrick, and Mark Langill were extremely helpful in securing interviews, press credentials, and research. So were Tim Mead with the Angels and Debbie Gallas with the Oakland A's.

The websites Baseball-Reference.com and Retrosheet.org are the greatest tools ever given to baseball writers. Without these sites, this book either wouldn't exist or would be filled with factual mistakes. The next time that readers of this book visit those websites, I'd encourage them to sponsor a page.

I'm forever in debt to the *Los Angeles Times* for making its archives available online, for free, and being so well organized. That newspaper's entire sports section was a daily masterpiece in 1988. It made researching this book fun and easy.

Dodgers beat reporter Sam McManis was an ironman that year. When did he ever take a day off? His coverage was rich with details, full of drama, and always balanced. Bill Plaschke's playoff coverage and his story of Don Drysdale on the night Hershiser broke the record showed why he was a future media superstar. National baseball writer Ross Newhan, columnist Scott Ostler, and the legendary Jim Murray delivered features and opinions that helped me bring 1988 back to life.

Peter Gammons' reporting in *Sports Illustrated* was an incredible resource. His late 1987 article about the lowly state of the Dodgers' organization helped the off-season chapter come together, and his Sportsman of the Year article on Hershiser assisted in telling the story of Hershiser's life in the six shutout chapters.

Ken Levine, Josh Rawitch, and David Feldman are friends who read a few chapters of this book, providing feedback and encouragement. Matt Hurst read the entire book, even when his own life was incredibly busy and he had much better things to do. His line-by-line notes caught many mistakes. I can't thank them enough for their overall excitement for the project.

Adam Motin at Triumph Books told me, "We like this story and we like your credentials." Those are the best words an author can hear and inspired me to reward that confidence.

I'd also like to thank my agent, Debbie Spander, for putting up with the hundreds of emails I send her every month, Ben Platt for getting me rare videos from the 1988 season, Jerry Gardner for having audio of the final out of Hershiser's scoreless streak, Eric Winter for his advice and being the big brother I never had, and my mom for always being my biggest cheerleader (even if she never cared much for baseball).

Introduction

The Los Angeles Dodgers broke my heart in 1988. I was 15 years old and a rabid fan of the Oakland Athletics. My real home was Pleasanton, California, a suburb 20 miles east of Oakland. But my practical home was the Oakland Coliseum.

My dad annually bought tickets to 20 games from a friend of his who had season tickets. The seats were amazing: Section 123, Row 2, Seats 12 and 13—on the aisle, just to the left of the A's dugout.

Even when we didn't have those choice seats, I'd go to games with a handful of good friends from Foothill High. We'd take the bus from Hopyard Road in Pleasanton to the Hayward BART station and ride it for three stops to the Coliseum exit. We'd leave right after school, arriving to get autographs in the parking lot, chase down batting practice home runs, watch the game, and stay late for more autographs.

We'd buy $2 bleacher seats or third-deck seats (I could pass for under age 12 to buy half-price tickets that cost $3). Then we'd think of creative ways to annoy the ushers by sneaking into seats that didn't belong to us.

I went to 53 regular season games in 1988. I know that number precisely. I saved the ticket stub from each game and kept them in my wallet, chronologically. If somebody at school didn't believe me, I'd show the ticket stubs for proof. If there was a day game, my friends and I usually skipped school to attend. Sometimes our parents knew. Usually, they didn't know.

When the 1988 playoffs began, I skipped school to watch Game 1 of the American League Championship Series against the Boston Red Sox on TV at home. I went to Game 4 of that series in Oakland and chanted "SWEEEEEEP" along with the sellout crowd.

For the World Series, I watched Games 1 and 2 from home. When the series shifted to Oakland, I snuck into Game 3 without a ticket. It was actually miserable not having a seat and walking around the whole game looking for an empty seat. I barely saw Mark McGwire's game-winning home run off Jay Howell. I watched Game 4 at home when the A's fell behind 3–1 and was dreading the elimination game.

We had tickets for Game 5. As usual, I took public transportation to the game with friends (who had seats elsewhere) and met my dad at "the good seats." I remember getting Bobby McFerrin's autograph in the parking lot before the game, and he wrote, "Don't Worry Be Happy." Still, I was worried. It felt like going to a funeral. I knew this night would end miserably for my beloved A's.

Sometime around the seventh inning, when the end was inevitable, my dad was losing his patience. Can't remember exactly what he yelled, but it must have been awesome and totally inappropriate because I vividly recall Mary Hart, from *Entertainment Tonight* fame, hearing it and turning around to see who would say such a thing.

In the ninth inning, my dad had seen enough. He wasn't going to watch the Dodgers celebrate on "our" field. He was leaving. I wanted to stay, just in case. After what Kirk Gibson did in Game 1, I wasn't going to miss the A's comeback. The conversation went something like this:

Dad: "We're leaving."

Me: "We should stay. You never know."

Dad: "If you want to stay, find your own way home."

Me: "Fine. I will."

Honestly, I didn't really think he'd leave. But he did. This wasn't poor parenting. Remember, I went to games without adult supervision routinely. We were experts at taking public transportation. Plus, one of my friends worked in the visitor's clubhouse, and he had a car, so there was a ride home available.

The A's didn't have a miracle comeback in them. Orel Hershiser finished them off in the ninth inning. I watched the inning with red eyes. When I saw the Dodgers celebrating on the field, tears filled my eyes and ran down my cheeks.

Eventually, I'd wipe the tears off my face and wander around the stadium in a daze. Instinctively, I walked toward the hallway that leads to the clubhouses and ran into my friend Corey Kell. His favorite player was Tony Phillips, who struck out to end the game, and I remember Corey saying he gave "TP" a standing ovation for what might have been his last at-bat with the A's.

I remember thinking everything about life sucked right then. The A's had lost the World Series to the Dodgers. I was going to be ridiculed at school for all the boasting I'd done. I owed a lot of money to kids from bets that I made. And, oh yeah, I had to find my own way home because I was stubborn.

Worst of all, baseball season was over. No more games to attend. No more school to cut. No more autographs to obtain. No more BP home runs to chase. No more fun.

As these thoughts swirled in my head, I was just about to start crying again. Then I heard a commotion. Security guards were clearing the way. Somebody was behind them.

It was Hershiser.

Before I even realized what was happening, I yelled, "You were lucky, Hershiser!" as he walked by, trailed by reporters as he was taken to the interview room.

◆ ◆ ◆ ◆

I'm guessing it was about a week later when my friend Corey Kell called me after school. The conversation went something like this:

Corey: "You get the new *Sports Illustrated* in the mail today?"

Me: "Yeah."

Corey: "Did you read it?"

Me: "Hell no. Why would I want to read about Hershiser beating us?"

Corey: "You should read the final paragraph on page 37."

I hung up the phone, grabbed a copy of the magazine, and couldn't believe what Peter Gammons wrote:

"But the Bulldog in him came out when, after the Athletics were disposed of, he walked down the hallway to the interview room in the Oakland Coliseum and an A's fan yelled, 'You were lucky, Hershiser!' A couple of dozen steps later, Hershiser blurted out, 'Oh yeah—grab a bat.' He wasn't smiling."

Only one person on the planet knew that I was the idiot who told Hershiser—after 59 consecutive scoreless innings and after dismantling the Mets and A's in the playoffs—that he was lucky.

It was Corey Kell. It just so happened Corey had a subscription to *Sports Illustrated*. And unlike me, he decided to read the magazine. If it wasn't for Corey, I'd have probably thrown the issue in the trash and never known about the paragraph.

At least my name wasn't used. But the only thing worse than knowing that my words were in the most famous sports magazine in the world, saying something utterly stupid, was that Hershiser taunted me by saying, "grab a bat."

I'd never heard the "grab a bat" line. We were walking opposite directions and he was past me in a second. I'm sure security tossed me out of the way, as well.

◆ ◆ ◆ ◆

Seven years later, in 1995, I was doing a summer internship at ESPN in Bristol, Connecticut. It was a Sunday afternoon and I was in the cafeteria alone when I spotted baseball reporter Peter Gammons. We were the only two people in there. I was about to turn 22 years old. If the place had been full of people, I'd have never approached him.

But I had to tell him about the article he wrote in 1988 and ask if he remembered some kid yelling that Hershiser was lucky.

Gammons remembered it well. We spent the next 30 minutes talking about Hershiser, Kirk Gibson, that series, the 1989 World Series, the earthquake, and how Gammons will always remember Dave Stewart going down to the site of the collapsed freeways to bring coffee and donuts to workers as they searched for bodies.

Six years later, in 2001, it was my second year as the San Francisco Giants beat writer for the *Oakland Tribune*. I was now 28 years old. I'd told the story to a couple of my colleagues, and they thought it was hilarious. One of them was Jeff Fletcher, who worked at the *Santa Rosa Press Democrat* at the time, and sat next to me in the press box.

One day during batting practice, Fletcher told me that he was here. Who? Hershiser.

The conversation went something like this:

Fletch: "You have to tell him the story."

Me: "Really? Do I really have to do it?"

Fletch: "Yes."

Hershiser was there as a TV analyst for ESPN. Bashfully, my heart racing, I went over and introduced myself—first, as a reporter. Then I told him that I was the kid who told him he was lucky. Hershiser was more excited than me to hear this story.

His response was something like this: "No way! This is awesome! We need a bat! Who's got a bat? We need a picture! My wife would love this! We need a photo for my wife. This is awesome!"

Hershiser went on to say he always regretted saying, "Grab a bat." He was reminded of the famous Coke commercial with "Mean" Joe Greene when he threw a jersey to the kid. He wanted to throw something toward me. But it was too late. He was whisked away, and I was gone.

Honestly, I thought it was a bunch of crap. But I appreciated Hershiser being so kind and saying something nice.

In 2006, I was the A's beat reporter at the *Trib*, and Hershiser was one of the candidates to be their new manager. We talked on the phone before his job interview, and we both laughed at how hysterical it would be if he got the job and one of the reporters covering him was the kid who called him lucky.

Deep down, we both knew Bob Geren was going to get the job—and Geren did. A few months later, I decided it was time to switch careers. I left the newspaper business and became a minor league play-by-play announcer for the Modesto Nuts.

♦ ♦ ♦ ♦

It's strange how often life comes full circle.

A year after leaving the majors for the minors, I was back in the majors, this time as the reporter for the Dodgers Radio Network and the cohost of *Post Game Dodger Talk* after every game on 790 KABC in Los Angeles. I held that job from 2008–11.

A few times every year, I'd run into Hershiser. Whenever possible, I wouldn't say hello. I'd just walk past him and say, "You were lucky, Hershiser" without stopping. It always made us laugh. Then we'd end up talking more and invariably tell the story again to whoever was around us.

The first time I got the idea to write this book was during the 2009 playoffs. I was on the Dodgers' charter flight to Philadelphia and was reading Joe Posnanski's magnificent book on the 1975 Reds, *The Machine*.

I wanted to write a similar book about a World Series champion from decades past. It seemed only natural to write about the 1988 Dodgers. That team crushed me as a teenager living in the Bay Area. But as an adult now living in Los Angeles, I could appreciate what an incredible story it would be to tell.

When I told Hershiser about this book, I could see what made him such a good teammate. He thought it was a great idea and encouraged me to do it. He made sure I had his cell phone number. When Hershiser entered my number into his iPhone, he typed "you were lucky" as my company name.

In the summer of 2012, as I worked on this book, I paid Hershiser a visit at Angel Stadium before a game he broadcasted on ESPN. When our conversation was over, I started to walk away and Orel stopped me.

"Hey Josh," he said, "grab a bat."

This time, he was smiling.

Chapter 1

The Off-Season

October 1987 to February 1988

Before the improbable streak, before the impossible home run, there was the indispensable reality: the Dodgers were a franchise in turmoil.

It wasn't just that the Dodgers finished with back-to-back losing seasons for the first time since 1967–68, or that they were under .500 for the third time in four years, or that their longtime rivals in San Francisco won the division title in 1987.

Just as concerning, the Dodgers were losing the interest of a city that fell in instant love when they arrived in 1958 but now had flashier, cooler, and better sports teams taking away attention.

The Lakers ruled the town. From 1980–87, the Lakers won four NBA titles and lost in the finals twice. They were the odds-on favorite to win again in 1988 (and did), behind the Showtime stars of Magic Johnson, Kareem Abdul-Jabbar, and James Worthy.

The Raiders were arguably the second-most popular team in town. They won the Super Bowl played in 1984, their second year in town. They weren't a threat to win another Super Bowl in 1987, but the NFL was the most popular sport in the country, the Raider lifestyle resonated in urban areas and the suburbs, and they now had a star—albeit a part-time star—in running back Bo Jackson.

Attendance at Dodger Stadium was down, at least by L.A. standards. The Dodgers drew less than 2.8 million fans in 1987 for an average of 34,536 a game. That still ranked third-best in the National League.

But the 1987 season was the first non-strike season the Dodgers had finished with less than 3 million fans in attendance since 1979. They'd led the league in attendance 10 straight years and for 13 of the last 14. Now they were bad and boring, and the fans were looking elsewhere for entertainment.

"In '86 and '87, we were awful," infielder Dave Anderson reflected. "We needed to make some changes."

In mid-August 1987, Peter Gammons penned a 2,969-word scathing indictment on the state of the Dodgers for *Sports Illustrated*. The headline, "Oh For Those Glory Days of Yesteryear." The subhead, "The Dodgers have lost the way that Branch Rickey laid out for them, and the future could be threadbare."

Al Campanis, the Dodgers' general manager since 1968, was fired after making racist comments live on ABC's *Nightline* early in the 1987 season. The firestorm over his racial remarks glossed over a painful truth: he'd been terrible on the job for the last half-decade.

The vaunted Dodgers farm system was no longer producing stars. Actually, it was. Those stars just weren't staying in Los Angeles because of poor trades.

Rick Sutcliffe was traded to the Indians in 1981 for Jorge Orta and two minor leaguers who never did anything. Sutcliffe was an All-Star in 1983, and he won the Cy Young Award in 1984 for the Chicago Cubs. Ted Power was traded to the Reds in 1982 for Mike Ramsey. The durable Power led the league in appearances in 1984 and racked up 27 saves in 1985.

John Franco was traded to the Reds in 1983 for Rafael Landestoy. Franco was an All-Star in 1986 and 1987. Dave Stewart was traded to the Rangers in 1983 for Rick Honeycutt. Stewart needed two more organizations to find himself, but he'd just won 20 games for the A's.

Sid Fernandez was traded to the Mets in 1983 for Carlos Diaz and Bob Bailor. Fernandez was an All-Star in 1986 and 1987, helping the Mets to the 1986 World Series championship. Candy Maldonado was traded to the Giants in 1985 for Alex Trevino. Maldonado hit 20 homers and drove in 85 runs, while batting fifth as the Giants won the 1987 division title.

The recent Dodgers drafts weren't any better, and scouting director Ben Wade was taking a ton of heat. Pitcher Dennis Livingston, the first-round pick in 1984,

2

was a bust who never reached the majors. Outfielder Michael White, the first-round pick in 1986, quit baseball a year later. He came back and played for seven years in the minors. Pitcher Dan Opperman, the first-round pick in 1987, blew out his arm in his first minor league bullpen session.

Going back further, the Dodgers brought a high school outfielder from their own backyard for a tryout at Dodger Stadium in 1980. Mike Brito, the same scout who signed Fernando Valenzuela, recommended they draft the kid from South Central. Despite an impressive tryout, the Dodgers ignored Brito's recommendation. Instead, the Reds drafted Eric Davis in the eighth round.

Wade claimed the Dodgers would have drafted a highly touted pitcher from the University of Texas in 1983. But because of Steve Howe's ongoing drug problems, there was a need for a left-handed reliever who could be in the majors soon. So the Dodgers selected lefty Erik Sonberg from Wichita State with the 18th pick.

With the 19th pick, the Red Sox drafted Roger Clemens.

It isn't known if that claim by Wade is the truth or revisionist history by somebody trying to deflect criticism elsewhere. Wade, who overall had a distinguished career with more scouting hits than misses, retired in 1990 and passed away in 2002.

Just about every poor decision was blamed on Howe, and usually it was true. Cardinals manager Whitey Herzog told Gammons, "[Howe] screwed them up more than any one player screwed up any other organization."

Believing that Howe was recovered from his drug problems in 1983, the Dodgers figured a minor league lefty was expendable and made the Franco-for-Landestoy trade. In fairness, Franco hadn't developed the screwball that would make him an All-Star closer. Why they'd even want Landestoy was another topic. He was coming off a .189/.250/.243 slash line.

Howe's departure for drug rehab forced Ken Howell into a closer role sooner than he was probably ready. Howe's third drug suspension forced the Fernandez-for-Diaz trade. Diaz couldn't fill the need in the bullpen. He had one awful year, two bad years, and was released after 1986.

The snowball impact of Howe continued. Needing a lefty reliever, the Dodgers sent backup catcher Steve Yeager to the Mariners in 1985 for lefty Ed Vande Berg. That didn't work, and Vande Berg was released a year later. Meanwhile, a backup catcher was now needed, so the Dodgers made the Maldonado-for-Trevino swap.

3

Not every trade was Howe's fault. After the 1981 World Series title—which Howe closed out—the vaunted infield of Ron Cey at third, Bill Russell at short, Davey Lopes at second, and Steve Garvey at first was broken up.

Lopes was traded to make room for Steve Sax—a wise decision. Lopes was 36 years old and didn't have much trade value. Still, all they got in return from the Oakland A's was a minor leaguer named Lance Hudson, who never played in the majors.

After the 1982 season, when Joe Morgan's home run on the final day of the season eliminated the Dodgers, the corner infielders departed. Greg Brock would take over at first base. Pedro Guerrero would play third base.

Garvey signed a five-year contract with the Padres and led them to the 1984 World Series. Cey, who still had three good years left in him, was traded to the Cubs for minor leaguer Dan Cataline and pitcher Vance Lovelace—neither had any impact in the majors. At least Lovelace is now one of current general manager Ned Colletti's more trusted talent evaluators.

There was fighting within the farm system, too.

Tommy Lasorda commented during the tumultuous 1987 season that there weren't any replacements coming out of the farm system. Terry Collins, then the Triple A manager at Albuquerque, fired back, "That's his opinion. Sometimes I think what Tommy Lasorda is doing is wrong. But that's his decision, and he's going to have to live with it."

There was another problem with the farm system, and while it's convenient to connect the dots to Howe, it was a widespread problem throughout all of society— substance abuse, specifically drugs and alcohol.

The story would get buried come October for obvious reasons, but the context is important to note as the 1987–88 off-season was beginning. The Associated Press quoted Dr. Forrest Tennant, the Dodgers' drug adviser, as telling a Rotary Club in Alaska, "The drug problem wiped us out."

Tennant said minor leaguers brought cocaine, marijuana, and alcohol onto the field, into the dugout, and into their hotel rooms. He said in 1983, 45 percent of the Dodgers' minor league players tested positive for marijuana, cocaine, or a high level of alcohol.

By 1988, that number was less than two percent. It's impossible to know what impact the unchecked drug and alcohol problem had on the Dodgers' minor league teams earlier in the decade. Certainly, it didn't help the shaky development track record.

Then there was the matter of Lasorda's well-documented longing for the GM job and powers that Fred Claire now held. Lasorda always denied that he was looking for a dual manager-GM job, saying he turned down millions from the Yankees and Braves. The industry thought otherwise.

But even Lasorda's star had faded. The second-guessing from his decision to not intentionally walk Jack Clark in the 1985 playoffs was still fresh in people's minds. He was entering the final season of his contract, and no extension was offered in the off-season. Lasorda's future was filled with more question marks than ever.

Claire went into his first off-season as general manager needing to fill a lot of holes. The farm system wasn't bursting with potential answers. The industry had its doubts about Claire, based on his background. The press reviews of his first five months of the job weren't kind, and optimism wasn't high for the future.

"I was never swayed by what was written or what was said," Claire reflected. "That didn't really have a major impact on what I saw that needed to be done. There was a lot written because of Steve Howe and the problems he had, that it set off a whole scenario of problems that you mentioned. I don't prescribe to that feeling. In Steve's case, it was very sad because it was drugs that played the role that totally derailed his career and caused his life to end too soon. But you have players with injuries, players with remarkable ability who simply aren't able to break through. No matter whatever happens, your job as an organization is not to dwell on that; it's to move on and fix it. There were a number of things that happened, but I didn't see that as a burden that we'd have to bear moving forward."

Claire didn't even know how long he would be the general manager. He'd been on the job for five months, didn't have a multiyear contract, and didn't have any public reassurances from owner Peter O'Malley.

"The [reporters] would ask Peter O'Malley, 'How long does he have the job?' and Peter would say, 'He has it today,'" Claire reflected. "I figured that's what I had. From day one, that's how I looked at the job, 'I got it today.' I'm going to do everything I can today to make our team better."

Claire told O'Malley they had three areas to address that off-season: a shortstop, a closer, and a left-handed reliever. In the last two years, they couldn't close games and they couldn't catch the ball at shortstop. If they didn't fix those holes, they wouldn't win.

◆ ◆ ◆ ◆

It was one of those rarest of trades where everybody was getting rid of players they no longer needed and everybody got better.

It was announced on December 11, 1987, at the Baseball Winter Meetings— the same day Magic Johnson baby hooked a shot off the glass to beat the Celtics at the buzzer inside the Boston Garden. The trade involved eight players, and seven were pitchers. All three teams had either recently been in the playoffs or felt they were one or two pieces from making the playoffs.

The Dodgers sent starting pitcher Bob Welch and lefty reliever Matt Young to the A's and minor league pitcher Jack Savage to the Mets. The Dodgers received shortstop Alfredo Griffin and closer Jay Howell from the A's, plus lefty reliever Jesse Orosco from the Mets. The A's also sent minor league pitchers Kevin Tapani and Wally Whitehurst to the Mets.

The A's didn't need Griffin because they had rookie Walt Weiss ready to take over at shortstop. They didn't want Howell closing out games because he was coming off an injury, the fans hated him, and they were going to experiment with Dennis Eckersley as their closer (against his own wishes, by the way).

The Mets didn't want Orosco because he wasn't the same after his 1986 playoff heroics, manager Davey Johnson didn't trust him, the fans constantly booed him, his contract was for $1 million, and everybody thought he was hurt. In return, they got three pitching prospects. The prize of the trio turned out to be Tapani.

The Dodgers didn't need Young because he wasn't very effective and they were getting Orosco. They didn't want to get rid of Welch. But they had young pitchers ready to contribute to the rotation, and they needed to give up something to stabilize the bullpen and the middle of their infield.

It was the fourth straight year the Dodgers traded for a left-handed reliever to fill the void of Steve Howe in the bullpen. Howe's drug use had cost the Dodgers wins, money, respect, and top prospects. Now, it cost them the highly popular, very talented, and very hyper Bob Welch. Tommy Lasorda said he cried at the decision.

Claire addressed his team's biggest needs at shortstop and the bullpen. But all three new players were either coming off an injury or suspected to be hurt. The national reviews were not kind, as illustrated by Gammons' review in his "winners and losers" column from the Winter Meetings.

"'The meetings were Fred Claire's *Nightline*,' wrote one observer, referring to the Waterloo of Claire's GM predecessor, Al Campanis. Claire was publicly ripped by other club officials for being 'unprepared' and 'unprofessional.' The Dodgers ended up trading Welch, Young, and a good young reliever (Jack Savage) for Griffin, a 30-year-old (or older) shortstop with his left thumb in a cast; Howell, a sore-armed reliever; and Orosco, who carries a $1 million contract and was available for the asking."

Claire knew his performance was being watched closely. He wasn't a scout. He wasn't a traditional baseball man. The other general managers in baseball weren't chummy with him. He was not only a rookie. He was a former sportswriter-turned-publicist who inherited the GM job after Campanis' meltdown on live TV eight months previous.

It was widely known in the meetings that Claire would entertain offers for Welch. But no trade was made after a few days. Throughout the hotel hallways, GMs and other baseball front-office men whispered about Claire's inexperience. They said he was afraid to make a move. The headlines said that Claire was holding up the trades at the winter meetings.

Claire defended himself to the Los Angeles media: "It wasn't our intention to hold up the meetings, and I don't think we did.… Everyone has a right to their opinion, but we haven't intended to do anything but improve the club and keep people informed. We identified our needs and stayed after them.… Whatever judgments or comments have been made, that's up to others, but we never once told another club not to do anything until they talked to us again.… Some clubs may have decided that we had the player they wanted and that they didn't want to talk to any other club, but that's their decision.… The bottom line is that in any trade discussion there are many factors. Some are more complicated than others, and many of those go beyond the basic issue of player evaluation."

The Blue Jays were interested in Welch. As a Blue Jays staff member told the *L.A. Times*, "We'd give them two names, and they'd want three. We'd give them three names, and they'd want four," Blue Jays GM Pat Gillick stated on the record. "The Dodgers have a new general manager. They may be moving slowly because of that."

The rumor at the time was that the Blue Jays were offering shortstop Manny Lee and pitcher Dave Stieb. The Dodgers asked for lefty John Cerutti instead, because they were concerned about Stieb's health and his contract, which had seven years remaining and an escalating salary. The Blue Jays wanted a combination of Welch and a skinny 19-year-old kid who pitched in the Florida State League. His name was Ramon Martinez. The Dodgers weren't trading Ramon Martinez.

One night, when the Dodgers called the Blue Jays, they were told Pat Gillick had gone to bed early. Claire felt he was being strung along. He moved on.

The Mets wanted Welch. They dangled Orosco, outfielder Mookie Wilson, and shortstop Rafael Santana. The Dodgers wanted Rick Aguilera instead of Wilson. If Aguilera was involved, the Mets wanted Ramon Martinez. Again, the Dodgers weren't trading Ramon Martinez.

"There did seem to be some indecision and confusion there," Mets executive vice president Joe McIlvaine said, before the trade. "We thought we had a deal, kept waiting for an answer, and never heard. We're dealing with new people. They're afraid to put the pedal to the metal."

By late Friday afternoon, the final day of the winter meetings, it appeared Claire would head home without making a trade.

What made the trade possible was that Fred Claire and Athletics general manager Sandy Alderson were avid runners. At various baseball meetings, the two would run together and developed a friendship. At the 1987 winter meetings in Dallas, Claire and Alderson did their usual run and got lost at one point. When they returned to the hotel, it was pitch black and much later than expected.

Two days after trading minor league pitchers Jose Rijo and Tim Birtsas for soon-to-be designated hitter Dave Parker, the Athletics made a push for Welch. When a deal couldn't be reached involving two teams, they got creative and included the Mets.

As Thursday night turned to early Friday morning on December 11, the blockbuster three-team deal was almost complete in the Dodgers' suite. Then Lasorda spoke up.

"We can't give up Savage," Lasorda said.

"Yes we can, Tommy," Claire said. "We didn't come this far to let Jack Savage stand in the way of this deal."

Claire remembered a conversation he had with trusted scout Carl Loewenstine, who told him, "I don't think Savage will ever be the type of pitcher who will make a difference for anybody."

Claire asked scout Reggie Otero, who signed Griffin out of the Dominican Republic in 1973 at age 16, "Would you give up Bobby Welch in a deal that would bring us Alfredo Griffin?"

Without hesitation Otero said, "Fred, I'd do it."

♦ ♦ ♦ ♦

Another trade was still on the table. It involved fewer players, but it was a bigger blockbuster—Pedro Guerrero for Kirk Gibson, straight up.

The Dodgers were tired of Guerrero's act. Yes, he produced. But the stories of his partying ways are legendary. As one longtime member of the organization recalled, "Those trips to San Francisco, he would go wild. Wow."

Guerrero admitted, in 2010, that he cared more about partying than baseball for most of his career. In addition, management felt Guerrero was a horrible influence on the team's young Latin players. Defensively, he was a below-average left fielder and a liability everywhere else.

"I really liked Pedro," Claire reflected. "I can remember when we signed him to a significant contract. I told him, 'Pedro, look, after you get the biggest house, after you get the biggest car, think about what you want to represent.' I don't think Pedro, because all of what was happening with his celebrity, I don't know that message got through. I do know this: Pedro was a remarkable hitter, but I'd see him walk down the tunnel way with a cup of coffee and a cigarette, and I'd say to myself, 'This is not the guy, and with his lifestyle, this is not the player I want being the influence for our young players.' That's not the way, in my view, that we're going to approach the game. As much as I recognized his talent, he wasn't the leader that I wanted."

The Tigers were ready to depart with Gibson. He feuded with Tigers owner Tom Monaghan, who felt his production was starting to slip, he was missing more and more games with injuries, and he wasn't very good defensively, and it drove Monaghan crazy to see Gibson's perpetually shaggy facial hair. Gibson even hinted it was time for him to move on, after his contract expired.

The hiccup was that Gibson was the central figure in the collusion cases from the 1985 and 1986 off-seasons. He was the premier free agent of the 1985 winter market, but a bidding war never took place. Gibson could have been declared an immediate free agent, or received financial compensation, or both.

The Dodgers needed certain protections from the Tigers or the owners' Player Relations Committee before they'd agree to the Guerrero-for-Gibson trade. Claire talked to Tigers general manager Bill Lajoie numerous times during the Winter Meetings.

"I called him one morning after a long meeting the previous day, and they said Bill had checked out of the hotel," Claire reflected. "I think he decided, perhaps for good reasons, this was too much to try and do at this time. There were too many unknowns. We weren't just making a trade based on ability, 'I'll trade you this player.' There were a lot of unknowns."

Speculation was the Dodgers would extend Gibson's contract by another 2–3 years, if he waived his penalty rights. The other protection discussed was whether or not the Tigers would return Guerrero to Los Angeles if Gibson was declared a free agent.

The decision was as much in the hands of the lawyers and the accountants as it was in the hands of the baseball men.

◆ ◆ ◆ ◆

Fred Claire needed a fax machine.

It was 10:00 PM on the night of Monday, December 14 and Claire was trying to find one at Dodger Stadium. The fax machine—the only fax machine—was in the stadium's library. Claire didn't have keys to the library. The publicity department usually had the keys but couldn't find them.

Free-agent outfielder Mike Davis was close to signing a contract with the New York Yankees. Claire didn't want Davis in the Bronx. Claire wanted him patrolling right field at Dodger Stadium. Claire wanted him so bad that he called a locksmith to come out to Dodger Stadium late at night to unlock the door to the library.

Once inside, Claire wired a facsimile of a proposed contract to Jonathan Moseley, the assistant to Louis Burrell, the agent who represented Davis. The contract was for two years and $1.95 million.

Davis thought he was going to New York. It's not like he wanted to go there. The Yankees hadn't reached the playoffs in six years. The fans were brutal, constantly booing Dave Winfield. Davis was born and raised in San Diego. He was drafted by the Oakland A's in the third round of the 1977 draft. He was a California kid.

But the A's no longer wanted him. They traded for Dave Parker and were moving Jose Canseco to right field. Billy Martin said, "I want that kid." So did George Steinbrenner.

Then came the late-night fax.

That was proof how badly the Dodgers wanted Davis—and it didn't hurt that the Dodgers' offer was slightly higher than the Yankees' offer. Instead of signing with the Yankees, Davis flew to Los Angeles and signed with the Dodgers.

Davis hit a combined 43 home runs and stole 51 bases in 1985 and 1986. He was hitting .292 with 20 home runs in 1987 at the All-Star break, coming into his own as a star at age 28. Oakland fans wanted him representing their team as they hosted their first All-Star Game. Davis was snubbed. Jay Howell and rookie Mark McGwire were the A's representatives.

On the first game after the All-Star break, Davis kicked a dugout door at Fenway Park, suffered a hyperextended knee, missed the next three games, and never fully healed. He hit two home runs and batted .224 over his final 214 plate appearances.

Davis would play right field for the Dodgers. Did this mean Mike Marshall or Pedro Guerrero were expendable? Claire insisted no. One would play left field. The other would play first base. Besides, Claire wanted the depth. He said at the time Davis brought, "power and one of the best arms in the game. He wants to play every day."

◆ ◆ ◆ ◆

Since the three-way trade that sent Bob Welch out of Los Angeles, Fred Claire knew he needed another starting pitcher. Fernando Valenzuela and Orel Hershiser were a solid 1-2 punch. After that, it was question marks.

Tim Leary was a former No. 2 overall pick in the 1979 draft. He'd spent parts of six years in the majors. The Dodgers acquired him after the 1986 season from the Milwaukee Brewers, along with Tim Crews, after finally giving up on the enigma that was first baseman Greg Brock.

Leary responded by going 3–11 with a 4.76 ERA while giving up 121 hits in 107⅔ innings. If this had been the Dodgers from the late 1970s, he wouldn't have stayed in the majors. But this was a sub-.500 team, and he was versatile. Leary started 12 games, relieved in 27, and that swingman role had his name written all over it again in 1988.

Tim Belcher was a promising rookie. He looked good in a six-game, five-start audition in 1987. But that was September, and he was unproven.

Sean Hillegas was another promising kid who was also unproven. The fourth overall pick of the 1984 secondary draft, Hillegas would be 23 years old. He was 4–3 with a 3.57 ERA in 12 games (10 starts) as a rookie in 1987. He struck out 51 in 58 innings but also walked 31.

Alejandro Pena and Ken Howell were also possibilities for the starting rotation. But they were probably better suited in the bullpen. There was also that tall skinny kid tearing it up in the minors that every team at the Winter Meetings wanted. Ramon Martinez would not be traded. But he wouldn't be ready by Opening Day, either.

Claire wanted a veteran for his starting rotation. To get him, Claire dipped into the Dodgers' past and made some modern-day concessions.

The media was called to a downtown restaurant on January 5 to introduce reliever Jesse Orosco to the team. When they saw Don Sutton, the joke—half-serious, half-joking—was that Sutton was joining the broadcast booth or some other front-office position. Nope.

The 42-year-old Sutton had debuted with the Dodgers in 1966, was taught his curveball by Sandy Koufax, left after the 1980 season as a free agent, played with the Astros, Brewers, Athletics, and Angels, and was now signed to pitch for the Dodgers.

Under the leadership of Al Campanis, the Dodgers didn't include performance incentives to contracts. The last time they'd done that was 1976, when Tommy John received incentive clauses in his return from a never-before-tried elbow surgery that revolutionized sports medicine.

Sutton had earned $890,000 the year before with the Angels—$550,000 in salary and another $340,000 for incentives based on games started. He went 11–11 with a 4.70 ERA, averaged 5⅔ innings per start, and was held to 100 pitches per start by Angels manager Gene Mauch at a time when pitch counts were rarely mentioned in the press. Sutton's contract with the Dodgers included incentives based on starts, relief appearances, and being on the roster at certain points of the season.

The Dodgers now had a No. 3 starter. The kids could fill out the next two rotation spots, and the fifth starter wouldn't be needed until the 11th game of the season anyway.

Claire wasn't done, though. He needed a third baseman. He offered a two-year, $2.3 million contract to Gary Gaetti, one of the heroes from the reigning

World Champion Minnesota Twins. Gaetti took less money to remain with the Twins and said at a news conference, "I used to hate the Dodgers. I still do. I can say that now. I hate the Dodgers."

There was another former Dodger who wanted to come home. Steve Garvey's five-year, $6.6 million contract with the Padres had just expired. Garvey barely played the final year, reduced to 76 at-bats because of injuries. He would be 39 years old.

Garvey was Dodgers royalty, though paternity suits forever tarnished that All-American clean-cut persona. He wanted one last hurrah. Claire had some discussions with Garvey's agent but never came close to an agreement. The Dodgers already had more first basemen than they needed. They had Franklin Stubbs. They had Mike Marshall and Pedro Guerrero on the roster. One would play left field. The other would play first base. There was no room for Garvey.

◆ ◆ ◆ ◆

The name Thomas Roberts isn't known by many Dodgers fans. But without him, the 1988 world championship wouldn't have happened.

Roberts was a native of Chicago and the son of a banker and he received bachelor's and law degrees from Loyola Marymount University of Los Angeles. He was the arbitrator in labor-management disputes involving General Motors, NBC, Hughes Aircraft, and the University of California system.

But the item listed in the first sentence of his 2008 obituary in the *New York Times* was his role as the arbitrator in the collusion rulings against Major League Baseball owners. Roberts' name had first appeared in sports sections in 1983, when he ruled in favor of Dodgers pitcher Fernando Valenzuela in a salary arbitration hearing. Valenzuela became the first baseball player to earn more than $1 million through the arbitration process.

Three years later, Roberts was fired by baseball owners after ruling that teams couldn't negotiate drug-testing clauses with players individually. Roberts ruled owners had to deal with the players' union on that issue, under a collective agreement. Roberts was reinstated after the players appealed.

Roberts' most famous ruling was that after the 1985 season, baseball owners violated Article XVIII, Paragraph H of the Basic Agreement: "Players shall not act in concert with other players, and clubs shall not act in concert with other clubs."

In layman's terms: collusion.

On January 22, 1988, Roberts declared that seven aggrieved players were entitled to become free agents immediately. They had until March 1 to sign with a new team.

The first six players were older and didn't have much of a market: catcher Carlton Fisk, reliever Donnie Moore, starter Joe Niekro, catcher Butch Wynegar, infielder Tom Brookens, and infielder Juan Beniquez.

The seventh player was 30 years old, signed to a contract that would pay him $1.3 million for 1988, and coming off of a season in which he posted a slash line of .277/.372/.489 with 24 home runs and 79 RBIs. His name was Kirk Harold Gibson.

Within hours of the decision, Fred Claire was on the phone with Doug Baldwin, Gibson's agent. So were the San Diego Padres. Gibson's first choice was to remain with the Tigers. But the Tigers didn't want to pay more money to a player already under contract.

Baldwin indicated there were four key points to the Dodgers' negotiations with Gibson.

- Gibson wanted to know his projected role and where he'd bat in the lineup.
- Gibson wanted a three-year contract in the neighborhood of $4.8 million with a no-trade clause.
- Gibson wanted to speak with Steve Sax first.
- Gibson wanted to know the language in the contract related to a looming strike and/or lockout that was expected after the 1989 season (and ultimately occurred).

Four days later, on January 26, the parameters of a three-year, $4.5 million contract were in place with the Dodgers. Gibson would be paid $2.5 million, more than half, in the first year. The Tigers countered with a modest raise from $1.3 million to $1.33 million.

"The way the Dodgers structured the deal, with so much of the money up front, I'd have been an idiot to turn it down," Gibson said.

The Dodgers wouldn't give a no-trade clause, per club policy. Gibson relented on that request. Claire wanted to include what he called two more "small clauses" into the deal:

The Dodgers could suspend Gibson without pay if he was not in first-class physical condition because of the use of illegal drugs, alcohol, or prescription medicine. (This clause is almost certainly because the team had been burned by Steve Howe so many times and perhaps because of the drug problems in the minors.)

And the Dodgers could stop paying Gibson in the event of a lockout when the basic agreement expired on December 31, 1989.

These weren't "small clauses" in the Gibson camp. They were deal breakers. For 48 hours, the deal looked dead. But the language was softened. As the *L.A. Times* reported:

"Gibson, it was learned, agreed to the conversion clause but only after the Dodgers agreed to a stipulation that would prevent them from voiding the guarantee without 'probable cause' and a now-mandatory examination by a doctor agreeable to both sides.

"In the modified version that will appear in Gibson's contract, Gibson will be paid in the event of a lockout but won't be paid if there is a strike by the players."

On January 29, Gibson became the first free agent player to change clubs as a result of the ruling by the arbitrator Roberts.

Tom Monaghan was the owner of the Detroit Tigers and Domino's Pizza. Monaghan used a weekly Domino's newsletter sent to corporation employees as his vehicle to rip Gibson: "I didn't like Gibson's grooming," Monaghan wrote. "I thought he was a disgrace to the Tiger uniform with his half beard, half stubble. I didn't like his long hair. His best talents, hitting home runs against right-handed pitchers and stealing bases, are not worth a million-and-a-half dollars a year. Which means the best he could do for the Tigers would be to serve as a designated hitter against a right-hander. He has one of the weakest arms in baseball for an outfielder and cannot field well. He was a liability in the outfield. We do not need to replace Kirk Gibson."

Gibson's reaction? "A cheap shot. I wouldn't have expected it from a guy of his stature. He didn't seem to mind what I looked like and played like in '84."

The Dodgers hadn't signed a free agent from another team since the 1979–80 off-season, when they spent $5.1 million on Dave Goltz and Don Stanhouse and were burned. They were burned so bad, they went nearly a decade without even considering a free agent, including the 1986–87 off-season, when Tim Raines was available to fill their most glaring offensive need.

Now the Dodgers were trying free agency again. They tried and failed to sign Gaetti. They thought about bringing back Garvey. Before trading for Howell and

Orosco, they tried to sign Yankees closer Dave Righetti, and Claire reflected, "Dave probably doesn't know how close he came" to signing with the Dodgers.

But they signed outfielder Mike Davis for his power and speed, they signed Don Sutton for his leadership and experience, and after flirting with the idea of trading Pedro Guerrero straight up for Gibson, they signed Gibson without having to give up a player in exchange.

The Dodgers now had five players capable of hitting 20 or more home runs. They also had five players for just four spots. Gibson would play left field. John Shelby would patrol center. Davis was in right field. Either Pedro Guerrero or Mike Marshall would get moved to first base.

But who was going to play third base? Would somebody get traded? Would somebody sit on the bench? How would this affect the team's chemistry?

Those were questions for manager Tommy Lasorda to figure out in spring training. For now, the Dodgers were rejoicing in the massive makeover that improved their offense, their middle infield defense, and their bullpen.

A few weeks before spring training began, Claire and Gibson had dinner. They discussed the team, the Los Angeles market, the history of the Dodgers, the two straight losing seasons, and the expectations for Gibson in Dodger Blue. Claire remembers one exchange vividly.

"I've done some homework," Gibson said. "I may have to kick some ass on this team."

"Why do you think you're here?" Claire replied.

Chapter 2

Spring Training

Vero Beach, Florida

The newspaper reporters covering the Dodgers annually held a pool for what day Pedro Guerrero would arrive to spring training.

In 1988, even a couple of players joined the "Pedro Pool," as well. Pedro was always late. Maybe it was problems with his visa, or the roof caving into his house in the Dominican Republic, or simply wanting to celebrate Dominican Independence Day in Santo Domingo instead of Vero Beach.

This year, it was almost certain Guerrero would be late. He was upset about the off-season trade rumors. Fred Claire and Tommy Lasorda couldn't reach him by telephone. Dodgers scout Ralph Avila visited him during a Latin America scouting trip and reported back that Guerrero was working hard...by playing softball. At 9:54 PM on February 25, Guerrero arrived. You know that money was on the line if the exact minute was reported in the Los Angeles papers. Guerrero was on time.

The next morning, Guerrero told reporters he didn't have hurt feelings anymore, his chronically sprained left wrist still hurt, it was fine if he got traded, he wanted to finish his career with the Dodgers, he understood that it was a business, but if he were the GM, "No way I would trade Pedro Guerrero."

Guerrero also considered himself a changed man after becoming a father three months earlier. "I stay at home more, spend more time with my family. Now that we have a baby, I have something to play with. Before, we didn't even have a cat."

The narrative that spring concerned how all the power hitters would fit into the lineup and how all the new egos would blend together. Players whispered to the reporters—off the record—doubts about how Guerrero would react to Mike Marshall and Kirk Gibson in the clubhouse.

"I think it'll be an interesting clubhouse, but that should be the least of our worries," Steve Sax offered. "We are all grown-up people, and if we can't get along, let's at least fake it."

The biggest question was who the hell was going to play third base.

Since Ron Cey departed, the Dodgers used 21 different players at the hot corner from 1983–87. It was mostly Pedro Guerrero the first three years. Bill Madlock arrived the final month in 1985 and was there most of 1986.

In 1987, it was a revolving door of Mickey Hatcher (42 starts), Tracy Woodson (33 starts), Phil Garner (29 starts), Jeff Hamilton (23 starts), Madlock (16 starts), Dave Anderson (11 starts), Mike Sharperson (seven starts), and Craig Shipley (one start).

Tommy Lasorda's first idea was moving Sax from second base to third base. He called Sax at his Manhattan Beach home on December 12 and invited him to lunch. Sax knew Lasorda wasn't just hungry. He knew something was up. Sax was initially reluctant. The more Lasorda explained the situation, the more Sax was receptive to the idea. A month later, Sax began taking grounders at third base.

On February 1, another idea was brewing. Sax was hunting doves in a Mexico desert, Gibson was getting introduced to the Los Angeles media, and now Mike Marshall was taking grounders at third base. Lasorda shouted encouragement from behind third base. All the encouragement in the world wasn't going to help Marshall play third base. A week later, Marshall told reporters he had no desire to play third base, and Lasorda scrapped that idea.

The ideal third baseman was Jeff Hamilton. He hit .360 in 65 games for Triple A Albuquerque the year before but only .217 in the majors. Lasorda considered Hamilton his "project" for spring training. Lasorda would correct the flaws in Hamilton's swing and fill him with confidence. Hamilton agreed there was a confidence problem. But it wasn't his lack of self-confidence. It was Lasorda's lack of confidence in him.

"Until he plays me and lets me show him how I can play, he won't have it in me," Hamilton said. "I can't do anything more than confront him and say, 'Yeah, I got confidence. Now, play me.'"

The infield conversion was such a constant topic that Sax stopped an approaching reporter in his tracks on February 29.

"I know what you're going to ask already. I'll give you the answers." Sax paused then went into his routine. "The spring's going good for me.... I feel good at third base.... I'm not competing for a job.... They are just going to decide who they're going to put where."

Sax liked Hamilton, knew he hit .360 in the minors, and considered him a great fielder. If Hamilton could just hit .260 with 10–15 home runs, Sax thought the Dodgers would be satisfied with Hamilton at third base, and he could move back to second base.

Hamilton figured he was the starting third baseman. He even issued a quote to the Dodgers' public relations staff, "I don't think it's a big challenge, because I don't think Steve wants to play third. I think it's too big of a transition."

Lasorda, in full Lasorda mode, said Sax could play third base like Hall of Famer Brooks Robinson, and Hamilton could hit like Steve Garvey. Even if Hamilton started at third base, there were still five power hitters for four spots. Kirk Gibson wasn't going to be platooned, so it was four players for three spots. And nobody could play center field like John Shelby, so it was three players for two spots. Either way, Marshall or Guerrero would get moved from the outfield to first base.

The Dodgers didn't break their no free agent rule by signing Mike Davis to be a fourth outfielder. Davis didn't think he was fighting for a job. He fully expected to start in right field, unless he was filling in for John Shelby in center.

Shelby read his name in the papers as the definitive starting center fielder but didn't take that for granted. He figured he'd know when spring training was over.

Marshall was incredulous at the idea of not having a starting job. Maybe it would be first base. Maybe it would be right field. Or maybe he'd be somewhere else. But he was starting somewhere.

◆ ◆ ◆ ◆

March 3, 1988
Vero Beach, Florida

Outside of trips to Anaheim to play the Angels with the Tigers, the only other time Kirk Gibson had been to Los Angeles was as a college football player, when Michigan State played USC at the Coliseum. Since his college days, he was close with a Mariners scout named Mel Didier. When Didier took a job scouting for the Dodgers, the two talked about Gibson joining the Dodgers one day.

Gibson knew about the Dodgers' history in New York and moving to Los Angeles. He played against Bob Welch in college. He watched Welch strike out Reggie Jackson in the World Series, and watched Jackson hit three home runs in a single World Series game. Gibson was excited to join the organization and add to that history.

But right away, Gibson was uncomfortable when he arrived at the Dodgers spring training complex in Vero Beach, Florida.

"The only manager I ever knew was Sparky Anderson," Gibson explained. "The way he did things was stricter, more black and white. We had a meeting in [the Dodgers] clubhouse. Guys were jumping out of trunks. It was not something that I was used to. It was very loose on the field, as well. They just always had jokes going on. What is this? With Sparky, you showed up, you got right to work. It wasn't very loose at all. It was very structured. I was uncomfortable with the jokes."

On the morning of March 3, the *Los Angeles Herald-Examiner* ran a story that Mike Marshall and Pedro Guerrero's feud had flared up as the two exchanged heated words. Marshall denied there was a problem, saying Lasorda brought them both into a meeting in his office and insisting he had no problem with Guerrero.

Lasorda was busy putting out more fires that spring. Another day, Gibson had an incident with infielder Mariano Duncan in the clubhouse. Gibson explained what happened at the batting cage the morning of March 3 to the *Los Angeles Times*, "What we basically had was a stare-down. I didn't know why, so I said to [Duncan], 'What the fuck are you staring at?' And he walked away. The next day, I go up to him and asked him what was wrong.

"We had a meeting. Tommy was there mainly as an interpreter because Mariano speaks better Spanish than English. We settled it. He said he was just joking with me, but I didn't know it. How would I know unless he tells me?

"I'm not here to start any—or settle any—differences they've had before. I just want to get along with everybody. I know that over the years, there's been a lot of bull going on in [the Dodgers'] clubhouse. I don't want that."

Gibson wasn't sure what to make of his new teammates, and the feeling back then was mutual.

In the decades that followed, as well as in his book, Gibson frequently told a story about the team working on bunt plays one day. Pedro was playing first base. Pedro did what Pedro did a lot in the infield. He made an error. The Dodgers' players laughed. They were used to Pete making errors. Gibson fumed. But for now, he was keeping it to himself.

The Dodgers did laugh. They laughed a lot. They loved practical jokes. Those jokes and laughs were usually done in the clubhouse and the dorms on campus— not on the field.

The favorite was having a rookie lay on the floor of the clubhouse under the guise that a player would lift him into the air, using just a belt, in a feat of strength. Players would bet money if it could be done. Once the ruse was set up, the rookie would get drenched with shaving cream and other items from the bathroom.

Newcomer Jesse Orosco was used to pulling pranks with the Mets and was intent on showing his new teammates how funny he could be.

The first clubhouse prank involving Gibson actually went well. A few days earlier, a teammate put shaving cream on a clubhouse phone and told Gibson he had a phone call. Gibson put the phone up to his ear, felt the shaving cream, and everybody had a good laugh. Gibson didn't seem to mind.

The second prank didn't go as well. It happened a few days after the laughs over Guerrero's errors in a workout, and a few hours after Gibson vented about "all the bull going on" in camp. Gibson was already seething.

It was about noon, an hour before the Dodgers' first exhibition game against the Chunichi Dragons of Japan.

"Little did those guys know, it was like the seventh game of the World Series to me," Gibson reflected. "They didn't know that about me. They learned shortly."

Gibson was running wind sprints in the outfield to get ready for the game, and he had built up a pretty good lather of sweat. Done with his running, Gibson put on his Dodgers cap. The inside had been covered with black shoe polish, and now that was all over Gibson's face.

"I was running in the outfield with him," infielder Dave Anderson remembered. "I told him, 'Gibby, you've got some black stuff on your head.' His reaction was not good."

Gibson flew into a rage in front of about 1,000 fans at Holman Field. He started running to the dugout. The only coach there was Bill Russell. Gibson was going nuts, throwing his hands in the air. Russell pointed to where Lasorda was located.

Lasorda was kissing babies and talking to fans by the dugout. Gibson yelled at Lasorda in front of the fans, then charged into the clubhouse, yelled at several teammates, and threatened offenders.

"No wonder you fuckers were in last place last year!" Gibson screamed. "Bunch of fucking comedian motherfuckers! You're laughing all the way to fucking last place!"

Gibson tore off his uniform. Buttons flew left and right. Eye black remained all over his face. Nobody in their right mind was going to intervene. Gibson took a shower, went into Lasorda's office, and demanded the culprit. Lasorda couldn't believe Gibson was making a big deal out of a practical joke and tried to smooth it over.

"Oh, Kirk, come on," Lasorda said. "You know the media's going to get this."

Gibson didn't care. Gibson gave Lasorda another 10 minutes to deliver the prankster. When nobody came forward, Gibson went home and fumed more. He was scratched from the starting lineup.

"We played the game and we're kind of laughing about it," said Jay Howell, in the 2001 book *True Blue*. "I mean, we don't know this guy yet. There were some comments like, 'We got a bad ass, but we'll break him.'"

Mickey Hatcher heard that some people thought it was him. Hatcher had a reputation as a prankster. One spring when he was with the Twins, the Dodgers came to visit Orlando. Hatcher shredded Tommy Lasorda's pants. Lasorda was livid, especially since he had to ride back on the bus to Vero Beach in his underwear. Later that spring, when Hatcher came to Vero Beach, he was in the outfield when he noticed the American flag getting lowered. Then he saw his pants getting raised on the flag, also all shredded up.

Hatcher was innocent of Eye Black–Gate, but he was worried that he'd get blamed for it.

"When it happened, I knew it was a pitcher," Gibson recalled. "Pretty self-explanatory. They have more time on their hands."

The next morning about 6:00 AM, Lasorda called Gibson. The manager and player had virtually no history at this point. They didn't know what made the other person tick. Lasorda asked Gibson to stop by his on-campus room before going to the clubhouse. Gibson walked right over.

For 20 minutes, Lasorda used classic Lasorda diplomacy in explaining that the Dodgers try to stay positive with the press, the Dodgers were a family, and that the joke was pulled because the players wanted him to feel like one of the guys and get comfortable with the new environment.

At the end of his pitch, Lasorda said he had a plan to tell the press, "I'd like to say that I excused you, that something personal came up, that it's all taken care of, and that you'll be in the lineup."

So far, Gibson hadn't said a word. When it was his time to talk, Gibson said he wasn't going along with the plan. He was going to tell the press the truth. Lasorda moaned. Lasorda thought Gibson was being stubborn and tried again. Gibson said no. Gibson wanted the prankster to come forward, and he wanted to talk with the team. Lasorda could tell Gibson was serious, and he agreed to the newcomer's demands.

The clubhouse was tense that morning. Nobody knew how to approach Gibson. They didn't dare say something that might cause the volcano to erupt again. Most avoided eye contact with him.

Jesse Orosco timidly approached Gibson to apologize. His hands were shaking.

"You don't know me," Gibson told Orosco. "Get out of my face."

Lasorda convened the usual morning meeting. This meeting was not usual, though. Lasorda told the players Gibson wanted to say something. Gibson wasn't sure how his message would go over. He didn't care, either.

In his 1997 book, Gibson recounted what he told his teammates:

> "On a bunt play, you guys throw balls into right field. You laugh, even though we've got to execute it correctly in a game. I've watched you guys on TV. Blowing plays like that is why, when you play St. Louis, they just keep running the bases.
>
> "What are we here for? We're here to be world champions. You know what? I've been a world champion. You don't become world champions by just stumbling into it.

23

"We're getting ready to enter the marathon race. We're going to see how much heart we have. If we haven't got heart, we haven't got a prayer. We've got to start challenging ourselves mentally—now, because it's going to get a lot worse than this.

"If I'm wrong, then I'm on the wrong team, the front office will move me, and you guys can go your own route. Now if anybody's got a problem with what I've said, *tough*. I'm standing right here. If you want me—one of you, all of you—I don't care. I will do anything to prove to you that I'm here to sacrifice in order to become world champions."

Nobody dared challenge Gibson. Besides, they knew what Gibson said was true.

"It was a big turning point for that team to gel and understand who our leader was on the team," infielder Dave Anderson reflected. "Up to that point, I don't think we really had a guy that was, well…intimidating for one."

Pitcher Tim Leary added, "Ultimately, that set the tone. This is not a practical joke team anymore. We're here to win, period."

Gibson reiterated his stance to the reporters. He admitted he has no sense of humor when he's the butt of the joke. He had that reputation in Detroit, too. It was duly noted in the L.A. papers that Gibson had the reputation of pulling pranks on others. He once pulled a chair out from pitcher Dave Rozema, Gibson's best friend on the Tigers, when Rozema tried to sit down. A bottle that Rozema was holding shattered. Another time, shortstop Alan Trammell required stitches after one of Gibson's pranks.

Orosco was genuinely sorry.

"Let's just say I won't be doing it again," Orosco told reporters. "That's because I don't want to read my name in the obituaries. It was just a typical practical joke. Kirk and I talked, and I hope he understands. I felt bad after I did it, and I felt really bad after [Gibson's] reaction."

Later in the season and over the course of the last 25 years this incident has been hailed as the galvanizing moment when the Dodgers realized they weren't serious enough. The story is now legendary for how Gibson changed the culture of the franchise. But for many longtime members of the organization, the impact is overstated.

Former teammates don't want to dispute Gibson's story that teammates laughed when Guerrero made an error in a fielding drill one day. However, not a single person interviewed for this book could remember that ever happening, although many said it wouldn't surprise them at all.

As one player put it, "It's not like we were a bunch of idiots wandering around and all of a sudden, he changed everything. We won a division in 1985. We had a lot of injuries in '86 and '87. In '88 we were rebuilt and moved forward. That was the first year Jesse Orosco was with us. That might have been a reflection of the things going on with the Mets, not with us. I'm not going to dispute that drill. I don't agree with the assertion that we were guys just flipping the ball around and didn't care about our craft. That's 180 degrees from what it was."

In hindsight, they know that Gibson's reaction worked, it was needed, and what Gibson said was true. Mike Marshall's reflections were mixed. Marshall loved Gibson, said it was "a dream come true" to play with Gibson, but he couldn't help point out the double-standard.

"I thought it was ironic," Marshall said, "that I was always known for being too serious, and not having a good time, and always taking the game too serious, and not having a smile on my face, and not being happy-go-lucky. Then [Gibson] comes in and sets it straight the way it's supposed to be. It goes one of two ways. If we have a lousy year and Gibby did what he did, he comes across [looking bad]. It all just worked itself out. I'm not a prankster, either. But I took ridicule for it my entire career. Whereas, Gibby was a catalyst for the rest of the season, which he should have been."

Three-thousand miles west, Dodgers fans in Los Angeles weren't taking Gibson's side. The letters to the editor in the Saturday *L.A. Times* were not kind to Gibson.

"I am embarrassed for Kirk Gibson. He acknowledges that he doesn't enjoy—and will not accept—pranks played on him. That's too bad, Kirk. I suppose he doesn't like losing his hair, either. These things happen, and they are part of everyday living. Practical jokes can bridge gaps between people. I can't wait to see his reaction when every fan in Candlestick Park wears shoe polish on his forehead."
—Steve Sugarman, North Hollywood

"Aw, did poor wittle Kirkie get his feewings hurt when bad ol' Jesse pwayed a twick on him? Grow up, Gibson."
—Ellen Schroder, Oceanside

"What's wrong with the Dodgers? It appears that they checked their brains at the door. They spent millions for a known malcontent prima donna crybaby who can give it out but not take it. Kirk Gibson's first act in his first game in Dodger Blue is to walk off the field and out of the park. I've always thought that pranks were dumb, but this guy knew about the Dodgers before he came here and, more importantly, he is a pro who is paid to play. Where will he be when the game, or the season, is on the line? At home, sulking."

—Bruce Epstein, Glendale

"So, Kirk Gibson has a history of playing practical jokes, sometimes causing injury to teammates. However, he is such an important fellow that no one would dare play a practical joke on him. Well, la de da. All of us have seen this type before. They're so unrelentingly arrogant and unlovable that they find little acceptance anywhere. Unless he can hit .325 this year, Gibson would do well to ask the Dodgers to release him so he can play in Japan. The Japanese are so polite, they won't even say 'shoe polish' to him."

—Marshall J. Garrott, Glendale

◆ ◆ ◆ ◆

The overwhelming attention that spring was directed at Kirk Gibson's tantrum, the competition for the fourth and fifth starting pitcher jobs, the reserves who wanted to be traded, if Guerrero or Marshall would get traded, and how all the newcomers would blend together.

For home games, the starters worked out and took batting practice on the main field at Holman Stadium. The reserves were on the back fields—the dreaded Field One. For away games, the starters would play 6-to-7 innings, get 3-to-4 at-bats, and call it a day. The reserves would enter in the seventh inning or later and maybe get one at-bat.

Peter O'Malley, Fred Claire, and Tommy Lasorda made a decision to try winning more spring training games than usual. After two losing seasons, with so many new players and after Gibson's tantrum, they felt it was important to get in the habit of winning. That's why the starters played longer than usual.

On the back fields in Vero Beach and on those long bus rides for one measly at-bat the reserves bonded over their situation. They made up songs and sayings. They challenged each other to little games in batting practice. They had fun with it. Most important, the games occupied their minds with thoughts other than the lack of playing time.

The reserves entered those spring training games in the final innings and often rallied the Dodgers to victory. They started calling themselves the Stuntmen. You didn't want to risk the stars playing in inclement weather or late in a meaningless game, so the Stuntmen filled in.

The leader was Mickey Hatcher. The charter members were outfielder Danny Heep, shortstop Dave Anderson, catcher Rick Dempsey, infielder Mike Sharperson, outfielder Jose Gonzalez, and infielder Tracy Woodson. You couldn't be part of the Stuntmen unless you worked out on the back fields—unless you came to the ballpark each day not knowing if you had a job.

"In spring training, these guys would get their two at-bats and take it in," Hatcher reflected. "They'd leave it up to us to win a game. I started to say, 'Don't get any more than two at-bats because we want to win this game today. Get the right guys in there, and we'll win this game.' We took pride in it. Let the superstars think they can do it, but the Stuntmen will come in and do a lot this year. We started building on that in spring training."

Hatcher had a game-winning RBI single in the 10th inning for one spring victory. Dempsey's double keyed a five-run eighth inning for another win. Heep's ninth inning home run tied another game they won in 10 innings. Hatcher came to the plate for one at-bat with the sun setting and not much light remaining with a flashlight duct-taped to his batting helmet. A photo of that scene was posted in the clubhouse the next day, and a teammate wrote as a caption, "The light is on, but nobody's home."

The Stuntmen were a big reason the Dodgers started the spring 14–3 and finished 21–11.

"Our clubhouse guy drew up an unbelievable shirt with all of us on it," Hatcher said. "Tommy was holding a detonator. We're all sitting on bombs ready to go off. It was a tremendous shirt. I wish we could have kept it. We'd have made a lot of money."

♦ ♦ ♦ ♦

Lost in the middle of Eye Black–Gate, a curious thing was happening at third base.

Pedro Guerrero was taking ground balls. Ever since Guerrero had made his major league debut in 1978, he never truly had a position. He played the two corner infield positions a little but mostly left field and right field up through 1982. He was moved to third base in 1983 to replace Ron Cey.

It was an all-around disaster at the hot corner, and Pete knew it. During a famous clubhouse meeting in 1983, initiated because of the team's losing ways, Lasorda asked Guerrero what he thinks about before the pitch is delivered.

"Two things," Pete said. "First, I look up to the sky and say, 'God, please don't have them hit the ball to me.'"

Stunned, Lasorda asked, "What's the other thing?"

"Please don't hit it to Sax."

That was the year Sax suddenly couldn't throw the ball to first base. The story is so legendary, it has to be fiction. Right? No. It's very true.

"I thought it was pretty funny," Sax said. "I appreciated him being honest about it."

Even after that admission about his inadequacies at third base, it took two years before the Dodgers moved Guerrero away from the hot corner. Guerrero was taken out of his defensive misery on June 1, 1985. On that day, he was batting .268 with four home runs and 16 RBIs. Lasorda moved Guerrero to center field for eight games before settling Guerrero in left field for the duration of that season.

Guerrero responded by hitting .344 with 15 home runs in June alone. He finished the year third in MVP voting—behind Willie McGee and Dave Parker—with a .320 batting average, 33 home runs, and 87 RBIs.

"Pedro was a very flamboyant ballplayer," said Jaime Jarrin, the Hall of Fame Spanish-language announcer for the Dodgers. "Personally, he didn't manage his personal affairs very well. He made good money, and he spent every penny. He loved to play. He wasn't good enough to be a regular at any position. He tried third base and he wasn't good. He tried left field and he wasn't good in left field. As a hitter, he was a really solid hitter. He was an asset in the dugout because of his behavior. He was always happy and kidding everybody. He was laughing and loud and everything. He kept everybody relaxed."

In 1986, Guerrero missed virtually the entire season after tearing up his knee in the final spring training game in Florida. Healthy in 1987, he finished 15th in

MVP voting with another solid season: a .338 average that was second to Tony Gwynn's league-leading .370, plus 27 home runs and 89 RBIs to lead the team.

Lasorda was hell-bent on getting all five of his power bats in the starting lineup together. To achieve this, Lasorda crafted out a slow plan to convince Guerrero to play third base again. Like most things with Lasorda, it started with food.

On March 7, Guerrero didn't play in the Dodgers' exhibition game against the Mets. Instead, he was the designated hitter for both teams in an intra-squad game, leading off every inning for each team. Guerrero was wholly uninterested in the plan to get him more at-bats. Lasorda observed this from about 20' from behind home plate.

"Hey Pete, how many hits do you got?" Lasorda yelled.

"I'm 0 for the morning," Guerrero moaned.

"I bet you a dinner you don't get a hit," Lasorda said. "I bet you don't even hit it out of the infield."

Guerrero's next at-bat was against Ramon Martinez, the phenom who would not be traded. Guerrero cleared the infield easily. He launched the ball over the outfield fence and a few of the trees lining a nearby golf course. Pete dashed around the bases with unusual quickness. He crossed home plate and smirked at Lasorda. Later, he was asked where Lasorda was taking him to dinner.

"Probably McDonald's," Guerrero cracked.

"No Pete," Lasorda said. "It's that French place, Jacques in the Box."

Actually, it was do-it-yourself takeout. In his office that day, Lasorda handed Guerrero two pounds of boxed linguine from Abruzzo, Italy, and two quarts of pasta sauce from Norristown, Pennsylvania. It was a plea. It was practically a beg. Lasorda needed Guerrero to play third base.

Guerrero and his agent, Tony Attanasio, considered asking for an extension on his $1.7 million contract in exchange for giving third base another try. As it turned out, they never asked for more money. (If they had, they wouldn't have gotten it.)

"Pedro at third was hold your breath," Claire reflected. "But there were a lot of guys at third who you held your breath [for]. Pedro didn't get hung up on that stuff. [His philosophy was], 'Give me my at-bats. I can't play a good left field, what makes you think I'll play a good third base?'"

Sax was the most relieved person in Vero Beach.

"I didn't want to play third base," Sax said, upon reflection. "I said I'd give it a try. I'd never played third base in my life. I think they knew all along. I was a last-ditch fill-in until they got somebody."

Marshall was also a brief desperation idea that he happily told them wouldn't work: "They tried to throw me at third base. Physically, I could have done it. Mentally, I wasn't into it. I probably should have been. Somebody had to play it. The fact that Pedro even gave it a go, that's a positive. It really helped us."

It made sense to Orel Hershiser, "If Pete plays third, there's only one guy out of position, and that's Pete."

Back in 1988, catcher Mike Scioscia said, "Pete's a liability at third. So, the decision is whether you go for offense over defense, because we're going to be sacrificing something."

Twenty-five years later, Scioscia was more diplomatic, "When Pete applied himself, he was okay at third. He was just more comfortable playing the outfield. But I think to try and get the bats in the lineup that we saw, trying to get some guys like Mike Davis and Kirk Gibson, the new guys who came over. You saw a team that got an injection of much-needed talent. We were fine. We never paid attention to where guys were playing, as much as what you had to do. That's the only way Tommy could figure it. We were okay with it."

An interesting domino effect occurred with Guerrero playing third base. Sax would move back to second base, and Mariano Duncan was out of a job. Duncan didn't want to return to the minors. Duncan was hoping to get traded.

Hamilton knew that he wouldn't be playing third base and even admitted he'd use the same lineup as Lasorda if he was in charge. Hamilton was hoping to get traded, too.

And with Marshall at first base and Mike Davis in right field, Franklin Stubbs knew that he wouldn't be playing much first base. Stubbs was hoping to get traded, as well.

Lasorda tried to claim the decision wasn't final. It wasn't because he didn't like what he'd seen from Sax or Hamilton at third base. He was just looking at the lineup with Guerrero at third base. But that was just a ruse.

It was clear this decision was final by March 15. The Dodgers were in Puerto Rico for two games against the Expos. The games would raise money for the Roberto Clemente Sports City. On the first day, Mike Davis stepped into a pothole in right field during batting practice and suffered a severely sprained left ankle. Davis would be out two weeks. But even with Davis out, Guerrero remained at third base and Marshall remained at first base.

By the end of spring, Lasorda began calling a lineup of Gibson-Shelby-Davis-Guerrero-Marshall his "awesome fivesome."

Dodgers management always claimed they didn't give Guerrero preferential treatment. But because he was moving to third base for the good of the team, they'd look the other way at one incident that spring and throw Guerrero a couple of bones. First, Guerrero was allowed to leave camp a few days early for a trip home to the Dominican Republic, and then he met the team in Puerto Rico. Second, Guerrero and Duncan missed the team bus on March 22 to Kissimmee. Guerrero said he overslept and then said he was taking care of Duncan, who had a headache. Considering his reputation for partying, the Dodgers were naturally suspicious of Pete's story and assumed they were both hungover. Third, when the team broke camp in Vero Beach for the start of the season in California, Guerrero got off the team charter when it stopped to refuel in Dallas. Guerrero took a commercial flight to Albuquerque, where his wife is a native, and met the team a day later in Los Angeles.

There was no collateral damage to Guerrero for missing the bus, but Duncan's involvement (and his .100 spring batting average) cost him a job in the majors. Duncan was sent to Triple A Albuquerque and blasted Lasorda on his way out of camp.

"When he told me today, I called him a fucking liar," Duncan told reporters. "I want to go somewhere else. I don't want them to trash my career. I cannot believe this guy [Lasorda] anymore when he says anything. He's a liar."

Lasorda denied that he promised Duncan a job in the majors. "The guy did not hit this spring," Lasorda said. "He did absolutely nothing. I didn't like his work habits. How do you warrant keeping a guy like that?"

Despite all the requests and rumors, no additional trades were made. Guerrero and Marshall weren't traded. Hamilton, Duncan, and Stubbs weren't traded, either.

The Dodgers liked their depth as they began the season. They had no idea how much that depth would be needed.

Chapter 3

April

April 4, 1988

Los Angeles

Giants vs. Dodgers

It was the 31st year for Major League Baseball in California. The Dodgers and Giants arrived from New York in 1958. It was a one-sided rivalry for most of those 30 years. The Dodgers had the clear advantage in postseason appearances (10–3), World Series titles (4–0), head-to-head results (284–269), and finishing the year with a superior record (21–10).

The rivalry script was flipped in 1986. The Giants hired Roger Craig, a former Dodgers pitcher, to be their manager. Craig started rookies Will Clark and Robby Thompson on the right side of his infield. He taught the split-finger fastball to all his pitchers. He brought a positive "Humm Baby" attitude to the team. He loved to squeeze, and he managed boldly.

In Craig's first year, the Giants won 83 games, a 21-game improvement, and stayed in the race until mid-September. In Craig's second year, the Giants won the division title, their first since 1971, held a 3–2 lead over the Cardinals in the NLCS, but lost in seven games.

Now it was Craig's third year, and the skipper declared his ballclub the best in the majors. In 1987, general manager Al Rosen strengthened the Giants by acquiring starting pitcher Dave Dravecky, reliever Craig Lefferts, and third baseman Kevin Mitchell from the Padres in July, then reliever Don Robinson and starter Rick Reuschel in separate trades with the Pirates.

The Giants would have all four pitchers for the entire 1988 season, plus thunder in the lineup with Clark, Thompson, Mitchell, Jeffrey Leonard, and former Dodger Candy Maldonado. Rosen unabashedly said the Giants were going all the way.

In fact, the Giants couldn't wait to open defense of their division title. When Mitchell arrived in the visiting clubhouse at Dodger Stadium on Opening Day at 8:00 AM for the 1:05 PM game, the clubhouse was already full.

No team had won consecutive National League West titles in a full season since the Dodgers of 1977 and 1978.

The Astros were still a threat. They'd won the division in 1986, taking the Mets to six heart-stopping games. They still had Mike Scott and Nolan Ryan in the rotation, plus the underrated Bob Knepper and Jim Deshaies. They still had Dave Smith and Larry Andersen in the bullpen. And they still had a lineup led by Glenn Davis and Kevin Bass, which would get better with speedster Gerald Young in his first full season leading off and playing center field.

The Reds finished six games behind the Giants in 1987 and looked improved on paper. They had a potent outfield with Kal Daniels, Eric Davis, and Paul O'Neill, a blossoming star at shortstop in Barry Larkin, and a potential rookie star at third base named Chris Sabo. Danny Jackson came over from the Royals in a trade to lead a rotation with Tom Browning, veteran Mario Soto, and rookies Jack Armstrong and Jose Rijo. John Franco was a proven closer with help from a young Rob Dibble and Rob Murphy. Pete Rose thought the Reds were the team to beat.

The Sporting News predicted a fourth-place finish for the Dodgers. So did *Sports Illustrated*. Both magazines thought the Giants would defend their title. Around the country, writers, announcers, and columnists listed the Dodgers between third and fifth place.

The Dodgers knew they would be better. They just weren't sure how much better they'd be. They had power and speed in the lineup but at the expense of a now questionable defense. The pitching staff had some question marks, and they had a roster full of players with a history of injuries.

Introductions were not just a formality on Opening Day at Dodger Stadium. Thirteen of the 24 players on the roster were not in the organization a year earlier. The only two starters in the same position from the 1987 Opening Day roster were catcher Mike Scioscia and second baseman Steve Sax.

When the players lined up along the third-base line for introductions, Mickey Hatcher took off his cap, and black shoe polish was all over his head. This was not Kirk Gibson getting revenge on the wrong teammate. This was a self-inflicted prank by Hatcher.

Dave Dravecky started for the Giants. The year before, the lefty held lefties to a league-low .142 opponent's batting average. Opening Day isn't the time for splits and platoons. Lasorda wanted to show off his "awesome fivesome" on Opening Day. Including Valenzuela, Lasorda put five lefties into his starting lineup.

Claire and Lasorda loved the combination of power and speed on the roster. This was the Dodgers' Opening Day lineup, with their age for that season, the salary they were making, and key stats from the 1987 season:

Steve Sax, 2B	Age 28	$ 838,182	6 HR, 37 SB, .280/.331/.369
Alfredo Griffin, SS	Age 30	$750,000	3 HR, 26 SB, .263/.306/.348
Kirk Gibson, LF	Age 31	$1,833,333	24 HR, 26 SB, .277/.372/.489
Pedro Guerrero, 3B	Age 32	$1,720,000	27 HR, 9 SB, .338/.416/.539
Mike Marshall, 1B	Age 28	$760,000	16 HR, 0 SB, .294/.327/.460
John Shelby, CF	Age 30	$465,000	21 HR, 16 SB, .277/.317/.464
Mike Davis, RF	Age 29	$987,500	22 HR, 19 SB, .265/.320/.468
Mike Scioscia, C	Age 29	$1,000,000	6 HR, 7 SB, .265/.343/.364
Fernando Valenzuela, P	Age 27	$2,050,000	14–14, 3.98 ERA

Valenzuela was the second highest paid pitcher in baseball. Gibson was the ninth highest paid player in the National League. The Dodgers' payroll was the highest in the majors at $17.5 million. The great Jim Murray wrote in the *Los Angeles Times,* "This team cost Dodger owner Peter O'Malley $17.5 million. Now, I can remember when you could buy a railroad for that. Or a coal mine. Or a Manhattan skyscraper. A small country. Peter got a whole bunch of .270 and .260 hitters for it."

Valenzuela was given the Opening Day start for the sixth time in his career. The top of the first inning was typical for that stage of Valenzuela's career. A fly-out. A strikeout. A walk. A single. Another walk. A fly-out to escape the inning.

Steve Sax knew the book on Dravecky. He had an uncanny knack for breaking bats. In a minor league game at Double A Amarillo, Dravecky once broke a combined five bats between Steve Sax and his brother, Dave. In one game.

Sax rarely swung at the first pitch of any at-bat. Swinging at the first pitch of any game was even more rare. But he didn't want Dravecky to get ahead in the count and run that cutting fastball on his hands to break a bat.

"I thought, *First pitch of the season, he's going to try and just lay a fastball in there*," Sax reflected. "He didn't throw a cutter. He threw a straight fastball, and I was sitting on it. I thought, *If he throws anything but a cutter, I'm going to wail on it.*"

Sax wailed on the inside fastball and walloped a home run into the left-field bleachers. Sax sprinted around the bases, pumping his fists with exuberance that went beyond the usual level of Sax enthusiasm.

"I was as surprised as everybody else was, believe me," Sax recalled. "I didn't hit home runs. I was beside myself. It was like a renaissance for our club. We hadn't been to the playoffs since 1985. It was my last year. I was really hyped up. I thought, *This is the way we want to do it.* I'm all about momentum."

In the Dodgers' dugout, Tim Belcher thought to himself, "*Maybe this can be the start of something special.*"

In the Giants' dugout, they steamed at Sax. The Giants never liked Sax. They pretty much hated Sax. Dravecky didn't see the pumped fists and didn't care when told later. Dravecky just went back to work. He retired the next 11 batters in a row and allowed just two more hits the rest of the game.

Brett Butler had always wanted to be a Dodger. He was born in Los Angeles, grew up a Dodger fan, and dreamed of wearing Dodger Blue. Butler was the consummate leadoff man of the 1980s. He played center field. He bunted. He stole bases. He worked the count and drew walks and racked up a high on-base percentage before those skills were in vogue.

The Indians were willing to trade Butler in the spring of 1987. The Dodgers weren't interested. They already had a leadoff hitter in Sax. Ken Landreaux was the returning center fielder, and he was shifted to left field so a rookie named Mike Ramsey could play center.

Neither of those options worked, so Claire went shopping for help. He didn't call Cleveland. He called Baltimore. The fans had never forgiven Tom Niedenfuer for the home run to Jack Clark in 1985, and Niedenfuer was never the same. Niedenfuer was sent to Baltimore in exchange for John Shelby.

Butler played the entire year in Cleveland, filed for free agency, and hoped the Dodgers would call. They didn't. Instead, the Dodgers signed Kirk Gibson and Mike Davis. The Giants lost center fielder Chili Davis to the Angels via free agency and replaced him with Butler. Now the defending champs had a superior defensive center fielder and the leadoff hitter they lacked. Craig, the "Humm Baby," considered Butler the final piece to a championship team.

As if Butler didn't have enough motivation to stick it to the Dodgers, the team that twice rejected acquiring him, another story was still simmering in the back of his mind.

In late August 1983, Butler's third year in the majors, the Braves acquired pitcher Len Barker for three players to be named later. It was widely known that Butler, Brook Jacoby, and Rick Behenna were the players who would eventually get sent to Cleveland. A few weeks later, the Dodgers were in Atlanta, and Tommy Lasorda called over Brett Butler for a chat.

"I was thinking, '*Tommy likes me as a player, he's going to tell me this and that,*'" Butler recalled. "When I walked over, Tommy said to me, 'Brett, do me a favor, would ya? Send me a postcard from Cleveland and tell me how bad it is.' And he started to laugh. I thought he was going to say, 'You're a good young player and you're going to do well.' He was trying to make a funny ha-ha. That's something that always stuck out in my mind."

On Opening Day, Butler showed the Dodgers what they were missing and showed Lasorda what he'd learned in Cleveland. In the fourth inning, Butler tripled home two runs off Valenzuela to make the score 4–1. When Mike Aldrete hit a shallow fly ball to left, Butler challenged Gibson's suspect throwing arm and scored another run easily. Gibson's throw was 5' up the first-base line. The score was 5–1. That would be the final score.

"Let's face it: We didn't play good," Gibson said that day. "It's nobody's fault but our own. Let's learn from it. It may take us a while to get going. People got to understand this isn't the end of the world. You can't call it a season after this. Tomorrow is a new day."

And tomorrow, Orel Hershiser was starting.

April 5, 1988
Los Angeles
Giants vs. Dodgers
Team record: 0–1

Orel Hershiser's first start of 1988 wasn't a big deal. The big deal was that it was the one-year anniversary of what had become known as "the Campanis thing" to Dodgers players and staff. It wasn't a big deal when Hershiser started. Not yet.

Hershiser was good—very good. He finished third in Rookie of the Year voting in 1984, third in Cy Young Award voting in 1985, reached his first All-Star Game in 1987, and finished fourth in the Cy Young race in 1987. He was paid well for his performance, $1.1 million for the 1988 season.

Even with all that, Hershiser wasn't special. He called himself "a nobody" and while that was a stretch, that was Orel. He was the No. 2 starter, behind Valenzuela. He was the guy who usually sat next to Lasorda and the coaches on days he wasn't pitching, volunteering to pitch in relief, and giving off the impression of the grade-school kid who sits in the first row of the class and always raises his hand to answer every question the teacher asks.

These were the career numbers for Hershiser entering the 1988 season.

Year	Tm	W	L	W-L%	ERA	G	GS	GF	CG	SHO	SV	IP	H	R	ER	HR	BB	IBB	SO
1983–1987	LAD	60	41	.594	2.91	161	124	17	35	11	4	933.1	806	360	302	48	284	29	655

Hershiser was 29 years old and looked younger. He always looked younger than his age. He was tall and thin. He wore glasses. He was pasty white. He was a Christian, and he knew what others thought of Christian athletes, especially those who were tall and thin and pasty white and wore glasses and looked really young.

Even if they didn't say it to his face, Orel wondered if others thought he was soft, thought he had no guts, thought he couldn't be counted on when the games really mattered.

In spring training, Hershiser's name rarely appeared in the newspapers. The most ink he received was over an emergency appendectomy in early February. Earlier that day, Orel played 18 holes of golf. He'd hit a shot, felt pain in his stomach, leaned against a tree for balance, and assured the guys in his group that he was okay. Hershiser figured it was just something he ate.

After the round, Orel drove himself across town from West Los Angeles to Pasadena (an hour's drive, if you're lucky in traffic), stopping a few times to relieve himself, and tried to take a nap when he got home.

When the pain didn't go away, his wife, Jamie, called Dr. Mickey Mellman, one of the Dodgers' physicians, and explained the symptoms. Mellman ordered Orel to the hospital immediately. Orel's brother, Gordie, was in town and helped get him into the car.

Four days after the appendectomy operation, Orel was out of the hospital. He flew to Florida a few days later and started throwing batting practice on his second day in camp.

There wasn't much publicity after that. He was mentioned as the reliable No. 2 starter, mostly within the context of the question marks after him and Valenzuela in the rotation. His spring performances were dot-dot-dot items in the notes section. Hershiser wasn't much of a story in March—not with Gibson's arrival and subsequent tantrum and the decisions regarding who would play where.

Hershiser's personal goals were the same every year—he wanted to pitch more than 200 innings, and he wanted to win at least 20 games.

After the 1987 season, Hershiser publicly stated that management needed to bring in better players. It did. Hershiser knew the team would be better in 1988. He didn't know how much better. He didn't care about preseason predictions by anybody, and he didn't think about rebuilding, or master plans, or anything else. He called it "putting on blinders" and just doing his job.

The departed Bob Welch was starting in Oakland the same night as Hershiser made his season debut. Hershiser's opponent was Kelly Downs, another one of those Giants pitchers who was good enough to make the majors but entirely hittable until Roger Craig taught him the split-fingered fastball. Now Downs was a threat, and after five innings in the second game of the season, Downs was throwing a perfect game.

This was a Giants-Dodgers game, so naturally, there was added drama. On an 0–2 pitch in the second inning, Downs threw a fastball over Mike Marshall's head before striking him out. During the next inning, with two outs and nobody on base Hershiser plunked Will Clark in the right leg. Umpire Jim Quick quickly warned both benches.

It was still scoreless in the sixth. Mike Scioscia dropped a soft single over shortstop Jose Uribe's head, becoming the Dodgers' first base runner. Then the Giants tried one of those plays that Roger Craig loved, the kind of play you see in college or maybe in high school.

The first baseman, Will Clark, sprinted home anticipating a bunt. The second baseman, Robby Thompson, sprinted to first base, and the pitcher tried to pick off the runner, who took a big lead once he saw the first baseman abandon his position. It's a play to make the other team look careless and stupid as much as it's a play to get an out and stop a rally. They tried it again now.

Only this time, Downs' throw was off target. It hit Scioscia, who threw Thompson out of his way and advanced to second base. Hershiser watched all this from the batter's box. Hershiser was no longer bunting. Now he was swinging. On a 2–2 pitch, he flied out to center field for an apparent out. But second-base umpire Dave Pallone called a balk on Downs, and Scioscia advanced to third.

The 1988 season would be known as "the year of the balk." The increase in calls stemmed from the 1987 World Series when Cardinals manager Whitey Herzog argued adamantly that Twins pitcher Bert Blyleven wasn't coming to a complete stop from the stretch. The league offices sent an edict to umpires that pitchers must come to a "discernible" stop. This was the first of numerous Dodgers games in 1988 in which balks played a major role.

Now it was Lasorda's turn to get creative. Even with two strikes, even with the catcher Scioscia at third, Lasorda signaled for a suicide squeeze. Hershiser got the bunt down, Scioscia scored, and it was 1–0 Dodgers.

Same score in the eighth. Craig took out Downs and brought in Scott Garrelts, another of those pitchers who went from pretty good to very good when he learned the split-finger fastball. The Giants were constantly moving Garrelts from the rotation to the bullpen. This year, he was pitching in relief. He opened the eighth by walking John Shelby, and then a passed ball moved him to second. Scioscia dumped another hit into shallow left, a replay of his earlier hit, and it was 2–0.

Hershiser bunted Scioscia to second. The crowd gave Hershiser a standing ovation. Pallone called another balk, this time on Garrelts. The crowd roared again as Scioscia went to third. Rattled, Garrelts walked Sax. Griffin doubled to right, scoring two runs for a 4–0 lead.

Craig didn't want to mess with Gibson and walked the slugger intentionally. Jeff Hamilton was batting cleanup because he pinch ran for Guerrero in the seventh and remained in the game for better defense. Hamilton hit a ground ball to third baseman Kevin Mitchell—yes, he was still an infielder—and the time was ripe for Kirk Gibson to show Dodgers fans and his teammates what it was like to have Kirk Gibson on your team.

Gibson was forced out at second base, but he took out Thompson with his slide. Thompson dropped the ball as he attempted to turn the double play. Griffin scored all the way from second base. It was 5–0 Dodgers.

Hershiser went the distance, needing 111 pitches. Three hits. Two walks. Six strikeouts. No runs.

The season-opening, two-game series was a draw.

"We definitely need nights like this," Scioscia said that night. "We aren't always going to get our big hammers to hit three-run home runs. We have to manufacture [runs] sometimes."

◆ ◆ ◆ ◆

April 14, 1988
San Diego
Dodgers vs. Padres
Team record: 6–2, ½-game behind Houston

Eight games into the season, Kirk Gibson had more strikeouts than hits. He was 8-for-33, and had a .242 batting average with 13 strikeouts. He'd hit just one home run and admitted it was meaningless because it came in the eighth inning of an 11–3 win over the lowly Atlanta Braves.

The ninth game was another tough night for Kirk Gibson. The Dodgers were shut out 2–0 by Padres pitchers Jimmy Jones, Mark Davis, and Lance McCullers. Gibson threw his bat after Jones struck him out to end the fifth inning.

A better chance arrived in the seventh inning. There was a runner at second base and two outs. It was the type of situation Gibson craved—the type of situation that Gibson was brought over to hit in.

Padres manager Larry Bowa went to the mound to check on his starting pitcher.

"You know the next hitter is Gibson?" Bowa asked.

"Yeah. I've walked him twice," Jones said.

Bowa didn't like that answer. As soon as he heard it, he motioned for the bullpen. Bowa brought in lefty Mark Davis, who would win the Cy Young Award a year later.

Gibson grounded weakly to first baseman John Kruk to end the inning. It was already the third time in 1988 that Davis had retired Gibson in late-game situations. Gibson's bat was silent, but his tongue was sharp after the game that night.

On Jimmy Jones, Gibson said, "We know we can beat this guy. We will beat him next time. It's not like Roger Clemens on the mound, blowing away 13 hitters."

On Mark Davis, Gibson commented, "He better enjoy it while it lasts. I'm not afraid of him. I'm going to get him next time."

Davis represented exactly what the Dodgers had been seeking since Steve Howe's drug problems—a reliable left-handed reliever for late in the game.

Lasorda's left-handed reliever on this night was starting pitcher Fernando Valenzuela. Even after Davis retired Gibson, it was still 1–0 Padres. In the bottom of the seventh, Valenzuela loaded the bases on two singles and a walk. His pitch count was at 126. Lasorda left him in. Valenzuela walked Kruk to force in a run. The score was 2–0. Valenzuela finished the inning without any further damage. He pitched the eighth inning and finished with a whopping 150 pitches in the game.

After the game, Lasorda was asked if he felt like he had to leave Valenzuela in the game.

"Absolutely," Lasorda said. "Who should have I brought in? [Brad] Havens?"

Once the reporters had retreated to the press box to file their stories, Lasorda approached Gibson. Like most high-profile free agents, Gibson was pressing at the plate.

"Let's go out for one drink," Lasorda told Gibson.

Gibson sipped two beers. Lasorda nursed one vodka. The two just talked. Lasorda did most of the talking. He reminded Gibson he doesn't have to hit the ball to Pasadena, just hit the ball up the alleys. But most of the conversation wasn't even about baseball. They talked about family, about Gibson's parents, his wife, and his newborn child. This was Lasorda's gift. He knew the name of every player's wife, the name of his parents, and the name of his children.

Lasorda bonded with his intense, ultracompetitive new star. Gibson saw the fire in Lasorda, how badly he hated to lose, how much family mattered to him as well, how he viewed the Dodgers as his family, and how much he cared about his players.

It was that night that Gibson started to visualize what it would be like to win a World Series with Tommy Lasorda.

◆ ◆ ◆ ◆

April 23, 1988
San Francisco
Dodgers vs. Giants
Team record: 9–4, first-place tie with Houston

They hadn't played a game in five days. They say it never rains in Southern California? Well, it rained three straight days at Dodger Stadium.

The first rainout wasn't bad. Sax, Gibson, and Shelby were all unavailable due to injuries. The second rainout was convenient, too. All three still weren't available, and Shelby was headed to the disabled list. The third rainout led to moments of stir crazy. Danny Heep went onto the field wearing flippers, a snorkel in his mouth, and carrying a kickboard. This wasn't New York in April. This was Los Angeles.

The Dodgers flew north to San Francisco and finally got to play…for all of six minutes. After batting in the top of the first, the rain hit Candlestick Park. The players were waved off the field. After a 95-minute delay, the game was postponed.

"At least we got to bat tonight," a laughing Lasorda said that night. "This is unbelievable. Four rainouts? I can't even remember three."

The Giants wanted to make up the game three days later, on a Monday that both teams were off. The Dodgers players voted against that plan, opting to play a doubleheader later in the season. Why the veto? The *San Francisco Chronicle* reported that numerous Dodgers players were going to a Bruce Springsteen concert at the L.A. Sports Arena and didn't want to miss The Boss.

Four rainouts meant four makeup games, possibly four doubleheaders down the road. It meant the hitters were rusty and all the pitchers needed work. Valenzuela was supposed to start on the 19th, then on 20th, and then on the 21st. He warmed up on the 22nd but never threw a pitch in the game.

The Dodgers finally played on the 23rd. Hershiser started on seven days rest against Mike Krukow. It was 1–1 after six innings, and Hershiser was lifted for a pinch hitter in the seventh. Two batters later, Griffin tripled home three runs for a 5–1 lead.

In the ninth inning, Mike Marshall hit a grand slam, right after Craig had intentionally walked Guerrero. Craig had tried the same thing a year earlier at Candlestick. Marshall hit a three-run homer that time too, and pointed at Craig in the dugout afterward. Those Giants fans couldn't stand the way Marshall feasted on Giants pitching. They hated Marshall.

Craig didn't second-guess himself for either intentional walk. "Ninety percent of the people in this room would have made that move," Craig said.

The Dodgers won 10–3. Their record was 10–4.

Hershiser was 4–0 in four starts with a 1.11 ERA.

◆ ◆ ◆ ◆

April 24, 1988
San Francisco
Dodgers vs. Giants
Team record: 10–4, one-game lead over Houston

Jay Howell was used to getting booed in Northern California.

The Oakland A's acquired him after the 1984 season from the New York Yankees—along with Tim Birtsas, Stan Javier, Eric Plunk, and Jose Rijo—for Rickey Henderson. Howell was an All-Star in his first year, saving 29 games, posting a 2.85 ERA, and throwing a whopping 98 innings in 63 relief appearances.

Injuries reduced Howell to 38 games and 53⅓ innings in 1986, although he still saved 16 (of 20) games and posted a 3.38 ERA.

Then the 1987 season came along. Howell blew the save in his first appearance of the year, and again in his fifth appearance. He settled into a better groove, racking up 14 saves by July 1, not allowing a run the entire month of June, and he was selected to his second All-Star Game, which was played in Oakland.

Then his elbow started to flare up. He tried to pitch through the pain and lost his effectiveness. Howell blew a save on July 1 at Chicago. Then he blew another save on July 12 at home against the Brewers, the final day before the All-Star Game.

A's fans were already frustrated with Howell. They took out those frustrations on Howell at the Midsummer Classic, booing their own player during pregame player introductions. They booed him again when Howell entered the scoreless game in the 12th inning. Howell pitched a clean 12th inning and then allowed a two-run triple by Tim Raines in the 13th inning for the only runs in the National League's 2–0 win.

After the All-Star nightmare, it went from bad to worse. Howell blew the save in each of his next four appearances over a nine-day stretch. He allowed 10 runs and 19 base runners over 5⅔ innings the rest of July. His eighth blown save was August 2. His final appearance was August 23, before undergoing season-ending elbow surgery. That led to the off-season trade.

The Dodgers were thrilled to get Howell. Al Campanis had tried to get him the previous off-season. They offered first baseman Greg Brock for Howell, but the A's weren't interested. The Dodgers offered Brock for center fielder Dwayne Murphy, but again the A's weren't interested. They tried Brock for pitcher Steve Ontiveros, and the A's continued to show no interest.

The A's didn't want a first baseman because they had high hopes for a rookie entering the 1987 season. His name was Rob Nelson. There was also a kid who played third base in the farm system that could get moved to first base, if needed. His name was Mark McGwire.

Still recovering from the elbow surgery in spring training, Howell was also slowed by back problems. Lasorda used Howell sparingly to begin the 1988 season, just twice in the first 13 games.

Howell's first real test came on April 24. Fernando Valenzuela pitched seven crafty scoreless innings and took a 4–0 lead into the eighth. Jose Uribe and Kevin Mitchell singled. Jeffrey Leonard walked. Bases loaded. Two outs. Candy Maldonado was due up. What was Lasorda to do? A year earlier, there was no doubt he'd leave Valenzuela in the game. Earlier that month, Lasorda left Valenzuela in the game.

This time in San Francisco, Lasorda took out Valenzuela. He brought in Howell. These were the situations the cost the Dodgers in 1987. This is why Howell was acquired in that trade from Oakland that made Lasorda cry because Bob Welch was gone.

Giants manager Roger Craig was hoping to see Howell in the game. Hell, the entire Bay Area was hoping to see Howell in the game. The boos only got worse for Howell after the All-Star Game. Craig wanted Howell in the game because that meant he could bring Will Clark off the bench. Clark didn't start because of food poisoning. Clark felt dehydrated and weak. But he was still Will "the Thrill" Clark.

The Candlestick crowd was on its feet, hooting and hollering and yelling at Howell. That's what happened in the Bay Area. Howell was booed. It didn't matter what side of the Bay. Howell was booed—always.

Howell would rather walk in a run than give Clark a fastball. He threw five straight sliders. The count ran full, 3–2. Here came the sixth straight slider. Clark swung and missed. The crowd went silent. Howell pitched a clean ninth inning to complete his first save as a Dodger.

"Now that is Jay Howell," said Mike Davis, who knew what his former teammate had endured in the Bay Area. "If he had done it in Oakland, it would have been awesome. But it doesn't matter where he did it. It shows he's a very good reliever."

If Howell felt any extra vindication, he wasn't going to admit it publicly.

"I was just glad to be able to go in in that type of situation," Howell said that day. "I didn't have the time or really wanted to think about that other stuff. It's the Giants I faced [not the A's]. That's over, as far as I'm concerned."

◆ ◆ ◆ ◆

April 30, 1988
Los Angeles
Cardinals vs. Dodgers
Team record: 13–6, ½-game ahead of Houston

A few days into spring training, Fernando Valenzuela approached a reporter. "What happened with me? Nobody comes to me anymore?" He looked at another reporter. "You want to talk with me? No? Okay, no interviews today."

Valenzuela walked off in mock disgust. Valenzuela was no longer "a story" in 1988. But he was still Fernando Valenzuela, still loved, and still a cult figure.

"Nobody in the world doesn't like Fernando," teammate Tim Leary reflected. "He would get recognized in a mall in Montreal by people who couldn't speak English. People loved the guy, to this day. He's the Pope."

But it was now his eighth full year in the majors. On the days he pitched, there wasn't a dramatic spike in attendance that characterized his incredible 1981 rookie season.

Valenzuela always threw a lot of pitches. He always threw a lot of innings. All those innings and all those pitches—especially all those screwballs—were taking a toll. It was inevitable.

Valenzuela didn't make the All-Star team in 1987 for the first time in his career. He led the league in hits allowed (254) and walks allowed (124). He managed a 14–14 record and never missed a start, but his 3.98 ERA was the highest of his career, and the 190 strikeouts was his lowest total in four years.

"You started to see a toll from the innings," Scioscia reflected. "It probably started in '86, even though he won 20 games. Toward the end of the year, he was laboring a little bit more but still effective. In '87, he still threw a full season of starts, but the stuff just wasn't as crisp."

Valenzuela's average start in 1987 was 7.4 innings, 7.5 hits, 3.6 walks, 5.6 strikeouts, and 3.98 earned runs. Pitch counts aren't available for 1987. If they were, they would be stunning. Pitch counts are available for 1988, however. After that 150-pitch game against the Padres, all those rainouts meant Valenzuela had nine days between starts. Perhaps that was a good thing.

It was cold and windy in Los Angeles on April 30. It felt like Candlestick but looked like 1981 in the stands. Dodger Stadium was sold out, no doubt in part because Fernando was pitching, but it was also a Saturday night and the defending National League champion Cardinals were in town, too.

Valenzuela had become a nibbler, working the edges of the plate and walking too many hitters. That's dangerous against any team, especially a team with the speed of the Cardinals. Valenzuela walked Vince Coleman and Ozzie Smith to start the game. He struck out Willie McGee, and then Coleman and Smith executed a double steal. Bob Horner, the Cardinals' answer after losing Jack Clark to free agency, hit a sacrifice fly for a 1–0 lead.

In the third inning, Valenzuela walked Smith again, and two runs would score. Of his first 62 pitches, only 31 were strikes.

After the third inning, Valenzuela wore glasses on the mound for the first time in his life. It was primarily because of the wind. But those glasses would appear on his face more often than not during the rest of his career. The Cardinals won the game 5–2.

All told, Valenzuela walked six in eight innings, gave up five runs (four earned), and struck out four. All that work led to 137 pitches. But this was before pitch counts were obsessed over. As usual, Valenzuela got better as the game went on. That's one of the reasons Lasorda left him in games so often. The other reason on this night?

"It just seemed like he couldn't get loose," Lasorda said, thinking the weather conditions were the reason. "That might have been a factor. Fernando had that nine days off between starts [because of four rainouts], then had five days off before tonight, and will have six days off before his next start, so we wanted to keep him in there and let him get in a groove. Otherwise, I would have pulled him for a pinch-hitter."

Chapter 4

The First Shutout

Sunday, September 4, 1988
New York
Dodgers vs. Mets
Team record: 77–57, first place by 5½ games over the Astros

The first time Orel Hershiser visited New York City was at age eight. That was also the year he started wearing glasses. He competed in a local contest for running, throwing, and hitting. His score was high enough that he was selected for the finals at Yankee Stadium.

Hershiser finished third in the nation in the 1967 Personna contest in the Bronx. He took home a trophy and decided he was going to be a Major League Baseball player when he grew up.

Born on September 16, 1958, in Buffalo, New York, Orel Leonard Hershiser IV played mostly baseball as a kid. At age 12, the Hershisers moved to Canada, and Orel picked up ice hockey. He was a defenseman and wore glasses. That made him a target.

"Picture a kid with a helmet on, with glasses on underneath, and being a string bean, and put 4" inches of skates under his 6'3½" body," his father, Orel III, once said. "He was a real gangler out there. [Opponents] would take a run at him once or twice—until they found out that, 'Hey, this wasn't going to be easy.'"

The Hershiser family was always into sports. Orel III played baseball as a kid and semi-pro hockey as an adult. He and wife Mildred remained avid golfers into their sixties.

Older sister Katie played college volleyball on a scholarship at Kentucky. Younger brother Gordie pitched at Alabama, was drafted four times before signing with the Dodgers as a free agent, and went 7–0 with a 2.35 ERA for the Dodgers' short-season Salem club in 1988. Youngest brother Judd earned a golf scholarship to Alabama-Birmingham.

The family moved to New Jersey when Orel started high school. He tried out for varsity baseball as a freshman but was assigned to the freshman team. He tried out for the varsity as a sophomore but was assigned to the junior varsity team. He made varsity as a junior where he pitched and played shortstop.

In the summer, he played Babe Ruth League ball—and on July 3, 1974, Hershiser pitched a no-hitter. Even back then, his last name was tough on news people. On page 20 of the *Cherry Hill (N.J.) News*, the headline read: "Nerheiser Hurls No-Hitter."

Hershiser was good at Cherry Hill East High School. Not good enough to get drafted, however, and certainly not good enough to pitch for one of those big-time college baseball factories. He went to Bowling Green State University in Ohio, which was a member of the Mid-American Conference.

◆ ◆ ◆ ◆

Orel Hershiser was back in New York on September 4, 1988, for what was supposed to be his 153rd career start and 29th start of that season.

Hershiser would face a Mets lineup that featured Lenny Dykstra, recent minor league wonder boy Gregg Jefferies, Keith Hernandez, Gary Carter, Darryl Strawberry, Kevin McReynolds, and Howard Johnson—a lineup that would lead the National League in runs scored and home runs.

David Cone was scheduled to start for the Mets. He would face a lineup without Kirk Gibson (strained right buttock) and without Mike Marshall (strained right thigh muscle). The Dodgers had lost three straight games overall, including the first two of the series in Queens. In 11 games against the Mets that year, the Dodgers scored just 18 runs and lost 10 times.

It seemed like the only thing that could stop the Mets from beating the Dodgers in the regular season was rain. And that's why the Mets finished the year 10–1 against the Dodgers instead of 11–1. After nearly a two-hour delay, the game was rained out.

Hershiser was relieved. Not because he feared another beat-down that the Mets were handing out to the Dodgers. He was relieved because he didn't want to pitch after sitting around for three hours and not doing anything.

The weekend "possible playoff preview" made it seem like the Dodgers had no chance in the playoffs. Hershiser turned philosophical to reporters after the game was canceled.

"Even if we had won today, people still would've said the Mets had dominated us," Hershiser said that day. "I don't think one game would have erased it. If this team could get anything out of the past, it's two things: One, it'll make us bear down if we get to the playoffs. And two, to forget about the past and think about the job at hand. If we execute the fundamentals, reduce the game to its simplest form, escape all the hype that will be there, the game will be easier."

Hershiser's next start would be easier. It was the next day against a Braves team that was in last place, 31 games out of first place, and would score the fewest runs in the league that season.

◆ ◆ ◆ ◆

Monday, September 5, 1988
Atlanta
Dodgers vs. Braves
Team record: 77–57, five-game lead over the Astros

DODGERS	BRAVES
2B Steve Sax	2B Jeff Blauser
SS Alfredo Griffin	LF Dion James
LF Kirk Gibson	1B Gerald Perry
RF Mickey Hatcher	RF Dale Murphy
CF John Shelby	SS Andres Thomas
1B Franklin Stubbs	C Ozzie Virgil
C Mike Scioscia	3B Paul Runge
3B Jeff Hamilton	CF Terry Blocker
P Orel Hershiser	P Rick Mahler

Pitching on five days rest, one more than usual, Hershiser felt too strong. The sinker wasn't sinking the way he preferred, and he knew it in the bullpen. Three years earlier, Hershiser didn't have the confidence to leave the bullpen without his best stuff. He'd have thrown and thrown until he felt right.

At age 29, Hershiser knew he could still get outs with location and making adjustments. Hershiser's strategy was to intentionally overthrow for the first four innings, figuring he would wear the edge off. Besides, he already led 2–0 on a two-run Mickey Hatcher single when he took the mound.

Sure enough, the best stuff wasn't there in the early innings of the game. In the first inning, Jeff Blauser grounded to short, and Dion James grounded to second. But then first baseman Gerald Perry doubled to left, and two-time Most Valuable Player Dale Murphy dug into the batter's box. With the count 2–1, Hershiser hung a curveball.

Murphy swung and missed.

Hershiser felt fortunate. He knew that type of pitch could have easily resulted in a two-run homer. Murphy swung and missed at the next pitch, too, ending the inning.

Including the final 4⅓ innings from his previous start against the Expos, Hershiser's scoreless streak was at five innings.

Andres Thomas led off the second inning with a ground-ball single to left field. He was erased on a 6-4-3 double play off the bat of Ozzie Virgil. Paul Runge struck out looking. The streak was six.

In the Dodgers' third, Sax doubled, stole second, and scored on an errant throw. Hershiser had a 3–0 lead. He didn't have to be precise. He didn't have to think about a shutout. He just had to get outs.

Terry Blocker started the third inning with a single just like Thomas'. Pitcher Rick Mahler laid down a successful sacrifice bunt, moving Blocker into scoring position. Blauser lined out sharply to center. James walked. On a 2–2 pitch, Perry flied out to deep right-center. The streak was at seven.

In the fourth, Hershiser hung another curveball to Murphy, and again Murphy missed it. Murphy struck out swinging. Thomas grounded to third. Virgil struck out looking. The streak was at eight.

By the fifth, the edge was off. Hershiser felt like his usual self, and the ball was moving the way he wanted. Runge flied out to right field. Blocker grounded out to first with Hershiser covering. Mahler grounded out to second. The inning took six pitches. The streak was nine.

The sixth inning required 10 pitches. Blauser grounded to short. James grounded to second. Perry struck out looking. The streak was at 10.

Murphy led off the seventh inning, and with the count at 2–2 Hershiser made his pitching coach cringe. He dropped down for a side-arm curveball to strike him out. Hershiser looked into the Dodgers' dugout and smiled at pitching coach Ron Perranoski. The smile was not returned.

"I cringe every time he does that," Perranoski said. "I don't think it's healthy for him, number one. And two, it can [mess up] the mechanics on his other pitches. But he still does it. Even once is too much."

Hershiser returned to his usual delivery. Thomas struck out swinging. Virgil flew out to right field. The streak was at 11.

Albert Hall pinch hit for Runge to begin the eighth. He grounded weakly to second. Blocker grounded to first. Ron Gant pinch hit for Mahler and grounded to third. The streak was 12.

Hershiser had retired 16 batters in a row when Blauser singled to left to open the ninth. James grounded to first, and Blauser moved to second. Perry lofted a high fly ball to deep center, but the ballpark held it, and John Shelby squeezed it. Hershiser's 109th and final pitch of the ninth struck out Murphy for a fourth time.

The streak was at 13 scoreless innings.

Pitching	IP	H	R	ER	BB	SO	HR	ERA	BF	Pit	Str	Ctct	StS	StL	GB	FB	LD
Orel Hershiser, W (19–8)	9	4	0	0	1	8	0	2.73	31	109	69	35	10	24	16	6	2

The Dodgers won 3–0. Their lead remained five games over the Astros. The postgame topics were Hershiser's pursuit of 20 wins and the Cy Young Award. The word "streak" was never used.

Hershiser won his final five starts in 1985 to reach 19 wins and pitched in relief on the final day but wasn't able to win his 20th. He won 14 games in 1986 and 16 games in 1987. He wanted 20 wins—badly.

Now, in 1988, Hershiser was 19–8.

"I've got five more starts to do it," Hershiser said. "Hopefully, I won't stop at 20. I want to win as many as possible and help the team win our division."

The top candidates for the Cy Young Award race at the end of play September 5 looked like this:

Player	W-L	ERA	IP	H (BABIP)	BB	SO	Opp. Slash line
Danny Jackson, CIN	20–6	2.49	224.1	169 (.245)	59	143	.210/.264/.291
Orel Hershiser, LAD	19 8	2.73	221.0	182 (.251)	65	152	.223/.281/.335
David Cone, NYM	15–3	2.31	190.2	144 (.265)	68	166	.211/.284/.293

Not surprisingly, manager Tommy Lasorda, catcher Mike Scioscia, and other teammates lobbied for Hershiser. But they don't have a vote. Hershiser knew who did have a vote—two sportswriters in each National League city.

An hour after the game, once the scribes had retreated to the press box to file their dispatches, Hershiser and Dave Anderson stopped by the press box.

"You guys need any more quotes?" Hershiser asked.

Chapter 5

May

Tuesday, May 10, 1988
Chicago
Dodgers vs. Cubs
Team record: 18–9, two games ahead of the Astros

Kirk Gibson was tired. Kirk Gibson was pissed. Kirk Gibson was hungry.

Gibson hadn't eaten since 9:00 AM. The game started at 1:20 PM. It had lasted more than four hours, and Gibson blamed himself that it was still going.

Gibson had two singles, two runs scored, and a stolen base to help the Dodgers take a 5–1 lead into the sixth inning. Their lead came at the expense of Chicago Cubs pitcher Rick Sutcliffe, who exchanged words with Pedro Guerrero after a 3–0 fastball was too high and too far inside to Guerrero's liking. The two had once been minor league teammates. Guerrero homered off Sutcliffe the year before and had eyeballed him as he trotted around the bases.

Guerrero threw his bat toward the Dodgers' dugout in anger after Sutcliffe's pitch nearly hit him. Teammates needed to restrain Guerrero from charging after Sutcliffe.

The Cubs scored three runs in the sixth. The big hit was a two-run double by Rafael Palmeiro. The Dodgers still led 5–4 in the ninth, and Jesse Orosco was trying to close out the victory. Orosco had two outs and Vance Law at first base.

Shawon Dunston smoked a ball to left field. Gibson got a late jump on it but raced back to make the game-ending catch. Only he didn't. He reached his glove up and just missed it. Gibson crashed into the ivy, the ball hit the top of the wall, and Law scored the tying run.

"The Cardinal rule is you don't let anything go over your head in the ninth," Gibson said that night. "I felt it was my fault. I blew the play. I couldn't have missed the ball by much, maybe 6"."

Jay Howell pitched a scoreless 10th but took himself out because of pain in his surgically repaired elbow. The game kept going. Brian Holton pitched a scoreless 11th, 12th, and 13th inning.

Les Lancaster was one out away from a fifth scoreless inning of relief in the 14th inning. But he hung a curveball, and Gibson absolutely crushed it. Even with the wind blowing in at 14 mph, the ball landed in the fifth row of the right field bleachers. Andre Dawson actually went back on the ball, like he had a chance to catch it.

Gibson muttered to himself, "No way Andre. Don't even bother."

The only pitcher left in the Dodgers' bullpen was Brad Havens. Lasorda didn't trust Havens. Lasorda hadn't trusted Havens since that grand slam to John Kruk back in April. It's hard to manage a five-person bullpen when you don't trust one of the pitchers. Still, Lasorda wasn't using Havens.

Instead, he sent Orel Hershiser, who was scheduled to start the next day, into the bullpen to get loose. Hershiser pitched the bottom of the 14th, needing just five pitches to get three outs and record the save.

"Win them today, and you don't have to win them next time," Lasorda explained to reporters.

That's how Lasorda managed. Bold and daring. Unafraid of hurting somebody's feelings. Not thinking about tomorrow's game when there's a game to be won today. Pitchers were pitchers. Starting pitchers were expected to pitch in relief when needed, and all of his starting pitchers would be used in relief that season.

That wouldn't fly nowadays. But it wasn't all that uncommon in 1988. In fact, 500 miles north of Los Angeles, Tony La Russa was inventing the modern bullpen in Oakland that season. In the years that followed, every manager would follow his formula. But not Lasorda—he managed on instincts, with his heart, with his eyes, he didn't care about pitch counts, he didn't care about egos, and he didn't care about conventional roles.

It wouldn't be the last time in 1988 that Gibson hit a home run in extra innings, and it wouldn't be the last time Orel Hershiser was needed in relief.

♦ ♦ ♦ ♦

Wednesday, May 11, 1988
Pittsburgh
Dodgers vs. Pirates
Team record: 19–9, three games ahead of the Astros

After his surprise relief appearance to save the game in Chicago, Hershiser didn't start the next game in Pittsburgh as scheduled. He was pushed back to the next day. Instead, the start went to Fernando Valenzuela, who was still on his normal rest.

Valenzuela was like Muhammad Ali on the ropes, bobbing and weaving but refusing to get knocked out. It took him 90 pitches to get through four innings. By the end of the seventh, he'd struck out eight and allowed seven hits and four walks. Despite those 11 base runners, Valenzuela took a 1–0 lead into the eighth inning.

The only run scored in the fifth inning on a Mike Scioscia double, a sacrifice bunt by Alfredo Griffin, and a single by Valenzuela.

In the eighth, Valenzuela walked Darnell Coles on four pitches to start the inning. Valenzuela's pitch count was at a whopping 137 pitches, and that was finally it.

"I'm having trouble almost every inning, especially with the walks," admitted Valenzuela that night. "When you walk and strike out so many guys, you have to throw many pitches. I've been having trouble the last two years with that. I'm not a power pitcher. I have to move the ball around."

Even though Jesse Orosco had blown a lead the day before, he had saved three straight before that one, and he was summoned to replace Valenzuela. It was Orosco's seventh appearance in 12 days.

Orosco walked Randy Milligan and struck out Matt Diaz. Then Junior Ortiz hit a single to left, scoring Coles with the tying run. Orosco induced a double play grounder to escape further damage in the eighth inning. He also worked a scoreless ninth, as well. The Dodgers went to extra innings for the second straight game.

Jay Howell's elbow was barking. He would go on the disabled list within a few weeks, but he was still pitching now. Howell walked two in the 10th inning but didn't allow a run. Howell wouldn't risk pitching another inning of relief, especially since he'd been getting warmed up from the seventh inning on.

In the 11th, it was left for Alejandro Pena, who normally didn't pitch on consecutive days after his shoulder surgery three years earlier. But with a 10-man pitching staff (and a five-man bullpen), on the heels of 14 innings the day before, Pena was needed.

Pena walked Andy Van Slyke with one out, and a wild pitch moved him to second. Bobby Bonilla was walked intentionally. John Cangelosi struck out, then Randy Milligan doubled home Van Slyke with the game winner. It was the first run Pena had allowed in 15 innings that year.

Lasorda was testy after the game. He didn't like the questions about Valenzuela's growing pitch count. "We thought maybe he was getting tired. The amount of pitches doesn't make my decision."

Lasorda didn't like the questions about overusing Orosco, either. "He said he felt fine. Otherwise, we wouldn't have put him in there, pal."

◆ ◆ ◆ ◆

Thursday, May 12, 1988
Pittsburgh
Dodgers vs. Pirates
Team record: 19–10, three-game lead over the Astros

The bullpen needed a rest. If ever there was a time for Orel Hershiser to pitch nine innings, it was after a 14-inning victory and an 11-inning loss. Hershiser gave his team seven innings—and seven runs allowed.

Barry Bonds, still a leadoff hitter, took him deep to leadoff the game and added a two-run home run in third inning. Bobby Bonilla hit a three-run homer in the seventh inning.

Hershiser insisted his worst outing of the year had nothing to do with pitching in relief two days earlier. "Not at all," he said that night. "I felt great. I had no problems other than my location. The home runs were all poorly located, and I wish I had them back. Physically, I felt good. Mechanically, I felt all right. But something's missing."

What was missing was the sink on his fastball, the bite on his curveball, and the location of his fastball. In total, he gave up 12 hits and three walks.

At least he gave the bullpen a breather. Lasorda finally found a spot where he would trust Brad Havens—trailing 7–3 in the eighth inning. Havens pitched a scoreless eighth then was optioned to the minors after the game to make room for Tim Crews.

In all, the Dodgers went 3–3 and were rained out on a seven-game, three-city road trip.

◆ ◆ ◆ ◆

Tuesday, May 17, 1988
Los Angeles
Expos vs. Dodgers
Team record: 21–12, two games ahead of the Astros

Dodgers fans weren't sprinting back to the ballpark. Through 18 games, the Dodgers attendance was down 84,968 from a similar time a year before. They were still averaging 37,051 fans a game—numbers that teams in most cities would drool over—but it was part of an overall decline.

Remember, attendance had dropped for two straight years. In 1987, the Dodgers failed to draw 3 million fans (in a non-strike season) for the first time since 1979.

George Bush, the vice president on the campaign trail, stopped by Dodger Stadium on May 17. Bush was flanked by Secret Service agents in gray suits. Steve Sax wasn't impressed. "That Secret Service doesn't look so secret," Sax said. "They look obvious to me."

Lasorda gave Bush a tour of the clubhouse and talked about Bush's playing days at Yale. Lasorda gave the VP an autographed bat, two Dodger warm-up jackets, and a T-shirt.

Seated in owner Peter O'Malley's box, Bush lasted as long as Fernando Valenzuela did in the game, and his reception was the same. Normally, that would guarantee a victory on election night. Not in 1988.

Fernando went seven innings. So did Bush. Fernando heard more boos than cheers. So did Bush. Yes, the great Fernando Valenzuela was actually booed at Dodger Stadium. It was another rough night for Valenzuela. He allowed 10 hits and six walks in seven innings. It took all of Valenzuela's guts and guile to limit 16 base runners to just six runs scored.

What was more astonishing, seeing Valenzuela struggle to get hitters like Johnny Paredes out? Looking at another box score and seeing just 61 strikes in 118 pitches? Or hearing boos from the home fans at Dodger Stadium who once worshipped him?

"I remember they booed a lot in 1982 when I showed up in spring training after the holdout," Valenzuela reflected. "I went there after a week [holding out]. I came out in relief, then I came up to hit and got a base hit. That changed everything. It was over. Here in Dodger Stadium, that happened. The fans want to see the team win and sometimes they get frustrated, like we are sometimes. That's part of it.

"Nothing is perfect. I have more good memories than bad. I understand. It was not a big deal. Of course, the fans pay the money for a ticket. They come out to see a good game. If we're not performing, of course it's going to be frustrating for them. They want to see the home team win. I understand that. The only thing is try to do better the next time, and I'm pretty sure it will change the whole thing."

Decades later, ask the question about Valenzuela getting booed at Dodger Stadium, and the looks on the faces are almost painful; the pain is evident in the voices.

"That was sad for all of us," fellow pitcher Tim Belcher said. "I had some great times with Fernando. Me and Tim Crews were his running buddies on the road. He was one of my all-time favorite teammates. He was one of the best humor guys I ever played with. He was a jokester. To see him struggle and be hurt and be booed by Dodger fans after Fernando-mania, it was hard to watch. It was hard for him."

◆ ◆ ◆ ◆

May 20–22, 1988
Los Angeles
Mets vs. Dodgers
Team record: 22–16, ½-game behind the Astros

The Mets were in town, and that meant the Dodgers weren't playing very well.

The Mets won the opener 5–2. They also won the second game 4–0, and that loss would be felt for months. In the fifth inning with two outs and Alfredo Griffin batting, Dwight Gooden threw a pitch up and inside.

"It was a fastball up near my head," Griffin recalled. "I put my hand up, so it wouldn't hit my face. It was just a reaction. I didn't get hit much. I was really quick. I had people throw at me on purpose, and they couldn't hit me. I was that fast. Gooden could bring it. He threw it hard. He threw the ball at my head, and I just reacted to it, I put my hand up."

The ball hit Griffin flush in the right hand. Griffin was upset but stayed in the game. He wondered if the pitch was on purpose. Still upset, he swiped second base. As the minutes passed, the more Griffin felt the pain. The hand was numb. He couldn't move the hand. X-rays showed the hand was broken. Griffin would be out 6–8 weeks.

Griffin was batting .167, with a .214 on-base percentage and a .243 slugging percentage. He was giving the team nothing offensively and everything defensively. Now he was out for two months.

Third-base coach Joe Amalfitano said simply, "I thought we were dead." That's how good a shortstop Alfredo Griffin was.

"I think Alfredo is the one guy who came over that probably had as big an impact as Kirk Gibson," catcher Mike Scioscia reflected. "We had seen Alfredo play from afar. He was in the other league. But from day one in the practice fields, we saw what Alfredo was. I don't know if we were ever more excited about getting such a presence at shortstop in the years that I was playing there. When he went down, we absolutely knew that would be a big void on our team."

One inning after Griffin was hit in the hand, Dodgers reliever Brian Holton hit Mets infielder Howard Johnson in the right leg with his first pitch in the sixth inning. Holton offered the usual response. It was a fastball inside, which just got away. Umpire Dave Pallone, a few weeks after Pete Rose was suspended 30 days for bumping him, warned both benches. No further incidents occurred in that game.

In the series finale, the Mets were looking for the sweep, and the bad blood resurfaced.

Valenzuela didn't make it out of the second inning, giving up five runs on eight base runners. It was the shortest outing of his career. Dodgers fans booed the great Fernando Valenzuela—again. For the first time, Lasorda admitted publicly that he wasn't sure if Valenzuela was healthy.

The Mets led 5–0 in the sixth inning, when Pedro Guerrero stepped into the batter's box. David Cone's first pitch was a fastball up and inside that Guerrero just avoided. The next pitch was a slow curve that hit Guerrero on the shoulder.

An enraged Guerrero threw his bat at Cone. Thankfully, the bat went way left and missed Cone. Guerrero charged the mound. Cone retreated backward, yelling, "It was a curve! It was a curve!" Teammates rushed to Cone's aide. Both benches emptied. Guerrero was ejected and needed to be restrained by Gibson before he did anything stupid.

"I was in disbelief," Cone told reporters that day. "I was in shock. I could not believe he would come after me after that. I threw a curve he had to duck into. He could have gotten out of the way. If I'm going to hit somebody, it'll be a 90 mph fastball. That first pitch wasn't even close [to hitting Guerrero], and he was standing over the plate. It's my job to pitch him inside."

Upon reflection Griffin said, "It was a rival. Everybody was upset. A lot of people thought [Gooden] tried to hit me on purpose. Pedro was upset. If you come close to me, I'm going to throw the bat and get in a fight. I tried to tell him, 'No, we have to win this game.' It happened. It came close to him, he threw the bat, and here we go. That tells you the type of teammate he was. He was letting them know, if you hit my teammate, I'm not happy with it."

A lot of people weren't happy. The league office wasn't happy. Guerrero was suspended for four days. The Mets weren't happy that it was only four days.

"It's a joke," reliever Roger McDowell said at the time. "Some justice. I mean, this guy [Bart Giamatti] is going to crack down on the balk rule, and Guerrero gets only four days?"

Added Mets pitcher Bob Ojeda, "The embarrassment [Guerrero] must feel in looking at his wife and kids after doing something that unmanly is probably punishment enough because he's going to have to live with it for the rest of his life."

◆ ◆ ◆ ◆

May 25, 1988
Philadelphia
Dodgers vs. Phillies
Team record: 23–17, one game behind the Astros

Tim Leary's career was resurrected somewhere between Pacific Palisades and Tijuana.

In the winter of 1987, he made that commute in an old pickup truck to pitch for the Tijuana Potros in the Mexican winter league. The trips were necessities. His career was on the line.

Leary had made his major league debut on April 12, 1981. He was the second overall pick by the New York Mets in the 1979 draft out of UCLA, he signed for a six-figure bonus, and he was the MVP of the Double A Texas League in 1980.

It was 41 degrees in Chicago on the day of Leary's debut. In the second inning, he felt something give in his elbow. He knew it wasn't good that day. He knew it was even worse the next day when he couldn't shave.

Two months later, baseball went on strike. Instead of getting the top care that a top prospect would receive from the top rehabilitation therapists available, Tim Leary received no care. Leary was left to his own remedies and admittedly had no idea what he was doing. He should have rested. Instead, he kept throwing.

The result was learning to pitch without using an elbow. That's essentially what he did at Triple A Tidewater after the strike ended. You can guess how successful that idea was—it led to an inflamed pinched nerve in his shoulder. He missed the entire 1982 season.

In 1983, he was back at Tidewater. He lost 16 games and his ERA was 4.38. In 1984, he spent half the year back at Tidewater (4.05 ERA in 10 starts) and half with the Mets (4.02 ERA in 20 games, seven starts). A writer once quipped that Leary's best pitch was "a single to right."

The Mets gave up on Leary, including him in a four-team trade that involved six players. Leary ended up with the Brewers along with pitcher Danny Darwin and minor leaguer Bill Hance. Don Slaught went to the Rangers, and catcher Jim Sundberg headed for the Royals. The Mets ended up with pitcher Frank Wills.

In 1985 the Brewers sent Leary to Triple A Vancouver where his ERA was 4.00 in 27 starts. He was given five major league starts after September 1 that year, and his ERA was 4.05.

In 1986, the Brewers finished next-to-last in the division, and Leary finally got a chance to pitch every fifth day in the majors. The results were similar to the previous years. His record was 12–12, and his ERA was 4.21.

Leary's ERA was 4.38, 4.05, 4.02, 4.00, 4.05, and 4.21 for his last six teams. At least he was consistent.

The Dodgers didn't necessarily see greatness in Tim Leary. They were just trying to unload Greg Brock. The shadow of Steve Garvey had engulfed Brock so much that he first requested a trade after the 1985 season. Players didn't request trades from the Dodgers very often. It illustrated how frustrated Brock was and how much he needed a fresh start elsewhere. The Dodgers found no takers to their satisfaction that off-season.

In '86, Brock was 6-for-59 with one RBI against lefties. The numbers were so bad, the Dodgers had no choice but to make him a platoon player. The Dodgers tried again to trade him. One proposal was Brock to the Mariners for lefty reliever Matt Young. Another was Brock and Bill Madlock to the Royals for Bud Black. Neither team would bite.

The Dodgers' philosophy in trades was always "when in doubt, take a pitcher" when getting rid of players. So that's what they did. They took a pitcher, Leary, and another pitcher, Tim Crews, in exchange for Brock. The trade was made on December 10, 1986, at the winter meetings. It was the last trade ever made by Al Campanis.

Leary felt like he'd won the lottery. Born and raised in Santa Monica, a product of UCLA, Leary was coming home. Whether he'd actually play for the Dodgers wasn't a guarantee. Campanis considered flipping Leary for a center fielder. Leary even told his mother, "Don't get too excited, I could be traded tomorrow."

Campanis held onto Leary. The homecoming wasn't very impressive. Leary began the year in the bullpen. That didn't work out too well. They tried him in the starting rotation. That didn't work out too well, either. One day, Leary was stretching on the outfield grass, and a reporter asked what he was doing. A teammate explained, "He's practicing to duck."

Leary went 3–11. He allowed 121 hits in 107⅔ innings, including 15 home runs. His ERA was in the 5.00s for most of the year. In the last five weeks, he pitched just good enough to drop the ERA to 4.76 for the year.

Tim Leary was about to turn 29 years old. His place in the major leagues was tenuous at best. He was embarrassed by his performance. He was shocked. The shock wasn't that he was still in the majors. The shock was why he wasn't getting more people out. He knew the talent was there. He just needed to figure out why it wasn't happening.

Leary swallowed his pride and told the Dodgers after the 1987 season that he wanted to pitch in winter ball. He chose Mexico over the Dominican Republic because it was closer to L.A., he was trying to finish his degree at UCLA, and he wanted to be there for his pregnant wife. Leary did get some big-league treatment. He was allowed to commute to work. He'd leave his house in the Pacific Palisades at 2:00 PM, stop for a hamburger along the way, and get to the Mexico border about 5:00 PM.

The Tijuana Stadium had no clubhouse, so Leary dressed at home and drove in his uniform. A couple times, border patrol stopped him because you didn't see people come across the border wearing a baseball uniform very often.

For road games, Leary drove to Tijuana and flew to Mazatlan or Culiacan or Hermosillo or Navajoa. Once, it took him 20 hours to reach his destination after flight delays and bus rides and driving. Leary didn't mind. He was trying to save his career. He was also trying to impress scouts in case the Dodgers released him or traded him.

Leary stopped throwing his curveball that winter. He dominated hitters with a four-seam fastball and a split-fingered fastball that he learned after reading an article about Roger Craig in *Sports Illustrated*.

"It was working for Jack Morris and Mike Scott; it seemed like a no-brainer for me," Leary recalled between bites of his breakfast at a restaurant in Santa Monica just down the street from where he grew up. "It was a complete swing-and-miss pitch, and a good ground ball pitch, and good for righties vs. lefties. It wasn't a hard pitch to throw because I had big enough fingers. It was just a matter of you don't want to hang it. If your arm speed isn't real good, nothing is going to work. If you're throwing hard with a 95 mph arm and the ball is going 95, then the split becomes one of the best out pitches you can possibly have."

In the Mexican Winter League, Leary went 9–0. His ERA was 1.24. The arm strength returned for the first time in years. Just as important, Leary rediscovered something that had been missing since that 41-degree day in Chicago when he made his major league debut—confidence.

Former teammate Mark Knudson also shared with Leary the proper grip of the split. The team most impressed, ironically, was the Brewers. They made an offer to Fred Claire, trying to re-acquire Leary. After the Bob Welch trade, there was no way Claire was trading Tim Leary.

In the spring, Leary led the team with a 1.71 ERA. He struck out 22 and walked six in 32 innings. That earned him the fourth spot in the rotation after Fernando and Orel and Don Sutton.

◆ ◆ ◆ ◆

Leary's confidence was in full bloom entering his start on May 25. He was coming off a seven-hit, no-walk, 10-strikeout shutout of the Expos. His ERA was no longer in the 4.00s. It wasn't even in the 3.00s. It was 2.90, with just seven walks in 49⅔ innings. He was working on a 19-inning scoreless streak, a 0.82 ERA over his last 33 innings, and hadn't walked a batter in 24 innings.

But he walked Milt Thompson to start this game. Then the umpires came to the mound to check his hand and glove. Curious teammates walked over to see what was happening. An unusual substance was on the baseball. This was not an illegal substance, however, it was blood. Leary wasn't doctoring the ball. He'd somehow cut the tip of his middle finger on his pitching hand on a pebble. It gave new meaning to the terms cut fastball and split-fingered fastball.

Dodgers trainers stopped the bleeding with a product called Tough Skin, and Leary made Phillies hitters red-faced the rest of the night. It's not like the Phillies (.225 team batting average) had a lot of tough outs in their lineup in those days. Still, the only thing between Tim Leary and a no-hitter on this day was a Darren Daulton third-inning single. No Phillies reached third base.

"I'm pitching better than any time in my life," Leary said that night. "There's no comparison between this year and last year.… As long as my arm feels strong, it's just a matter of not making a stupid pitch. When you get a lead like tonight, that's a bonus. That helps your confidence."

With the suspended Guerrero out of the lineup, Jeff Hamilton was back at third base. He hit a two-run homer. Mike Scioscia also hit a two-run homer. They were the first home runs of the year for both players. It brought back the old conversation about Hamilton's confidence and his ability to hit. Hamilton said he knew he could hit. He just needed the playing time to prove it.

◆ ◆ ◆ ◆

May 26, 1988
Philadelphia
Dodgers vs. Phillies
Team record: 24–17, tied for first place with the Astros

During the 1981 players' strike, Tommy Lasorda visited the Dodgers' top minor league affiliates to do some first-person scouting. Lasorda visited Double A San Antonio and fell in love with second baseman Steve Sax.

If ever a player and manager were meant to be paired together, it was Steve Sax and Tommy Lasorda. Sax was 21 years old in 1981, a ninth-round pick from Marshall High in West Sacramento who shot through the Dodgers' farm system.

Sax would do whatever it took to get on base—he could run like hell, he was smart, and he played with an energy that's hard to describe. Put it this way: Steve Sax is never in a bad mood. He never had a bad day in his life, and his energy is contagious.

Lasorda knew that when the strike ended—if the strike ended—he wanted Sax in the major leagues. Davey Lopes was 36 years old and in the final year of his contract. Lopes saw the writing on the wall. In spring training that year, Lopes took Sax under his wing, knowing he was helping the guy who would take his job.

A week after the strike ended, Lopes was hurt and Sax was in the majors. Sax hit .364 in his first eight games and stole two bases. The Dodgers had their second baseman for the future, the kid who would break up The Infield. But the future could wait.

Once healthy, Lasorda decided that Lopes would start the final weeks of the regular season and start in the playoffs. The Infield went out winners. The Infield occupied the top four spots in the batting lineup for Game 6 of the World Series, the night the Dodgers won the world title.

The next spring, Lopes was traded to Oakland. Sax won Rookie of the Year in 1982, with a .282 average, 88 runs scored, and 49 stolen bases. The 1983 season was the year of Sax's throwing problems. He made eight errors in April, four in May, 11 in June, and another for·all the world to see in the All-Star Game.

Sax can laugh about it now. But he's also fiercely proud of the way he rebounded from the mental block. He made four errors in July, three in August, and none in September. The last 37 games were error-free that year. In 1989, his first with the Yankees, Sax led the American League in fielding percentage.

Most players who are stricken with "the yips" or "the thing" never rebound. Pitcher Steve Blass had to retire. Dale Murphy moved from catcher to right field. Mike Ivie moved from catcher to first base. Chuck Knoblauch moved from second base to the outfield and retired prematurely. Catcher Mackey Sasser had to retire.

Sax stayed at second base. He played 17 years in the majors. He became a utility infielder late in his career, but he survived "the thing" and lived to tell about it. Sax was never going to be a Gold Glover—not when the award is based on reputation, and his reputation was sealed for life in those first three months in 1983. But his errors dropped to 16 in 1986, 14 in 1987, and advanced defensive measures now show his defense from 1984 to the rest of his career as league average to slightly above average.

"Everybody wants to make fun of Saxy for the throwing issue he had," teammate Mike Marshall reflected. "But he was self-made, a hard-worker. Played every day. Out-worked everybody on the field. All they want to do is make fun of him. Mentally, he struggled because he's a very strong and muscular guy. He lost the feel for throwing a little bit. What a competitor. What a great player. And what a hard worker."

When Griffin arrived in 1988, he noticed that Sax never had an errant throw turning a double play. His theory was that Sax didn't have time to think. On a routine grounder to second, he'd have time to think. Griffin's advice to Sax was treat every grounder like it was a double play. Catch it and throw, as fast as you can.

Griffin doesn't know if his advice made any difference, but he knows that Sax's throwing was never an issue in 1988. What was also never an issue was Sax's un-human energy level.

"He was a machine, Saxy, in and out every day," Griffin said. "I don't know how he did it. He gave 100 percent one day. The next day, he comes back and gives 110 percent. I thought, *Where does this guy get all this energy*? It was unbelievable. He'd hit a grounder, and he's flying to first base. Doesn't matter if we're down one run or up 10 runs. This guy was the best."

Everybody liked Sax. It didn't matter what position you played or where you were from. It was impossible not to like Sax. He was a great player, a great teammate, and he was hilarious. It didn't hurt that he was a lady magnet, either.

With his good looks and relentless energy, Sax became one of the biggest fan favorites in Dodgers history. In 2008, the Dodgers' 50th season in Los Angeles, hundreds of players returned on Opening Day for introductions. Behind Sandy Koufax and Fernando Valenzuela, Steve Sax drew the most cheers of any returning player.

On the road, Sax was hated, especially in San Francisco.

"I remember how much they hated me, and it couldn't be a better compliment," Sax reflected. "I have people today who come up to me because I'm a motivational speaker, and I'll have somebody in the audience who will say, 'Man, I loved your speech, but I hated you when you played for the Dodgers. I'm a Giants fan.' I say, 'Thank you so much.' I know one thing, nobody boos a nobody. If they hated you, they must have feared you or respected you because they wouldn't pay you any attention."

The two people Giants fans hated the most were Sax and Lasorda. They were perfect together.

"Steve Sax could crack up Lasorda on a moment's notice," Leary said. "He could keep the team loose. He was as intense a player as Gibson but also just really quick-witted. Sax could recite every word to *Caddyshack*. He could do imitations to everything. Once somebody can make you laugh, you can just laugh by looking at them."

Sax and Lasorda. They'd go to war against each other in the afternoon and do anything they could to win a game together at night.

"We treated Tommy like one of our teammates," Sax recalled. "We did shit to Tommy that we can't tell you about. We used to strip him naked in the clubhouse and scribble on his nuts. But you know what, did the players play like hell for him, or what? We loved him. We'd do anything for Tommy."

◆ ◆ ◆ ◆

After the game on May 26, Tommy Lasorda was exhausted. Lasorda had a splitting headache. Just imagine if he'd lost the game.

Don Sutton was given a 1–0 lead in the first, but that was erased. The Dodgers led 4–1 in the sixth, but Sutton gave up two more to cut the lead to 4–3. The Dodgers tacked on a run for a 5–3 lead, but Tim Crews gave up three runs in the seventh. The Dodgers answered again, but Jesse Orosco helped to blow a 7–6 lead.

Finally, the Dodgers scored three runs in the top of the ninth inning, and Jay Howell pitched two scoreless innings to beat the Phillies 10–8.

"Hey, we won," said Orosco, who had blown two of his last three save opportunities. "That's all I care about. If we'd lost, I'd have felt like shit. But we won. The guys picked me up."

The guy who picked up Orosco the most was Steve Sax. On the first pitch of the game, Sax connected on Shane Rawley's pitch and smacked it over the left-field fence. In the fifth, his two-run homer off Rawley made it 3–1. It was the first two-homer game of his major league career but not his life.

"Little League, 1972, Sacramento," Sax said that day. "I hit two off Roger Matsumoto. I swear. I'm not making it up."

Three decades later, Sax's memory was just as sharp: "I still remember the home runs off Roger Matsumoto. Roger was just a local kid here. I was 12 years old. I remember the second one was way farther than the first one. I was surprised then, too, because I didn't hit many home runs in Little League, either. I remember the pitch. It was a fastball up and in, and I just cranked on it."

Sax doubled in the seventh, advanced to third, and scored on a sacrifice fly to the shortstop in foul territory to make it 5–3. Yes, a sac fly to the shortstop. In the eighth, Sax hit a run-scoring grounder to the shortstop for a 7–6 lead. You think Tommy hugged Sax a few times that day?

After the game, Guerrero told Sax, "You're going to replace me. You'll hit 25 home runs."

Chapter 6

The Second Shutout

Saturday, September 10, 1988

Los Angeles

Reds vs. Dodgers

Team record: 79–60, four-game lead over the Astros

REDS	DODGERS
SS Barry Larkin	2B Steve Sax
3B Chris Sabo	SS Dave Anderson
LF Kal Daniels	LF Kirk Gibson
RF Eric Davis	RF Mickey Hatcher
1B Paul O'Neill	CF John Shelby
CF Herm Winningham	3B Jeff Hamilton
C Jeff Reed	1B Tracy Woodson
2B Ron Oester	C Rick Dempsey
P Norm Charlton	P Orel Hershiser

Orel Hershiser started college in the fall of 1976 in Bowling Green, Ohio, which is 184 miles from Riverfront Stadium in Cincinnati where the Big Red

Machine called home and dominated baseball. Shortly after Hershiser started attending classes, the Reds won another National League West title, their second in a row, and fourth in five years.

The Reds overwhelmed their playoff opponents, sweeping the Phillies in three games in the National League Championship Series and sweeping the Yankees in four games in the World Series. The Reds had defended their World Series title in astonishing fashion, not losing a playoff game. It was the peak of the Big Red Machine.

Hershiser lived in the dorms at the time and watched the playoffs whenever possible. Like a lot of college students, sometimes Hershiser went to class, and sometimes he played pool instead. Sometimes he woke up early to attend class, and sometimes he drank too many beers with friends and slept in late.

In the spring semester, Hershiser was academically ineligible, his girlfriend broke up with him, and he wasn't ready for finals. In a panic, he left campus during finals and hitchhiked home to Cherry Hill, New Jersey.

From a pay phone at a hotel in mid-Pennsylvania, he worked up the courage to tell his parents the truth. He cried through the phone call, admitted failure, and asked for help. His parents were disappointed, but they welcomed him home and worked on solutions.

Hershiser went to summer school to get his grades up and pitched in late summer on a team that won the All-American Amateur Baseball Association national championship. Hershiser started the title-winning game.

As a sophomore, Hershiser still wasn't even on the Bowling Green traveling squad. As a junior, however, he was the ace of the pitching staff. In two years, Orel had grown three inches, added some weight (but not much), and picked up about 5 mph on his fastball. The scouting report on Hershiser read, "Good curve, decent fastball, mediocre control, but a lot of potential."

Potential. Hershiser hated that word. That meant he hadn't reached a level others thought he should have reached.

On draft day in 1979, Hershiser waited by the phone. It rang earlier than he expected. The Padres selected him in the first round. Hershiser couldn't believe it. The first round? That was beyond his imagination. He looked for friends to share the news. Nobody was around. They arrived later, and their congratulations were lukewarm. Were they jealous?

No, they weren't jealous. They were laughing. Hershiser wasn't drafted in the first round. That phone call wasn't from the Padres. It was from one of his Sigma Phi Epsilon fraternity brothers. He'd been duped, and he fell for it.

In reality, Hershiser was drafted in the 17th round by the Dodgers. A part-time bird dog scout for the Dodgers—Mike Trbovich—recommended Hershiser to full-time scout Boyd Bartley. Hershiser might have hated the word potential. But he was drafted on potential and given a $10,000 signing bonus based on his potential.

◆ ◆ ◆ ◆

The Dodgers-Reds rivalry in 1988 wasn't anywhere close to the rivalry in the 1970s. But that history meant it was still something special when the Reds came to Dodger Stadium.

Danny Jackson opened the three-game series on September 9 with a complete-game 5–2 victory. It was Jackson's 21st victory of the season. As Reds manager Pete Rose noted Jackson had more wins, fewer losses, more complete games, and more shutouts than Hershiser—so the Cy Young Award vote should easily go to Jackson.

The Reds were red hot. They'd won 8-of-10 and 11-of-16 games. They were now in third place, just 5½ games out of first and making a late move for the division title. The Dodgers had lost three of their last four. Hershiser knew his team needed a win in the second game of the series.

Hershiser, pitching on normal rest, started the game with an abnormal four-pitch walk to Barry Larkin. Chris Sabo bunted the first pitch he saw over to third, to sacrifice Larkin to second. Kal Daniels struck out swinging, but next was Eric Davis.

It was Eric the Red's third full season in the majors, and the pride of Fremont High in South Central Los Angeles always seemed to put on a show when he returned home. He was 26 years old, in his prime, not yet damaged by injuries, coming off a Gold Glove and Silver Slugger season in 1987, and he had 11 RBIs in his previous nine games.

On a 1–1 pitch, Davis flied out to center field. The scoreless streak was 14 innings.

Hershiser settled down in the second inning. Paul O'Neill struck out swinging. Herm Winningham grounded to second. Jeff Reed swung at the first pitch and flied to left. Just 10 pitches were needed, and the streak was at 15.

More trouble came in the third inning. Ron Oester struck out, and starting pitcher Norm Charlton grounded to short. Then Larkin grounded a single to right.

Sabo grounded a single to left, and Daniels walked on five pitches. The bases were loaded, and here was Davis again.

Hershiser jumped ahead 1–2, and Davis struck out on a check swing. The streak was 16.

The game was scoreless after three innings. O'Neill grounded to short, and Winningham flied out to left to start the fourth. Reed grounded a single up the middle on the at-bat's seventh pitch. Oester struck out looking to end the inning. The streak was 17.

This was two years before Norm Charlton was part of the Reds' "Nasty Boys" bullpen. At this time, he was a rookie making his sixth career start and his first at Dodger Stadium in the pressure of a playoff race. In the fourth inning, Charlton walked three, allowed a single and a sacrifice fly for a run, and uncorked a wild pitch for a second run.

Given the 2–0 lead, Hershiser needed eight pitches to cruise through the fifth inning. Charlton struck out swinging. Larkin popped to short. Sabo grounded to second. The streak was 18.

A hit-by-pitch of Kirk Gibson, a balk, and a Mickey Hatcher single gave the Dodgers a 3–0 lead and sent Charlton to the showers.

In the sixth, Daniels reached on an infield single to begin the frame, so Davis was at the plate with a runner on base for a third time that night. Davis grounded a sinker to short, Dave Anderson flipped to Steve Sax, and Sax made the pivot for a double play. O'Neill grounded to short, as well. The streak was 19.

Hershiser became noticeably more animated on the mound as the game continued, scolding himself for mistakes and pumping his fist after big plays.

Winningham grounded to third to begin the seventh. Reed walked on five pitches, leading to a self-scolding by Hershiser. Oester singled to right field, Reed advanced to third base, and now it was really time for Hershiser to bear down.

Rose went to his bench, calling on 38-year-old Ken Griffey to pinch hit in the pitcher's spot. Griffey lofted a fly ball to left field, and teams loved to run on the arm of Gibson. But this was a catcher at third base, and the ball just wasn't deep enough for Reed to challenge Gibson's arm. Reed stayed at third. Larkin struck out swinging, the ball bounced away from catcher Rick Dempsey but not far, and Dempsey threw out Larkin at first base. The streak was at 20 innings.

Not that pitch counts mattered in 1988, but Hershiser was at 93 pitches as he entered the eighth inning. He was at 99 pitches when he ended the eighth inning.

Sabo reached on an infield single to short. Daniels grounded to shortstop but not hard enough to turn a double play. Davis batted with a runner on base for the fourth time and also grounded to short. This time, the 6-4-3 double play was turned. Davis was 0-for-4, made six outs, and left four runners on base in the game. Hershiser's streak was at 21 innings.

Dempsey hit a two-run home run in the eighth inning. The Dodgers' lead was now a comfortable 5–0.

Nowadays, perhaps a manager thinks about the upcoming playoffs and wants to save a bullet in the arm of his ace pitcher by taking him out. If Lasorda had removed Hershiser at that point, the nearly impossible task of breaking Don Drysdale's record would have been even more impossible.

But nobody was thinking about Drysdale yet. His name didn't appear in the game stories the next day. The math on available innings left in the season for Hershiser wasn't being counted. If it was added up, and if Hershiser ran the table with shutouts the rest of the season, he would still be one inning shy of the record. If removed after eight innings on this night, Hershiser would have been two innings short.

None of that was considered. Hershiser remained in the game because this was 1988, this manager was Tommy Lasorda—and there wasn't time to warm-up somebody else. Dempsey's homer came with two outs, just before Hershiser's turn to bat. There would be no doubt that Hershiser would hit for himself and pitch the ninth inning.

Hershiser grounded out at the plate, then went back to the mound and induced more groundouts. O'Neill grounded to short to start the ninth. Winningham flew out to center. Reed lined a double to left field. Hershiser was thinking shutout, not scoreless streak. On a 1–2 pitch, he froze Oester for a called strike three.

The streak was at 22 innings.

Lasorda said the mantle had fallen on Hershiser to be the team's stopper. Fernando Valenzuela was on the disabled list. Bob Welch had been traded. Tim Belcher was a rookie. John Tudor was new, and his arm was being held together by a thread.

"You get the label of being the stopper, of being the ace, and it seems like everything has come into focus in the pennant drive," Hershiser said that night. "I don't know if this is the best groove I've ever been in, but it's the most animated, the most energetic I've ever been in. I feel like every pitch is my last pitch."

The night before, Hershiser said winning his 20th game wouldn't mean that much to him unless they reached the playoffs. Now that he had reached 20 wins, Hershiser admitted he was excited.

"I'm excited because it was a shutout," he said that night. "I'm excited because Houston lost, and this was a chance to gain ground on both the Astros and Reds. I'm excited personally because the world sets a standard of 20 wins, and now I've attained it. I went into the season with a goal of making the All-Star team. Then, halfway, I had 13 wins and began to feel that I would be letting the team down if I didn't win 20. Now I don't want to stop here. I have four more starts, and I want to keep going."

Pitching	IP	H	R	ER	BB	SO	HR	ERA	BF	Pit	Str	Ctct	StS	StL	GB	FB	LD
Orel Hershiser, W (20–8)	9	7	0	0	3	8	0	2.62	35	109	67	38	10	19	17	7	1

"The amazing thing is it was happening at the end of the season, after a lot of innings under his belt," infielder Dave Anderson reflected. "It's not like he did it at the beginning of the season. It was right at the end. I can't remember a time there was a runner on third and two outs, where there was pressure on us defensively. The stuff he had back then, a lot of balls weren't centered. A lot of easy ground balls to catch. You just knew how he was going to pitch, how he wanted things to happen. It was amazing to be part of that, to see a team with big-league hitters not get a guy to second base."

David Cone also threw a shutout that night in Montreal, so the top candidates for the Cy Young Award race, at the end of play September 10, looked like this:

Player	W-L	ERA	IP	H (BABIP)	BB	SO	Opp. Slash line
Danny Jackson, CIN	21–6	2.43	233.1	178 (.248)	60	151	.212/.265/.289
Orel Hershiser, LAD	20–8	2.62	230.0	189 (.253)	68	160	.223/.282/.333
David Cone, NYM	16–3	2.21	199.2	151 (.267)	71	176	.211/.284/.290

"I've been around several Cy Young winners," Reds manager Pete Rose said. "I played with Steve Carlton. I played with John Denny. I'm not taking anything away from Hershiser, but I think it would be a mistake not to vote for Danny Jackson."

Chapter 7

June

June 3, 1988
Los Angeles
Reds vs. Dodgers
Team record: 28–20, 1½-game lead over the Astros

The Lakers were pushed to the brink again. They were pushed to Game 7 in the Western Conference semifinals by the Utah Jazz. Now it would come down to another Game 7, at the Forum, to decide the Western Conference finals between the Lakers and the Dallas Mavericks.

The Raiders decided to finally end the Marc Wilson era, releasing their much-maligned quarterback. Wilson did not report to the team's recent mini-camp, and owner Al Davis—who had signed Wilson to a five-year, $4 million contract to prevent him from bolting to the USFL—decided enough was enough. The shocking release was given to wire outlets late Friday afternoon with little fanfare.

Across town, Fred Claire was defending another decision. Claire was always defending decisions. This time, it was about a player the Dodgers drafted. Or in this case, didn't draft.

Andy Benes was taken first overall by the Padres. The Indians followed with a high school shortstop named Mark Lewis. The Braves took high school pitcher Steve Avery third overall, and the Orioles selected Auburn closer Gregg Olson fourth.

With the fifth overall pick, the Dodgers selected right-hander Bill Bene. It was a gamble. Bene posted a 5.80 ERA at Cal State Los Angeles, with more walks (51) than strikeouts (45). But the Dodgers were impressed with Bene's fastball, which was in the 90s. Claire was questioned about the more accomplished players the Dodgers bypassed.

The Angels drafted Jim Abbott eighth, and the White Sox took Robin Ventura (he of the 58-game hitting streak at Oklahoma State) at 10th overall. Tino Martinez went 14th to the Mariners. The Giants drafted Royce Clayton at 15, the Indians took Charles Nagy at 17, the Brewers took Alex Fernandez at 24th (and did not sign him), and the Blue Jays selected Ed Sprague at 25th.

"Our feeling was just to take the best player with the most potential," Claire said at the time. "[Bene] has maybe the best arm in the country."

It was a confusing time. There was an Andy Benes, Bill Bene, Billy Bean, and Billy Beane all playing baseball.

The decision to draft Bene would backfire, tremendously. Bene never found any control. He walked 96 batters in 57 innings one year. He spent nine years in the minors, never reached the majors, and finished his career with 543 walks in 516 innings. In 2012, Bene would plead guilty on federal charges of operating a counterfeit karaoke business and not paying taxes on sales.

Claire and his scouts missed on Bene. They compensated with results later in the draft. Eric Karros was drafted in the sixth round. Mike Piazza was drafted in the 62nd round.

A barely mentioned international signing took the sting out of the Bene selection. A little over two weeks after the draft, Claire signed Ramon Martinez's younger brother. He was just as skinny and not as tall, but he could throw pretty hard, he would grow, and he had a big heart—and he was Ramon's brother.

So that's why Pedro Martinez was signed.

♦ ♦ ♦ ♦

Mickey Hatcher thought his career was over. He came up with the Dodgers, played in 1979–80 and was sent to Minnesota in a trade for Ken Landreaux just before the 1981 season. Hatcher spent six seasons with the Twins and was released at the end of spring training in 1987. He returned to his house, a 3⅓-acre lot in the desert community of Apache Junction, Arizona.

Just in case another team was interested, he woke up early every morning to run and stay in shape. But the phone wasn't ringing. Nobody was interested in a 32-year-old utility man coming off a slash line of .278/.315/.366 in 317 at-bats for the Twins. His stats weren't bad. They just weren't great, and he didn't profile at any specific position.

One morning after his usual run, Hatcher stopped at the house of a neighbor. He grabbed the neighbors' paper off the driveway and read it on their porch. They were an older couple. The wife came outside and brought him coffee. In the sports section, Hatcher read that Bill Madlock was injured. He thought the Dodgers could use a utility player with the ability to fill in at third base.

Hatcher asked his agent to call the Dodgers and gauge their interest. His agent said he had called two weeks earlier, and the Dodgers weren't interested. Hatcher begged his agent to try again. Things had changed. Madlock was hurt. Al Campanis was out. Fred Claire was in charge.

"Tell them I'd love to go to Triple A, and I'll pay my own expenses," Hatcher told his agent. "I'll just play Triple A, see if they like me, just trying to find a job. My agent said, 'Okay, I'll do it.'"

The date was April 10, 1987.

Remember, Fred Claire never knew how long he would be the general manager. After "the Campanis thing" earlier in the week, the sportswriter-turned-publicist-turned-executive was tabbed the general manager. On his second day on the job, Claire told owner Peter O'Malley that he wanted to release pitcher Jerry Reuss and sign Mickey Hatcher.

O'Malley asked Claire how much the team owed Reuss. Claire told him it was $1.35 million—$950,000 this year, and a $400,000 buyout for next year. O'Malley asked where Hatcher had been. Claire told him the Twins just released him. O'Malley swallowed deep and said, "You better call Sam Fernandez."

Fernandez was the general counsel. Put another way, Fernandez was the money man. Fernandez arrived in the room. Claire repeated to Fernandez what he wanted to do.

"I want to do it today because Bill Madlock pulled a hamstring," Claire said. "Peter said, 'Wow. Well, you're the general manager. I don't know. But it's up to you.' Sam and I are walking back to my office. He said, 'What are you going to do?'

79

I said, 'When I get back to my office, I'm going to call Jerry Reuss and release him. I'm going to sign Mickey Hatcher and get him here for tonight's game. Sam looked at me and said, 'Holy cow.'"

Claire pulled the trigger. Reuss was released. The Dodgers ate his contract. Hatcher was signed.

Hatcher recalled, "My agent calls me back and says, 'Mick, get on a plane.' I said, 'I'll be in Albuquerque in a few hours.' He said, 'No, you're going to the big leagues.' I said, 'Holy shit.' The Dodgers were the start of my whole career. This is the whole organization that taught me everything. It was great. At that time, I felt like I was coming home."

Hatcher was in uniform that night, and he hit a ground ball that went through the legs of third baseman Chris Brown that helped tie the game. Hatcher was the consummate utility man. He started 42 games at third base, 29 at first base, and six in right field for the Dodgers in 1987. He batted .282 in 287 at-bats and showed a tiny bit of pop with seven home runs and 19 doubles.

In 1988, after all the new additions, Hatcher knew his playing time would drop considerably. He was the ringleader of the Stuntmen. The first rule of the Stuntmen: "We're never happy. You show me a guy happy to be on the bench, and I'll show you a loser."

Five weeks into the season, the Stuntmen weren't very happy. Alfredo Griffin and Mike Marshall didn't miss any of the first 33 games. Pedro Guerrero and Mike Davis missed one game each. Kirk Gibson missed two games.

Hatcher started twice in April and four times in May. Things began to change in June. He started the first day and again on June 3. Two starts in three days was rare for Hatcher. But he was needed because Reds manager Pete Rose started lefty Dennis Rasmussen, so Lasorda sat the slumping Mike Davis and stacked his lineup with righties. Hatcher batted second and played right field.

In the first inning, Steve Sax singled and Hatcher singled. Three more singles, a hit batter, and a wild pitch produced four runs.

In the second inning, Hatcher singled again. Two more singles, two stolen bases, a walk, and an intentional walk led to two more runs.

In the third inning, Hatcher singled again. He was erased on a double play.

In the fourth inning, Hatcher singled again. Five more singles and an error contributed to five more runs.

In the sixth inning, Hatcher singled again. Two more runs scored.

In the eighth inning, Mickey Hatcher was 5-for-5 and had a chance to go 6-for-6. No Reds pitcher was able to get him out that day. Not Dennis Rasmussen. Not Tim Birtsas. Not Jose Rijo. Not John Franco. All that stood between Mickey Hatcher and a six-hit day was shortstop Dave Concepcion.

All out of pitchers, or not wanting to burn up any more pitchers, Rose put his shortstop on the mound to finish the seventh inning and let him pitch the eighth inning too. Sax singled to start the inning, his fifth hit of the game.

In the modern era (1900-on), only 44 players had recorded six hits in a nine-inning game. It had been 13 years since Rennie Stennent became the only player in baseball history to go 7-for-7 in a nine-inning game.

However, it was not meant to be for Hatcher. He flew out to center field and ended the day 5-for-6.

"I think he scuffed the ball," Hatcher joked, after the game. That's what Hatcher did. He joked.

"He probably used spitters, too." Hatcher said it with a smile, of course.

The Dodgers had 22 hits in the game, all singles. They won 13–5. They weren't all the most aesthetically pleasing singles. Two of Hatcher's were bloopers. Two others were softly hit.

"I know that," Hatcher said. "But a week from now, they'll look like line drives."

♦ ♦ ♦ ♦

June 4, 1988
Los Angeles
Reds vs. Dodgers
Team record: 29–20, 1½ games ahead of the Astros

Pete Rose was only half-kidding when he said it in spring training. If Rose was right, he was serious. If Rose was wrong, or somebody was upset, he was just joking.

Rose's prediction: "Lasorda will use Orosco so much he won't be able to salute the flag by June."

Orosco was used only five times in April. He saved three games and allowed one run all month. Then came May. Orosco was used seven times in 12 days early in the month. He pitched two innings May 31 and two more innings on June 1.

On the evening of June 4, the Reds were threatening to score in practically every inning, yet Orel Hershiser found a way to scuttle most rallies. Two runners were stranded in the sixth. Two runners were stranded in the seventh, but not before a Chris Sabo RBI double tied the score. Two more runners were stranded in the eighth.

Through it all, the Dodgers' bullpen stayed quiet. Brian Holton made a few token tosses. That's it. Lasorda was sticking with Hershiser, his bulldog, his ace.

Hershiser took the mound to start the ninth inning with 135 pitches. The game was tied 2–2. Barry Larkin singled, Chris Sabo flew out to center, and Hershiser's pitch count was at 140. Jay Howell started to get loose.

Kal Daniels grounded out, Eric Davis was hit by a pitch, and Hershiser's pitch count was at 142. The left-handed batting Paul O'Neill was due up. Orosco was not getting loose because of tenderness in his left elbow. Brad Havens had been demoted weeks earlier, so there were no other lefties available.

Hershiser went to work against O'Neill. The count went to 3–1. Hershiser was trying to pitch around O'Neill to face Dave Concepcion. On his 147th pitch of the game, Hershiser hung a curveball, and O'Neill hit a three-run home run into the right-field bleachers. Hershiser finished the game with a season-high 153 pitches and his third loss of the year.

The postgame opinions that night were interesting.

Lasorda: "You have to think of the bullpen in that situation. We didn't want to pitch Orosco today. He wasn't available, so I'm not going to answer all these 'What if?' questions from you [reporters]."

Hershiser: "Tired? No, not at all. I felt great. I could've gone 10 or 11 innings. I don't think Tommy even thought about going to the bullpen. He asked me how I felt, and I said 'Okay.'"

Orosco: "Yeah, I could've been used, but [Hershiser] was pitching fine. And I'm not sure they would have used me in that situation."

Catcher Mike Scioscia said that Hershiser "struggled all day" and also added, "Orel's such a good pitcher that every mistake is magnified. If you say Hershiser gave up the home run and that's why we lost the game, you're missing the point. The real story is that we scored only two runs. Orel gave us six more innings to pad a 2–1 lead, and we didn't do it. That's the story."

In the Reds' clubhouse, Rose wasn't gloating about his spring training prediction about Orosco's ability to salute the flag by June. At least, not on the record.

"That's the other guy's decision," Rose said. "[Hershiser] didn't look any less [effective] in the ninth than in the second."

◆ ◆ ◆ ◆

June 6–9, 1988

Los Angeles

Astros vs. Dodgers

Team record: 30–21, 2½-game lead over the Astros

It was no longer just a slow start. Mike Davis still wasn't hitting. The free-agent signing of Davis, which pushed Mike Marshall to first base and Pedro Guerrero to third base, wasn't looking good.

Lasorda tried giving Davis some mental days off. He didn't start him four straight games, from May 31 to June 3. Back in the lineup on June 4, Davis managed a single in four at-bats and made an error in right field. The next day, he went 0-for-4 and exchanged angry words with a Dodgers fan after making another error. Lasorda needed to restrain Davis with a giant bear hug.

It was one-third of the way through the season, and the numbers on Davis' stat line could no longer be ignored:

G	GS	Result	PA	AB	R	H	2B	3B	HR	RBI	BB	IBB	SO	HBP	SH	SF	ROE	GDP	SB	CS	BA	OBP	SLG
48	43	27–21	183	165	17	34	4	1	0	9	16	0	40	0	2	0	1	4	5	1	.206	.276	.242

On the same night 4-to-1 underdog Iran Barkley stunned Thomas Hearns with a desperation right hook to win the welterweight title, it was time to KO the "awesome fivesome" experiment that was failing miserably. Marshall wasn't comfortable at first base, and it was affecting his hitting. Guerrero wasn't comfortable at third base, and he was missing games with a pinched nerve in his neck.

On June 6, Mickey Hatcher started in right field, and Davis was back on the bench. Not that it mattered. Don Sutton fumed about another quick hook after six innings, the Astros scored nine runs in the final three innings off the Dodgers' bullpen, and the final was 10–4. The Astros ran like wild, stealing six bases in the game. The Dodgers' lead was down to 1½ games.

On June 7, about two hours before the game started, Marshall requested a move back to right field. Lasorda obliged and moved Danny Heep to first base.

Heep had limited experience at first base, and it showed. He made one error. Several other hard-hit grounders got past him. It led to five runs in less than three innings in a 5–2 loss. Heep was furious at the last-minute switch.

"It wasn't fair to me, to [starter Tim] Belcher, and to the team," Heep said that night. "Changing the lineup like that—maybe, it's only me—but it's real bad timing. This is a big series. We've got to put our best lineup out there. I didn't know what was going on. When you get two hours' notice you're going to play, you have to learn first base. Most first basemen make those plays I missed. But I'm not making excuses. I'm no Keith Hernandez, but a first baseman should make those plays."

Marshall had been steady at first base. But playing the infield took a toll on his chronic bad back, and it was affecting his offense. Lasorda suggested it was *possible* the move would be permanent, which in baseball clubhouses meant it would be permanent.

When Guerrero was healthy, he could return to first base. In the meantime, Franklin Stubbs received more playing time at first base, and Jeff Hamilton now had another chance at third base.

The other fallout was that Mike Davis was out of a job. He talked to Lasorda before the game, made it clear he wasn't happy about the switch, and insisted he still had confidence in himself. He thought regular playing time was the only way to come out of his slump.

"Pinch-hitting won't do it," said Davis, who would start just 20 games the rest of the season, usually in a doubleheader, or if Marshall was banged up and needed a blow. "I'll guarantee you that. I can't get into any kind of a groove. You look at my numbers and they're terrible. I know that as much as you, but I can't improve sitting over there [on the bench]."

The Dodgers' lead was down to a half game. Mike Scott was pitching the next day. Nolan Ryan was starting the day after that.

Two decades later, Marshall was more candid about the switch. Sitting in the old wooden seats at Albert Park in San Rafael where he manages an independent league team, Marshall admitted the move to right field was more about his bat than his back.

"I don't know if it was the rebel in me," Marshall admitted. "Here I come up a first baseman my whole career, and I wasn't good enough to take over for [Steve] Garvey. A little selfish. Probably stupid at the time. If they pay you, you do whatever they want you to do. I worked so hard and was so committed to becoming the best right fielder I could, then when they switched me back to first base, yeah, mentally and physically it took its toll a little bit. I was at a comfort level in the outfield."

The numbers proved it.

Marshall from Opening Day to June 6, before the switch:

G	GS	Rslt	PA	AB	R	H	2B	3B	HR	RBI	BB	IBB	SO	HBP	SH	SF	ROE	GDP	SB	CS	BA	OBP	SLG
52	50	30–22	217	204	23	49	5	0	6	28	12	5	35	0	0	1	4	11	0	0	.240	.281	.353

Marshall from June 7 to season's end, after the switch:

G	GS	Rslt	PA	AB	R	H	2B	3B	HR	RBI	BB	IBB	SO	HBP	SH	SF	ROE	GDP	SB	CS	BA	OBP	SLG
92	89	53–38	360	338	40	101	22	2	14	54	12	2	58	7	0	3	5	6	4	1	.299	.333	.500

On June 8, Kirk Gibson watched videotape of Scott before he faced him for the first time, something Gibson rarely did. The payoff came in the third inning, when Gibson hit a towering home run that landed halfway up the right-field bleachers and bounced out of Dodger Stadium. Marshall followed with a home run off Scott as well.

Marshall went 4-for-5 and scored three runs. The Dodgers won 11–1 to remain in first place. And there was optimism that Valenzuela had turned a corner. He went the distance in an efficient 105 pitches. He walked three, struck out none, and allowed a run on six hits. The crowd saluted him with a standing ovation afterward.

Asked if he appreciated the ovation, Valenzuela smiled that night and said: "Yeah, but two games ago, they booed me. But that's the game. The fans change when you change. You do well, they cheer."

On June 9, the Lakers evened their best-of-7 NBA Finals series at 1–1 with the Pistons at the Forum, and Pedro Guerrero was sent to the hospital. The pain in his neck was preventing him from swinging, sleeping, eating, and everything else. The prognosis was that Guerrero would spend 3–5 days in traction, at least 15 days on the disabled list, and possibly be out longer than three weeks.

The lineup remained the same—Marshall in right, Stubbs at first, Hamilton at third, and Davis on the bench. Hershiser spotted Nolan Ryan and the Astros a 2–0 lead. The Dodgers fought back with a run-scoring single by Hamilton in the fourth. Marshall doubled off The Express to tie the game in the fifth then scored the go-ahead run on John Shelby's double. Scioscia's single made it 4–2 Dodgers, and Hershiser did most of the rest.

An ill-fated attempt at an inside-the-park home run prevented Hershiser from going the distance. With two outs in the eighth, Hershiser hit a line drive that center fielder Gerald Young misplayed. Young dove, and the ball sailed over his head. Hershiser reached third base, and the relay throw was just getting to shortstop Craig Reynolds in shallow right-center. Third-base coach Joe Amalfitano waved Hershiser home.

"I was kind of hoping for the hold sign at third because I was really puffing," Hershiser said that night. "But when he waved me in, it was, 'All right. How many times will I have a chance for an inside-the-park home run?'"

Hershiser, exhausted, was out easily at home plate. He dusted himself off, pointed to the dugout and motioned for the bullpen. Hershiser took his warm-up pitches in the ninth, but that was just to give Jay Howell time to get loose in the bullpen. Howell picked up his sixth save, although Hershiser regretted his animated pointing at home plate.

"Too much Hollywood, I know," Hershiser said. "I should've let Tommy manage the club."

◆ ◆ ◆ ◆

Tuesday, June 21, 1988
Los Angeles
Braves vs. Dodgers
Team record: 38–29, 2½-game lead over the Astros

It was the 222nd playoff game in the career of Kareem Abdul-Jabbar. He'd been through some wars in his lifetime but nothing compared to this year. The Lakers needed seven games to beat the Jazz, seven games to beat the Mavericks and were facing a Game 7 against the Pistons for the NBA Title.

Isiah Thomas needed some help to play in the game, so he went to the Raiders' training facility in El Segundo to get treatment on his ankle. Raiders owner Al Davis gave his blessing, Thomas' ankle allowed him to play, and Davis watched Game 7 from courtside seats. (Davis cheered for the Lakers.)

"Big Game" James Worthy lived up to his nickname, or earned his nickname, depending on your perspective. Worthy went for 36 points, 16 rebounds, and 10 assists as the Lakers won their second straight NBA title and fifth of the decade at the Fabulous Forum in Inglewood.

Across town, the Dodgers hosted the Atlanta Braves. The paid attendance was 18,485. The actual crowd was even smaller. It was all about the Lakers. Even those in attendance were following the Lakers' game on portable TVs and radios.

In the second inning, just as Tim Leary delivered a 2–0 pitch to Ozzie Virgil, the crowd roared in delight at a Lakers basket. The cheers went to silence, however, as Virgil hit a home run at the same moment.

The Dodgers answered with two runs in the bottom of the second inning on a Scioscia RBI single and a Dave Anderson RBI groundout. Leary did the rest. He went the distance for the 2–1 victory, lowering his ERA 2.92 in the process. The complete game was welcomed because Jay Howell had joined Griffin and Guerrero on the disabled list. The domino effect went deep. Tim Belcher was moved to the bullpen to replace Howell. Sean Hillegas was moved into the starting rotation.

◆ ◆ ◆ ◆

June 24–26, 1988
Cincinnati
Dodgers vs. Reds
Team record: 39–30, 1½ games ahead of the Astros

In the series opener, Orel Hershiser won his 11th game, a 5–3 victory over the Reds. Tim Belcher, the reluctant new closer, struck out the side to get his first save. Dave Anderson, still filling in for Alfredo Griffin at shortstop, drove in two more runs. The Astros lost, so the Dodgers' lead was 2½ games.

In the second game of the series, Fernando Valenzuela didn't make it out of the first inning. Valenzuela allowed home runs to Barry Larkin, Eric Davis, and Paul O'Neill. Four runs in two-thirds of an inning ballooned his ERA to 3.96.

Outside of Hershiser and Leary, the rotation suddenly had question marks. Don Sutton hadn't made it out of the fourth inning in his previous start, on June 22, against the last-place Braves. Sutton's ERA was 3.70 overall, and he'd walked 20 in his last 36 innings.

It was time to start taking fliers. You can never have enough pitching, especially with two veterans struggling and Hillegas replacing Belcher in the rotation. Those struggles were taxing the bullpen.

Mario Soto was a flier. He was an All-Star in 1982, 1983, and 1984, and the Cy Young Award runner-up in 1983 to John Denny. Soto underwent shoulder surgery in late 1986, missed all of 1987, and was released by the Reds on June 20 with a 3–7 record and 4.66 ERA in 14 starts.

Reds manager Pete Rose essentially said that Soto had "lost it." Soto was 31 years old, still in Cincinnati, and not ready to retire. The Dodgers happened to be in Cincinnati. Claire met with Soto to gauge his state of mind and how much was left in his arm.

"I liked Mario," Claire reflected. "I knew the type of person he was. The influence he could be on our young Latin pitchers. You don't know how much somebody has left. I was there when the Dodgers signed Juan Marichal. You never know. When somebody is that skilled, despite the age, it was worth a try."

The Dodgers had used a rigorous rehabilitation program on Alejandro Pena after he had the same shoulder surgery as Soto, and the velocity returned to Pena's fastball. They would try the same with Soto and see if he could help later in the season.

The results with Pena made it worth the risk of the pro-rated $62,500 minimum salary. Why not? It was looking like one of those years when anybody in uniform found a way to help win a game and no deficit seemed too much.

Even after Valenzuela gave up four runs in the first inning, the Dodgers scored five runs in the second inning. Dave Anderson singled home a run. Pinch-hitter Danny Heep singled home a run. After Gibson was intentionally walked, Mike Marshall singled home two runs to tie it. John Shelby singled home a run to make it 5–4 Dodgers.

Tim Crews pitched four scoreless innings, and Pena pitched 3⅔ scoreless innings with five strikeouts. Jesse Orosco got the final out to save a 6–4 win. The Astros lost, so the Dodgers lead was 3½ games in the standings.

In the series finale less than 24 hours later, the Dodgers trailed 6–5 in the ninth. John Franco entered to save it. He hadn't blown a save all year.

Gibson led off the ninth inning. As he came off the field after the eighth inning, he visualized himself as the catalyst for the game-winning rally. He couldn't wait to get to the plate. Gibson slashed a ball into the left-center gap, put his head down, and thought double instantly. The problem was that the ball didn't get past center fielder Eric Davis.

"No, no, no!" first-base coach Manny Mota yelled, because Davis backhanded the ball and quickly threw to second base. Gibson wasn't going to stop. Gibson's arrival at second base wasn't pretty. Gibson's slides were rarely pretty. But he was safe. The tone was set.

Marshall grounded out for the first out, but Franco left a fastball up in the zone and Shelby pulled it into left field. It was one of those hits by Shelby that was big but not big enough to get headlines and reporters surrounding him afterward. Gibson scored to tie the game and Shelby went to second on the throw. Gibson was now pacing up and down the dugout as head cheerleader.

Hamilton was walked intentionally. Rick Dempsey's infield single loaded the bases. Mike Sharperson forced Shelby at home for the second out, but the bases were still loaded.

Steve Sax didn't start because of a badly bruised left ankle suffered the night before, but he could pinch hit. On a 1–0 pitch, Sax hit a liner down the right-field line that scored all three runs. Sax barely made it second base when he was lifted for a pinch runner. He barely survived his return to the dugout, after the way Gibson mauled him in celebration.

"It should have been a triple, but I couldn't run," recalled Sax, who didn't mind the dugout mauling. "Enthusiasm is something that you can't buy. Enthusiasm was contagious. Enthusiasm overcomes a lot of mistakes. It's also something you can't fake. People have enthusiasm, and that overcomes a lot of things."

Pena wasn't available because of his work the day before. Orosco had already been used. Howell was on the disabled list. Belcher had pitched the seventh and eighth innings.

It was left for Brian Holton to pitch the ninth inning. He retired the Reds in order for his first save. Of course he did. It was that kind of year.

"One of the last steps to make this a great team is to win games later, which we hadn't done until the last couple days," Gibson said that day. "Obviously, we're getting that belief in ourselves now. That is very contagious. We were behind in these two games, but we got the wins and everybody should be happy."

◆ ◆ ◆ ◆

Wednesday, June 29, 1988
Houston
Dodgers vs. Astros
Team record: 43–31, 3½-game lead over the Astros

You knew it was a big game because Tommy Lasorda couldn't shut up. He was extra loud and extra boisterous—even by Lasorda standards—in the clubhouse before the game. Lasorda was trying to pump up his players, inspire them. Really, it was just his own anxiety coming out.

Orel Hershiser heard all of Lasorda's words, walked by him calmly, and said in passing, "Don't worry."

Hershiser wasn't worried. He was facing Nolan Ryan in the rubber game of a three-game series. Ryan was 41 years old, but he was still The Express and still threw between 92–94 mph. Hershiser lacked Ryan's fastball velocity, the reputation, and the pizazz. But in 1988, he was the better pitcher, and games like this were the opportunity for Hershiser to make people take notice.

Craig Biggio made the fourth start of his major league career. Biggio's first career hit came in the third inning, after Hershiser had retired seven straight to begin the game. The next time Hershiser allowed a hit was an infield single to Billy Hatcher in the fifth inning. Hatcher was quickly erased on a double-play grounder.

The only other Astros base runner came on a walk to Kevin Bass in the sixth. Hershiser retired the final 10 batters he faced in a 2–0 complete-game shutout. It was the second time Hershiser defeated Ryan, head-to-head, in the month of June.

"There's an intensity about going out there against Ryan," Hershiser said that night. "Nolie's an outstanding competitor, and I feel fortunate to be on the same field with him. For me to beat him twice is, well, a dream come true. I remember watching guys like him when I was growing up."

The shutout was needed because Ryan was in vintage form. Mike Marshall had both RBIs. Ryan hit Marshall with the bases loaded to score a run in the third. Kirk Gibson walked, stole second, and scored on Marshall's single in the eighth inning.

"That was as good as I've seen [Ryan] in quite a while," Marshall said. "He was overpowering, exceptional. When he's pitching like that, you just hope your pitcher is throwing zeros up on the board. Even though we weren't hitting, we knew we could still win because Orel was out there."

Maybe Orel Hershiser was getting a reputation after all.

Chapter 8

The Third Shutout

Wednesday, September 14, 1988

Los Angeles

Braves vs. Dodgers

Team record: 83–60, first place by 6½ games over the Astros

BRAVES	DODGERS
3B Ron Gant	SS Alfredo Griffin
2B Jeff Blauser	2B Steve Sax
1B Gerald Perry	LF Kirk Gibson
RF Dale Murphy	RF Mike Marshall
SS Andres Thomas	CF John Shelby
LF Dion James	1B Franklin Stubbs
C Ozzie Virgil	3B Jeff Hamilton
CF Terry Blocker	C Mike Scioscia
P Rick Mahler	P Orel Hershiser

When you get drafted in the 17th round, you're not considered a top prospect. At best, you're a project. At worst, you're a roster filler. Orel Hershiser was a little of both. What stands out most about his minor league statistics was how often he pitched in relief. Closers weren't groomed in the early 1980s. If you pitched out of the bullpen in the minor leagues in the '80s, it was because you weren't good enough to pitch in the starting rotation.

Year	Team	Lg	Level	Unif	Org	Age	Rk	W	L	ERA	G	GS	CG	SH	GF	SV	IP	H	R	ER	HR	BB	SO
1979	Clinton	Midw	A	-	LAD	20	-	4	0	2.09	15	4	1	0	0	2	43.0	33	15	10	2	17	33
1980	San Antonio	Tex	AA	-	LAD	21	19	5	9	3.55	49	3	1	0	0	14	109.0	120	59	43	7	59	75
1981	San Antonio	Tex	AA	-	LAD	22	14	7	6	4.68	42	4	3	1	30	15	102.0	94	54	53	12	50	95
1982	Albuquerque	PCL	AAA	-	LAD	23	46	9	6	3.71	47	7	2	0	20	4	123.2	121	73	51	10	63	93
1983	Albuquerque	PCL	AAA	-	LAD	24	23	10	8	4.09	49	10	6	0	32	16	134.1	132	73	61	16	57	95

It was tough to crack the starting rotation on the 1980 team at Double A San Antonio. It included first-round picks Ricky Wright (second overall, 1980 secondary draft), Brian Holton (22nd overall, 1978 regular draft), and Rusty McDonald (eighth overall, 1978 secondary draft). It also had a lefty from Mexico named Fernando Valenzuela.

In 1981, Hershiser was sent back to San Antonio, Texas, for another season. It's never a good sign when an organization asks you to repeat the same level, so it's clear that Hershiser wasn't high on the Dodgers' priority list that year. The only benefit to pitching at the same level in consecutive seasons is that Orel had met his wife, Jamie, the previous season, and San Antonio was her home.

Early in the 1981 season, the *San Antonio Light* wrote a story about Hershiser that included the following passage: "Orel Hershiser made everyone at the ballpark hold their collective breath last season when he entered the game as a relief pitcher. Fans never knew if he would serve the pitch that would be hit for the game-winner or the one that would retire the side.

"This season, Hershiser is in love with his new bride and he's confounding the opposition with regularity. Hershiser admitted there is a correlation between the two."

Hershiser's hot start, which included a 0.51 ERA and the league lead in saves, didn't last. On a road trip, he allowed 20 runs in seven innings. The worst point was giving up eight earned runs in 3⅔ innings at El Paso.

It was the lowest point of Hershiser's professional career. He wanted to quit. That night, at the Ramada Inn in El Paso, Hershiser knocked on the door of trainer Charlie Strasser. Hershiser was practically in tears and said he was going to quit.

Manager Ducky LeJohn and pitching coach Gary Wheelock came into the room. They talked Hershiser out of quitting. They told him he had the potential to become a major league pitcher. Deep down, Hershiser thought they were trying to be polite.

Hershiser was better the rest of that season but still ended the year with a 4.68 ERA. Statistically, he didn't look like a future major league All-Star. He barely looked like a major leaguer. The best you could say was he might be a decent middle reliever.

The 1982 season was Hershiser's fourth in the minors. Finally, he was promoted to Triple A Albuquerque to begin the season. His numbers don't look spectacular. He was 9–6 with a 3.71 ERA. He pitched 40 games in relief and got seven starts.

But keep in mind, the high altitude (4,943') in Albuquerque made it a notorious hitters' park. Hershiser was a sinkerball pitcher, and the summer heat dried up the infield and made it easier for ground balls to turn into singles. The entire Pacific Coast League was known for inflating ERAs. In that context, a 3.71 ERA is actually very good.

The Texas Rangers were impressed and asked for Hershiser in a potential trade. The Dodgers would obtain catcher Jim Sundberg and would give up pitchers Dave Stewart and Burt Hooton, plus outfielder Mark Bradley and Hershiser. Both teams agreed to the trade.

Sundberg needed to approve the trade, though. He asked for his contract to be rewritten. The Dodgers refused to extend his contract. The trade was nixed, and Hershiser remained a Dodger.

In the spring of 1983, Hershiser was determined to win a job in the majors. He won the Mulvey Award, which is given to the Dodgers' top rookie each spring. Those college days playing pool paid dividends as he won the Walter Alston billiards tournament, as well.

Hershiser thought for sure he was headed to Los Angeles. But on the final day at Vero Beach, Lasorda told Hershiser that he was going back to Albuquerque. Hershiser was devastated, frustrated, and growing impatient.

That was the problem of being in the pitching-rich Dodgers organization. The 1983 major league rotation was loaded with Valenzuela, Bob Welch, Hooton, Jerry Reuss, and Alejandro Pena. The bullpen consisted of Steve Howe, Tom Niedenfuer, Joe Beckwith, Pat Zachry, and Dave Stewart.

Once again, Hershiser's numbers at Triple A Albuquerque didn't look great in 1983. But in the rarefied thin air, they were actually not bad. His ERA was 4.09. He finished 32 games and saved 16. Perhaps most impressive, although he was primarily a relief pitcher, Hershiser was given 10 starts and went the distance six times.

Hershiser had always considered himself a starting pitcher. He knew he didn't have an overpowering fastball or splitter. He needed to be creative to get outs, and cherished the opportunity of working through a lineup four times.

◆ ◆ ◆ ◆

All those years in the minor leagues spent primarily as a relief pitcher with occasional starts forced Hershiser to be versatile. He never got locked into a routine between starts, and was accustomed to starting games with shorter rest.

Schedules were now being consulted. Days were being counted. But it wasn't due to a scoreless streak. Manager Tom Lasorda and pitching coach Ron Perranoski wanted Hershiser to pitch when the Dodgers played the second-place Astros the next week.

To make that possible, Hershiser made his next start on three days rest. It was the third time Hershiser pitched on three days rest at that point in the 1988 season. The first time—on May 4 against the Pirates—he allowed 10 hits and only lasted 6⅓ innings but limited the damage to two runs, and the Dodgers won 8–5. The second time—on June 19 in the first game of a doubleheader against the Padres— Hershiser went the distance in a 12–2 victory. The second time was a two-inning, eight-run debacle against the Giants on August 14.

The timing was also good for Jamie Hershiser. Pregnant with the couple's second son, she was scheduled for induced labor the day after her husband would face the Braves, a day off for the Dodgers. Jamie watched the game from the stands with a few friends, who were ready to provide a ride to the hospital in case the baby couldn't wait until the morning to arrive.

◆ ◆ ◆ ◆

Ron Gant struck out looking to begin the game. Jeff Blauser struck out swinging. Gerald Perry grounded out to Hershiser. The streak was at 23 scoreless innings.

Dale Murphy had struck out four times against Hershiser nine days earlier. To begin the second inning, Murphy lined a 1–2 pitch into center field for a single. He didn't stay on first base for long. Andres Thomas hit a comeback to Hershiser, who started a 1–6–3 double play. Dion James grounded to second. The inning took eight pitches. The streak was at 24.

"One thing I always remembered is I've never seen a pitcher move infielders exactly where he wanted them," first baseman Franklin Stubbs recalled. "He was so locked in that year, he would actually move our defense around to where he thought the ball was going to be hit. And pretty much, 99 percent of the time, that's where they hit it. It was the best thing I saw him do.

"That was unique. He was the only one who would move infielders around. Nobody else would take a chance. The other guys were young. Hershiser had a status that he was putting the ball where he wanted to put it. You trusted him. If he said move, you moved."

The third inning was the biggest threat yet to the scoreless streak. Ozzie Virgil lined an opposite-field single to right, and Terry Blocker singled to right. With two on and nobody out, Mahler tried to bunt the runners over, but he struck out on a two-strike fouled bunt attempt. Gant struck out looking. Blauser flew out to left field. The streak was 25.

In the fourth, Perry grounded out to short. Murphy struck out swinging, and it was his fifth whiff in his last six at-bats against Hershiser. Thomas singled to center on an 0–2 pitch, no doubt drawing Hershiser's ire toward himself. It didn't matter. James flew out to left field. The streak was 26.

Mahler was matching Hershiser with zeroes, retiring 12 of the first 13 batters he faced. Virgil grounded to short to begin the fifth. Blocker bounced out to Hershiser. Mahler flew to right field. It was a six-pitch inning, and the streak was 27.

Still scoreless in the sixth, Hershiser walked Gant to begin the inning. Blauser sacrificed him to second. Perry, the No. 3 hitter, flew out to center for the second out. Murphy, incredibly, struck out for a sixth time in seven at-bats against the Bulldog. The streak was 28.

The next biggest threat to the streak, to date, came in the seventh inning. Thomas doubled into the left-center gap to start it. James grounded to Stubbs at first, but his throw pulled Hershiser off the bag. Thomas moved to third. James was safe at first. And there were no outs.

Virgil was only a .247 hitter with minimal power, but Hershiser considered him a potential menace. Virgil hit another grounder to Stubbs, who looked back Thomas at third, made the putout at first, and allowed James to advance to second base. With first base open, Hershiser pitched carefully to Blocker. When the count reached 2–0, an intentional walk was issued.

Now it was decision time for Braves manager Russ Nixon. His pitcher, Mahler, was due up but was also working on a shutout. Mahler was the ace of this staff.

Mahler was also an above-average hitting pitcher. Four years earlier, he had 21 hits and a .296 batting average. Nixon elected to let Mahler hit for himself. Hershiser struck him out on three pitches. Two outs.

Hershiser's first pitch to Gant, who would hit 19 home runs and finish fourth in Rookie of the Year balloting, was a ball. On the second pitch, he hung a curveball. As soon as it left Hershiser's hand, he shouted, "No!!!"

Gant lofted a long fly ball to left. Hershiser held his breath. The game, the streak, and the Cy Young Award were on the line. Kirk Gibson went back to the track, to the wall, crashed into the wall … and made the catch. The streak reached 29.

If this was a day game or mid-summer, Gant would have hit a grand slam. Hershiser thought.

There was no drama in the eighth. Blauser tried to bunt his way on, and Hershiser threw him out. Perry struck out swinging. Murphy finally made contact again, but it was popup to short. The streak was at 30.

The game was still scoreless in the ninth.

Thomas fouled out to third. James flew out to center. Virgil lined a two-out single to right. Blocker hit a sharp grounder into the hole. Shortstop Alfredo Griffin backhanded it, threw off-balance, and second baseman Steve Sax scooped the low throw for the force out at second base. The streak was at 31 scoreless innings.

Mahler was at 85 pitches to begin the bottom of the ninth. Gibson led off the inning, and worked him for a seven-pitch walk. As Mike Marshall came to the plate, Hershiser told Lasorda he was ready to pitch the 10th inning.

"Oh, no you're not," Lasorda said. "Not on three days' rest, you're not. I'm not gonna take the chance of your gettin' hurt."

Turned out, it was a moot point. Marshall was sitting on a fastball, since Gibson was a threat to steal second base. With the count 2–2, Marshall hammered Mahler's 97th pitch into the left-field corner. Gibson ran the bases like a tight end. Nobody was going to stop him. He wasn't going to slow down until he crossed home.

The newspapers described it as a hit-and-run. Marshall reflected, "Let me tell you, it wasn't a hit-and-run. Gibby was probably going with two strikes. We never would hit-and-run with us. You can call it a run-and-hit. Gibby would tell me many times, 'Hey, early in the count, you get a breaking ball, give me a shot [to steal].' Later in the count, Gibby didn't mind me swinging when he was going. I would give him some time early. I don't remember the play. But I guarantee it wasn't a hit-and-run. Gibby was going, and I hit it."

The Dodgers won 1–0.

Pitching	IP	H	R	ER	BB	SO	HR	ERA	BF	Pit	Str	Ctct	StS	StL	GB	FB	LD
Orel Hershiser, W (21–8)	9	6	0	0	2	8	0	2.52	35	103	70	42	15	13	14	12	3

Hershiser was still only halfway to breaking Don Drysdale's record of 58⅔ innings, but it was now time to talk about it. "In my view, [the Drysdale record is] an unbelievable feat, one of the records that may not be broken," Hershiser said that night. "It's hard enough to throw a shutout, and he threw six and then some. I don't know if I have enough innings left in the season and enough pitches left in my arm to do it. But I'll settle for three more [shutouts]. I don't want to give up a run until I have to."

Publically, Hershiser called Drysdale's streak untouchable.

Privately, yes, Hershiser thought about the streak. He talked about it only with his wife, Jamie, and it wasn't a frequent conversation. It was still too far away. They actually laughed at how improbable it would all be. Something fluky needed to happen to get another inning.

Three more complete-game shutouts would leave Hershiser at 58 scoreless innings, still ⅔ of an inning shy of the record.

Danny Jackson pitched that night as well, and gave up his most runs since May 21. Glenn Davis and Rafael Ramirez took him deep, and the Astros won 7–1. It was the day the Cy Young Award race evened up.

These were the updated numbers after play on September 14.

Player	W-L	ERA	IP	H (BABIP)	BB	SO	Opp. Slash line
Danny Jackson, CIN	21–7	2.64	238.2	185 (.249)	63	152	.215/.269/.302
Orel Hershiser, LAD	21 8	2.52	230.0	195 (.253)	70	168	.222/.280/.328
David Cone, NYM	16–3	2.21	199.2	151 (.267)	71	176	.211/.284/.290

"I've got three more starts, then hopefully the playoffs," Hershiser said. "I'm really looking more at the Mets than Danny Jackson and the Cy Young."

But his immediate thought wasn't even on baseball.

Jamie had a 6:30 AM appointment the next morning at the doctor's office.

Chapter 9

July

July 4, 1988
Los Angeles
Cardinals vs. Dodgers
Team record: 45–33, 4½ games ahead of the Giants

Kirk Gibson jumped up and down and screamed. That's when he was happy. Kirk Gibson jumped up and down and screamed. That's when he was unhappy, too.

The polar opposite of left fielder Kirk Gibson was located about 90' to his left each night in the outfield. John Shelby didn't get excited or depressed. He didn't play pranks or freak out after pranks. He just showed up every day with the same attitude and quietly went about catching everything in center field and getting big hits.

In spring training, when a lot of players were expecting to start or wishing they were traded when they realized they weren't going to start, John Shelby didn't expect or wish. He just quietly got ready for the season. If somebody had told Shelby that he was no longer the starting center fielder, he wouldn't have been too surprised. That was the story of his career so far.

Shelby was born in Lexington, Kentucky, and was drafted in the first round by the Baltimore Orioles in January 1977 as a shortstop. He'd never played the outfield before in his life, but the Orioles converted him to center field instantly.

Six years later, he still had only 37 plate appearances in the major leagues. Shelby's path to the majors was first blocked by Al Bumbry. Shelby didn't do much with his first chance to be a regular in 1984 (.209/.248/.313 slash line in 415 plate appearances).

The Orioles signed free agent Fred Lynn to play center field in 1985, and Shelby's plate appearances were cut in half. He was the fourth outfielder who could play any position and hit for a little power, but not a lot of power, and not much of a batting average.

One day in the spring of 1986, former Dodgers outfielder "Sweet" Lou Johnson was in the press box at Holman Stadium in Vero Beach, Florida, talking to PR guy Fred Claire. Shelby came to the plate, and Sweet Lou made an innocent comment, something like, "Shelby is better than the Orioles realize. He just needs a change of scenery." It wasn't a recommendation. It was just a random statement one day in spring training.

Besides, this was a full year before "the Campanis thing" made Claire the general manager. Claire always remembered what Sweet Lou told him but didn't do anything with it. After all, he wasn't making player personnel decisions.

About 14 months later, Claire was in charge, and he needed a center fielder pretty badly. They tried to promote a kid from Double A named Mike Ramsey, but he wasn't the answer. The final straw for Claire was a May 16, 1987, game in Montreal when Ramsey committed an error and also misplayed a run-scoring double.

"It was just one of those days, man," Ramsey told reporters that night. "What am I supposed to do, run everything down? I just didn't get that ball. You expect me to get everything, man?"

Claire read that quote and thought to himself, *Hell yes. You're the center fielder of the Los Angeles Dodgers. I expect you to catch everything. That's your job.*

The next day, Claire started looking for a center fielder. He remembered what Sweet Lou Johnson had told him a year earlier. His target was Shelby.

Claire's trade piece was reliever Tom Niedenfuer. Oh yeah, Niedenfuer. Can you mention Niedenfuer's name without mentioning the home run to Jack Clark in the 1985 playoffs? Or the home run to Ozzie Smith earlier in the same playoff series? Fair or not, Niedenfuer was never the same after that series. At least, his numbers were never the same. More important, Dodgers fans were never going to let Niedenfuer forget it.

It came to a head when Niedenfuer gave up a three-run homer to Willie McGee in St. Louis on May 1, 1987—another go-ahead home run to another Cardinals player. After that, it seemed Tom Lasorda didn't trust him, either. He wasn't used for 10 days. Niedenfuer heard the rumors. There was a spring training rumor about a trade with Cleveland for Brett Butler. Another rumor was Niedenfuer to Boston for Dave Henderson.

Niedenfuer heard so many trade rumors that when Fred Claire called him up to his suite on May 21, Niedenfuer walked inside the room and said, "Which team was I traded?"

The trade had taken a couple weeks to finalize. Claire dispatched trusted scout Mel Didier to Triple A Rochester. Shelby's teammates discussed that if Didier was there, a trade with the Dodgers was likely. But Shelby had no idea that Didier was scouting him. The games that week were freezing cold. Didier was impressed that Shelby was preparing for a game as if it were a World Series game.

That was Shelby. He wasn't the typical bitter major leaguer demoted to the minor leagues who pouted and loafed. He didn't hit in the cage and retreat to the warm clubhouse. He hit, then returned to the outfield and tried to catch everything hit in batting practice. In his mind, he was still a shortstop learning all the nuances of center field.

On May 21, Shelby wasn't in the starting lineup. He asked his manager—future general manager John Hart—why he wasn't playing. Hart said, "You're going to be traded tomorrow." The trade was originally Niedenfuer for Shelby and Jim Dwyer. But from May 15–20, the five days before the trade was completed, Dwyer went 8-for-22 (.364) with four home runs and seven RBIs.

Orioles general manager Hank Peters called Claire and said he couldn't include Dwyer. Not now. Not after those five games. Instead, the teams settled on lefty swingman Brad Havens as the second player coming to the Dodgers. When in doubt, the Dodgers always took a pitcher. Claire and Lasorda called Shelby on the phone. They wanted Shelby in uniform that night.

"I've got an apartment in Rochester," Shelby said. "My wife is pregnant. I need three days to get to Albuquerque."

"You're not going to Albuquerque," Claire said. "You're going to be the starting center fielder for the Los Angeles Dodgers."

The phone was silent. Claire wasn't sure if Shelby was still on line. Shelby was speechless.

Finally able to talk, Shelby said simply, "I've been waiting my entire life to hear those words."

It's safe to say, however, that Dodgers fans and the Los Angeles media were not waiting their entire lives to hear those words. Claire was panned by writers and fans for acquiring a recently demoted outfielder.

Shelby had spent parts of six seasons with the Orioles, posting a career .240/.274/.363 slash line entering 1987. In 491 career games, the equivalent of about three full seasons, he had 30 home runs, 135 RBIs, 260 strikeouts, and 63 walks. Shelby was the Orioles' Opening Day right fielder in 1987, but a 6-for-32 (.188) start with 13 strikeouts sent him to the minors. Now, this guy was the answer?

The Dodgers knew he would catch everything in center field. Didier felt Shelby was trying to hit too many home runs because that's what the Orioles valued, but his swing could be corrected. Once Shelby heard he was going directly to the majors, he didn't need those three days to report. Besides, the Dodgers were in New York. Shelby arrived at Shea Stadium about 45 minutes before the first pitch, started in center field, and batted second.

In the fourth inning of Shelby's first game, Darryl Strawberry hit a home run off Fernando Valenzuela that went over the center-field wall. Valenzuela had yet to say hello to Shelby because Shelby arrived just before the game and Valenzuela was getting ready to pitch. After the inning, Valenzuela waited for Shelby at the dugout.

"I thought we got you to catch the ball," Valenzuela said, dead serious. "Can't you jump?"

Shelby was stunned. He had no chance to catch the ball. He wasn't sure how to react. Then Valenzuela broke into a big smile and laughed. "I'm just kidding. It's okay. Welcome to the team."

The next day, Shelby proved he could jump. He robbed Kevin McReynolds of a game-tying home run, bringing Claire's wife out of her seat in excitement. Shelby went 8-for-25 (.320) with a double and home run in his first six games. Claire smiled and thought, *We've got ourselves a center fielder.*

National League pitchers kept pumping fastballs to Shelby, and he kept whacking them. Shelby hit 21 home runs and drove in 69 runs in the final 4½ months of the 1987 season and continued to catch everything in center field. Pedro Guerrero welcomed him with the ultimate wisdom about playing for the Dodgers.

"I'll never forget the first time we were in the outfield together in L.A.," Shelby reflected. "We're talking and Pedro said, 'I'll give you some advice. Never forget this. Whatever you do, when Freddie is pitching, don't mess up. Don't miss the ball.' Freddie was Fernando Valenzuela. I kinda laughed. Then I looked into the outfield. The entire outfield pavilion was all Mexicans. Then I knew what Pedro was talking about. I will never forget that."

In a clubhouse filled with larger-than-life personalities and flamboyant characters, Shelby fit in well. Meaning, he didn't talk much. He wasn't very loud. He didn't mind that reporters avoided his locker after most games. He was perfectly content when the reporters gathered around Gibson and Hershiser and filled their notebooks with quotes from Sax and Scioscia.

But sometimes he did things that required him to speak, and July 4, 1988, was one of those nights.

◆ ◆ ◆ ◆

Bill Krueger started the game for the Dodgers, in place of the injured Don Sutton. Krueger allowed three runs and six stolen bases in less than three innings. Krueger, even though he was left-handed, had no answer for those jackrabbits on the Cardinals. The Dodgers' bullpen held down the fort to keep them in the game, though.

Mickey Hatcher was trying to get Tommy Lasorda to wear the Stuntmen's official hat. Hatcher made it himself. Hatcher loved hats. He had a million of them. This one was a helmet liner with a pinwheel on top. The Stuntman had their own shirts—designed by clubhouse attendant Mitch Poole—that they wore under their uniforms. Now they had a hat, too.

Hatcher told Lasorda, "If you wear the hat, we'll score."

Lasorda told Hatcher, "If we don't score, I'd break it into a thousand pieces."

Down 3–1 in the fourth inning, Lasorda agreed to wear the hat. Dave Anderson started the inning with a single. Gibson immediately hit a two-run home run. Lasorda couldn't help but laugh. The Stuntmen's hat was safe. The game was tied.

It was still 3–3 in the eighth inning, and there were two on and two out. Whitey Herzog intentionally walked Mike Marshall to load the bases for John Shelby. The strategy was sound. Marshall was more feared than Shelby. John Tudor was still in the game, so that created a lefty-lefty matchup.

Tudor made Kirk Gibson look calm with some of his antics over the years. Tudor was once so mad, he cut his hand punching an electric fan in the Cardinals' dugout during the 1985 World Series. Tudor threw Shelby a low fastball, and Shelby lined it back up the middle. Two runs scored, and the Dodgers led 5–3.

At first base, the strangest thing happened. Shelby softly pounded a fist into his other hand. Pounded isn't even the right word. It was like a love tap. For John Shelby, softly pumping a fist into an open hand was the equivalent of storming out of spring training because somebody put eye black in his cap.

"I can remember a couple times when I actually pumped my fist," a retrospective Shelby said, laughing. "It was a big series against St. Louis, and it was a big hit. It was one of the few times that I was more emotional than others. Believe me, I was always excited and emotional when I got a hit. A couple of times, it actually came out."

When Tudor returned to the Cardinals' dugout, he chucked his glove against a wall. A television camera captured the whole thing. Tudor realized this, and now he was more pissed. He picked up his glove and stuffed it inside the camera's lens.

Tim Belcher was still in the Dodgers' bullpen because Jay Howell was still on the disabled list. Belcher, the apprehensive closer, worked a scoreless ninth inning for his save. After the game, Shelby was in the position he didn't enjoy—talking to the press.

"Usually, I hope other people get those hits, so they can give the interviews," Shelby said that night. "I don't enjoy talking about this."

Noticing the crowd of reporters around Shelby afterward, backup catcher Rick Dempsey quipped, "Maybe John's coming out of his shell. He didn't say five words when he and I were in Baltimore."

Three decades later, Shelby laughed and said, "If you listen to somebody like Rick Dempsey, you don't get a chance to say more than five words. I'm sure I said more than five words. He just never heard me."

◆ ◆ ◆ ◆

July 6, 1988
Los Angeles
Cardinals vs. Dodgers
Team record: 47–33, 5½ games ahead of the Giants

It's Los Angeles, so you never knew who would be on the field during batting practice.

Tom Berenger and Charlie Sheen showed up on July 6. They took batting practice and worked out with the Dodgers. They were preparing for some upcoming movie with a baseball theme—something about a team in Cleveland whose owners were trying to lose.

The Dodgers' season was starting to feel like something out of a Hollywood script, especially the way they were winning games lately.

Fernando Valenzuela pitched his best game in a month, giving up three runs in seven innings. He needed only 93 pitches. The concerns about Fernando would go away for another five days. Fernando needed a start like this, especially after throwing 138 pitches in his previous start on July 1 where he gave up six runs, six walks, and eight hits in seven innings.

Still, the Dodgers trailed 3–0 entering the bottom of the eighth. Tim Crews replaced Fernando in the top of the eighth.

Starter Jose DeLeon was still in the game. Gibson, of course, got the rally started with a single. Marshall flied to right, and Shelby got another one of those singles that was important but not so important that he'd have to talk with reporters about it.

Herzog went to lefty Ken Dayley. Lasorda sent up righty Rick Dempsey to hit for lefty Mike Scioscia. It worked. Dempsey doubled down the left-field line to score two. The Cardinals' lead was down to 3–2.

Herzog went to his closer, Todd Worrell. Lasorda went back to his bench for another lefty. Danny Heep flew out for the second out. Dave Anderson just avoided getting hit in the head by a Worrell fastball. On the next pitch, Anderson singled up the middle to score Dempsey and tie the game at 3–3.

Mickey Hatcher batted for reliever Tim Crews and reached on an infield single. Steve Sax walked to load the bases and set the stage for first baseman Franklin Stubbs.

◆ ◆ ◆ ◆

The ghost of Steve Garvey was very powerful.

Garvey had been part of The Infield, won the MVP in 1974, was named an All-Star every year from 1974–81, hit .393 in 10 Midsummer Classics, reached 200 hits in six different years, won four Gold Gloves, hit 10 of his career 11 postseason home runs, batted .301 as a Dodger, and didn't strike out very often.

Mike Marshall posted a .373/.445/.675 slash line at Triple A Albuquerque in 1981, winning the Triple Crown with 34 home runs and 137 RBIs. Marshall's

105

reward was another trip to Albuquerque because of Garvey. Marshall was moved from first base to the outfield and reached the majors for good in 1982.

Greg Brock was the next power-hitting phenom to challenge for Garvey's job. Brock's slash line was .310/.432/.663 at Triple A Albuquerque in 1982, adding 44 home runs and 138 RBIs. That performance convinced the Dodgers to let Garvey leave for San Diego in free agency. However, Brock wasn't up to the challenge of the majors.

Pedro Guerrero could hit, and because he struggled at third base, he was tried at first base. You held your breath with him everywhere defensively, and left field was probably the best spot.

Franklin Stubbs was next in trying to chase away the ghost of Steve Garvey.

"It was probably harder for Greg Brock more than anybody," Stubbs said. "Greg came right after Garvey. The pressure is just trying to get to the big leagues and stay there. There's enough pressure playing in L.A. when the spotlight is always on you because they always have a chance to win. That's pressure itself. Forget about the Garvey stuff. There's pressure just to win in L.A."

Stubbs was born in Laurinburg, North Carolina, and grew up on a farm in Hamlet, North Carolina. He played ball and worked in the field as a youth. His family didn't have much money. But his mother and grandparents kept clothes on his back and provided fresh food to eat that they grew themselves.

"We had a mule and I plowed him," Stubbs recalled. "When my grandfather got old, he couldn't do it, so I did it most of it myself. He taught me how. I became very close to my grandfather from about age eight on. We were inseparable until he passed away. During that time, we plowed any kind of food that you can grow in the ground—corn, beans, okra, tomatoes, squash, watermelons, cantaloupes, sweet potatoes. You name it, we grew it.

"I tell you what, when you grow the food yourself, you harvest it, it's a different feeling than just going to the store and buying something with a whole bunch of chemicals they have on the food. It's more natural. It's better for your body. You feel more appreciative when you do something like that.

"What we'd do is stock it up for the winter. We bought our meats from the grocery store and bread. We had eggs. We pretty much had our own stuff because we lived in the country. I thought it was a great life, and I miss it. I didn't like getting up at 6:00 in the morning and hooking up that mule. But I loved the winter when we had all that food to eat."

A Dodgers scout named Jim Garland stopped at a diner with his wife to get something to eat one day in the mid-1970s. He noticed an American Legion baseball team was inside. The coach was George Whitfield, and he told the scout he should follow a kid named Franklin Stubbs. The kid was only a sophomore, but he was worth following. The scout did.

Five years later, Stubbs was the Dodgers' first-round pick (19th overall) in the 1982 draft out of Virginia Tech.

Hamlet (population 6,400) was once the hub of the old Seaboard Coastline Railroad. It was virtually unused by the mid-1980s, and the town was in jeopardy of drying up without the railroad. Hamlet residents took great pride in their professional athletes, though. At the cornerstone of Hamlet Memorial Park are four names:

Louis Breeden, cornerback, Cincinnati Bengals.
Mike Quick, wide receiver, Philadelphia Eagles.
Perry Williams, cornerback, New York Giants.
Franklin Stubbs, outfielder, Los Angeles Dodgers.

Stubbs was in the majors by 1984 and blasted eight home runs in 217 at-bats. But he wasn't ready. He was rushed because of an injury to Brock, batted just .194, and struck out 63 times in 217 at-bats.

In 1985, he was back in the minors for more seasoning. In 1986, Stubbs was finally in the majors—as an outfielder, because Brock was still at first base. He hit 23 home runs, the most on the team but had only 58 RBIs to show for those home runs. He batted just .226 and struck out 107 times back when it was embarrassing to strike out 100 times.

After the 1986 season, Brock was traded to Milwaukee for pitchers Tim Crews and Tim Leary, and first base was finally Stubbs' job. He started 86 times in 1987, and a slash line of .233/.290/.415 didn't justify further playing time. In roughly the same amount of plate appearances (42 fewer) as a year earlier, Stubbs had seven fewer home runs and six fewer RBIs.

When 1988 began, Stubbs was one of those unhappy young players who didn't want to demand a trade, but sure hoped he would be traded somewhere to get more guaranteed playing time. Instead, he was a reserve—a reserve who didn't play much but played too much to be considered one of the Stuntmen.

On June 7, just past the one-third mark of the season, Stubbs had started four games and had 37 plate appearances. But then Mike Marshall said his back felt better when he was in right field instead of at first base, and Pedro Guerrero was out with that neck injury.

Mike Davis became the odd-man out in right field, and Franklin Stubbs became the odd-man in at first base.

♦ ♦ ♦ ♦

Now Franklin Stubbs was battling Todd Worrell—the Cardinals' 1985 playoff savior and 1986 Rookie of the Year—with the bases loaded in the eighth inning of a tied game as the Dodgers attempted to rally from a three-run deficit to sweep the defending National League champions.

The count went full. Stubbs fouled off a pitch. Then he fouled off another. On the eighth pitch of the at-bat, Stubbs launched a ball into the right-field pavilion for his first career grand slam.

"I definitely remember that one," Stubbs recalled. "I knew [Worrell] didn't walk many people. He was their closer. He was a tough pitcher. For some reason in that at-bat I fouled off his high fastball, and I felt like I had a pretty good chance to get a pitch to hit. If he couldn't throw that pitch by me, I could pretty much hit anything else he threw. He did throw a nasty slider, on like a 2–2 count. To this day, I don't know how I fouled it off. Then he gave me a 3–2 fastball, and I hit it over the right field wall."

Stubbs received a hero's welcome at home plate. You'd have thought Sax had hit the home run, as excited as he was. Sax tried to lift Stubbs into the air and actually got both feet airborn for a moment, too.

"Here's the deal," Sax explained. "You're with these guys 7–8 months a year. You know their families. You know them very well. You know their kids. When somebody struggles and then they come out of it or they do something really tremendous, those things just really got me excited. I was so happy for my teammates. I loved being around my teammates. There was nobody happier than me. I loved being on a team. To share that with your teammates, there's really nothing better. That's why I got so excited about it. I loved my teammates."

◆ ◆ ◆ ◆

July 7
Los Angeles
Day off
Team record: 48–33, 5½ games over the Giants

Kirk Gibson didn't like All-Star Games.

Sparky Anderson wanted to bring Gibson to the 1985 Midsummer Classic in Minnesota. Sparky was the manager, after the Tigers had won the World Series in 1984 and Gibson hit that "other" huge World Series home run. Gibson declined that invite. His pattern was set. He didn't do All-Star Games.

The pattern continued in 1988. Gibson was the Dodgers' catalyst. He was batting .298 with 15 home runs and 46 RBIs at the time All-Star rosters were announced. He was a popular choice for MVP in those mid-season national baseball writer columns. Cardinals manager Whitey Herzog submitted Gibson's name to the league office to be a reserve.

Gibson preferred the time off and asked Tom Lasorda to speak with Herzog on his behalf.

"Kirk told me that his leg has been bothering him," Lasorda explained to reporters. "He's been running, but not 100 percent. He said he wanted to have the time off to get treatment. I talked to Whitey. I think he would have been selected if he had felt his leg was 100 percent."

The fans elected the Mets' Darryl Strawberry, the Cubs' Andre Dawson, and the Cardinals' Vince Coleman. Herzog added three more outfielders to his 28-man roster: Willie McGee of the Cardinals, Andy Van Slyke of the Pirates, and Rafael Palmeiro of the Cubs.

Gibson didn't want to talk with reporters about it. He rejected interview requests and released the following statement from the public relations office: "I feel that each player selected to the All-Star team deserved that honor. Personally, I am focused on the success of our team this year. That has been and will continue to be my goal."

Ten years later, when the *Los Angeles Times* did a retrospective on the 1988 Dodgers, Gibson gave one of his most revealing quotes, "I tell people that I was an average ballplayer who did some exceptional things at the right time. You know what? That's how I saw myself. I never cared about making the Hall of Fame. I never cared about hitting .300 or .400. I never cared about making the All-Star team. And you know what? I didn't do any of that and I won't do any of that. But I did care about becoming a world champion and sacrificing for the team, for the fans, for the organization, for the city."

Pitcher Orel Hershiser was the only Dodgers representative for the All-Star Game in Cincinnati. "On one hand it's a slap in the face to a team that's in first place and has been in first place for more days than any other team," Hershiser said. "On the other hand it's a compliment in that no one player is having an unbelievably brilliant year and everybody is chipping in. You would think we'd be better represented, but it shows a team effort, and if a guy like John Shelby hadn't been injured for a while, his statistics might be so good they would have had to pick him."

The Dodgers had won 14-of-19 games, were 15 games over .500, had a run differential of plus 79, and were 5½ games ahead of the Giants, the team that unabashedly called itself the team to beat in spring training.

Three home games against the surprising Pittsburgh Pirates remained until the All-Star break.

The first game was July 8. The script was all set for another comeback. Down 4–0, John Shelby hit a three-run home run to close the gap—another one of those important hits, but no so important that he'd have to answer a lot of questions. The next inning, Tracy Woodson hit a drive into the right-center gap. Out of nowhere, right fielder Darnell Coles made a diving catch on the warning track. His body ended up on top of center fielder Andy Van Slyke. Both were motionless. The umpires ruled it was a catch. Lasorda argued to no avail.

But that was just one loss.

The next game, July 9, Sean Hillegas started instead of Bill Krueger in Don Sutton's place in the rotation. Hillegas walked five in five innings and allowed three runs. He allowed home runs to Mike LaValliere and Barry Bonds. The final was 8–2.

But that was just two losses.

The Sunday before the All-Star break, July 10, was Orel Hershiser's turn to start. He allowed two runs in the fourth inning, including an RBI triple by former Dodger R.J. Reynolds. Then he allowed four more runs in the sixth inning, including a two-run single by Reynolds. It was Hershiser's shortest outing of the year to date. The final was 7–2.

The Giants swept the Cardinals during the same weekend. The Dodgers' lead went from 5½ games to 2½ games in three days. Maybe it would be a race after all.

◆ ◆ ◆ ◆

July 14–17, 1988
Chicago
Dodgers vs. Cubs
Team record: 48–36, 2½ games in first place over the Giants

On the original schedule, it was a brutal four-city, 14-games-in-14-days road trip to begin the second half. Due to earlier rainouts, it became a four-city, 16-games-in-14-days road trip.

"If we go 15–1, it will be very important," Hershiser predicted. "If we go 1–15, it will be very important. If we win about half, people will talk like we've survived it. I think it'll be a telltale trip, simply because of its length."

On the first day, they played a doubleheader at Wrigley Field. Tim Leary pitched seven scoreless innings, singled home the only run, and the Dodgers won the opener 1–0. In the nightcap, Sean Hillegas didn't last three innings, but the bullpen held the fort, Gibson hit two home runs, and the Dodgers won 6–3.

On the second day, Alfredo Griffin wasn't ready to come off the disabled list, but he threw batting practice. Griffin struggled to throw consistent strikes, driving Gibson crazy. "This is horseshit," Gibson yakked. "Why do we take BP if we're not going to get anything out of it?"

An overweight baseball card photographer was next for Gibson's wrath, "Get out of here! We told you to quit bothering us!" Lasorda told the photographer, "When he's like that, you just walk away from him." Rick Dempsey explained, "Gibby's always upset before games. That's how he gets himself psyched up."

The Dodgers won that game, too. Sax hit a sacrifice fly in the eighth inning to tie the game off Greg Maddux, and Tracy Woodson singled home the go-ahead run in the 10th for a 3–2 win.

On the third day, the Dodgers trailed 2–1 in the sixth inning but had the tying run at third base with one out. The Cubs removed lefty starter Jamie Moyer and brought in reliever Les Lancaster to face Woodson. Lasorda was ready to counter with lefty Franklin Stubbs.

"Tommy goes, 'Stubby, get ready,'" Woodson remembered. "I said, 'Tommy, no, I'm going to get this fucking guy in. I'll get him in.' I hit a sacrifice fly to center, and he scored. Gibson came up to me later and said, 'I'm glad you got that guy in, because your ass would have been sent back to Triple A if you hadn't.' I didn't want to be pinch hit for. You brought me up for a reason. Tommy was surprised that I said that. He had no choice. I think I backed him into a corner a little bit."

In the top of the ninth inning, with the game still tied 2–2, rain pummeled the field. The first night game at Wrigley Field was still a few weeks away. One hour and 42 minutes later, it was dark, and the umpires called the game. Because the game was tied, it was ruled a rainout and therefore would be not resumed. The teams would start all over again and play a doubleheader the next day.

The Roadtrip from Hell was now 17 games in 14 days.

"This game didn't take place in the history of the National League," said Hershiser, who allowed two runs in seven innings. "Only in the history of time."

On the fourth day, Franklin Stubbs hit a three-run homer in the seventh inning to break a 1–1 tie, and the Dodgers won the opener 4–1. In the second game, Hillegas started again. It was two days after Hillegas lasted less than three innings. Nowadays, another pitcher would get called up from the minors to make the start—but not on the 1988 Dodgers.

Hillegas allowed two runs in the first inning. But Mike Davis hit a two-run homer to tie it, one of just two he'd hit all year, Hillegas lasted five innings, Sax singled home the go-ahead run in the seventh, Jeff Hamilton singled home two more for insurance in the ninth, and the Dodgers won 5–2.

"That was a big series because people thought we were going to fade after the All-Star break," Stubbs recalled. "We went in there and won all those games."

Over four days, the Dodgers completed a five-game sweep, in a six-game series, against a Cubs team that had sent six players to the All-Star Game. The 2½ game lead turned into a seven-game lead in four days. When they returned to the clubhouse, Lasorda had a message for his players that turned into a mantra. He would repeat it, over and over, at least five times.

"What a fucking team!" Lasorda hollered. "What a fucking team! What a fucking team! What a fucking team! What a fucking team!"

◆ ◆ ◆ ◆

July 19
St. Louis

Dodgers vs. Cardinals

Team record: 54–36, eight-game lead over the Astros and the Giants

In the never-ending quest to find a replacement for the injured Don Sutton, the Dodgers tried Bill Krueger and tried Sean Hillegas. Now they were trying William Brennan, a 25-year-old who looked a little like Orel Hershiser. Brennan signed a minor league contract in 1984 after 51 rounds came and nobody drafted him out of Mercer University in Macon, Georgia.

It was 1–1 in the fifth inning, two outs, and leadoff hitter Vince Coleman walked. Brennan kept throwing over to first base, delaying the inevitable. When he finally threw home, Coleman stole second base. Still thinking about Coleman's speed, Brennan balked and Coleman went to third base. Yes, it was the year of the balk. Ozzie Smith singled to right to score Coleman. Brennan uncorked a wild pitch, and Smith went to second.

Terry Pendleton hit a grounder to first base. Brennan was slow covering first base. Pendleton was called safe. Brennan argued the call with first-base umpire Charlie Williams, and during the argument, he forgot all about Smith, who scored from second base.

The score was 3–1, and that was it for William Brennan's big-league debut.

The Dodgers had their chances. In the seventh, Davis doubled, Sax singled, and Danny Heep hit a sacrifice fly to make it 3–2. Gibson struck out, stranding the tying run at second.

In the ninth, Hamilton singled to start a rally. Anderson struck out, and so did pinch-hitter Franklin Stubbs. Sax singled to put the tying run at second. Heep grounded out to first to end the game, as Gibson watched from the on-deck circle.

That ended the Dodgers' six-game winning streak. Gibson didn't like losing. He really didn't like losing one-run games when he struck out to end the seventh and was in the on-deck circle when the game ended. So you know he was already pissed off.

Then came The Showdown.

Several Cardinals players came into the Dodgers' clubhouse after the game to chat with Pedro Guerrero, who was still on the disabled list. Entering the other team's clubhouse is considered one of *the* cardinal sins in baseball. That it was happening after a tough one-run loss and that it involved an injured Dodgers player being chummy with Cardinals players made it all the worse.

Gibson and Guerrero never hit it off. Gibson was intense. Guerrero could be aloof. Guerrero liked to play his music, and nobody told him to turn it off or turn it down because Guerrero was the best hitter, had been around a long time, and was a pretty big intimidating dude.

Kirk Gibson wasn't intimidated by anybody. He got up and walked over to where Guerrero and the Cardinals players were talking.

"If you fuckers want to be in our locker room, why don't you tell your agents to trade you here?" Gibson said.

"Who invited you into this conversation?" Guerrero replied.

"Tell your buddies to get the fuck out of our locker room!" Gibson said. "And if they don't, I'll throw them out myself.... If you want to go, get your little buddies together and I'll take all of you on, right now!"

Guerrero made a move toward Gibson. It wasn't a serious move. Gibson held his ground. Guerrero knew a couple teammates were holding him back. Nobody wanted to take on Kirk Gibson—not even Pedro Guerrero. The staredown didn't last long. Guerrero and the Cardinals' players left peacefully.

It was only a matter of time before Guerrero would leave permanently.

"My mentality was not made for that," Gibson said. "It wasn't that I didn't respect those players. That's just how I was. When I'd get ready for a game, I would always be the first one on the field. I was so tightly wound, I'd snap at the dumbest thing. I was the same way after a game. I'm like, 'get the fuck out of here. What are you thinking?'

"I didn't think it was the time for that. It's nothing against Pete. That's who he was. But I can tell you, in that instance, I didn't care that it was okay with him. It wasn't okay with me. I wasn't looking for a confrontation. But it needed to be said. If it needed to be more aggressive, that's okay, too."

Gibson knows he wasn't always perfect when he challenged teammates and management.

"There were times in my career that I spoke up and I was wrong," Gibson said. "I have a tendency to snap. I was as guilty as Pete in certain situations of doing the wrong thing. Fortunately, I was right in that situation."

◆ ◆ ◆ ◆

July 24, 1988
Pittsburgh
Dodgers vs. Pirates
Team record: 56–39, five games ahead of the Astros

Alfredo Griffin's hand was healed. He was coming off the disabled list shortly. The injury could have doomed the Dodgers. But it didn't because of the performance of Dave Anderson.

Never flashy, always lauded by teammates, Anderson played all six of those games in those four days in Chicago. He played almost every inning at shortstop with Griffin out. His numbers offensively were more than enough, and what he did defensively was immeasurable.

Mike Marshall said at the time, "I think [Anderson's] been our MVP. Without him, who knows where we'd be? He waited a long time for his chance, and he's made the best of it."

These are Anderson's numbers during the two months that Griffin was on the DL.

G	GS	Rslt	PA	AB	R	H	2B	3B	HR	RBI	BB	IBB	SO	HBP	SH	SF	ROE	GDP	SB	CS	BA	OBP	SLG	OPS
59	58	35–23	220	189	22	50	7	2	1	17	27	4	32	1	1	2	2	7	3	1	.265	.356	.339	.695

The team's won-loss record probably stands out most—35–23. Defensively, he made three errors. Two didn't lead to unearned runs. The other came when the score was already 8–3.

"It was the best I ever played for an extended period of time," Anderson reflected.

In Anderson's mind, it all started with a conversation right after Griffin was injured. "Tommy called me into his office and said, 'We're thinking of getting another shortstop. But I told Fred Claire that you're going to play.' When a guy shows that much confidence in you, it's hard not to go out there and do what you can to play well."

Was it true? Was Fred Claire really thinking of getting another shortstop? With Lasorda, you never knew.

Griffin was a magician at shortstop, but he was hitting only .167/.214/.243 at the time that a Dwight Gooden fastball broke his hand. Anderson wasn't Cal

Ripken Jr. at shortstop. Still, he was giving the Dodgers more offense than Griffin and doing the job defensively. There was no doubt, however, who would play shortstop when Griffin came off the disabled list.

"I know how Tommy operates," Anderson reflected. "He's always been the same. That was my sixth year playing with Tommy. His rule was always a guy never lost his job because of an injury. I knew as soon as Alfredo came back, I was going on the bench. It wasn't a surprise to me. Alfredo was a really good solid player, switch-hitter, and added a lot of things that I couldn't do. It was best for the team. Plus, now I'd played a lot and I could go in, and I was ready to play third base or second base or give Alfredo a day off. It wasn't that big a deal. I knew it was going to happen before it happened."

The final game before Griffin returned was an example of what Dave Anderson did.

Leading off the third, Anderson doubled off Pirates starter Brian Fisher down the left-field line. Two batters later Steve Sax went the other way, dropping a single into right-center, and Anderson scored to make it 1–0.

With two outs in the sixth, Andy Van Slyke tied the game with his 16th home run, a deep drive to right-center.

In the seventh, Fisher retired the first two batters. Anderson worked the count full, fouled off a number of pitches, and drew a walk on the ninth pitch of the at-bat. Danny Heep pinch hit for starting pitcher Sean Hillegas, also worked the count full, and also drew a walk. Sax lined a 1–1 pitch into left field for a single, Anderson scored ahead of Barry Bonds' throw, and it was 2–1 Dodgers.

The bullpen did the rest. Alejandro Pena pitched a scoreless seventh. Jesse Orosco got two outs in the eighth. With Bobby Bonilla coming up and a runner at second base, Lasorda went to Jay Howell to get the last four outs. Bonilla popped to third to end the eighth, and Howell worked a clean ninth to save the 2–1 victory.

On their epic 14-day, 17-game road trip, the Dodgers were off to a 9–3 start. The lead was 2½ games when the trip started. Now they led the Astros by six games and the Giants by seven games. Four more games remained—in three days—up in San Francisco.

◆ ◆ ◆ ◆

July 26, 1988

San Francisco

Dodgers vs. Giants

Team record: 57–40, 5½ games ahead of the Astros

Back in April, when the Dodgers were rained out four straight games, the final rainout came in San Francisco. The Giants wanted to make up the rainout on a mutually open date later in April. The Dodgers voted against it because they wanted to see Bruce Springsteen in concert on that same day.

That meant a doubleheader in San Francisco in late July during the Dodgers' epic road trip. The rained-out game was rescheduled as a twi-night doubleheader, the first game starting at 5:35 PM.

Orel Hershiser started the first game, and he was in somewhat of a slump—somewhat. Hershiser hadn't won in three games, he had averaged six innings in those three starts, and he allowed 11 runs (nine were earned).

The bigger issue was the innings pitched. Hershiser was used to going at least seven, if not eight innings, or the distance. He needed to go deep in the first game of the doubleheader. Remember, this is when rosters held only 24 players and pitching staffs went just 10 men deep.

It was a raucous night by the Bay. Fights broke out constantly. The actions of more than 100 unruly fans would have long-term consequences for traditions at Candlestick. Typical for San Francisco in July, the temperature at first pitch was 60 degrees.

"The atmosphere in San Francisco, you just have to remember one game, and it was like that every game," Scioscia recalled. "You had a smattering of brave Dodgers fans there. For the most part, and they were drawing well, you had a stadium full of people that wanted nothing more than for the Dodgers to not only lose but be humiliated. They were going to be very vocal. Occasionally, you're going to get an orange coming out of the stands. That was pretty much the environment every time going into Candlestick."

The Dodgers struck first. Sax singled off Terry Mulholland, went to second on a groundout, and scored on Marshall's two-out single. The Giants answered with a run in the bottom of the first. Brett Butler walked, stole second, and scored on Candy Maldonado's double. In the seventh, Jeff Hamilton doubled, and Rick Dempsey homered for a 3–1 lead.

In the bottom of the eighth, Hershiser loaded the bases with one out. Lasorda went to his bullpen, calling on lefty Jesse Orosco. Roger Craig sent righty Joel Youngblood to hit for lefty Mike Aldrete. Youngblood scored a run with a fielder's choice. Jay Howell put out another fire, getting Kevin Mitchell on a fly ball to center to keep the score 3–2.

Hamilton led off the ninth with a solo home run off Craig Lefferts. Dempsey walked and Franklin Stubbs singled. Craig went to Scott Garrelts, another one of those Giants pitchers who went from good to great after Craig taught him the split-finger fastball. Sax tripled into the left–center field gap, scoring two runs.

Then, in the year of the balk, home plate umpire Jerry Crawford called a balk on Garrelts that scored another run. The lead was 7–2.

In the bottom of the ninth, Howell allowed three singles, Crawford called another balk, and a run scored. But Howell struck out Robby Thompson and Will Clark to end it.

"San Francisco was always a tough place for us to play," Stubbs recalled. "It's still a hard place to play because of the rivalry. Every time you play San Francisco, I don't care what place you're in, you can throw the records out the window. It's a flat-out war."

Between games, Giants manager Roger Craig told the newspaper men the next game was the most important of the season. The temperature dropped from 60 degrees at first pitch of the first game to 49 degrees at first pitch of the second game.

The nightcap began at 9:08 PM. No rules existed at that time for cutting off beer sales.

In the third inning, Chris Speier hit a solo home run for a 1–0 lead. The Dodgers answered immediately off starting pitcher Don Robinson. With two on and two out, Hamilton reached safely on an infield single, and Gibson scored all the way from second base. Griffin dumped a single into right field to score a run, and Dodgers pitcher Tim Belcher ripped a double down the left field line to score two runs and build a 4–1 lead.

The game was far from over. In the sixth, Mike Aldrete and Ernest Riles doubled to make it 4–2. Alejandro Pena replaced Belcher and put out the fire, working a scoreless seventh. Maldonado and Riles singled in the eighth inning, and Lasorda went back to Howell for another four-out save. Bob Melvin greeted Howell with a triple to right-center, and the game was tied 4–4.

In the ninth, Hamilton reached on an error by shortstop Jose Uribe, and Anderson bunted him to second. Dempsey grounded out, and Sax came through once again, beating out an infield single to make it 5–4 Dodgers.

The Giants wouldn't go away. Thompson singled, Butler sacrificed him to second, and Speier reached on a throwing error by Griffin. Now Lasorda needed Orosco to bail out Howell, as Will the Thrill came up. Clark hit a grounder to short, but the Dodgers couldn't turn two. It was tied again at 5–5 and headed to extra innings.

It was past midnight in San Francisco. The kids who would run down from those bleachers toward the left-field wall to snag home runs balls were literally climbing the fence on routine fly balls, and they refused to return to their seats. The crowd of about 50 young males hung on the outfield fences, and shook them in an attempt to knock them down.

Now the game was going extra innings. Yes, near the end of 17 road games in 14 days in four cities and after 18 innings in the past six hours, the Giants and Dodgers were going to extra innings.

Garrelts and Holton retired the side in order in the 10th. In the 11th, Stubbs doubled to right-center to start the inning. Tracy Woodson grounded to second, and Stubbs went to third. Anderson came to the plate, with another chance to be a hero.

On the first pitch home plate umpire Greg Bonin called a balk on Scott Garrelts. Yes, another balk. This was the year of the balk. Stubbs scored the go-ahead run. Craig lost his mind, argued like crazy, got ejected, and then argued even more. Pitcher Mike Krukow, on the disabled list at the time, was ejected from the dugout, as well.

"It was just an incompetent call," Craig said that night. "Let the players decide the ballgame, not the umpire. We come back twice, battle like hell, play seven, eight hours of ball, and a balk has to be the deciding factor in the game. We lose the first game and then the second on a balk call, and the ump says I got the fans excited. If a guy is a good pro umpire, he's not going to make a borderline call at a point like that. He lets the players decide the game."

What remained of the 49,209 fans at Candlestick—perhaps half—was absolutely livid. One fan to the left of home plate chucked a baseball that just missed umpire Bonin's head. The fan was led away by police. Other fans pelted the field with balls, batteries, bottles, hot dog wrappers, and rolled up soda cups. Gibson was one of the biggest targets in left field.

Holton returned for the bottom of the 11th inning. He got two quick outs, pitched around Will Clark with four straight bad ones, and struck out Maldonado to end it at 1:21 AM. The Dodgers shook hands and ran for their lives across the outfield to the safety of their clubhouse.

The Dodgers had played seven hours and 10 minutes of baseball against their biggest rivals and won both games. The Astros were seven back. The Giants were eight back. But the fallout from that night in Candlestick went beyond the standings.

In all, 75 fans were ejected by San Francisco police. Another 2–3 dozen were ejected by Candlestick security personnel. Eighteen were arrested for fighting and throwing objects at Dodgers players and umpires.

Dodgers general manager Fred Claire called National League president Bart Giamatti the next morning and met with Giants president Al Rosen.

"I talked to Bart Giamatti because it's frightening," Claire said the next day. "That's the only word for it. The Giants and Al assured us they'd take all the steps they can. There's a problem that's here. I called upon the National League to put a stop to it. Al Rosen is very concerned. You can't put players in a position of danger. I think it's worse now than it was before."

Rosen agreed. He also called the events "frightening" and added, "This was the worst I've seen since I've been born, and I've been in World War II. The beach at Okinawa was safer."

That was the final night fans at Candlestick Park were ever allowed to run down from the left-field bleachers to get home runs. Starting the next day, additional security was in place. Protective steel barriers prevented the time-honored tradition.

That night was also the turning point in the year of the balk. An important game was decided in extra innings, between the sport's two best rivals, on a balk call. The outrage in the stands led to a dangerous scene for players, umpires and innocent bystanders. No official memo was sent to umpires, but the number of balks called the rest of the season dropped considerably.

◆ ◆ ◆ ◆

July 30, 1988
Los Angeles
Astros vs. Dodgers
Team record: 59–42, 4½ games ahead of the Astros

It looked like one of the best outings of the year for Fernando Valenzuela.

Valenzuela took a 2–0 lead into the fifth inning and was working on a one-hit shutout. He wasn't throwing his signature pitch, the screwball, very often. That was weird. He was mostly using his fastball, and even with declining velocity, he spotted it well enough to shut down the Astros.

Billy Hatcher grounded to short for the first out in the fifth inning. Ken Caminiti grounded out for the second out. But something was wrong, and Valenzuela knew it. Valenzuela stepped off the mound. Trainer Charlie Strasser and pitching coach Ron Perranoski visited the mound, and so did all of the infielders.

Valenzuela tried a couple of warm-up pitches. It still didn't feel right. But his shoulder never felt totally right. It was his eighth year in the majors. He'd averaged 266 innings from 1982–87. Nobody had thrown more innings or pitches in baseball than Valenzuela in that time. He just didn't leave games when something felt a little off. So he stayed in.

Rafael Ramirez singled to center. Alex Trevino, who had been cut by the Dodgers at the end of spring training to make room for Rick Dempsey, hit a deep two-run home run.

Fernando's afternoon was done. It wasn't known at the time, but Fernando's season was essentially done, too.

That day Valenzuela told reporters, "It's not just the shoulder; it's the whole arm that feels weak. I don't know when I will throw again. I felt good when the game started. But on the fastball to Hatcher, the arm felt weak. I got the next batter [Caminiti], but I knew my arm was weak. I thought I could get the next out, but I couldn't. I had to leave."

The game imploded from there. The Astros scored four runs that inning, then 10 runs in the next three innings. It was so bad, outfielder Danny Heep pitched the final two innings to save the bullpen. The final was 14–6. But the game was irrelevant. The story was Valenzuela.

The next day, after 255 consecutive starts, Valenzuela was placed on the 21-day disabled list. Dr. Frank Jobe said he thought Valenzuela would need more than three weeks rest but would return before the season ended. Considering the way Valenzuela struggled and the drop of 5–10 mph on his fastball, it was just a matter of time before this happened.

"I always felt that something was wrong," Lasorda said that night. "But he would never tell you because he's such a tremendous competitor."

Twenty-five years later, Valenzuela continued to insist he was never hurt until that fateful night.

"That was it, that was the only time I started feeling it in my shoulder," Valenzuela said. "Before, I never felt any pain in my arm. Of course, you get normal tired after games. Nothing like that pain. I still remember that game against Houston. That's when I started feeling in the middle of the game. I remember those first two hitters. I felt something in my arm. At first, I thought it was my elbow."

Valenzuela was scared. "Yeah, that's a scary feeling," he reflected. "I'd never felt that kind of experience or pain in my arm. I wasn't sure what it was. At first, I didn't think it was major. I didn't think it would be the whole season."

Jaime Jarrin, the Spanish voice of the Dodgers who was Valenzuela's interpreter in 1981 and longtime confidant, advised Valenzuela to have the same shoulder surgery that had saved Alejandro Pena's career and would later save Orel Hershiser's career.

"His shoulder was really in shambles," Jarrin recalled. "I told him he should have surgery. If he had that surgery, I think he could have pitched five more years. They blame Lasorda for allowing him to make so many pitches. [Fernando] doesn't believe that. He never complains. He always wanted the ball. To take him off the mound was a tough call for a manager."

Mike Marshall reflected, "This was no one's fault. You just can't pound the 130s and 140s [in pitch count] and throw the screwball and take a lot of pitches to get a lot of outs. Fernando was just not an easy-out guy. Fernando was not going to lay it in there and let you hit the ball. Fernando was going to work and work and nibble and nibble. It took its toll. For five to six years, he was one of the best pitchers in baseball. It didn't surprise us that he would slow down. Maybe I'm wrong. From the outside looking in, his pitch count had to be enormous."

Valenzuela saw a printout of his pitch count totals from 1988—which included games of 150, 137, 137, 121, 138, and 128. (Accurate pitch-count totals are not available up through 1987.)

"When I'm on the mound, I never think about how many pitches I have," Valenzuela said in 2012. "I don't think the numbers at that moment mean anything. I'm just concentrating on the game. I want to keep going and going. I never realized that was going to do damage for the future. At that moment, I never thought, 'I don't want to pitch more than 120 pitches.'

"But that is a lot of pitches. Over 250 innings for eight years. I think my arm said, 'That's enough.'"

Chapter 10

The Fourth Shutout

Monday, September 19, 1988

Houston

Dodgers vs. Astros

Team record: 86–61, first place by nine games over Astros and Giants

DODGERS	ASTROS
SS Alfredo Griffin	CF Gerald Young
2B Steve Sax	2B Bill Doran
LF Kirk Gibson	RF Kevin Bass
RF Mike Marshall	1B Glenn Davis
CF John Shelby	3B Buddy Bell
1B Franklin Stubbs	C Alan Ashby
3B Jeff Hamilton	LF Cameron Drew
C Mike Scioscia	SS Rafael Rarmirez
P Orel Hershiser	P Nolan Ryan

Orel Hershiser's first start in the major leagues, after 24 relief appearances to begin his career, was in New York on May 26, 1984.

An injury to Jerry Reuss moved Hershiser into the starting rotation to face the Mets in a nationally televised game. Hershiser allowed one run in 6⅓ innings—a home run to Hubie Brooks—but took a no-decision in a 2–1 loss. A month later, Hershiser was in the starting rotation for good.

Orel Hershiser's first significant scoreless streak began during that rookie season on June 29, 1984. It came a few weeks after the famous story of how the nickname "Bulldog" was born.

Hershiser was summoned into Tommy Lasorda's office for a meeting that included pitching coach Ron Perranoski. Hershiser feared he was being sent back to the minor leagues. Lasorda thought Hershiser could do much better. Lasorda scolded the pitcher for giving the hitters too much credit and not trusting his abilities.

Lasorda was in a rage as he delivered the message. His eyes bulged. His cheeks were red. Veins were sticking out. Hershiser felt the sweat on the back of his neck and on his forehead. He didn't dare move or wipe the sweat away. Spit poured out of Lasorda's mouth and landed on Hershiser's face. They were nose to nose.

The end of Lasorda's speech, "I've seen guys come and go, son, and you've got it! You gotta go out there and do it on the mound! Take charge! Make 'em hit your best stuff! Be aggressive! Be a bulldog out there. That's gonna be your new name: Bulldog. You know, when we bring you in in the ninth to face Dale Murphy and he hears, 'Now pitching, Orel Hershiser,' man, he can't wait 'til you get there. But if he hears, 'Now pitching, Bulldog Hershiser,' he's thinking, 'Oh no, who's that?' Murphy's gonna be scared to death."

When asked how to frame the importance of that meeting, three decades later, a few things came to Hershiser's mind. "It was the nickname that turned around my mentality and erased my memories of admiring and putting big leaguers on a pedestal. When you admire the talent of big leaguers your whole life, and now you have to get them out, the nickname Bulldog was almost like permission to say, 'You belong here. And you not only belong here, these guys fear you because you're that good.'"

Hershiser didn't always feel that way. "I hated the nickname. Hated it. Absolutely hated it. I don't know if Lasorda will ever tell you this, but he didn't give you a nickname until he thought you were a big leaguer. Dave Anderson was 'Honey-do.' Franklin Stubbs was 'Cadillac.' Mike Marshall was 'Moose.' He didn't call you by that nickname until he wanted you on the team. When Tommy thought you had big-league ability and he wanted you on the team, he gave you a nickname."

Hershiser had pitched 24 times in relief in that 1984 season, posting a 4.70 ERA, when Lasorda moved him into the starting rotation. In his third career start, Hershiser allowed one run (in the seventh inning) of a complete-game 7–1 win over the Cubs. Then he shut out the Pirates 9–0 on July 4, so the streak was 11 scoreless innings.

Four days later, on the final day before the All-Star break, Hershiser entered the game in relief. In the ninth inning of a one-run game with a runner at first, Hershiser allowed the tying run to score. He was charged with a blown save but didn't allow a run of his own in the ninth or the 10th inning. He was now at $12\frac{2}{3}$ scoreless innings.

On July 14, the third day after the All-Star break, Hershiser shut out the Cubs 8–0 at Wrigley Field. Five days after that, he blanked the Cardinals 10–0 in St. Louis. Now it was $30\frac{2}{3}$ scoreless innings, a stretch that included four wins and a blown save.

On July 24, Hershiser put up three more zeroes against the Braves, reaching $33\frac{2}{3}$ innings. With one out in the fourth inning, Claudell Washington singled and Dale Murphy—who was coming off back-to-back Most Valuable Player awards— hit a two-run home run to end the streak.

The difference between the 1984 and 1988 streaks?

"I really didn't know what I was doing in '84," Hershiser once said. "I was like that pitcher in *Bull Durham* when he throws a great pitch and says, 'God, that was beautiful. What'd I do?'"

Hershiser also learned valuable lessons from Burt Hooton that year. The pitchers carpooled together the 45-60 minute drive from Orange County to Dodger Stadium. They disagreed on musical choices. Hershiser enjoyed light rock. Hooton preferred country.

But they shared a bond over discussing the art of pitching. Hooton did most of the talking. Hershiser listened and asked questions. Hooton used a lot of sarcasm to get the point across. What Hershiser learned most from Hooton was the work ethic required, the endurance required to make 33 starts in six months.

Following the advice of Hooton, Hershiser followed up his rookie season by going 19–3 with a 2.03 ERA in 1985. He finished third in the Cy Young Award voting behind Dwight Gooden and John Tudor and established himself as one of the top pitchers in baseball.

His name, however, still gave people trouble. Frank Sinatra signed a photo for Hershiser and spelled his name "Oral."

In 1986, Hershiser's ERA climbed almost two full runs to 3.85, and his walks rose to 3.3 per nine innings, a rate he wouldn't exceed until he was 39 years old. That off-season, the Dodgers tried to obtain Expos reliever Jeff Reardon. The Expos asked for Hershiser. The Dodgers said, "No way." The Dodgers offered Bob Welch. The Expos said they wanted another player if Welch was involved. The Dodgers offered Rick Honeycutt. The Expos said, "No way." The talks stalled.

Hershiser bounced back in 1987, leading the pitching staff with 264⅔ innings pitched and 10 complete games, lowering his ERA back to 3.06 and reaching his first All-Star Game. He finished fourth in the Cy Young Award voting behind Phillies closer Steve Bedrosian, Cubs starter Rick Sutcliffe, and Giants pitcher Rick Reuschel.

Even though he was one of the best starting pitchers in baseball, and one of the best paid, Hershiser never lost his fondness for pitching in relief.

"I remember in '87 in St. Louis, in probably August or July," Fred Claire said, "Orel came to me because we didn't have anybody to close games and said, 'I'll close for you. I'll become the closer for you.' I told him, 'You've got about as much chance of closing games as I do. That's not going to happen.'

"With Orel, you just came to expect perfection. Orel was the composite of all that you would look for in terms of being extremely competitive, extremely intelligent in his approach, and he understood all parts of it. He was using a computer before anybody was using a computer. It was just part of what came from him. He was always prepared to do the job, to deliver that type of performance."

Hershiser laughed when he recalled why he started using a computer, an early IBM model. "There were a lot of IBM commercials back then," Hershiser reflected. "In one of them, they'd design a play in football, they'd print it out on the sidelines, and give it to everybody. The play was taped to the rear end of the center, and the quarterback fades back and looks for the receiver by which route, and he throws it, and they score a touchdown.

"I don't know why, but I remember that introducing me to computers and sports. I thought, *I should have one of those.* I [previously] took the notes in a notebook. But that always got trashed in your bag with your spikes and the dirt. I was never smart enough to put it in a plastic bag."

By 1988, the nickname Bulldog was no longer needed to convince Hershiser that he could get major league hitters out. Hershiser reflected, "It was warm and friendly, you know, 'That's the Bulldog.' It wasn't, 'Act like a Bulldog.' It was, 'That's Bulldog.' I didn't need a reminder anymore. That just happened to be my name."

Hershiser still hated the nickname.

◆ ◆ ◆ ◆

What happened in the five days since Orel Hershiser had last pitched? His son, Jordan, was born. Orel celebrated his 30th birthday. Tom Browning threw a perfect game against the Dodgers in Cincinnati. Wayne Gretzky made his debut with the Los Angeles Kings. Janet Evans won her first gold medal at the Seoul Olympics.

Hershiser never joined his teammates in Cincinnati. Jordan's birth came with complications. With fluid in his lungs, the newborn was placed in intensive care. Tubes and wires engulfed his frail body. Blood was taken from his heel, and he was fed intravenously.

Orel and Jamie asked their family and friends to pray. Orel did his usual throwing and between-starts workouts in Los Angeles. He flew directly to Houston the day before his start, the same day Jordan pulled out of danger and was moved from intensive to intermediate care.

Hershiser knew his son was in good hands back home, and there was nothing more he could do. He knew everybody was concerned, but he didn't want to keep dwelling on Jordan's condition as person after concerned person asked him for an update.

So at the usual pre-series scouting meeting, Hershiser told his teammates, "I'm glad to be back. I want you to know Jordan's okay, and I just want to concentrate on beating these guys."

On the other side of the globe at the Seoul Olympics, Greg Louganis hit his head on the 3-meter springboard in his ninth dive of the qualifying round, dropping him to eighth place. Less than an hour later, with four stitches in his head, Louganis rallied with the best dive of the day to easily reach the finals.

Back in Houston, Hershiser was facing Nolan Ryan for a third time that season. He'd moved himself to the upper echelon of pitchers by beating Ryan twice, and now he was looking for a third win against the certain Hall of Famer.

Gerald Young and Bill Doran flew out to left field to start the game. Kevin Bass lined a single to left and stole second base on a 1–2 pitch. Glenn Davis grounded to short, but Alfredo Griffin committed an error to prolong the inning. Buddy Bell bounced to second to end the inning, and Griffin breathed a sigh of relief. The scoreless streak was at 32 innings.

In the second inning, Hershiser struck out catcher Alan Ashby after a seven-pitch duel, Cameron Drew (in his 11th career at-bat) popped to short, and Rafael Ramirez grounded to second. The streak was at 33.

Ryan struck out two Dodgers hitters in the top of the first and two more in the top of the second, but then he departed the game with a cramp to his left hamstring. Danny Darwin replaced Ryan and grounded out to short to start the third. Young struck out swinging. Doran grounded to first. It took Hershiser just 11 pitches. The streak was 34.

In the fourth, Bass hit a fly ball to deep left, but it was no threat in the spacious Astrodome. It was just a long out. Davis struck out looking. Bell lined a two-out single to shallow center, but Ashby grounded to second on the first pitch. The streak was 35.

Drew opened the fifth inning with a routine ground out to first. Ramirez lined a single to right-center. Darwin tried a sacrifice, but the slick-fielding Hershiser got the lead runner at second base. Young grounded to first, but the inning was prolonged when Stubbs misplayed it. Casey Candaele, who had entered the game at second base in the top of the fifth, flew out to deep left. Stubbs exhaled. The streak was at 36.

The game still scoreless, Hershiser breezed through the middle of the Astros lineup in the sixth, needing just nine pitches. Bass lined out to center. Davis struck out looking. Bell grounded to third. The streak was 37.

Enough offense arrived in the seventh—meaning, one run. John Shelby led off the inning with a home run to right-center. Hershiser knew the way the offense was going, he needed a shutout to keep winning.

After the seventh-inning stretch, Hershiser was back in the dugout after just 12 pitches. Ashby struck out swinging. Drew popped to short left field. Ramirez grounded to short. The streak was 38.

Astros manager Hal Lanier went to his bench to begin the eighth, calling on Harry Spilman to bat for Darwin. Spilman popped to short. Young flew out to center. Candaele flew out to center. Shelby caught everything in center. The streak was 39.

Vin Scully on Koufax and Drysdale

"The difference between Koufax and Drysdale was not just left and right," broadcaster Vin Scully said. "They were that different. There was an awe about Koufax. If we were on the road, Sandy would have dinner with either Dick Tracewski, a backup infielder, or a third-string catcher. They'd go off quietly. Don was the pied piper. On the road, if Don was going out to dinner, there would be six other guys out there with him, at least. With Sandy, everybody just couldn't believe how good he was. I think it might be equated to the way the Yankees treated Joe DiMaggio. It was above and beyond the call."

Drysdale's reputation carried over through the decades.

"The thing the players loved about Drysdale is there was never an excuse," Scully said. "He would pitch hurt. He pitched with shingles. You know, shingles are excruciating. He still pitched with them. I can just imagine Hershiser admiring Drysdale because he knew he wasn't just a winner. He wasn't as good as Koufax, but he was a grinder. Anybody in that business would really admire him."

Hershiser was at just 90 pitches after eight innings. Bass lined a single to center field to start the ninth inning. Davis hit a hard grounder to short, but Griffin fielded it cleanly, made an off-balance throw to second, and Steve Sax completed a double play. Bell fouled out to catcher Mike Scioscia to end it.

The scoreless inning streak was at 40. The shutout streak was at four. The complete-game streak was at seven. The Dodgers' magic number to clinch the division was five.

Pitching	IP	H	R	ER	BB	SO	HR	ERA	BF	Pit	Str	Ctct	StS	StL	GB	FB	LD
Orel Hershiser, W (22–8)	9	4	0	0	0	5	0	2.43	32	96	67	41	5	21	12	15	5

Don Drysdale didn't ask Hershiser about the record during his TV interview after the game. But when the newspaper reporters asked him later in the broadcast booth, Drysdale was already preparing to see his record broken.

"Oh, yes, I'm pulling for him," Drysdale told reporters, chuckling. "Hey, that's what records are for—to be broken. At least it's another guy on the Dodgers [trying to] do it, and one with his [uniform] number in the 50s."

No. 53 was happy for No. 55, but there remained a problem reaching 59.

"It's hard enough to throw one shutout, let alone two more in my last two starts," Hershiser said. "Even if I did, I still would come up short."

Two more shutouts would give Hershiser 58 innings. The record was 58⅔ innings. The reporters asked Hershiser about pitching in relief.

"Oh yeah, I can just see me asking Tommy to do that on the last day of the season with the playoffs coming up," Hershiser said.

Lasorda's take? "That's a hell of a question you're asking me. To paraphrase the words of a great leader, we'll cross that bridge when we come to it."

At 40 innings, the Elias Sports Bureau determined Hershiser's streak was the fourth-longest in National League history. Bob Gibson threw 47 straight scoreless in 1968, the same year Drysdale set the record. Carl Hubbell pitched 46 scoreless in 1933, the record that Drysdale broke.

"I doubt it can be done," Hershiser said. "I really do. I've always said that that might be the one record that would never be broken. I'm not just trying to jinx myself or anything. But it's true."

Meanwhile in Cincinnati, Danny Jackson allowed two runs in 7⅓ innings to win again. Here are the updated numbers for the three Cy Young Award candidates:

Player	W-L	ERA	IP	H (BABIP)	BB	SO	Opp. Slash line
Danny Jackson, CIN	22–7	2.63	246.0	192 (.248)	66	154	.216/.270/.306
Orel Hershiser, LAD	22–8	2.43	248.0	199 (.249)	70	173	.218/.275/.321
David Cone, NYM	17–3	2.18	206.2	156 (.269)	74	186	.211/.284/.287

Hershiser's next start would be against the Giants, the same Giants that shelled him for eight runs (five earned) in just two innings 36 days earlier. With all the history in the Giants-Dodgers rivalry, a little more history would need to be revisited for history to be made again.

That was still four days away. For now, Hershiser had more modest goals. "I'm just going to go out in my next start and try not to embarrass myself," he said.

Chapter 11

August

August 10, 1988

Cincinnati

Dodgers vs. Reds

Team record: 62–49, ½-game ahead of Astros

As usual, Kirk Gibson was blunt about the state of the team.

"You look at every aspect of our game, and it's terrible right now," Gibson said. "Everything's going against us, from A to Z. How to get out of it? I don't know. But I don't feel like it's the end of the season. We're fortunate to be playing as poorly as we are and still be in first place. Maybe it will do us good to get out of first place and get something to fight for again."

All the momentum from that 11–5–1 road trip after the All-Star break was gone. The Dodgers had lost three in a row and 9-of-12. They were shut out in the last two games. Their eight-game lead was down to ½-game.

If people in Los Angeles weren't paying attention, it was understandable. The team was on the road. Not every game was on television. The sports section was dominated by the blockbuster trade that sent hockey icon Wayne Gretzky to the Los Angeles Kings and the news of the first night game in Wrigley Field history.

The fifth spot in the Dodgers' rotation was a mess. Two days earlier, Sean Hillegas was bombed in a 10–0 loss. One day earlier, Don Sutton came off the disabled list, made his first start in 42 days, and allowed six runs in seven innings. Lasorda called it "poor." Sutton called it "progress."

After the game, Fred Claire met with Lasorda in the manager's office. Lasorda was adamant that Sutton couldn't help the team anymore. Claire agreed.

Sutton was a future Hall of Famer with 324 wins. But the end was coming soon. Everybody knew it—even Sutton. He knew he couldn't pitch forever, and he was thinking about a job the next season in the front office or broadcasting booth. A few days earlier in Houston, Sutton ran into Astros general manager Bill Wood and talked with him informally about an assistant GM job.

Informal or not, Claire wasn't happy. He considered it a form of tampering.

"Don has expressed his desires," Claire said then. "But there are precise rules as to what clubs can and can't do and what players can and can't do. He should not have had any discussions with anyone. He's playing for the Los Angeles Dodgers."

The next morning, Claire met with Sutton and told him his services were no longer needed. It wasn't easy delivering the news. Sutton was part of Dodgers royalty. But it was time. It wasn't about the Astros job next year. It was about his pitching this year.

Claire presented Sutton with two options. One, he could announce his retirement and the Dodgers would present the news in that fashion. Two, the Dodgers would release him.

Sutton wanted to know if he'd still get paid the rest of his contract if he announced his retirement. Claire said no. That was bad business and would set a bad precedent. In August 1969, when Don Drysdale announced his retirement, he was not paid the rest of the season.

The only way Sutton would get paid is if he was released. Sutton asked for his release.

"I would have liked this year and this relationship to end on a more successful note," Sutton told reporters in a quickly arranged press conference at the team hotel. "I would have not wanted the injury, would have wanted more wins. I had one perfect scenario for the time somewhere near the end of my career. I would pitch seven perfect innings, then call out the manager and call in the infielders, hand them the ball and then get in my car and go home."

Decades later, Claire regretted how the situation was handled. With history on his side, Claire would have paid Sutton the rest of the season and allowed him to retire as a Dodger.

Claire always felt Sutton never forgave him for how the departure was handled. He had an idea for how to make it up to Sutton, but the idea would have to wait.

That night, the temperature was in the upper 90s in Cincinnati, which made the temperature on that artificial turf exceed 100 degrees. Orel Hershiser was on fumes at the mound, his uniform drenched in sweat. Each time he returned to the dugout, Hershiser lied to Lasorda about his actual condition.

Hershiser later said it was his "worst stuff" all season. But he had to find a way to win. These were the games he would lose in prior seasons. Now he was the Bulldog, the ace of the staff with Fernando Valenzuela on the DL, and he needed to win these games. He gutted his way through eight innings with an 8–2 lead. He allowed his third solo home run to start the ninth, and Jay Howell finished the victory for him.

The Dodgers remained in first place for another day. It was the eighth time that year the Dodgers snapped a three-game losing streak before it reached four. Hershiser was responsible for the last two of them.

In the Reds' clubhouse, Pete Rose wasn't impressed. "I personally don't think the Dodgers are going to win it," Rose said that night. "I said a couple of weeks ago that I want to catch the two teams in front of us, which are Houston and San Francisco."

Lasorda shook his head and laughed. "Pete's entitled to his opinion," Lasorda replied. "He's picked his two teams now. But Pete's picked horses that haven't won before, hasn't he?"

◆ ◆ ◆ ◆

August 13, 1988
Los Angeles
Giants vs. Dodgers
Team record: 64–50, 2½ games ahead of Astros

Ramon Martinez was not going to be traded. Ramon Martinez was going to make his major league debut at Dodger Stadium. It was the most anticipated major league debut for a Dodgers pitcher since Fernando Valenzuela. Don Sutton was released to make room for Martinez, the 20-year-old kid from the Dominican Republic whose teammates called him "Ramon the Bone" for his skinny frame.

Martinez was born in 1968, the year of the pitcher, when Don Drysdale set the scoreless inning record, Bob Gibson posted a 1.12 ERA, and Denny McLain won 31 games. Martinez was signed at age 17, blitzed his way through the minors in three seasons with a 93 mph fastball, deceptive change, and good enough breaking stuff.

After a winter of teams trying to pry him from Los Angeles, Martinez began 1988 at Double A San Antonio, going 8–4 with a 2.46 ERA in 14 starts. Promoted to Triple A Albuquerque, Martinez went 5–2 with a 2.76 ERA in 10 starts in a notorious hitters' league, including a shutout in his final minor league game.

The debut came against the Giants, on a Saturday night, in front of a sellout crowd at Dodger Stadium. Ramon the Bone arrived at 4:00 PM and met with catcher Mike Scioscia to go over the signs in Spanish.

"His stuff was so explosive at that point in his career," Scioscia reflected. "He had unbelievable velocity and late life to his fastball. He had a changeup that came up there and just stopped. He was very young. You could see this guy had a just pitcher's body, that whip in his arm."

Martinez's first inning went 1-2-3, three straight fly balls. He retired nine of the first 10 batters he faced, including Will Clark and Kevin Mitchell.

Martinez walked Bob Brenly to start the fifth, and Brenly advanced to third base with one out. Brett Butler sent a fly ball to Kirk Gibson in left field. In the season opener, Butler had boldly challenged the suspect arm of Gibson on a fly ball to shallow left. On this night, Brenly would also challenge Gibson's arm. Brenly was a catcher, however, not a speedy leadoff hitter. Gibson threw a one-hopper to the plate, Scioscia blocked the plate like only Scioscia could, and Brenly was out. The shutout was still alive.

Mike Krukow, making his first start in seven weeks due to shoulder inflammation, matched Martinez with zeros into the sixth inning.

Pedro Guerrero had come off the disabled list 15 days earlier, on July 29, and wasn't doing much (.220 with two home runs and 12 strikeouts in 50 at-bats). He'd been shifted back to first base, so Franklin Stubbs was back on the bench.

With two outs in the sixth, the slumping Guerrero ripped a double down the left-field line. Krukow remained in the game. His first pitch to Mike Marshall was lined into center for a base hit. Guerrero scored to make it 1–0. It was Marshall's team-leading 68th RBI.

Martinez was four outs from a shutout in his major league debut. It would be just like Fernando on Opening Day in 1981. He'd allowed three hits—all singles—and struck out five. With two outs in the eighth, Martinez walked Butler. Craig put on the hit-and-run, and Robby Thompson executed it perfectly with a single to left, putting runners at the corners.

That was it for Martinez. There would be no complete-game shutout. The bullpen would need to save the victory. Martinez was given a standing ovation by the crowd. It wasn't the birth of Ramon-mania, but the Dodgers knew this was the start of greatness.

Jesse Orosco got the call. This is why the Dodgers had traded for Orosco. Matchups like this. Close game. Orosco against Will Clark. The night before, Orosco had faced Will the Thrill and struck him out looking. Roger Craig was livid at the call, and the Humm Baby was ejected.

Orosco wasn't happy afterward, however, because he wanted to remain in the game to get the save. He didn't consider himself a middle reliever or a situational lefty. It was a four-run lead, and there were two outs in the ninth. Instead, Alejandro Pena was brought in, and he struck out Kevin Mitchell for the final out. Orosco thought he'd be better off with another team.

By the next day, Orosco had calmed down. But his agent made it clear that Orosco wasn't happy with his role as a middle reliever because he thought he should be getting saves.

In the Saturday game, Orosco was unhappy again. This time, Clark ripped a single into right field. Butler scored. Game tied. Ramon Martinez would not get the win in his major league debut. In fact, now he was in jeopardy of getting the loss.

Craig had double-switched an inning earlier, removing his cleanup hitter, so now the pitcher's spot was due up. Joel Youngblood hit for Garrelts. Lasorda went to Jay Howell, and he struck out Youngblood.

Martinez would not lose his major league debut. In fact, Martinez's debut would be overshadowed (and forgotten by so many) because of what happened in the extra innings.

It was still 1–1 in the 11th inning when Guerrero led off the inning with a fly ball to right. Candy Maldonado—in shades of the 1987 playoffs—lost the ball in the lights, and Guerrero was safe at first base. Joe Price was the Giants' pitcher. As Guerrero took his lead, he thought Price had balked and let the umpires know he thought Price had balked.

No balk was called. Balks weren't being called as often anymore. It appeared to be a moot point because Guerrero advanced to second on a passed ball anyway. But then things got weird—Pedro weird.

Guerrero was still talking to second-base umpire Joe West about the balk. Guerrero thought they were kidding, or so he said later. But next thing you know, Guerrero was pissed, West was pissed, Guerrero called the ump, "A big-headed motherfucker," and Guerrero was ejected by West.

Lasorda couldn't believe it. He raced out to argue. He spent half the time arguing with West, and the other half trying to restrain Guerrero from attacking West. In the process, Lasorda was ejected, too.

Once order was restored, Stubbs pinch ran for Guerrero. Marshall walked. John Shelby tried to lay down a sacrifice bunt. The ball rolled foul, but the Dodgers thought Joe Price touched the ball, which would make it fair. Mike Davis and Alfredo Griffin were on the top step of the dugout arguing that Price touched the ball.

Home-plate umpire Paul Runge told them to sit down. Griffin did. Davis didn't. Davis continued waving his arms, and Runge ejected him.

"I didn't argue with him at all," Davis told the *L.A. Times* the next day. "I did tell him that [Price] bumped [the ball]. Runge then stared me down. I waved my arms, like saying 'Okay, I'm not going to mess with you.' He then screamed at me, 'Sit down.' I said, 'What's wrong with you?' He then screamed, 'You want a piece of me?' It was the worst thing I've ever seen. [The umpires] don't have anyone checking up on them. It's ridiculous. They can do whatever they want."

Shelby ended up flying out to right field for the first out. Tracy Woodson flew out to center field for the second out. The runners tagged up, putting Stubbs at third and Marshall at second base.

Craig intentionally walked Griffin to load the bases because the pitcher's spot was due up and he knew the Dodgers were out of position players. Davis was the last position player when he got ejected.

With nobody else left, the Dodgers turned to pitcher Tim Leary. He was more than ready. Once Davis was ejected, Leary saw the inning unfold and knew he'd be used. He went back into the clubhouse, put on his cleats, and grabbed his bat. Leary was no slouch. He was batting .306 at the time. The night before, Leary singled, hit a sacrifice fly, and pitched into the ninth inning in a 7–3 victory that was his 12th win.

Leary worked the count full. He knew Price was going to throw him a fastball. There's no way a pitcher was going to throw another pitcher something other than a fastball with the bases loaded and a 3–2 count. Indeed, Price threw another fastball. Leary was ready, and he ripped a single up the middle for the game winner.

"I swear, it was the most beyond cloud nine I've ever been," Leary recalled. "Driving home, I was just shaking my head like, 'This is ridiculous.' You grow up a Dodger fan. I liked hitting more than pitching growing up, like most people. That was a peak moment in my career."

How sweet it is.

"What a fucking team."

◆ ◆ ◆ ◆

August 16, 1988

Los Angeles
Phillies vs. Dodgers
Team record: 66–51, 2½ games ahead of the Astros, 4½ ahead of the Giants, 6½ ahead of the Reds

No team had utilized a four-man rotation on a regular basis since the 1970s. But that's what the Dodgers were trying to do. They weren't happy with the results of the fifth starter. The experiments with Bill Krueger, Sean Hillegas, and William Brennan had not worked. So they decided to scrap the fifth starter entirely.

When the Dodgers released Don Sutton and promoted Ramon Martinez, they also shipped Hillegas to the bullpen to be a long reliever. Now, it was a four-man rotation with Hershiser, the 20-year-old Martinez, the rookie Tim Belcher, and Tim Leary.

Fernando Valenzuela hadn't picked up a baseball in three weeks. The optimism that he would pitch again this season was fading by the day. Mario Soto hit a plateau with his rehab work. It was becoming clear Soto's career was over.

The Dodgers were among the leaders in nearly every pitching category. Fred Claire knew it wasn't enough, though. He wanted another starter, another lefty. He needed another starter. He knew they couldn't use a four-man rotation the final six weeks, especially since two of them were rookies.

Blue Jays lefty Mike Flanagan was scouted, and Claire had discussions with the Detroit Tigers, too. Other teams wanted Ramon Martinez. Of course they wanted Ramon Martinez. But if Ramon Martinez was not going to be traded in the off-season, he really wasn't going to be traded in August after nearly pitching a shutout in his major league debut.

A Detroit newspaper reported the Tigers rejected a Pedro Guerrero for Frank Tanana trade. A week later in *Sports Illustrated*, Peter Gammons reported the Dodgers had worked out a deal for Tigers minor league lefty Steve Searcy.

Then the Cardinals called and offered John Tudor for Pedro Guerrero—straight up.

Forget about an aging Mike Flanagan or Frank Tanana or unproven minor leaguer Steve Searcy. The Cardinals were offering the pitcher who had won 49 of his last 64 decisions and had the lowest ERA in the National League. The Dodgers couldn't believe it.

"Even though he had his physical problems along the way, [Tudor] was a flat-out big-game pitcher," Claire said. "I just felt the time was right to make the trade. I thought it was the right trade for us. I can remember meeting with Pedro that night in Tommy's office. That was not easy. He was a very sad guy, with his long connection to the Dodgers. He wasn't angry as much as he was just sad. The Dodgers were his connection. I'm sure he was stunned."

Claire insisted the Guerrero-Gibson clubhouse showdown in St. Louis three weeks earlier wasn't the reason for the trade. It was strictly about improving the pitching staff.

When asked what role he had in Guerrero getting traded, Gibson said in the book *True Blue*, "I didn't make that decision. You have to ask Fred. I didn't hide anything. There wasn't anything secretive about it. My opinion was asked, and I gave it. And we did get John Tudor for him. Now that's not to say we wouldn't have won it with Pete. But whoever made that decision, they knew there was a little bit of conflict there."

Guerrero wasn't having a good year. He played in only 59-of-118 games to that point, due to injuries and his suspension. When he did play, he still batted .298, but the power and production were missing. He had five home runs, 35 RBIs, and a career-worst .409 slugging percentage.

Usually, Guerrero's hitting was always so good that it made up for his defense, temper, and well-chronicled nightlife and attitude. This year, he wasn't hitting. It was never one thing with Guerrero. It was the culmination of everything.

Guerrero blew out his knee on the final day of spring training in 1986, so he took it easy on the base paths. It was a smart decision. But now that Kirk Gibson was on the team, willing to take out any second baseman trying to turn a double play, Guerrero looked especially bad when he veered sharply to the right and out of the way of the second baseman.

"He's trying to take out the center fielder," was the joke.

Truth is, Guerrero probably would have been traded earlier, if he had been healthy. The chronic pinched nerve in his neck shelved him much longer than anticipated. He was supposed to undergo daily traction treatments. But he just stopped.

"He didn't do it very religiously," Dodger trainer Bill Buhler said at the time. "He just stopped coming in, and we stopped nagging him about it."

At the time, the reaction was positive among Dodgers players.

"I'm very surprised Fred could make this big a deal this late in the season," catcher Rick Dempsey gushed. "It's a miracle. It's fantastic. It gives everyone a lift. No one has to wonder anymore if we have enough [to win the division]. We know now we do. We know we'll have a 20-game winner out there every four or five days. Tudor has to come out here and do the job, but his credentials say he will. It takes a lot of the pressure off. It helps everyone relax."

The reaction 25 years later was mixed.

Mike Marshall: "I loved John Tudor. I thought that was going to be a huge bonus. He was just a brilliant magician on the mound. Competitor and everything like that. But to say that I was happy that Pedro was gone or that I understood why they would get rid of Pedro, I have no answer for that. I really don't. Pedro and I had our thing. Just like I need Gibby, I needed somebody behind me. Pedro needed me. So when I wasn't in the lineup, Pedro voiced his opinion that I should play through some injuries. I don't have a problem with Pedro. Great hitter. Good teammate. I liked Pedro. He was a great hitter. He won a lot of games for the Dodgers."

Tim Belcher: "I liked Pete. I really did. He was off-the-wall and a loose cannon at times. He wasn't a very good fielder, but he was still a great hitter. Even though I liked Pete, that was a trade that put us over the top. I think it was addition by subtraction. I think Pedro leaving the team really put Orel and Gibby at the forefront of being the leaders of the team. It was no longer this guy who had been with the team for all these years [as the leader]. You know what I mean? It solidified Gibby as the go-to offensive guy and leader on the club. Once Pete was gone, from an emotional and mental and team chemistry standpoint, it was addition by subtraction. It wasn't that Pete was being disruptive by any means. I think subconsciously, it elevated Gibby to another level."

John Shelby: "The trade was shocking. I never really understood the trade. I guess they wanted more pitching. But when you have a hitter like him.… He was a pure hitter. He could swing the bat."

Mike Scioscia: "John Tudor was a very highly regarded pitcher. Great competitor. Just a winner. As much as you're shocked that Pedro gets out of your clubhouse, to have John Tudor walk into your clubhouse was a great feeling. You never have enough pitching, especially the caliber of John. He was a terrific starting pitcher."

Alfredo Griffin: "It was a sad moment for me. It was really exciting when I came to the Dodgers. We always wanted to play together. In the winter, we talked about it. The same [Indians] scout [Reggie Otero] signed us both. We prepared ourselves to play together one day. He was a good hitter, and I was a good defensive player. Pedro wanted us to play together and have that excitement. When he got traded, it was a sad moment. He cried like a little baby. I know it was good for him, and it was good for us. I take it half-and-half."

Franklin Stubbs: "You know what, it was tough because that's a big bat to lose. Pedro was a great power hitter. He was the best two-strike hitter I ever played with. Just a tremendous hitter. A great teammate. I thought it was hard to give him up. But I also thought when you have a chance to get a John Tudor, who I thought was a No. 1 on every team except ours because we had Hershiser, [you do it]. But it was hard to see him leave."

Jaime Jarrin: "He was crying. Honestly, he was crying. Because he didn't know anything else except baseball. He was strictly a baseball player. He spent all his life with the Dodgers. He didn't know how he would be received in St. Louis. He was crying. He was very sad to leave the Dodgers."

Columnist Scott Ostler wrote the following about the trade in the *Los Angeles Times*:

> "I just got the news that the Dodgers have traded Pedro Guerrero to the St. Louis Cardinals for a pitcher. Or maybe it was a batboy, or a veteran Clydesdale. Early reports are sketchy. It doesn't matter. Whomever or whatever the Dodgers get, they have significantly improved a team that is already leading its division.

"If I'm a Giant or an Astro, right about now I've got to be cursing and slamming my morning newspaper to the floor.

"What a week in baseball, as Mel Allen might say. Within a nine-day span, lights go on at Wrigley Field and in the Dodgers' front-office cerebrums. Not that Guerrero was a cancer on the team. That's pretty harsh terminology. But at this stage of his career, let's just say Pedro was at least an inflamed appendix."

Division opponents were not happy.

"The Dodgers get a top-quality pitcher for a minus," Astros pitcher Bob Knepper said.

The Giants wanted Tudor, as well. They had offered infielder Tony Perezchica and pitcher Trevor Wilson. The Cardinals had asked for Matt Williams, and the Giants said, "No."

Nine months earlier, Fred Claire was being accused of not having enough experience, for holding up the winter meetings, for being scared to pull the trigger. Now he pulled the trigger on a mid-August blockbuster totally out of the blue.

Guerrero might have cried when Fred Claire told him the news. But his tears went away eventually—especially when the Cardinals immediately signed him to a three-year, $6.2 million contract.

Guerrero packed his belongings in front of a throng of media members. It was Family Night at Dodger Stadium. The contrasting images were stark. On the field, the players' kids wore uniforms and the dads took turns pitching to them in a family game. In the clubhouse, Guerrero went through a decade of memories stashed in his locker.

He'd been with the Dodgers since 1978, shared the MVP award won in the 1981 World Series title over the Yankees, and once hit 15 home runs in June 1985. Guerrero packed Dodgers jackets and jerseys. He grabbed videotapes of his at-bats. He grabbed salsa and samba cassette tapes. He packed bats and gloves and batting gloves. He found a hockey stick belonging to Montreal Canadians center Shayne Corson and a Bible. In total, all his belongings filled two duffel bags, three cardboard boxes, and a trunk.

A television reporter asked him what he was thinking about when he was packing.

"I was thinking that I have to get all my things out of the locker," he replied. Classic Pedro.

Guerrero grabbed a tiny flag of the Dominican Republic and literally waved goodbye.

◆ ◆ ◆ ◆

August 17, 1988
Los Angeles
Phillies vs. Dodgers
Team record: 67–51, 3½ games ahead of Astros

It was the third time John Tudor had been traded in six years. The first time, in December 1983, the Boston Red Sox sent him to the Pittsburgh Pirates for Mike Easler. The second time, in December 1984, Pittsburgh sent him to the St. Louis Cardinals with Brian Harper for George Hendrick.

Now he was traded in the middle of the season. Tudor was known as a fierce competitor, very stoic, and wasn't thrilled about the trade. He was tired of getting traded, period. He felt getting uprooted in the middle of the season was a pain in the ass. He was an East Coast guy and didn't know what to expect in Los Angeles.

Before leaving St. Louis, Tudor told reporters, "My heart is in St. Louis, but my arm will be in Los Angeles. I really didn't foresee it happening, although I guess this is the logical time for contending teams to do something like that. I don't relish the idea of going over there as the guy who's going to try to pick it up for them. I'm not going to be the one to do that. It's going to be a team effort. This is hard. In my mind, I'm still a Cardinal."

On the day of the trade, Tudor was supposed to start for the Cardinals against the Astros. He flew to Los Angeles the next day, was escorted to the ballpark by Dodgers scout Steve Boros, and arrived at Dodger Stadium about 2:00 PM. He met with Claire, met with Lasorda, declined pregame interview requests, took the mound at Dodger Stadium, and threw a 122-pitch complete-game victory.

Tudor was greeted by polite applause to start the game. By the end, the fans were on their feet, chanting his name as Keith Miller flied out to left field to end the game. Tudor allowed 11 singles and two walks but just two runs (one earned).

With Guerrero in St. Louis and Marshall in right field, Franklin Stubbs was once again the Dodgers' first baseman. Mike Davis still thought the Dodgers' best lineup was himself in right field and Marshall at first base. But there would be no change. Marshall was hitting. His back wasn't hurting. Marshall wasn't going back to first base.

Tudor's new teammates welcomed him to the team with three runs in the first inning, straight out of the Cardinals' playbook. Sax singled, stole second, went to third on a groundout, and scored when Gibson beat out a high chopper in front of the plate. Three batters later, Stubbs ripped a two-run double to the right-center gap for a 3–0 lead.

In the third, John Shelby had another one of those hits that was important but not so important that the media would crowd around him after the game. Shelby pulled a Mike Maddux fastball to right field for a two-run homer. It was 5–2. The final would be 7–2.

The word on the street in St. Louis was the Dodgers got the better of the deal, and that's not how it usually worked. The Cardinals were the masters of swindling other teams. They got Jack Clark from the Giants for nothing. They got Willie McGee from the Yankees for nothing. They swapped Garry Templeton for Ozzie Smith when it seemed like Templeton was the better player, and that worked out perfectly.

Were the Cardinals losing their touch? They let Jack Clark leave in free agency. They signed Bob Horner to take his place, and that was a disaster. Now they traded Tudor for Guerrero and signed Guerrero to a three-year contract for twice the money Clark was requesting.

"I don't care if we had five John Tudors, we were never going to be anything again until we were in position to generate some offense," Cardinals manager Whitey Herzog said. "I know that people in Los Angeles are now saying that Guerrero is a bad apple and a cripple, but they're always saying that in Los Angeles. All of their players are great while they're still there, but then they give them up and they're horseshit. I'll take my chances with Pete."

◆ ◆ ◆ ◆

August 20, 1988
Los Angeles
Expos vs. Dodgers
Team record: 70–51, 4½ games ahead of Astros

"I'm not as big an asshole as people think."

Those were the words Kirk Gibson told *L.A. Times* columnist Scott Ostler in the summer of 1988. Ostler, the ultimate wordsmith, penned a column expressing disappointment that Gibson hadn't erupted more often since spring training. The headline read, "Gibson Is Not So Hot, Which Is Not So Bad."

The start of Ostler's column:

"Let's be honest here. Kirk Gibson has been a major disappointment as a Dodger. After an encouraging start in spring training, when he did his volcano act after a teammate sabotaged his cap, Gibson really hasn't exploded, not once. He hasn't torn apart any clubhouses or dugouts or teammates.

"All the guy has done is strike fear in opponents' hearts with his aggressive hitting and base running. All he has done is become one of the National League's most effective hitters and the key guy—who else can you point to?—in the Dodgers' return to respectability."

Given the lens of history, the spring training eye black incident was the turning point in the season. It was when Gibson asserted his leadership, made his point about the time to be serious, and his teammates followed. But it could have just as easily led to disaster, more clubhouse problems, and infighting.

In the immediate days afterward, even Lasorda was worried. Lasorda preached working hard and would throw batting practice all morning and all night— whatever was necessary to help a player. Lasorda also loved practical jokes, and the stories of players turning the tables on Lasorda are legendary. It was the Dodger Way—work hard and laugh hard.

It wasn't just about Gibson fitting into the Dodgers' culture. It was all the newcomers. Lasorda said, "It was like adopting seven kids. How are they going to fit into your family?"

The sheer force of Gibson's size and personality made him a natural leader. But it was his play more than his mouth. Gibson routinely took out infielders trying to turn double plays. He ran over catchers. He dove for fly balls. He busted his ass down the first-base line on routine ground balls. He started rallies, and he was one of the biggest cheerleaders when teammates delivered hits.

"I was his locker mate that year," Stubbs said. "He didn't care about stats. He didn't care about his individual numbers. He only cared about winning. Anything else was irrelevant to him. His whole thing is if I go 0-for-4 and we win, that's the bottom line. That's the attitude we took. It doesn't matter who gets the job done. At the end of the game, make sure we have the W. As great an athlete and as gifted as he was, as a leader, his thing was, 'Figure out a way to get the job done, and let's win and forget about who gets the credit.'"

Earlier in August, Gibson went 4-for-5 with three doubles, a home run, four runs and three RBIs. But the Dodgers blew a lead and lost 9–8 in 10 innings. Gibson was in no mood to celebrate his big night. "Big deal," he said that night. "We lost, didn't we? People talk about the MVP. I want to be a world champion. That's the only title I want."

Gibson intimidated the opposition. Truth be told, he also scared the hell out of his own teammates. "When I would come out from the bullpen, Kirk would be standing in left field," reliever Brian Holton once said. "I was actually fearful. Gibson would have his arms folded, he'd say to me, 'You better get their asses out!' I had to, he would've killed me."

Sax's locker was right next to Gibson's all year. Sax was the guy Gibson requested to talk to before he signed with the Dodgers. It was one of the four conditions. Sax saw the fury of Gibson, the passion, the humor, and the ego. He also knew when to call Gibson on his bullshit.

"You know, Kirk Gibson is a tough guy," Sax said, upon reflection. "There's no question about it. I know this: he respected people who told him how they felt. I remember some days that he would say whatever, and I'd tell him, well...you know. I would tell him my opinion of him, but I told him to his face. That's why we were such good friends. He liked people who were really real. He didn't like it when people cowed down to him. He liked it when people gave it back. A lot of people wouldn't do it because they were afraid of him. I wasn't afraid of him, not a bit. I think that's why he liked me. We got along real well."

Overlooked because of the bravado was Gibson's baseball intelligence. Mike Marshall said, "It was a dream to play with a guy who was that in tune with the game of baseball. That was Gibby."

Gibson taught the Dodgers it was cool to care and gave them a shot of intensity. In return, the Dodgers actually taught Gibson to mellow out. Gibson learned the time to smile and the time to growl.

"After that [spring-training incident], I changed, too," Gibson told *Washington Post* columnist Thomas Boswell that summer. "I told 'em, 'Do whatever you got to do to get ready to play. Just don't do it to me.' I guess there are times to goof around. You don't need to sit in here losing weight worrying. Tommy likes to have fun. But it also kills him when we lose. He's been good at showing [me] how the two can go together. He and I have become closer daily. It would really be fun winning with him."

Gibson still threw his helmet after he made the final out of an inning. He still beat up bat racks after strikeouts. But that was just his release, and then he was over it.

"I'm trying to keep my cool more," Gibson told Ostler. "That just comes with experience. It can be a detriment if you do it too much."

In the summer of 1988, when Kirk Gibson's teammates taught him when to smile, and he showed his teammates that he would do whatever it took to win a game, the defining moment of his sheer aggression was on August 20.

The Expos were in Los Angeles. They led 3–0 with two outs in the seventh inning.

Gibson started the comeback. Gibson doubled to left, and Marshall followed with a double into the right-field corner to make it 3–1. In the eighth, Tracy Woodson hit a home run off Andy McGaffigan to make it 3–2.

In the ninth, lefty Joe Hesketh tried to close out the Expos victory. Sax grounded out to start the inning. Lasorda went to a right-hander, Mickey Hatcher, to pinch hit for the lefty Mike Scioscia. Hatcher delivered his 10th pinch hit in 29 assignments, a double to left-center.

Dave Anderson ran for Hatcher, and he scored the tying run when Gibson looped a single over the dive of shortstop Luis Rivera. Marshall fouled out for the second out, and that brought up John Shelby.

On a 1–1 count, Gibson stole second base—his 23rd theft of the season. Gibson barely bothered to dust himself off. He started to visualize a scenario as he took a lead off second base. He'd been thinking about the huge amount of foul territory between home plate and the backstop at Dodger Stadium for quite some time.

Gibson had also done his homework. Hesketh suffered a broken leg earlier in his career while covering home plate on a wild pitch, and Gibson thought he would be hesitant at a recurring play. If a ball skipped past the catcher, Gibson would try to score from second base. The other team would never expect it.

On the next pitch, nanoseconds after the thought entered Gibson's mind, Hesketh bounced a pitch in the dirt that got past catcher Nelson Santovenia and went all the way to the backstop. Gibson was off like a caged animal unleashed, and he never slowed down at third base.

"If Hesketh was going to try to stop me at the plate, he was going to pay for it," Gibson wrote in his 1997 biography. "As I steamed around third, I liked my chances in what 10 years earlier would have been a gallop for the end zone. I practically left an excavation at the point where I began my slide."

Hesketh was standing on the first-base side of home plate, wanting no part of another collision, and made a half-hearted attempt to catch the throw from the catcher Santovenia. It wasn't close. Gibson was safe. The Dodgers had won again.

Gibson leaped into the air after his slide and jumped up and down. He thrust his left fist toward the earth, leaped into the air again, and pumped his fist skyward. Teammates stormed out of the dugout to celebrate, stunned at what they'd just witnessed yet not surprised at the man who had done it.

The celebration was something you might expect in October. In retrospect, it was a dress rehearsal.

"I've gone from first to third a few times [on a wild pitch]," Gibson told reporters that night. "I knew it would be close, and I said, 'Here I come.' If I make it, we win; if I don't, we're in extra innings. We had tied the game, and I was in the mood to be aggressive. My adrenaline was pumping with every stride. I mean, once I got going, there was no way I was going to stop. I just pumped my arms, and my legs followed."

Gibson had never tried to score from second base on a wild pitch in his life.

He never tried it again.

When he looks back on his career now, Gibson enjoys that play just as much as any game winning homer he ever hit.

"Oh yeah, absolutely," Gibson said. "I will always remember that play and my reaction. Good stuff. When the moment is right, you have to be ready for it."

How sweet it is.

"What a fucking team."

◆ ◆ ◆ ◆

August 30, 1988

Montreal

Dodgers vs. Expos

Team record: 76–54, 6½ games over the Astros

It was the day before teams needed to submit a playoff roster to the league office. This was before teams found loopholes to put pitchers who came up from the minors in mid-September on the playoff roster.

General manager Fred Claire wanted to make one more addition. Since the departure of Brad Havens, the only left-hander in the bullpen was Jesse Orosco, so the now quick-trigger Claire acquired Ricky Horton from the Chicago White Sox. A few days later, Hillegas was announced as the player to be named later.

"Through my years with the Dodgers, believe me, I knew every left-handed pitcher who ever pitched," Claire reflected. "I run into guys today that I know that I almost signed. There had to be hundreds of these guys. Ricky had a different type of delivery. I thought he was a guy who could help us. By adding him to the postseason roster, I had to remove Tim Crews. That wasn't easy. But those are the decisions you make."

◆ ◆ ◆ ◆

Orel Hershiser was in a slump. Not that he wanted to admit it.

In his first three starts in August, Hershiser allowed 17 runs (14 earned) in 15 innings. The worst was an eight-run drubbing by the Giants, in just two innings, which happened to be his first start with the four-man rotation.

It was so bad that game, the scoreboard at Dodger Stadium malfunctioned and briefly showed the Giants leading 95–4. The score was really 15–4, and that was humiliating enough.

Hershiser's ERA was 3.06, the first time all year it was over 3.00, and he'd already allowed more home runs (18) in 185 innings than he did the previous year (17) in 264⅔ innings.

"No, it's not a slump," Hershiser insisted. "I analyze baseball on a day-to-day, pitch-to-pitch basis. I'm throwing the ball well. I haven't thrown it poorly. Stats can't show everything. If I thought I had a slump, it would be when I'm not executing on my pitches and have mechanical problems."

Actually, it was a mechanical problem, and fate would intervene.

Dave Wallace, the Dodgers' minor league pitching supervisor, happened to be in Los Angeles to watch Ramon Martinez's debut. Wallace knew Hershiser's delivery better than anybody after working with him so closely in the minors. Wallace noticed that Hershiser was opening up his delivery too soon with his front foot, landing his front foot 6–8" too far toward first base.

It wasn't dramatic. But it was noticeable to Wallace, and he was in town to tell Hershiser himself. Hershiser trusted Wallace immensely and worked on correcting that flaw as he played catch the next few days and during his between-starts bullpen session.

The adjustment worked immediately. Hershiser's sinker began diving more dramatically. His curveball became sharper.

The first game after Wallace's discovery, Hershiser shut out the Expos 2–0 on August 19. He took another shutout into the eighth inning against the Mets on August 24 but allowed two runs and lost 2–1. The Mets had the Dodgers' number. That's just how it was.

On August 25, the Dodgers flew to Philadelphia. A handful of players drove to Atlantic City and hit the tables. Rick Dempsey played a variety of games, bet conservatively, and raised his bets as he got comfortable.

Hershiser pulled out $5,000 to gamble that night. On the first hand, Hershiser put the entire amount on a single hand of baccarat. Naturally, he won.

"And the thing about it is, win or lose, you can't tell what he's going to do or how he feels about it," Dempsey said in 1988. "That's exactly the way he pitches. He's not afraid of anything. He's a gambler. He'll go for broke on one pitch. Nothing fazes the guy. He's got nerves of steel.

"You wouldn't think of it to look at him, would you? He's kind of a bookworm-looking character. But, let me tell you, Orel Hershiser is one of the toughest characters I have ever come across. He's got the greatest attitude in the world—win, lose, or draw. Ten minutes before a game and 10 minutes after, he's in exactly the same mood."

Back in Philly, Hershiser didn't pitch in the series, and the Dodgers still swept the Phillies in three games.

♦ ♦ ♦ ♦

On August 30, Hershiser wouldn't need any relief help in Montreal. He doubled home two runs himself in the second inning and took a 4–0 lead into the fifth inning. Tim Raines broke up the shutout bid with an RBI double, and Dave Martinez singled him home to trim the lead to 4–2.

After that, Hershiser was back into a groove. He pitched a scoreless sixth, seventh, eighth, and ninth inning to record the complete-game victory. He retired 12 of the final 15 batters, the Expos managing a single and two walks. It was Hershiser's 18th victory.

Nobody knew it, but Orel Hershiser's scoreless streak was at four innings.

Chapter 12

The Fifth Shutout

Friday, September 23, 1988

San Francisco

Dodgers vs. Giants

Team record: 89–63, first place by eight games over the Reds

DODGERS	GIANTS
SS Alfredo Griffin	CF Brett Butler
2B Steve Sax	3B Ernest Riles
LF Mickey Hatcher	1B Will Clark
RF Mike Marshall	LF Kevin Mitchell
CF John Shelby	RF Mike Aldrete
3B Jeff Hamilton	2B Robby Thompson
C Rick Dempsey	C Kirt Manwaring
1B Tracy Woodson	SS Jose Uribe
P Orel Hershiser	P Atlee Hammaker

The San Francisco Giants went into the 1988 season believing they were the team to beat. With nine games left in the season, they were 10½ games back.

They'd been mathematically eliminated. Their storied rivals, the Dodgers, were days from clinching the division title.

Only one thing could salvage an otherwise highly disappointing season for the Giants: ending Orel Hershiser's scoreless streak.

"There's no doubt, are you kidding me?" Giants center fielder Brett Butler recalled. "I don't care what streak it is. We wanted to spoil that, any way, shape, or form. We knew there was a streak on the line."

A crowd of 22,341 was announced at Candlestick Park, which meant the actual turnout was less than 20,000 in a stadium that seated just over 59,000. The only reason to show up that night was to watch Hershiser's streak end.

"The rivalry, you have to know, it's intense," reflected Giants pitcher Mike Krukow, now a broadcaster for the team. "Because you know how much it means to your fan base. It's not a normal game. Because of that, the rivalry solves a lot of problems. If you're in the middle of a funk and going horseshit and you've won two of your last 12 games, you get into your rivalry series, and all of a sudden, you're not thinking about the slump. It takes your focus completely away from whatever you're doing. During the course of a season, guys can wonder. They might have problems at home or somebody is sick or ailing or they've got financial problems.

"When you go into your rivalry series, it all goes like this," Krukow continued, using his arms and hands to indicate tunnel vision. "That's the benefit of being part of an organization that has a rival. You don't want to lose. You know it hurts your fans more than any other game. So things do get said, because your intensity level goes up, it does get louder. When you're yelling, 'Fuck you!' across the diamond, you mean it. It's not just for a drill."

A few days earlier, prompted by the media seeking clarification, the league office changed Don Drysdale's record from 58⅔ innings to 58. The ruling was that parts of innings by a starting pitcher would not count. The league office also clarified that playoff innings would not count toward the streak. It would carry over the following season with an asterisk.

On September 24 in Seoul, Ben Johnson broke his own world record by running a 9.79-second time in the 100-meter final, beating the great Carl Lewis and two others who all finished in less than 10 seconds. Just before first pitch in San Francisco, Jose Canseco stole his second base of the night in Milwaukee, giving him 40 on the year and becoming the charter member of the 40-homer, 40-steal club.

Manager Tom Lasorda and pitching coach Ron Perranoski were aligning their starting rotation for the playoffs and wanted Hershiser to start Game 1. To do so, Hershiser started on three days rest again. They'd rather have Hershiser pitch on short rest the second-to-last week of the regular season than the final week.

Giants manager Roger Craig stacked his lineup with four lefties in the first five positions against Hershiser, including the first three. When Hershiser's sinker is sinking, however, it doesn't matter. And in the first inning, it was clear Hershiser's sinker was on. Brett Butler grounded out to third. Ernest Riles grounded out to second. Will Clark grounded out to Hershiser. The streak was 41 scoreless innings.

Kevin Mitchell started the second inning with a single to center. Mike Aldrete grounded to short, and Mitchell was forced at second. Robby Thompson grounded to second, and Steve Sax's play was at first base. With a runner in scoring position, Kirt Manwaring flew out to center. The streak was 42.

"As a defensive player, [the streak] put pressure on everybody behind him," recalled Mickey Hatcher. "You don't want to be the one who screws it up. You feel it as a player. I'm telling you, every ground ball hit to an infielder, every fly ball hit to an outfielder, you're wearing three glasses. You're doing everything you can not to screw up. Nobody talked when he walked off the field.

"If somebody is going to score, I'm going to throw as hard as I can. I don't care if I throw it over the backstop I'm going to try and stop that run from scoring. You think about all kinds of stuff like that before it happens. It's tough for a defense. It wasn't just tough for Orel. It was tough for everybody."

In the third inning, Jose Uribe singled up the middle, and it was back to the stretch for Hershiser. The pitcher, Atlee Hammaker, laid down a bunt, and Hershiser slipped trying to field the ball. Everybody was safe. Two on, none out. It was just the second time in the streak Hershiser had faced a situation like this.

Back to the top of the lineup, Butler pushed a slow grounder to third. Hamilton tried for a double play. He forced Hammaker at second base, but Butler was too fast and beat the throw. Runners at the corners. A runner was at third base for just the fourth time in the streak.

♦ ♦ ♦ ♦

Twenty years earlier, another scoreless streak was in the balance when the Giants and Dodgers played a game. This one was in Los Angeles. Don Drysdale was one inning from a fifth straight shutout, putting his steak at 44 innings. Among the impressionable kids in the stands during the streak was 9-year-old Tim Leary.

On May 31, 1968, the Dodgers led the Giants 3–0. Drysdale walked the dangerous Willie McCovey to open the ninth inning. Jim Ray Hart singled to right, and pinch runner Nate Oliver stopped at second base. Dave Marshall walked to load the bases. Still nobody out.

On a 2–2 pitch, Drysdale hit Dick Dietz with a pitch. The shutout was over. Or was it? Home plate umpire Harry Wendelstedt ruled that Dietz made no effort to avoid the pitch. Giants manager Henry Franks was livid. He argued and argued, got ejected, and argued more. The decision stood.

"I was on the air and I couldn't believe it," Dodgers announcer Vin Scully remembered. "As soon as Dick was hit, I thought, *There it goes.* And then Harry Wendelstedt said he did not make an effort to get out of the way of the pitch. I didn't really even think that counted. I thought guys could take one for the club. Harry interpreted it that way."

Given a new life, Drysdale went back to work. Dietz flew out to left field but not deep enough for Oliver to score. Pinch hitter Ty Cline grounded to first, and Wes Parker came home for the force out. Pinch hitter Jack Hiatt popped out to first to end the game. Drysdale's streak continued. He was at 45 innings.

On June 4, Drysdale blanked the Pirates at Dodger Stadium, and his streak was at 54 scoreless innings—two shy of Walter Johnson's record. Across town, Robert F. Kennedy was at the Ambassador Hotel making a victory speech after winning the California and South Dakota primaries. Kennedy congratulated Drysdale during his remarks. Kennedy was assassinated minutes later by Sirhan Sirhan.

On June 8, Kennedy was buried in the morning, and Drysdale pitched with a heavy heart about the loss of his friend. Drysdale pitched four scoreless innings to start the game, reaching 58 innings and establishing a new record.

After that inning, Phillies manager Gene Mauch approached umpire Augie Donatelli that Drysdale was using a foreign substance. Donatelli instructed Drysdale not to touch the back of his head for the rest of the game. The next inning, after the warning, the streak ended when Phillies pinch-hitter Howie Bedell hit a sacrifice fly to score Tony Taylor.

"I wanted the record so bad," Drysdale said that day, "but I'm relieved that it's over. I could feel myself go 'Blah' when the run scored. I just let down completely. I'm sure it was the mental strain."

◆ ◆ ◆ ◆

Harry Wendelstedt, meet Bob Engel.

Hershiser knew he was in trouble. Uribe was at third. Butler was at first. He needed a double play—needed one bad. Ernest Riles was at the plate. Will Clark was on deck, and Hershiser didn't want to face Will the Thrill with runners on base. Clark was one of the most dangerous hitters in the league. He had finished fifth in MVP voting the year before, and would finish fifth again in 1988 with 29 home runs and 109 RBIs.

If the streak was going to end, it was going to end with a sinker—a hard sinker. Hershiser pumped in two sinkers, and the count was 1–1. Next was a third straight sinker.

Riles hit a bouncer to second base. Hershiser held his breath. Steve Sax fielded it and flipped to Griffin for one out. Hershiser kept holding his breath. Butler dug hard for second and slid harder. Griffin's throw to first sailed way wide left of first baseman Tracy Woodson. Riles was safe. Uribe scored.

"I thought it was over," Woodson said.

"My heart sunk for Orel," Sax said.

"It was frustrating," Griffin said. "As soon as I threw the ball, I exploded, because I knew the streak was gone and it was my error."

Hershiser grimaced. He was still 16 innings short of Drysdale's record, but it felt so close. Hershiser let out a huge breath. It was a letdown, no question, but it was back to work. The Giants led 1–0. There was a game to win, a couple more games to clinch the division and celebrate, and the bigger goal was the World Series.

Hershiser was rubbing up a new baseball and turning back to the mound when he saw Bob Engel, the second-base umpire, signal that Butler and Riles were both out.

"It was a big relief," Griffin said. "It was a great call by the umpire. I knew this guy was too far [out of the baseline]. We talked about it, and the umpire knew right away. I went way wide [outside of second base]. I cheated, so I can clear him. He couldn't reach the base the way he was. If it was a regular game, I'd hit him in the face. I know he was coming into my body. I'd drop down and aim for his face. But I couldn't do that. I had to make the throw."

The Dodgers sprinted off the field before Engel could change his mind. Engel ruled that Butler slid too far away from second base to break up the double play and called him out for interference. Giants manager Roger Craig bolted from the dugout to argue, joining Butler for an argument that lasted more than five minutes.

Upon reflection, Butler said, "My immediate reaction to the umpires was, 'That's just wrong. If he's going to get a record, let him get it the right way. Don't do it on a bogus call like this. You and I both know this was a bogus call.' Again, it was unbelievable. Like, really? Really? Really? The umpire's discretion? Really? Okay. Whatever. Everybody knew. I should say, everybody on our side knew. On the other side, they probably thought the opposite."

The details of that fateful play were still vivid in Butler's mind, 25 years later.

"Let's clarify," Butler said. "It was a slow grounder to second. It was not a two-hopper. It was not a hard-hit shot. It was a slow, got jammed, hit off the end of the bat. Obviously, I'm three-quarters of the way to second base. They flipped it to second base.

"In all my 17 years in the majors, every time I've ever slid into second base or taken out a fielder, there's only one time that I was ever called out for not being able to touch the base, and it was right then. In all 17 years of my career. There was no way they could turn the double play. None."

The run was reluctantly taken off the Candlestick scoreboard. The streak was at 43 innings.

"Drysdale got his break. Now you got yours!" Lasorda said to Hershiser in the dugout, laughing at the absurdity of history repeating itself twice.

"Dietz revisited!" Hershiser said.

"When you're hot, you're hot!" Lasorda said.

Hershiser was hot, and the second life by the umpire made him hotter. To start the fourth, Clark lined out to left on the first pitch. Candy Maldonado replaced Mitchell and grounded to third. Aldrete grounded to first. A nine-pitch inning. The streak was at 44.

It was still scoreless in the fifth. Thompson dueled Hershiser for nine pitches before flying out to center. Manwaring also flew out to center. Uribe grounded to Sax at second base. The streak was 45.

"When they changed it back, it was a big boost," Sax said. "And it was the right call."

Hershiser was in one of those grooves. Hammaker bounced back to Hershiser to open the sixth. Butler hit the ball hard, but it was a liner to first. Riles struck out swinging, Hershiser's first whiff of the night. The streak was 46.

"I don't think [the umpire's call] took the wind out of our sails," Butler said. "It fired us up more. It probably fired us up too much. We tried even harder to get it done. It's a credit to Orel that he did what he did."

The game was scoreless in the seventh. Of course it was still scoreless. In the last 24 innings of The Streak, at that point, the Dodgers had scored two runs.

Hershiser had retired 11 in a row when Clark dug into the batter's box. Hershiser pitched carefully to Clark. He was worried about the wind blowing out to right field. He wouldn't give "The Thrill" anything to pull for a home run. He pitched him away and didn't mind the slightest when Clark singled to center.

Maldonado, who had seen his home runs drop from 20 the year before to 12, laid down a sacrifice bunt to move Clark to second base. Aldrete was intentionally walked, setting up the double play. Two on, one out, once again.

Craig, the Giants manager who loved to squeeze and play hunches, replaced Thompson with pinch-hitter Francisco Melendez. It was an odd move. Melendez was a career minor leaguer with 68 at-bats in the majors (this at-bat was his 69th), spread over four seasons. Melendez made the move look foolish.

Another hard sinker. Another grounder. This was a comebacker. Hershiser to Griffin to Woodson. The streak was at 47.

Kirk Gibson, mired in a 2-for-26 slump and getting treatment for chronic hamstring soreness, was not in the starting lineup. Utility man Mickey Hatcher started in left field instead. Hammaker came back out in the eighth inning. Woodson singled and Griffin singled, then Hatcher hit a three-run home run for a 3–0 lead. Foreshadow much?

Hatcher said he doesn't remember too many of his big hits, but he remembered that one. "A ball that was down and in, I pulled it down the line," he recalled. "Of course, I hardly ever watched any of my home runs because they always hit the top of the fence. I was always running hard. It was another one that I was surprised that went out."

Given the lead, Hershiser wouldn't be denied. It didn't matter that pinch-hitter Phil Garner reached on an infield single. Everybody knew Hershiser would pitch out of trouble again.

Uribe grounded to second, and Garner was forced out. Joel Youngblood batted in the pitcher's spot and grounded out to Hershiser, but Uribe moved to second. Butler grounded to third to end the eighth inning. The streak was at 48.

The Giants had one more chance, and so did Clark, in the ninth inning. Riles lined out to right. Hershiser pitched around Clark, walking him on five pitches.

Maldonado struck out swinging. Aldrete flew out to center on Hershiser's 112th and final pitch of a wacky Friday night in San Francisco.

All that remained were the postgame complaints from the Giants.

"It was a bad call," Krukow said, 25 years later. "It should have never happened. It was a call that I didn't think should be made. It was a ticky-tack call. He should never have been able to break Drysdale's record. You should know that I am biased. Drysdale was my guy. But you know what? Orel was everything that was good about pitching. In fact, we called him the Needle-Nosed Boy Scout because he was a little too good.

"But you know I definitely applauded the effort. Anybody that saw how dominant he was, the guy was amazing that year. Alfredo hit under .200 that year and he was unbelievable. Hershiser moved him over a little into the 5.5 hole, and that fucker got everything. He picked it clean. Those two guys were a great combo."

Paul Runge, the crew chief working third base that night, spoke to reporters after the game. He was asked about how far away from the base a runner must slide to get called for interference.

"It's not measured by feet or anything like that," Runge said. "You must make an attempt to slide to the bag. If the shortstop or second baseman is at the bag, you can hit him there, but you can't hit him when he leaves the bag area—once he's off to the right, two to three feet."

After the game, with his shirt off and his arm wrapped in ice, Hershiser said, "the Governor visited me in the third inning. I got called off the electric chair. It was unbelievable. It did not take me long to get off the field when I saw the call. I usually walk off the mound, just have a nice pace to myself. Some people call it a strut. I ran off that mound and was greeted by a bunch of guys who were just laughing at me. They couldn't believe it. Nobody can go that good."

Pitching	IP	H	R	ER	BB	SO	HR	ERA	BF	Pit	Str	Ctct	StS	StL	GB	FB	LD
Orel Hershiser, W (23–8)	9	5	0	0	2	2	0	2.35	32	112	73	45	8	20	20	8	4

The streak was at 49 innings. Hershiser knew that tying the record was more attainable than ever. Still, a sixth straight shutout?

"I'd have to pitch 10 innings in my last start anyway," Hershiser told reporters. "To say the record is breakable is crazy."

Even with the statistical change from 58⅔ to 58 innings, Hershiser felt everyone would know he'd fallen just short. He knew the record could be extended in 1989, but having six months of rest took away the spirit of a record. Plus, there would be an asterisk.

"I just want to put up as many zeroes as I can," Hershiser said. "Our magic number is two, and my streak seems to coincide with what the team has done."

Drysdale watched it all from the Dodgers' TV booth and described every moment—all of which added to a surreal and historical month. "Orel's pitching well, and he's in a great frame of mind," Drysdale said that night. "He's such a great kid that I'm having fun watching him. I'm happy for him, and I'm glad I'm around to see him do this."

In the next issue of *Sports Illustrated*, a letter to the editor listed the following connections between Hershiser and Drysdale's scoreless streaks:

- Both almost ended against the Giants.
- Both stayed alive on controversial umpire calls.
- Brett Butler was the interference. His initials are the same. Dick Dietz was hit by a pitch in 1968. His initials are the same.
- Both games were played on a Friday night.
- The Dodgers won both games by a 3–0 score.
- The shutouts were the fifth in each pitcher's streak.
- In each game, the Giants started a lefty. Mike McCormick in 1968. Atlee Hammaker in 1988.
- Butler wore uniform No. 2 and so did Dietz.

◆ ◆ ◆ ◆

Then there was the race within the race. David Cone had won his sixth straight game three days earlier 6–4 over the Phillies and had two starts left to reach 20 wins. Danny Jackson would start the next day on normal four days rest. Here are the updated stats for the top Cy Young Award candidates:

Player	W-L	ERA	IP	H (BABIP)	BB	SO	Opp. Slash line
Danny Jackson, CIN	22–7	2.63	246.0	192 (.248)	66	154	.216/.270/.306
Orel Hershiser, LAD	23–8	2.35	257.0	204 (.247)	72	175	.217/.274/.317
David Cone, NYM	18–3	2.17	215.2	162 (.267)	76	195	.210/.282/.286

The great Jim Murray wrote in the *Los Angeles Times*, "Five shutouts in a season is Cy Young stuff. Five shutouts in a row is Hall of Fame stuff."

Chapter 13

September

Saturday, September 3, 1988

New York

Dodgers vs. Mets

Team record: 77–56, 6½-game lead on the Astros

It was the NBC *Game of the Week*, so Vin Scully was broadcasting the game for a national audience, not just the Los Angeles audience. He opened the broadcast this way:

"Welcome to what most people are saying is a fall preview of the League Championship Series between the Dodgers and the Mets. If that's so, the Dodgers are certainly doing a great job of making the Mets overconfident. And why has New York been able to dominate during the regular season? Well, sometimes the obvious answer is also the best one. The Mets are simply the better team."

The Mets had won the opener of the series 8–0 the night before. Tim Leary gave up four home runs, and none of them were by the Mets' heavy hitters.

For Kirk Gibson, it wasn't just that the Mets were a pain in the Dodgers' ass. He literally had a pain in his ass. Gibson singled with two outs in the first inning and stole second base off Dwight Gooden. While on the bases, Gibson felt something in the back of his leg. It was a burning sensation. He feared it was a hamstring injury, which had bothered him in the past and had resurfaced earlier that year.

Gibson took his position in left field. The leg started to knot up, so he stood on one leg. After the inning, he came out. The official diagnosis was a strained right gluteus maximus.

"I didn't want it to be a situation where I'm out six weeks, four weeks, or even two weeks," Gibson said that day. "I think I got it early enough. I don't think it's severe. As much as we want to win now, it's not do-or-die. I don't want to be in a position where I'm out for a long time."

The Mets scored two runs in the second inning, when Gibson was standing on one leg. That's all they would need. Dwight Gooden went eight innings, allowed just one run, and picked up his 16th victory when Randy Myers struck out Rick Dempsey with the tying run at second base.

The Dodgers had no answer for the Mets. They were blown out one night. They lost by one run the next day. The Mets were now 10–1 against the Dodgers.

"It's amazing," manager Tommy Lasorda said that day. "They play their best against us, and we play our worst against them. Why, I don't know."

♦ ♦ ♦ ♦

September 7, 1988
Los Angeles
Astros vs. Dodgers
Team record: 78–58, five-game lead over the Astros

Alfredo Griffin was accustomed to grooming people to take his job. He was the Rookie of the Year in 1979 for the Toronto Blue Jays. He led the league in triples (15) in 1980, and he played all 162 games in 1982 and 1983. He didn't hit much and walked even less, but man, could he play defense.

The Blue Jays had an up-and-coming shortstop who could also play defense, and this one could hit, too. So once Tony Fernandez was ready for the majors, the Blue Jays traded Griffin and outfielder Dave Collins to the Oakland A's for relief pitcher Bill Caudill, who'd just saved 36 of the 77 A's victories.

Griffin came to the A's a career .249 hitter but hit .270 in 1985, played in every game, and won a Gold Glove. He played in every game again in 1986, raised his

164

average to .285, stole 33 bases, and became one of the most popular players in Oakland.

In 1987, Griffin's average dropped down to .263, and his salary rose to just over $600,000. Another young shortstop was ready, this one named Walt Weiss, so the A's were willing to include Griffin in that three-team trade that sent Griffin to Los Angeles and Bob Welch to Oakland.

Offensively, Griffin was a disappointment in his debut season with the Dodgers. He finished the year with a .199 batting average—59 points below his career norm. He was out from May 22 to July 25 with a broken right hand, courtesy of a Dwight Gooden fastball.

But even in the 95 games Griffin did play, shortstop-turned-infield coach Bill Russell called him, "The missing link."

The ghosts of The Infield affected all four positions. The drought at shortstop wasn't as long, because Russell was the last of The Infield to keep playing every day, but it had become the hardest position to fill. Russell was the regular up until 1983 and kept playing through 1986.

Mariano Duncan was a minor league second baseman who was rushed to the majors prematurely and tried to learn shortstop at the highest level, and big error totals followed—27 in 1985, 25 more in 1986, and 21 in just 67 games in 1987. Dave Anderson didn't make a lot of errors, but he didn't have great range and didn't hit enough to justify playing every day.

The Dodgers needed a shortstop who could change the game defensively. That's why they wanted Griffin. If nothing else, his presence just provided an attitude change for the pitching staff. If they made a good pitch, they didn't have to worry about the shortstop booting a grounder.

This is what Bill Russell told the *L.A. Times* about Griffin late in the season:

"There's nothing flashy to him, but he's given us the consistency and dependability we hadn't had. There's an awareness to him out there that everyone else draws from. He makes everyone more sure of himself, including the pitcher. It's a plus for the pitcher when he can walk out there confident of the defense behind him. I mean, Griffin just never makes a mistake. The pitcher sees that and the infielders see that, and everyone goes about their job more calmly."

Advanced defensive metrics didn't exist in 1988. There was no Ultimate Zone Rating or Plus-Minus to put a value on defense. Back then, a player was judged by his errors and what the baseball men saw with their eyes.

"It was like watching Baryshnikov out there," Leary would gush, three decades later.

Besides his defense, Griffin was the positive influence that Pedro Guerrero wasn't. The Dodgers wanted a positive role model for Ramon Martinez and three up-and-coming shortstops in the organization. All were age 20. All were fellow Dominicans. They would learn from Griffin, and one of them would take Griffin's job. They were Juan Bell, Jose Offerman, and Jose Vizcaino.

For now, the future could wait. There was still a division to win, and Griffin was finally starting to hit like he had in Oakland. He probably came back too soon from the broken hand. Now it was September, the hand was fully healed, and Griffin was in the middle of a seven-game hitting streak that would reach 12 games.

Facing Mike Scott to start the fourth inning on September 7, Griffin hit a double into the right-field corner. Gibson struck out. Mickey Hatcher hit a grounder to short, and Griffin was caught in no-man's land. Shortstop Rafael Ramirez misplayed the rundown, however, and the speedy Griffin made it safely to third. John Shelby hit a sacrifice fly to score Griffin, and the game was tied 1–1.

Tim Leary had been in the Cy Young Award discussion during the summer, but he hit a roadblock in September. On this night, Leary was pitching like he did in April and May when he had three shutouts. Leary dueled the great Mike Scott evenly. It was still 1–1 in the eighth inning.

Steve Sax snapped a 1-for-26 slump with a single to center. Griffin did his job, laying down a sacrifice bunt to move Sax to second base. Of course, that made it easy for Astros manager Hal Lanier to intentionally walk Kirk Gibson.

Mike Marshall had received an injection for a pulled muscle in his right leg, so he wasn't batting cleanup. Hatcher was, and he struck out, but not before Sax and Gibson executed a double steal.

Now it was up to John Shelby, the guy who had so many big hits that were mostly forgotten. On deck was Mike Davis, who had never found his swing all year, but Lanier wasn't walking another batter. He let Scott go right after Shelby. The first pitch was a ball. The second pitch was hit into the right-field pavilion for a three-run homer.

Back in July, Shelby did the unusual, lightly pumping his fist into his other hand after getting a big hit.

Now he did something incredibly unusual, pumping his fist as he rounded first base.

"It was just one of those things that came out," Shelby recalled. "That's probably the only hit I ever got off Mike Scott. It felt like every time I faced the guy, I struck out. I hit that home run down the right-field line. It was always tough facing him. I guess it gave me a big jilt to know that I can make contact. It was a big hit for us."

At home plate, Sax couldn't wait for Shelby to circle the bases. Sax lived for these moments. Sax never needed a reason to pump a fist or get excited. Now he had a big reason. He picked Shelby off the ground, he was so pumped up. Shelby was just glad that Sax didn't drop him.

Jay Howell got the final three outs in the ninth inning. The lead was six games over the Astros, 7½ over the Reds. The obituary had already been written on the Giants. The magic number was 19.

Champagne would be popped soon—just not by who you think.

◆ ◆ ◆ ◆

September 11, 1988
Los Angeles
Dodgers vs. Reds
Team record: 80–60, five games ahead of the Astros

Jeff Hamilton would have happily accepted a trade in spring training after Pedro Guerrero was moved to third base and he was out of a starting job. He wasn't going to demand a trade. But again, he'd have been in favor of a trade when he started once in the first 39 games of the 1988 season.

Sure, he was happy in the majors. He defied odds by simply reaching the majors. He was a 29th-round draft pick in 1982 out of Carman High in Flint, Michigan, and 29th-round draft picks don't make the majors very often. Los Angeles was better than Albuquerque, major league money was way better, and he spent parts of the last two years at Albuquerque.

Sure, he was happy to be on a winning team. But he was only 24 years old. Jeff Hamilton wanted to play.

Then Guerrero was suspended for throwing the bat at David Cone, and Hamilton had five hits in three games, including a two-run homer. See, he could hit major league pitching. Then Guerrero missed large periods of times with injuries. Then Guerrero returned and was moved to first base. Then Guerrero was traded.

Hamilton, at long last, was given the opportunity to prove he could hit in the majors, that his minor league numbers were not the result of the high altitude at Triple A Albuquerque. These were the results:

May 24, 1988 to Jul 26, 1988

Tm	G	GS	Rslt	PA	AB	R	H	2B	3B	HR	RBI	BB	IBB	SO	HBP	SH	SF	GDP	SB	CS	BA	OBP	SLG
LAD	57	52	37–19	212	201	26	52	11	2	4	24	7	1	31	2	11	4	5	0	0	.259	.289	.393

It wasn't bad. It just wasn't great. Not great enough to silence the critics during his two-month audition. It wasn't a three-month audition because Hamilton was sidelined with a sore rib cage for 35 games. That injury opened the window for Tracy Woodson to get called up from the minors, and now Woodson would try to prove his minor league numbers (17 home runs in 313 at-bats and a .556 slugging percentage) weren't inflated by the Albuquerque altitude.

When rosters expanded September 1, Hamilton was activated from the disabled list. He started his seventh consecutive game on September 11 against the Reds at Dodger Stadium.

If ever a game existed that showed the uncanny contributions from so many players in 1988, this was it. Starting pitcher Tim Belcher hit a home run in the third inning. Gibson cranked his 25th home run in the fourth inning for a 2–0 lead.

The Reds tied it in the sixth and took a 3–2 lead in the seventh inning. John Franco entered in the ninth inning. Franco hadn't blown a save since June 26, when Gibson started the comeback with his hustle and an injured Sax capped with a pinch-hit three-run double.

This time, Sax grounded out, but Gibson ignited another comeback with a single to center. Hatcher struck out. Shelby was down 0–2, the Dodgers down to their final strike. Shelby hit a grounder to third. Chris Sabo made a diving stop on the dirt. Sabo jumped to his feet, rushed his throw, and it skipped past first baseman Dave Concepcion.

Chugging hard from first base on his sore legs, Gibson didn't slow down at third base and raced home in a fury to score the tying run. It was reminiscent of his game-ending dash from second base on a wild pitch a few weeks earlier.

Gibson returned to a giddy dugout, and Jeff Hamilton walked to the batter's box using one of Gibson's bats. It was a heavier model that Gibson was too tired to swing himself. Gibson thought the 24-year-old Hamilton was strong enough to use them, so he offered them.

Hamilton worked the count to 3–2, then took a mighty swing with Gibson's bat, and whacked a two-run home run into the left-field pavilion to end the game. Hamilton was mobbed by his teammates between third base and home plate. It was just his fifth home run in 241 at-bats.

"I think I can swing the bat better than I have in the past," Hamilton said that night. "The injury let part of the season get away from me. I hated to go on the DL, but I simply couldn't play with the injury. This is something I'll remember for a lifetime. This is the biggest hit I've ever had. I had a home run last year to win a game against San Diego, but this one happened in the middle of a pennant race. It's much bigger."

How sweet it is.

"What a fucking team."

♦ ♦ ♦ ♦

September 16, 1988
Cincinnati
Dodgers vs. Reds
Team record: 84–60, seven games ahead of the Astros

It rained most of the day in Cincinnati. It rained in the late afternoon, canceling batting practice. It rained in the early evening, delaying the start of the game. It didn't look like the game would be played.

Tim Leary was scheduled to pitch the next day, and as all starting pitchers are allowed, he returned to the team hotel to get rest. The game wasn't on TV. He listened on the radio for a little while, assumed the game would be rained out, and went to bed expecting a doubleheader the next day.

Players waited out the rain delay in the dry clubhouse, playing cards and talking at their lockers.

The Reds' starting pitcher, Tom Browning, sat alone in the Reds' dugout. He watched the steady downpour at Riverfront Stadium. Browning looked over to the Dodgers' dugout, noticed that Tim Belcher was doing the same as him, smiled at his opponent and gave Belcher grief about the home run that he'd hit off him five days earlier.

"I don't recall the specifics," Belcher said. "I later played with the Reds and was a teammate of his. He was very loose. I can see him looking into the skies like,

'What the hell, am I going to pitch or what?' I know it was a long night. I'm from Ohio. I had people who gave up and left early and never saw the game."

Browning was a rookie three years earlier and finished second to Vince Coleman for the Rookie of the Year Award in 1985. He struggled in 1987, was demoted to the minors with an ERA above 5.00, and had rebounded from a sore elbow earlier in 1988.

The rain didn't stop, and Browning got irritated. The talk was a doubleheader the next day. Great, just what the Dodgers needed, yet another doubleheader? Browning wasn't too happy either. He just wanted to pitch.

At 10:02 PM Eastern Daylight Time, Browning finally got to pitch. The announced crowd was 16,591. The number of fans who actually waited through the two-hour, 27-minute delay were dramatically fewer.

Neither pitcher allowed a hit through five innings. The only base runner was a second-inning walk by Belcher to Eric Davis.

Barry Larkin broke up Belcher's no-hit bid with a two-out double in the sixth inning. Chris Sabo followed with a chopper to third base. Jeff Hamilton fielded the ball cleanly, just as Larkin passed him, but his throw to first base was in the dirt and Mickey Hatcher couldn't scoop it. Larkin scored for a 1–0 lead. Belcher would allow just one hit the rest of the game.

Meanwhile, Browning retired the first 12 Dodgers batters with ease. Mike Marshall led off the fifth inning with a sharp grounder to third, but Sabo fielded it cleanly. His throw to first base was off-line to the right, but first baseman Nick Esasky deftly scooped it up.

In the seventh, Kirk Gibson was called out on strikes. Immediately after hearing the call, Gibson got into home-plate umpire Jim Quick's face and started arguing. It was classic Gibson. He was genuinely pissed. He was also trying to fire up his teammates. It took Lasorda and Belcher to restrain Gibson but not before he was ejected.

Gibson's rage was well calculated. It was his last chance to spoil Browning's shot at history anyway.

In the eighth, Marshall drove a 1–2 fastball into the right-center gap. Paul O'Neill chased it down and made the catch. John Shelby struck out. Hamilton grounded to short. Three outs to perfection.

Rick Dempsey had decent swings his first two at-bats. In the ninth, he flied out harmlessly to O'Neill in right. Sax, batting eighth because he was in a slump,

The 1988 season was bittersweet for iconic pitcher Fernando Valenzuela. He was inconsistent for four months, heard boos at Dodger Stadium for the first time in his career, and missed the playoffs with a shoulder injury. (AP Photo/Lennox McLendon)

Umpire chief Harry Wendelstedt signals the ejection of Dodgers closer Jay Howell in Game 3 of the 1988 National League Championship Series for having pine tar on his glove. Howell insisted it was just to get a better grip on the ball. He was suspended for three games, which led to a surprise relief appearance by Orel Hershiser in Game 4. (AP Photo/Bill Kostroun)

If ever a player and manager were meant to be paired together, it was Steve Sax and Tommy Lasorda. "We treated Tommy like one of our teammates," Sax said. "Did the players play like hell for him, or what? We loved him. We'd do anything for Tommy." (AP Photo/Lennox McLendon)

Tim Belcher only lasted two innings in Game 1 of the 1988 World Series. He later recalled, "I can't think of a worse game that I ever pitched in the big leagues, on the biggest stage—and that was the best game that I was ever part of." (AP Photo/Bob Galbraith)

Kirk Gibson spent most of Game 1 of the 1988 World Series inside the trainer's room getting treatment on two bad legs. He did make a brief appearance in the dugout in the third inning. At the time, nobody thought he was available to pinch hit later in the game. (AP Photo/Bob Galbraith)

This is the famed scouting report of A's relief pitcher Dennis Eckersley that was prepared by Dodgers scouts Steve Boros, Mel Didier, and Jerry Stephenson. (Courtesy of Tim Leary)

DENNIS ECKERSLEY - RP - <u>STOPPER</u> - R/R

Low 3/4 to sidearm arm action. Throws across body - semi "Cross fire". FB down sinks and tails. SL is big, quick, at times flat, and it has some "bite". At times will get under ball and throws FB "uphill" and it climbs. *Likes to "backdoor" slider to LH hitters with 3-2 count. Throws strikes, excellent control. On RH hitters, will come inside to get you off plate (seldom throws a strike in there) but <u>mainly</u> likes to stay on <u>outside</u> part of plate for strikes. Hitters tend to chase pitches, especially slider, out of strike zone. Sliders are old "round house" curve ball. Great confidence (cocky). Does not like people bunting on him. SLOW TO home with runners on base. WE CAN RUN ON HIM QUICK move to 1B.

1988 - 4W - 2L - 45S - 70IN - 52H - 10W - 67K - 5HR.

Orel Hershiser is congratulated by catcher Mike Scioscia after shutting out the A's 6-0 in Game 2 of the 1988 World Series. Hershiser pitched a three-hit shutout while batting for three hits and an RBI. He also scored a run himself. (AP Photo/Eric Risberg)

John Tudor was the hired gun acquired in a mid-August trade for popular slugger Pedro Guerrero. But he departed Game 3 of the World Series in the second inning with an injured elbow and wasn't available for the rest of the Series. (AP Photo/Lennox McLendon)

Tim Belcher redeemed himself from a poor Game 1 outing by pitching into the seventh inning and getting the victory in Game 4 of the 1988 World Series. The A's traded Belcher a year earlier for pitcher Rick Honeycutt because Belcher walked too many hitters.
(AP Photo/Lennox McLendon)

Orel Hershiser had a shirt made before Game 5 of the World Series that read, "Don't Worry, I'm Pitching," and he wore it in the clubhouse to relax his teammates. Hershiser then threw a complete-game victory to clinch the world championship. (AP Photo/Lenny Ignelzi)

How sweet it is! General manager Fred Claire and manager Tommy Lasorda hoist the World Series trophy in the raucous Dodgers clubhouse. It was vindication for Claire after his peers didn't think he could handle the job. It took all of Lasorda's motivational tools to make the championship happen. (AP Photo/Bill Beattie)

Orel Hershiser earned a lot of hardware for his performance in 1988. He's holding the award for Most Valuable Player of the World Series. Teammate Mike Marshall commented, "After the Series, the league above the major leagues will draft Orel No. 1. Then he'll be the top pitcher in the Ultra League." (AP Photo/Lennox McLendon)

grounded out to short. Lasorda sent Tracy Woodson to the plate as a pinch-hitter for Belcher.

At 11:53 PM, Woodson swung and missed at a 2–2 fastball. The 14th perfect game in baseball history was complete. Tom Browning threw 72 of his 102 pitches for strikes. He never went to a three-ball count.

"I never expected anything like this to happen to me," said Browning that night, drinking California champagne straight from the bottle. "In the last few innings, the ball was really moving in and out for me. I started to think about it—to realize I could do it—in the eighth inning. Once I got to the eighth, I started feeling a little antsy. I was feeling the pressure, and I had to make sure that I calmed myself. After that, everything just seemed to fall in place."

The only other perfect game against the Dodgers, at that point in history, was Don Larsen's in the 1956 World Series. The previous no-hitter against the Dodgers was Nolan Ryan's fifth in 1981.

"He was throwing hard," Woodson reflected. "That's the hardest I'd ever seen him. He struck me out on a high fastball. He had a little more on it that night. Maybe he got stronger as the game went along. He threw harder than I remember."

Tim Leary woke up the next morning, grabbed a newspaper, and was surprised to see the game was even played. He was even more surprised to learn he'd missed the perfect game.

◆ ◆ ◆ ◆

September 20, 1988
Los Angeles
Astros vs. Dodgers
Team record: 87–61, 9½-game lead over the Reds

Tim Belcher knew he was going from prospect to suspect.

That's what happens when four organizations own your rights in five years. The start of his transaction page is a relic from baseball's complicated past.

Belcher was the first overall pick by the Twins in the June 1983 amateur draft out of Mt. Vernon Nazarene College in Ohio, but he didn't come close to terms of a contract. Six months later, Belcher was the first overall pick by the Yankees in the now-defunct Secondary Draft of 1984. His time with the Yankees lasted six days, based on a technicality.

At the time, baseball rules required teams to submit a list of 26 protected players by mid-January for the now-defunct free-agent compensation draft. Belcher signed the first week in February, leaving the Yankees no chance to include him. Athletics general manager Sandy Alderson selected Belcher in the free-agent draft, the compensation for losing pitcher Tom Underwood to the Orioles.

"Sandy Alderson made a pretty shrewd pick," Belcher reflected. "He got a two-time No. 1 pick and didn't have to pay the bonus. It was a loophole. There was an opportunity for me to file a grievance and go to the commissioner's office. If I went kicking and screaming, like I grew up a Yankees fan and really wanted to be a Yankee, blah blah blah, they might have ruled against that pick and asked Oakland to select somebody else.

"I thought it over. Number one, I'd just gone through the embarrassment of being a No.1 overall pick in June by the Twins and not signing. I took some heat for that publicly. I didn't want to go into another fight with two teams. I hadn't even put on a uniform yet. Number two, I thought my chances of getting to the big leagues with Oakland were quicker than with the Yankees."

In the A's farm system, walks were Belcher's biggest problem: 89 in 152⅓ innings with two teams in 1984, then 99 in 149⅔ innings at Double A Huntsville in 1985. In 1986, he was limited to nine starts back at Huntsville due to injury.

Promoted to Triple A Tacoma in 1987, Belcher's wildness got even worse. He walked a whopping 133 batters in 163 innings.

The A's were still lurking in the 1987 division race. It was August 29, and they needed pitching. Joaquin Andujar was hurt and wouldn't return. Moose Haas and Chris Codiroli were done. Gene Nelson and Dennis Lamp looked more suited for the bullpen. Dennis Eckersley wanted to start and was pissed that he spent virtually the whole year in the bullpen.

Fred Claire agreed to trade Rick Honeycutt to the A's for a player to be named later. Honeycutt was expendable. He was 2–12 with a 4.59 ERA for the Dodgers. He'd lost his spot in the starting rotation in July. The results weren't better in relief. Just before the trade, 13 of the last 24 batters he faced had reached safely.

The Dodgers wanted a minor league shortstop named Walt Weiss. The A's didn't want to trade Weiss, though. Weiss was their future. They could trade Griffin, but they'd want more in return than Rick Honeycutt. The A's offered pitching instead. When in doubt, the Dodgers acquired a pitcher in a trade. On

September 3, the Dodgers announced the player they received for Honeycutt was Belcher.

"In all the reports I got, I thought we have to get this guy," Claire reflected. "He had a great delivery, great body, great makeup. I was about as happy as you could be when we traded Honeycutt, with all due respect. We followed [Belcher] close. We saw his last 6–7 starts that he'd made at Tacoma. I said, 'I hope Oakland's watching more what's happening in Oakland than what's happening in Tacoma.' This guy is going to develop."

The A's were no longer waiting on prospects like Belcher to develop. The playoffs were possible, and they wanted experience. They had Dave Stewart, Curt Young, and Steve Ontiveros in the rotation. They'd just traded for Storm Davis and Honeycutt.

Belcher was buried on the minor league depth chart behind Darrel Akerfelds, Tom Dozier, Tim Birtsas, Jose Rijo, and Todd Burns. Belcher wasn't going to reach the majors anytime soon with the Oakland A's, especially with all those walks.

The Dodgers were hopeless in 1987. They brought Belcher directly to the majors. Belcher drove from Tacoma to Seattle, took a flight to Los Angeles, and had one of those career-changing, self-evaluations on the plane.

"I'm sitting there, and all the emotions are going through your head," Belcher said. "You're 26 years old. You've gone from prospect to suspect and now back to prospect. I was smart enough to realize the only reason I hadn't gotten called up to the big leagues from Oakland was that very fact. I was walking too many people. You know what, I'm going to L.A. They're out of it. They're going to pitch me all of September. I've got to throw the ball over the plate. Even if everything I throw goes off the wall or over the wall, I have to throw strikes."

Belcher made his major league debut on September 6 in the 15th inning of a game against the Mets. He pitched two scoreless innings for the win and earned five starts to close out a lost season.

What happened in those five starts was incredible. The kid who couldn't throw strikes in the minors was suddenly a strike-throwing machine. Belcher pitched 34 innings and walked just seven batters.

"We went to Cincinnati, and I invited his parents to sit with me," Claire reflected. "You saw Tim throw and you thought, *Wow, we've got ourselves a pitcher.* When you got to know him, you knew he could be a really big-time pitcher."

Belcher won the fifth starter's job in the spring of 1988, became the reluctant closer in June with Jay Howell on the disabled list, and returned to the starting rotation after the All-Star break. Because of his startling ability to suddenly do in the majors what he couldn't do in the minors—throw strikes—Belcher was now under consideration to start a playoff game.

When he took the mound on September 20, Belcher had just 47 walks in 158⅔ innings. He'd walked only 10 batters in his last seven starts, and his ERA was 3.20 overall. The knock on Belcher was that he couldn't pitch longer than six innings.

"I recall storming into Tommy's office with [pitching coach Ron] Perranoski and complaining about getting taken out in the sixth or seventh inning all the time," Belcher said. "Of course, Tommy's response was a typical manager's response. He said, 'Timmy, I don't take you out of games. You take yourself out of games.' It was frustrating."

Backup catcher Rick Dempsey thought he knew the reason. He noticed that as Belcher pitched deeper in the game, he stopped rotating his body as much. He lost velocity and movement on his pitches. Dempsey told the rookie pitcher, "Show me the numbers on the back of your uniform."

The adjustment worked. Belcher went eight innings on the night Tom Browning was perfect.

Now he was facing the Astros and continued the trend of Dodgers dominant pitching. Belcher walked none. He allowed six hits. All singles. Only one runner reached third base, and that was after a sacrifice bunt. In the ninth, Belcher completed his first major league shutout by getting Glenn Davis on a grounder to short.

"It was nice to finally get the first shutout," Belcher reflected. "I remember my first complete game was against the Phillies [in May]. I came out of that game and I thought, *My goodness, I'm exhausted. How can anybody throw consecutive complete games?* I was ready to fall over. Once you get there and you've done it once, it gets easier the second time."

Dempsey, getting a start as Mike Scioscia returned to Los Angeles for his first child's birth, had two hits and an RBI. The Dodgers—after scoring 10 runs in their previous six games and still going 5–1—scored six runs in this victory.

It was the Dodgers' 23rd shutout of the year and third in a row. Their magic number to clinch the division was four.

◆ ◆ ◆ ◆

September 26, 1988

San Diego

Dodgers vs. Padres

Team record: 91–64, seven-game lead over the Reds

The Giants prevented the Dodgers from clinching the division and celebrating at Candlestick Park, but it only delayed the inevitable. So the champagne was packed on the charter for the flight to San Diego.

The playoffs were a foregone conclusion. The questions centered around the playoff roster. In particular, who would be in the playoff rotation? Could a long-since-forgotten Dodger legend, Fernando Valenzuela, return from his injury to pitch in October?

"I wanted to pitch," Valenzuela recalled. "I wanted to find out if I could keep going in competition. I got the opportunity to pitch in that game. I didn't feel any pain. No problem."

Valenzuela took the mound to find out on September 26. It was his first appearance in 58 days, since walking off the mound with a stretched anterior capsule in his left shoulder on July 30. Even if the great Fernando couldn't be part of the playoffs, the Dodgers wanted him to be part of the division clincher.

It didn't start pretty. Alfredo Griffin made a rare error, and Randy Ready hit a screwball for a two-run home run before Valenzuela got an out. He didn't allow any additional runs. But he reached the 60-pitch limit after a mere three innings with two hits, two walks, and a wild pitch.

Nobody would say it publicly that night—and Valenzuela would pitch four innings in relief five days later—but Valenzuela's chances of pitching in the playoffs were over.

The rest of that game was textbook for 1988. Brian Holton pitched a scoreless fourth. Holton, Ricky Horton, and Tim Crews escaped the fifth without allowing a run. Alejandro Pena delivered three scoreless innings, allowing just one hit.

John Shelby homered in the fourth—another one of those hits that was big but not so big that Shelby would get mobbed by reporters afterward. Tracy Woodson homered in the fifth inning to tie it.

In the eighth inning, the game was tied at 2–2, and it was time for the leading Stuntman to shine again. Griffin reached on a two-base throwing error by Padres shortstop Dickie Thon to start the inning. Sax bunted him to third base. Mickey Hatcher was due up. Hatcher wasn't supposed to be at the plate. That was Gibson's spot in the lineup. It was the spot made for Gibson. It was the spot for which Gibson was brought over from Detroit.

But the playoffs were inevitable. Gibson's left hamstring was sore and needed rest, so Hatcher was a late insertion into the starting lineup. Even then, Hatcher figured he would get double-switched out of the game in the sixth inning. Nope. Hatcher remained in the game, and he was surprised.

Hatcher was surprised that he was still on the roster. The Dodgers traded Hatcher to the Twins at the end of spring training in 1981 then won a World Series. The Twins released Hatcher at the end of spring training in 1987 then won a World Series. He'd missed on two World Series titles by six months.

Hatcher thought the Dodgers would get rid of him. He spent every day in September fearful the grim reaper was going to take him away from the playoffs, when he was so close. He'd think it. Worst of all, Lasorda would say it—out loud.

"Mick, we have to get rid of you," Lasorda would say, shaking his head. "We've got a chance to win a World Series. We have to stay with the program."

Did Hatcher really believe Lasorda?

"You never know with Tommy," Hatcher reflected, with a laugh. "All I was doing was playing hard and making it tough on him to make that choice."

Hatcher just hoped to see his jersey at his locker each day. And now here he was, not only still on the roster but with a chance to clinch a playoff spot for the team that drafted him in the fifth round out of the University of Oklahoma in 1977. Hatcher's mind raced with delirium. "I thought, *Oh, thank you, thank you for letting me get a crack at this.* I was just where I wanted to be."

With the infield drawn in, Hatcher slapped the second pitch into left field to score Griffin with the go-ahead run. Jay Howell pitched the ninth for the save. The final out came when Marvell Wynne popped up to second baseman Steve Sax. The celebration was on.

Hatcher was in the clubhouse, soaked in beer and champagne, still wearing his black batting glove, and practically screaming. "Can you imagine that, my first playoff, and I get the hit that [puts the Dodgers into] it?" Hatcher said that night. "I was so happy I was able to do it. It makes this celebrating so much better."

The only person happier was Fred Claire. "It was particularly rewarding for this thing to end on a Mickey Hatcher hit," Claire said. "He was the first guy I brought here. He is where the building began."

Tommy Lasorda went from player to player, hugging them like only Tommy Lasorda can hug. They went through 15 cases of beer and five cases of champagne. The alcohol flowed for 30 minutes. Only small portions were consumed.

Drenched in booze, Howell called it his best moment in baseball. Howell dusted off a phrase from the spring to describe himself, Alejandro Pena, Jesse Orosco, Brian Holton, and Tim Crews. "We're the awesome fivesome," Howell said.

For somebody who spent half the season in the minors, Tracy Woodson was ecstatic. "I won championships in the minors," he reflected. "You threw a few beers on each other, that kind of thing. This celebration? I've never seen anything like it. You walk up and there's three huge trash cans of beer. There's champagne, and they told you, 'Make sure you drink the good champagne and squirt each other with the cheap champagne.' I went back to the hotel. I don't know how much money I spent. I know I spent at least 100 bucks. I have no idea what the other guys spent. We bought out everything. Guys were buying the most expensive champagne at the hotel. I've never seen anything like it. I'd never experienced it. They cover up the locker room with all the plastic. It was ridiculous. It was awesome."

Gibson was one of the most subdued. He called it "the first step"—and left his partying teammates in the clubhouse for some alone time on an empty baseball diamond. He stood on the third-base line at Jack Murphy Stadium, all alone, clutched a beer, and stared deeply at the full moon, a man alone with his thoughts.

His legs were aching. His entire body was hurting. But he knew this was just the beginning.

In eight days, the Mets and Dodgers would begin the National League Championship Series. All that remained was the hype, the playoff roster decisions, and Orel Hershiser's improbable pursuit of a streak that was almost mathematically impossible.

Chapter 14

The Sixth Shutout

Wednesday, September 28, 1988

San Diego

Dodgers vs. Padres

Team record: 92–65, first place clinched

DODGERS	PADRES
2B Steve Sax	2B Roberto Alomar
1B Franklin Stubbs	3B Tim Flannery
LF Kirk Gibson	CF Tony Gwynn
CF John Shelby	1B Carmelo Martinez
RF Mike Davis	RF Marvell Wynne
C Mike Scioscia	C Benito Santiago
3B Jeff Hamilton	LF Randy Ready
SS Alfredo Griffin	SS Garry Templeton
P Orel Hershiser	P Andy Hawkins

In order to break Don Drysdale's consecutive scoreless inning streak, all Orel Hershiser had to do was shut out a lineup with a rookie second baseman who would make the Hall of Fame, a center fielder who was days away from the third of his eight batting titles en route to the Hall of Fame, a first baseman with 18 home runs, a catcher who was the reigning Rookie of the Year, and a shortstop with three All-Star Game appearances.

Even that would have only tied the record.

Hershiser also needed the opposing pitcher, Andy Hawkins, and/or his bullpen, to throw nine shutout innings. Hawkins had thrown two shutouts that year. He'd also allowed 12 runs (10 earned) in his previous 16 innings over three starts. He'd faced the Dodgers twice that year, giving up a combined five runs in 11⅓ innings. Hawkins' ERA was 3.51. It was 5.05 the year before.

The afternoon of the game, Hershiser ate lunch with Tim Belcher at TGI Friday's. It was Belcher's goal to not bring up the record or discuss it. In order to keep Hershiser's mind occupied, he asked the waitress for a copy of *USA Today*. When the waitress brought it over, Belcher was eating soup. He passed it over to Hershiser. On the front page of the sports section were big pictures of Hershiser and Drysdale. It was the big feature story.

"I think it was me and Jay Howell and several of us," Belcher said. "Nobody wanted to bring it up. We wanted him to relax and just have fun. Then I hand him a newspaper and there's a big picture of him and Drysdale and a big article. Oh jeez, what have I done?"

Drysdale was cheering for Hershiser the whole way, but the old athlete in him was superstitious enough to refrain from talking about it with Hershiser. After the Dodgers clinched the division, Drysdale didn't mention the record in the champagne-filled clubhouse interviews.

The pressure of the pennant race helped Hershiser stay focused in the five shutouts to get to this point. What also helped is that there was no margin for error. In his three previous starts, the game was scoreless going into the seventh inning.

Now the division was clinched. It was all about the record, and Tommy Lasorda would be justified in managing differently to preserve the streak. If a runner reached third base with nobody out, Lasorda could bring the infield in—a move that you wouldn't normally do early in a game.

The other pregame storyline wondered if Hershiser threw another shutout, would Lasorda use Hershiser in relief to set the record before the season ended?

Hershiser's start was on a Wednesday, the fourth-to-last game of the regular season. He would start Game 1 of the National League Championship Series the next Tuesday, on five days rest. It was reasonable to use Hershiser in a relief appearance on the penultimate game of the season. That was the day of Hershiser's normal between-starts bullpen session anyway.

That game was held at Dodger Stadium. Only two of Hershiser's six starts in the streak occurred at home. So this would allow the home crowd to enjoy the record with Hershiser.

But that wasn't Hershiser's plan. He wanted to make a relief appearance, get two outs, tie the record, and leave the mound in a tie. Hershiser considered it a slap in the face to break Drysdale's record in relief.

Remember, the league office had already changed Drysdale's record from 58⅔ to 58 innings, so Hershiser's plan was actually pointless.

All the what-ifs made for interesting discussion. But unless Hershiser threw another shutout, they were a moot point.

All along, Hershiser simply wanted the chance at history. Now he had it. Many starting pitchers tell you that waiting around all day for a night game seems to take an eternity. Hershiser tried to tell himself that it was just another start, focus on mechanics and release points, and forget about scoreless innings. But who was he kidding?

"You know, I'm really pretty nervous," Hershiser told pitching coach Ron Perranoski, after a few warm-up pitches. "I can even feel it in my stomach."

"You'll be all right once you get out there and get the first couple of outs." Perranoski said.

A few pitches later…"Did you hear that?" Perranoski said.

"No."

"That was my stomach. I'm nervous, too."

During his final eight warm-up pitches on the mound at Jack Murphy Stadium, some Padres fans tried getting into Hershiser's head.

"You've been lucky, Hershiser! We're not only gonna score off you, we're gonna kill you!"

That just brought out the famed Bulldog even more.

With no local TV, Vin Scully had the play-by-play in the first inning. Drysdale wasn't an analyst. The Dodgers' broadcasting style was one voice talking to the audience. Drysdale sat next to Scully, but he didn't talk on the radio. He read a newspaper with his reading glasses perched on his nose.

As Drysdale read the paper, Roberto Alomar flew out to center to start the bottom of the first. Tim Flannery singled up the middle. Tony Gwynn grounded to second, and Flannery was forced out. Carmelo Martinez popped out to first base. The streak was at 50 innings.

In the second inning, Marvell Wynne flied out to center. Benito Santiago flied out to right field. Randy Ready reached first base on an error, but Garry Templeton hit a comebacker to Hershiser. The streak was at 51.

Hershiser singled to right field with one out in the top of the third. So much for at least one of the nine Dodgers hitters whiffing on purpose to help Hawkins throw nine scoreless. He was stranded at first, though.

The third inning was Drysdale's turn to take over play-by-play duties. An ABC-TV camera was in his face, looking for a reaction. There would be no reaction. Drysdale kept a straight face.

Hawkins grounded to third to open the third inning. Alomar tried a bunt and popped out to first. Flannery grounded to short. The inning took seven pitches. The camera backed away and Drysdale let out a "Ohhhhh" in relief. Scully laughed and poked Drysdale on the arm. The streak was at 52.

"Even in the booth, Don was still the same competitor that he was on the field," Scully said upon reflection. "By that I mean, he wanted to win. If we lost a game, he would be angry in the booth. I used to say to him, 'Hey, come on, relax. What are you talking about?' He'd say, 'Awwww, those bastards.' Then I'd make him laugh. I told him, 'I'm going to hire a plane that will say, 'Give the money back.' He would laugh and calm down.

"So I think in watching him during the game, he was much more interested in the Dodgers winning than his own record. It's not like he was sitting there thinking, *This guy is going to break my record that's lasted for 20 years.* Oh no. All he wanted to do was win. I don't think he had other feelings. That's the way he was."

In the top of the fourth, Mike Davis hit a deep fly ball to right field. If it cleared the fence, the best Hershiser could do on this night was tie Drysdale. But the ballpark held it. It was caught by Wynne and the game remained scoreless.

"Yes, we were trying to score," Sax said.

As Gwynn led off the bottom of the fourth, Drysdale left the booth and visited the press box cafeteria. He filled up on popcorn and soda. If the streak ended with one swing of the bat, Drysdale would have missed it.

Gwynn wasn't the home run threat like Will Clark was a start earlier. Still, Hershiser pitched Gwynn extra careful, throwing almost every pitch on the outside corner to him this at-bat and all game. Gwynn grounded to second for the first out. Martinez struck out looking. Wynne lined a single to center.

Next was Santiago. The year before, Hershiser ended Santiago's hitting streak at 34 games. Now was a chance for Santiago to get even. A double up the gap, or down the line, would score the speedy Wynne. But there would be no payback. Santiago grounded to short. The streak was at 53 innings.

With two outs in the top of the fifth, Alfredo Griffin doubled to left field. That brought up Hershiser with a runner in scoring position. Surely, Hershiser knew what was at stake if he singled again. The run would score, and he couldn't break the record. Hershiser swung away and grounded back to Hawkins for the final out.

Back on the mound, Hershiser needed eight pitches in the bottom half of the fifth. Ready grounded to second. Templeton flew out to left. Hawkins grounded out to Hershiser. The streak was at 54.

As each inning passed, more and more Padres fans went from rooting against Hershiser to rooting for him. They knew that history was possible.

Four hundred and sixty-seven miles north in Pleasanton, this book's author and his father searched for a radio station in Southern California, or any radio station, that could be found to hear the final innings. We couldn't get the Dodgers' station in Los Angeles but remarkably picked up the Padres' station in San Diego.

In the top of the sixth, a leadoff error and a two-out walk put a runner in scoring position for the Dodgers. Davis, getting a rare start, popped out to short to end the Dodgers' threat. It was probably a good thing that Davis made an out. He made so many outs that year, if he finally got a hit and ruined Hershiser's chance at history, Dodgers fans would have hated him more.

"Yes, we were trying to score runs," Shelby said. "We wanted to score as many runs as we possibly could. Even though there was a streak, that's not your main focus. It's trying to win a ballgame. If we had scored a run early in the game, it wouldn't be the end of the world."

Hershiser's nerves were gone by the bottom of the sixth inning. Now, Hershiser felt excitement. All he'd wanted was to get close to the record, to give himself a chance. Now he'd done that. Even if he fell short, he knew it was an impressive streak and there was honor in just coming that close.

Alomar flied to left field to start the bottom of the sixth. Flannery grounded to second. Gwynn battled Hershiser for seven pitches before grounding out to second, as well. The streak was 55.

Hershiser had thrown 65 pitches—45 for strikes—to that point. He'd allowed two hits and went to a three-ball count just twice. As he walked out for the seventh, the visiting fans (and Dodgers fans who made the two-hour drive south), greeted him with a standing ovation. Hershiser felt the adrenaline rush.

In the seventh inning, Drysdale went back on the air for his second and final inning of play-by-play. Martinez grounded to short. Wynne lined a single to left. Wynne was once a stolen-base threat, swiping 24 bags four years earlier. He only had three steals in 1988, but Hershiser had to pay attention to him.

Santiago flew out to right field. Ready grounded to short. Hershiser had passed the great Walter Johnson. The streak was 56.

"That's 56 innings in the book," Drysdale said on KABC-AM.

Off the air, Drysdale looked at his watch, shook his head, and said, "We might be here all night."

In the top of the eighth, Kirk Gibson hit a high fly ball to deep center. Once again, the ballpark held it. Incredibly, the game was still scoreless.

Hershiser avoided using his curveball almost completely in this game. He feared hanging one. He relied on his sinker and fastball instead.

Templeton grounded to second to open the bottom of the eighth inning. Jack McKeon, the Padres' general manager who had fired Larry Bowa during the season and replaced him with himself, didn't pinch hit for Hawkins. Hershiser struck out Hawkins on four pitches.

Alomar was in the batter's box. In the broadcast booth, a tiny hand slipped through the back door and an infant boy shouted, "Daddy, Daddy." The baby was 14-month-old Donnie Drysdale. He was brought into the booth by Drysdale's wife, Ann Meyers.

Scully continued calling the action, Drysdale got up to see his son, and Alomar bounced a single up the middle. Alomar was a big threat to run, and Hershiser knew it. He didn't want the go-ahead run in scoring position. Hershiser threw over to first base. And threw over. And threw over. He wanted to make Alomar so tired of throws over to first that he reduced his lead. With a 1–0 count, Alomar leaned the wrong way and Hershiser picked him off. The streak was 57.

Before the top of the ninth, catcher Mike Scioscia took off his equipment and asked Hershiser, "Do you want me to hit one out or just a base hit so you can have a chance at the record?"

They was the first words any teammate, including his catcher, had said to Hershiser the whole night. Scioscia, it should be noted, had three home runs that year.

"Yeah, I remember saying that," Scioscia said, "because me hitting a home run isn't what you would expect."

Shelby singled to start the Dodgers' ninth. Davis flew out to right. Next came Scioscia. He hit a line drive, but it was caught by Flannery at third. Hamilton grounded out.

Hawkins had done his part. He'd thrown nine shutout innings. Now Hershiser had a chance to not only tie the record but break the record. No relief appearances necessary. No carryovers to the next season. No asterisks. He could do it on this night in San Diego.

The inning to tie the record was one of the easiest of the streak. With the stadium on its feet, Flannery hit a comebacker for one out. Gwynn grounded to second for the second out. Martinez grounded to third for the third out. Eight pitches. The streak was at 58 innings.

"It was the best I've ever seen him pitch," Gwynn said. "I grounded to second base each time, each time on a sinker, although he set me up differently each time. He sure as heck knew what he was doing out there."

The announced crowd was only 22,596, but the atmosphere was electric.

Lasorda was the first to greet Hershiser as he came off the mound. With no walks and two strikeouts so far, Hershiser's pitch count was at just 98 pitches. Lasorda, Hershiser, Perranoski, and hitting coach Ben Hines gathered for a discussion about pitching the 10th inning.

"Let me tie it at home," Hershiser said.

"You hear this guy?" Lasorda asked. "No way! You're goin' out there, Bulldog! You owe it to yourself and to the team. And to baseball."

"Then let me just tie it and leave it there," Hershiser said.

"No. I'm not takin' you out," Lasorda said. "You're gonna pitch, and I want three outs."

Andy Hawkins went out for the 10th inning, as well. He started the inning by hitting Griffin. Hershiser came to the plate, and the crowd roared because they knew that meant he was staying in the game. Hershiser bunted Griffin to second base. Steve Sax grounded to short. Franklin Stubbs grounded to first. Still scoreless.

In the dugout, Belcher considered all the possibilities that were coming together.

"If he threw another nine-inning shutout, he's dead tied with Drysdale, right on the number," Belcher said. "The only way he can eclipse the number is to throw a 10-inning shutout. The only way that happens is if the other guy throws a shutout. And I'll be damned if that happens. We're sitting there thinking, *Are you shitting me? Is this actually going to happen? Is he really getting a chance to throw a 10-inning shutout?*"

As Hershiser took the mound in the 10th, and the crowd rose to its feet again, Hershiser looked for Drysdale. He was seeking approval of the pitcher whose record he was trying to break, a little nod or a glance for acknowledgment. Hershiser didn't see Drysdale in the press box—didn't see him in the dugout, either.

Hershiser gave up looking for him. He tipped his cap toward the press box, in recognition of Drysdale, and said to himself, "I'm going for it."

Drysdale was in the elevator, making his way down to the field for an interview on the KABC Postgame Show. He wasn't sad. He was smiling. Bill Plaschke, then the Padres' beat writer for the *Los Angeles Times' San Diego Edition*, rode the elevator with him.

"You know, I got in the Hall of Fame, and after that, nothing is as important," Drysdale told Plaschke. "That's it. That's the greatest. I don't feel bad. I feel good. I feel good just watching Hershiser pitch. He's in such a groove. I've been rooting for him, working hard, really rooting. I have been thinking, *Hit the ball at someone, hit the ball down.*"

Numerous times during the streak, Drysdale interviewed Hershiser. Not once did he ask him about The Streak.

"I told myself I would not say anything to him about it, and I haven't," Drysdale said. "On the postgame show, I've asked him how he feels, and things like that, but I've never talked to him about now it's 40, now it's 49, that kind of thing. I didn't want that monkey on my back when I pitched, and I wouldn't put it on his back."

Drysdale reached the Dodgers' dugout to watch the bottom of the 10th inning. What an inning it would be.

Wynne struck out swinging on a breaking ball, but the pitch got away from Hershiser, and more important, got away from Scioscia. Wynne reached first base on the wild pitch. Hershiser would need four outs in the final inning.

Next was Santiago, and he was asked to lay down a sacrifice bunt. He did. Hershiser fielded the ball, but his only play was at first base. Wynne was at second base. The game was on the line. The streak was on the line. A single would end them both.

On a 1–0 pitch, Ready hit a grounder to short. Griffin went to first base for the second out, and Wynne advanced to third. Now, even the bean counters would say Hershiser and Drysdale were tied at 58⅔ innings. A wild pitch would end the streak. A wild throw would end the streak.

The decision was made to intentionally walk Templeton. His run was meaningless, and that set up a force at second base. Plus, the pitcher's spot was due up next.

After the second ball to Templeton, Hershiser casually strode away from Scioscia's throw. He had to desperately lunge back to catch the ball, or else it would have gone into center field. Can you imagine the streak ending that way? It was inches from happening.

Hershiser looked at Wynne at third and smiled. Wynne smiled back.

Keith Moreland came off the bench to pinch hit. Moreland's batting average against Hershiser was less than .200 at that moment. Hershiser knew that Moreland would chase curveballs low and outside. Although Hershiser trusted his catcher to block balls in the dirt, he didn't want to chance the streak ending on a wild pitch or passed ball.

Instead, it was the sinker. Of course he would throw sinkers. The first two pitches were called strikes. The crowd rose to its feet, cheering on Hershiser. Moreland took ball one and fouled off a pitch. On the radio, Scully said the following:

"Eugene O'Neill wrote a great line. He said, 'There is no present and there is no future. There is only the past, over and over, now.' That's what we're looking at, the past. Twenty years ago, we're looking at it again. Remarkable. Hershiser ready and the 1–2 pitch…"

On his 116th pitch of the night, Hershiser threw a fastball, up and away. Moreland lofted a fly ball to shallow right field.

Jose Gonzalez, a 23-year-old who split the year between the majors and minors, camped under it. Hershiser watched the flight of the ball. He bent over slightly, hands on his knees. He stared at the ball and Gonzalez, the ball and Gonzalez, the ball… and Gonzalez caught it.

He'd done it.

The improbable was complete.

Hershiser's teammates on the field mobbed him. So did those on the bench.

"Where's Drysdale?" Hershiser said. "I've got to find Drysdale."

Drysdale, his hair now gray, his skin always tan, was beaming from ear to ear in the dugout. The new record holder and old record holder met at the dugout—and hugged.

Drysdale told Hershiser, "It couldn't have happened to a nicer kid."

Then, with a bigger grin, he told him, "I can't believe you didn't win that game. Just like the sixties."

Pitching	IP	H	R	ER	BB	SO	HR	ERA	BF	Pit	Str	Ctct	StS	StL	GB	FB	LD
Orel Hershiser	10	4	0	0	1	3	0	2.26	36	116	77	44	12	21	22	10	3

The game was still tied. It was going into the 11th inning. But the game's outcome was now meaningless. Drysdale interviewed Hershiser in the dugout on KABC radio, as the game was going on. Hershiser told Drysdale his plan was to tie the record at 58⅔ innings.

Drysdale responded, "If I'd known that, I'd have kicked you in the rear and told you to get your buns out there and go for it."

Hershiser retreated to the clubhouse to ice his arm. Dodgers public relations director Mike Williams requested his presence at a press conference.

"During the game?!" Hershiser asked.

Yep. The game's outcome didn't matter. The division title was clinched. It was past deadline for the East Coast papers. Deadline was approaching quickly for the West Coast papers.

"I know I said I never thought the record could be approached," Drysdale told more than 50 reporters. "But really, I thought it could be approached. And it has. My record—I mean his record—well, I guess it can be topped. At least it stays in the [Dodgers] family."

A few booths over from Scully and Drysdale, Spanish language announcer Jaime Jarrin felt more joy for Hershiser than he would any other player. Back in the 1960s, Scully gave Jarrin the same advice that Red Barber had given him.

"Vin advised me not to get too close to the players," Jarrin said. "I kept my distance with them. I tried to be very nice with them, but not very close. Except with Hershiser. He was special. When my son died, he was the first one to approach me, and say, 'Don't let the memory of your son fade away. Let's do something.' We founded a foundation, and we collected over $100,000 and gave away scholarships. Because of that and everything else, he was my favorite player. I was extremely happy to see what kind of year he had. The streak was unbelievable."

The game wouldn't be decided until the 16th inning. The Dodgers scored an unearned run in the top of the 16th. Mark Parent hit a two-run homer off Ricky Horton in the bottom of the inning to win it.

Hershiser wouldn't get a win, a shutout, or a complete game. But he'd get a record.

These are his numbers during the streak.

G	GS	CG	SO	W-L	IP	H	R	ER	BB	SO	1B	2B	3B	HR	HBP	ERA	Pit	Str	Str %
6	6	5	5	5–0	59.0	30	0	0	11	38	27	3	0	0	0	0.00	697	461	66%

♦ ♦ ♦ ♦

By the way, if people tell you they watched this game on TV, they either lived in San Diego or they're lying. The game, shockingly, was not televised in Los Angeles. The division clincher, two days earlier, was also not televised. The meaningless middle of the game series, commonly known as "the hangover" game after a division clincher, was televised.

L.A. Times radio-TV columnist Larry Stewart ripped Channel 11 two days later for these decisions. "Channel 11 asks viewers to watch games all season, then when special ones come along, the station ignores them. Instead, Channel 11 gave viewers two horror movies, Friday the 13th on Monday night and The Funhouse on Wednesday night. The real horror, however, was the decision not to televise the two big Dodgers games."

Hershiser's brush with history was not televised nationally, either. ESPN's contract with baseball didn't begin until 1990. There was no Wednesday night Game of the Week on rights holders NBC or ABC. The only television broadcast was the Padres' feed.

◆ ◆ ◆ ◆

The final numbers for the top three Cy Young Award candidates looked like this:

Player	W-L	ERA	IP	H (BABIP)	BB	SO	Opp. Slash line
Danny Jackson, CIN	23–8	2.73	260.2	206 (.249)	71	161	.218/.273/.312
Orel Hershiser, LAD	23–8	2.26	267.0	208 (.242)	73	178	.213/.269/.310
David Cone, NYM	20–3	2.22	231.1	178 (.272)	80	213	.213/.283/.293

The next morning, Sandy Koufax picked up the newspaper in Florida and didn't know how to feel.

"I cared so much about both of them, having worked with Orel and having played with Don for so long," Koufax said to a wire reporter. "I was proud of Orel but a little sad for Don. It's an amazing record, when you think about it. I can believe most anything that happens in a single game, but such sustained excellence over such a long period, with no margin for error, is unbelievable."

Chapter 15

NLCS

Tuesday, October 4, 1988
Los Angeles
Mets vs. Dodgers
NLCS Game 1

The space shuttle Discovery returned to earth, landing at Edwards Air Force Base in the Mojave Desert, and welcomed by more than 400,000 exuberant witnesses that included vice president George Bush. A NASA physician boarded the space plane, giving checkups to astronauts Frederick H. Hauck, Richard O. Covey, John M. Lounge, George D. Nelson, and David C. Hilmers. They exited the plane waving American flags. It was the first mission since the Challenger disaster 33 months earlier.

One-hundred fourteen miles to the south, doctors and trainers were checking on Kirk Gibson, as well. Gibson started six of the Dodgers' final 14 regular season games. Part of this was because the Dodgers had a big lead and they could afford to rest him. The bigger reason was his body—in particular, a pulled hamstring and sore knee—needed time to heal.

Gibson had run hard once in the last two weeks. He couldn't walk for two days afterward. It was the worst he'd felt all season. The hamstring was bothering him. But now his knee was killing him. Gibson thought he'd have to throttle down a little, if that was possible. He didn't want to end up crippled. But he knew one thing.

"I will be in the lineup," Gibson said. "I will be in the fucking lineup."

Gibson didn't fill out the lineup, though. Tommy Lasorda did. One factor would determine if Lasorda would start Gibson in Game 1 of the NLCS against the Mets.

"If he's breathing," Lasorda said, "he's in there."

The Mets won the season series—10-of-11 games—by a combined score of 49–18. One scout told the *Philadelphia Inquirer* the Mets should win in four games, all by the score of 10–0. But the Dodgers had Orel Hershiser. He would start Game 1, Game 4, and Game 7 if necessary. Hershiser not only couldn't lose, he couldn't give up a run. That made his starts crucial.

"If we beat Orel in the first game," Mets first baseman Keith Hernandez said, "we'll be in great shape. He has to win for them."

One area the Dodgers knew they could exploit was on the bases. The only Mets pitcher who held runners on effectively was Ron Darling. Catcher Gary Carter struggled throwing out runners for three years.

"That was the whole plan, really," second baseman Steve Sax reflected. "Disrupt their staff. We wanted to do anything we could on the base paths to cause disruption. Anything we could do to throw them off-kilter."

In the first inning of Game 1, Sax took advantage. He singled off Dwight Gooden, immediately stole second base, and went to third on Gibson's grounder to the right side. Mike Marshall stroked a single to right field, and the Dodgers led 1–0.

That's all Orel Hershiser needed, especially in the twilight with a 5:20 PM Pacific start, right?

Sure seemed like it. In the seventh, Mike Scioscia doubled, Jeff Hamilton grounded out, and Alfredo Griffin singled home a run. It was 2–0. Now it was really over, right?

Hershiser took a shutout into the ninth inning. The scoreless streak didn't officially extend into the playoffs, but it was now at 67 innings. He'd allowed five hits, one walk, and struck out six so far in Game 1. He'd retired seven batters in a row, faced four batters over the minimum, and only twice had a Mets base runner reached third base. His pitch count was at 90.

Gregg Jefferies had just turned 21 years old, had one month of big-league experience, and had somehow lived up to the enormous hype since he was named Minor League Player of the Year. He referred to the pitcher on the mound as "Mr. Hershiser." Jefferies was respectful but hardly intimidated.

Too young to realize what was going on, Jefferies did what most of the National League couldn't do—rake Hershiser. Jefferies singled in the first, singled in the sixth, and started the ninth inning with a clean single up the middle.

On the first pitch to Keith Hernandez, Mets manager Davey Johnson put on the hit-and-run, and Hernandez hit a hard grounder to first. Hernandez was out, and Jefferies advanced to second.

Jefferies didn't realize the ball was fair, though. He wandered off the base. Dodgers shortstop Alfredo Griffin slipped behind Jefferies and called for the ball, begged for the ball, but Franklin Stubbs didn't realize the opportunity. The Mets screamed from the first-base dugout at Jefferies, and he got back to second base safely.

Months later, Hershiser would still taste the situation—two outs, nobody on base. Instead, a runner at second base, one out, and cleanup batter Darryl Strawberry at the plate.

With the count 2–2, Strawberry fouled off two pitches. Lasorda paced in the Dodgers' dugout. The Mets wore their hats backward for a rally. Hershiser hung a curveball, but Strawberry was too eager to cream it. He nearly jumped off the ground, and he fouled it back. Hershiser came back with another curveball. This one had better spin, a better release. But he threw it too hard, not enough snap. Another hanging curve.

Strawberry smashed it into center field for a double. It was 2–1.

Hershiser had allowed a run, his first since August 30. He was human, after all. Hershiser was furious at himself for hanging two straight curveballs to Strawberry. His mind shifted to the next hitter, Kevin McReynolds, and closing out the victory. Then he saw pitching coach Ron Perranoski talking to the umpire. It took a moment to register what was happening.

Incredibly, Hershiser was being taken out of the game on a double switch. By the time Perranoski reached the mound, the move was made. Hershiser couldn't plead his case, couldn't talk his way into staying in the game. Jay Howell was coming into the game.

Howell pitched around McReynolds and walked him. Howell struck out Howard Johnson for the second out. Howell jumped ahead of Gary Carter with two curveballs. The crowd was on its feet, one strike from victory.

On the ABC telecast, analyst Tim McCarver said the Dodgers' outfield was playing too deep for Gary Carter. "They're playing the Gary Carter of five years ago," McCarver said.

Howell snapped off another curve, low and away. Carter reached his bat outside, feebly, and barely made contact. The bat was broken. It was a blooper into shallow center field.

John Shelby was playing deep, preventing a double that would score two runs. Shelby got a decent jump, charged at full speed, and thought he would catch it. He dove for the ball.

The ball was ever so briefly inside Shelby's glove, came out at impact with the ground, and rolled behind him.

"When the ball was hit, I ran in, and my first thought was that I wouldn't need to dive," Shelby reflected. "Then I realized I did need to dive. I actually got to the ball quicker than I thought. I actually extended too far. The ball hit me in the wrist. It handcuffed me."

Strawberry scored easily. McReynolds was running with two outs and charging home. Shelby double-clutched before throwing home. Scioscia blocked the plate. McReynolds ran him over. The throw was way late. McReynolds scored the go-ahead run. It was 3–2 Mets.

"That was very devastating to me," Shelby said. "But it wasn't enough that it was going to affect me the rest of the series. I took a lot of pride in my defense. I would have felt worse if I had let the ball drop in and never tried to catch it. Anytime I try something, I never have second thoughts. If I never try, then I'll second-guess myself the rest of my life."

Randy Myers pitched the bottom of the ninth for the Mets. Seven pitches later, the game was over. The unthinkable had occurred. Hershiser had allowed a run. Hershiser was lifted. Hershiser started, and the Dodgers didn't win.

Grilled by reporters, Lasorda said that Hershiser "definitely" was tired, referred to the hard-hit balls by Jefferies and Hernandez and the hanging curves to Strawberry.

Hershiser defended the decision, agreeing it was the right move. But he was adamant that he was not tired. Not in that game specifically. Not overall from a long season and all those scoreless innings.

Back at home, Hershiser couldn't sleep. He couldn't sit still. He was still angry, at himself, for those two hanging curveballs. It took Hershiser four hours to fall asleep.

"It's not your fault, honey," Jamie told her husband.

"Yes, it is."

◆ ◆ ◆ ◆

Wednesday, October 5, 1988

Los Angeles
Mets vs. Dodgers
NLCS Game 2

Dave Anderson didn't make the playoff roster because of a back injury. He'd done a yeoman's job subbing for Alfredo Griffin at shortstop for two months. In the playoffs, he'd have to find another way to contribute. Anderson arrived early for Game 2, and a Dodgers public relations member showed him an article from the *New York Daily News*.

"Ever heard the saying, 'Better to be lucky than good?' Trash it, because Hershiser was just lucky. Look what happened to luck in the ninth inning last night. It's called justice—catching up to luck and pummeling it into the ground. Trouble was, Orel was lucky for eight innings."

Those weren't the words of a New York columnist stirring things up. Those words were under a first-person byline of David Cone, the starting pitcher in Game 2 of the playoffs. Cone didn't "write" the column himself. He was interviewed by Bob Klapisch, who was responsible for putting his thoughts into print.

That wasn't even the most controversial part of the column, either.

"I'll tell you a secret: As soon as we got Orel out of the game, we knew we'd beat the Dodgers. Knew it even after Jay Howell had struck out HoJo. We saw Howell throwing curveball after curveball, and we were thinking, *This is the Dodgers' idea of a stopper?* Our idea is Randy ⌊Myers⌋, a guy who can blow you away with his heat. Seeing Howell and his curveball reminded us of a high school pitcher."

195

Anderson made copies of the column, underlined the key passages, and plastered the clubhouse with them. He put them in the trainer's room, on the walls of the clubhouse, on the chairs of teammates, and a stack was on Tommy Lasorda's desk.

"Trying to do something, you know, to motivate the boys," Anderson recalled, laughing.

The Dodgers arrived to the clubhouse an equal combination of down and angry. Then they read the article and became a combination of pissed and aggressive.

"We didn't have a good opinion of the Mets," Hershiser recalled. "Then Lasorda came into the locker room yelling, 'If this was a one-game series, I'd be depressed! But it's not! It's a seven-game series!' He was doing all the Tommy stuff and yelling at us."

The days of "bench jockeying" were mostly a lost art in 1988. There was more than what you'll see nowadays but far less than the 1960s and 1970s. Players didn't razz opposing players from the dugout. It's mostly a quiet place. But things would change on this night.

The game started later than usual due to the vice presidential debate between Senator Dan Quayle, the Republican nominee of George Bush, and Senator Lloyd Bentsen, the Democratic running mate of Michael Dukakis.

When questioned about his lack of experience, Quayle said, "I have as much experience in the Congress as Jack Kennedy did when he sought the presidency. I will be prepared to deal with the people in the Bush administration, if that unfortunate event would ever occur."

Bentsen replied, "Senator, I served with Jack Kennedy. I knew Jack Kennedy. Jack Kennedy was a friend of mine. Senator, you are no Jack Kennedy."

David Cone was no Jim Murray in the sports section. The Dodgers would ensure he would be no Orel Hershiser on the pitching mound, either.

Steamed from Cone's words, the Dodgers' players turned into high school or college players. They were all over Cone, giving him hell. Every player except for starting pitcher Tim Belcher was on the top step of the dugout. They heckled Cone worse than any fan in the bleachers could ever heckle.

Cone was rattled. In the first inning, he walked Mickey Hatcher, balked him to second, and Mike Marshall singled him home.

In the second inning, after getting one out, Cone dropped down sidearm, and Jeff Hamilton was hit by a pitch. Griffin struck out with a feeble swing on a splitter.

Belcher (an .091 hitter) singled up the middle to keep the inning alive. Sax singled up the middle to score a run, Hatcher doubled (just barely fair down the left-field line) to score two runs, Gibson was intentionally walked, and Marshall singled home another.

It was 5–0. Cone was done after two innings.

Tim McCarver on ABC, "I guess the moral to the story is if you're going to write a column in the playoffs, write it like Ann Landers. I tell you, this is a different Dodgers club."

"Everybody was geared up," Belcher reflected. "I remember virtually everybody standing on the top step, screaming at him in the bottom of the first inning. Everybody except me, I was the starting pitcher, so I'm sitting back and relaxed. I remember Rick Dempsey, top-stepping, screaming at him, all kinds of stuff. I think it really rattled David. I don't know if he would ever admit it. He was pretty early in his career, too. He had a tremendous career. I think that rattled him. We got to him."

Belcher started Game 2 because Tim Leary was inconsistent the last month of the season (5.13 ERA), and because John Tudor felt muscle spasms in his left hip in his final regular-season start. Tudor's elbow wasn't right, either. A scout clocked his fastball at 78–80 mph in his final three starts in September.

Belcher, who couldn't throw enough strikes in the minors *and* had no future with the A's *and* needed to win a job in spring training *and* was a reluctant closer in early summer *and* needed to shed the label of a six-inning pitcher in late summer, took a 6–2 lead into the ninth inning. The only runs he'd given up came on a two-run home run to Keith Hernandez in the fourth inning.

Lenny Dykstra doubled to start the ninth, Jefferies grounded out, and Hernandez singled home a run. Now it was 6–3. Belcher was removed, and he wasn't happy. Belcher calmly walked to the bat rack, picked out a model of his choosing, slammed it against the dugout steps, and flung it under the bench.

"It was frustrating," Belcher remembered. "Orel carried our club. From what I remember, it was like, 'Jeez, we've come this far. We got beat with our best pitcher on the mound, and now we're facing the prospect of going to New York down two-nothing?' It didn't sit well."

Hershiser walked over, put his arm around Belcher, and tried to calm him down. Hershiser told him, "Don't worry about the ninth, you did your job, you did what you were supposed to do." Belcher was still pissed at himself for giving the Mets a chance. He feared Game 2 would end just like Game 1 did.

Whether the Dodgers wanted to admit it or not, the Mets were in their collective heads. That's what happens when a team beats you 10-of-11 times in the regular season and rips your heart out against your ace and closer in the first game of the playoffs.

Now it was up to Jesse Orosco against his former teammates. Orosco would face Strawberry, lefty on lefty, the exact reason why the Dodgers acquired Orosco. On the third pitch, Strawberry singled to right field.

The tying run was coming up. Were the Mets really going to rally in the ninth? Again? The anxiety level permeated throughout Dodger Stadium and even inside the dugout. What was Lasorda going to do? Would he go back to Howell? Would he stick with Orosco?

Lasorda yanked out Orosco and called on Alejandro Pena to get the final two outs this time. Pena retired Kevin McReynolds, the hitter the Dodgers feared the most in that lineup, on a foul popup. Howard Johnson was more dangerous from the left side, and Pena knew it. He pitched him carefully and ended up walking Johnson.

Now the bases were loaded, and Gary Carter was up—again. The sinking feeling was there in the stomachs, a feeling of *deja vu*. Carter fell behind the night before on curveballs. He wasn't going to fall behind again. He was going to swing early. He swung at the first pitch, hit a line drive to right field, and Marshall caught it to end the game.

After the game, the biggest story for the newspaper men was the newest member of their profession. Before the game, Cone said he was misquoted. After the game, he said it was supposed to be a joke.

"Everything I said in there was meant in a facetious manner," Cone said. "For me to belittle a fine pitcher like Jay Howell isn't right, and it wasn't meant like that. The comments were made after a very emotional game. I take total responsibility. Nothing I can say will justify what was in the paper. But again, they were meant to be facetious."

As for the impact of the column on the game, Cone said four of the hits were "seeing-eye hits…I don't think that newspaper article made those grounders find holes."

In the next day's paper, Cone issued an apology. After consulting with Mets management and veteran players, Cone declared his journalism career was over.

The series was tied 1–1 and headed to New York.

◆ ◆ ◆ ◆

Saturday, October 9, 1988
New York
Dodgers vs. Mets
NLCS Game 3

The Mets were still steamed at the David Cone drama. They weren't happy about what he said and how those words appeared in print. But they were even more upset at the crude and obscene things the Dodgers yelled at Cone from their dugout.

"Sportsmanship is out," was the first sentence in a story in *The New York Post*. The Mets vowed they would get revenge. They had a pretty good idea how to do it. They just had to wait for the right moment.

They would wait through the travel day. They would wait through another day, after rain postponed Game 3 from Friday to Saturday. They would wait until late in Game 3, when the opportunity presented itself.

Because of the rainout, and because of the fragile condition of John Tudor's hip and elbow and shoulder, Orel Hershiser started Game 3 on three days rest. Hershiser considered it a blessing, not a detriment. Two of the shutouts during The Streak came on three days rest. The sinker worked better when he wasn't as rested. Plus, Hershiser was still angry about how Game 1 ended, and he was eager to get back on the mound.

In retrospect, Hershiser thought Game 3 should have been postponed yet another day. The temperature at first pitch was 43 degrees. The wind was blowing at 10 mph. The game started at 12:20 PM in New York, and it was so overcast, it looked like it was already a night game. In the official box score for the game, the field condition is described as "soaked."

Mets owner Nelson Doubleday wanted a night game so the field would have more time to dry out. Doubleday fumed to *Newsday* that television was "screwing the national pastime.... This is the Fall Classic and we have to change things because the networks want to make money off us and off college football and pro football? When do we start making sense? They should come to us and ask us when we are going to play the games. I don't want my guys playing on a soggy field. I don't want a game decided because somebody's outfielder slipped on wet grass. TV shouldn't want it, either."

Hershiser was convinced the only reason the game was played was because it was the playoffs and they needed to fit the game into the schedule. The A's beat the Red Sox that day to go up 3–0, and they were ready for a sweep in Oakland. Hershiser wrote the following in his 1989 book:

"Shea Stadium was so muddy and sloppy it was like playing in a pigsty. The tarp had protected the field before we started, but by the fourth inning it was a like a soup bowl. With the temperature in the forties, I wore long underwear, my long-sleeved sweatshirt, and a dickey. A lot of our guys moaned about having to play at all, but it was the same for both teams. I tried to encourage them, saying that whoever was the toughest was going to win."

Hershiser walked two batters in the first inning. He had trouble with his footing because he was worried that he would slip and fall. He also struggled to get a solid grip on the ball. Pitching coach Ron Perranoski noticed that Hershiser wasn't bending his back enough because his footing was tentative. Hershiser was able to get out of the first inning without any runs allowed.

Kirk Gibson, the native of Michigan, would call it the coldest game he ever played in. He compared it to taking an ice bath for nine innings. The conditions got worse as the game went along. Midway through at-bats, hitters would try to dry their bat by wiping it between their legs or under their arms. The grounds crew worked on the infield between every half-inning, spreading Diamond Dry on the ground to soak up the moisture.

Ron Darling struggled even more than Hershiser. He issued two walks to start the second inning. On a sacrifice bunt, 10-time Gold Glove–winning first baseman Keith Hernandez (he won his 11th in 1988) threw the ball away to score one run. Jeff Hamilton's groundout scored another run.

In the third inning, Sax went back to the blueprint. He singled to right, stole second base, went to third on a slow roller to Darling, and scored on a grounder to second base by Gibson. It was 3–0 Dodgers.

In the bottom of the third, the Mets answered. Gregg Jefferies, who walked in the first inning, singled to center. It was his fifth time reaching base in six plate appearances against Hershiser.

Hernandez crushed a ball to left field that he thought was a home run for sure. But with the wind blowing in, and in the damp conditions, the ball didn't carry. Gibson caught it on the warning track. Strawberry followed with a liner to right, a double that trimmed the Dodgers' lead to 3–1.

In the fifth, the field would nearly impact another play. Mookie Wilson hit a line drive to left field that Gibson pursued. Gibson slipped on the grass, fell to his knees, staggered back up to his feet, and made a diving catch. Gibson would change his shoes after the inning. But they just made bigger divots.

The sixth inning would bring more drama and more problems from the conditions.

Hernandez singled to start the inning. Strawberry singled to left, and Hernandez momentarily stopped at second base, until he saw Gibson bobble the wet ball. Hernandez started running again, slipped on the muddy field, stumbled on his way to third base, and fell on his chest. Ultimately, he tried crawling to third base and was easily tagged out.

The out proved to be crucial. Kevin McReynolds reached on a throwing error by third baseman Jeff Hamilton, another casualty of the poor field conditions. Howard Johnson hit into a fielder's choice for what should have ended the inning.

Instead, Carter singled to right to score a run. It was 3–2. Wally Backman hit a grounder between first and second. As Hershiser sprinted over to cover first base, he saw first baseman Mickey Hatcher just barely get a glove on the ball. If he missed the ball entirely, Sax fields it and throws out Backman. But by touching the ball, it slowed down too much. Everybody was safe. Game 3 was tied 3–3.

In the eighth, Roger McDowell struck out Mike Marshall and John Shelby. Scioscia hit a slow comebacker. McDowell backhanded the ball, slipped on the field, and threw the ball into right field. The field conditions were officially a joke.

Hamilton reached on an infield single. Then Mike Davis pinch hit for Alfredo Griffin and drew a walk. It wouldn't be the last time that month that Davis would hit for Griffin and draw a walk. The bases were loaded.

Lefty Danny Heep pinch hit for Hershiser. Davey Johnson countered with Randy Myers, a lefty. Lasorda countered that move, hitting Mike Sharperson for Heep. Sharperson worked a seven-pitch walk, forcing in a run. The Dodgers led 4–3.

Lasorda needed six outs to secure this one-run victory. Lasorda handed the ball to Jay Howell, who pitched two innings 15 times in the regular season, eight times getting a save. The first batter Howell faced was Kevin McReynolds.

The game was three hours old, and the weather had gotten worse. It was colder. A steady drizzle had fallen the entire game, and this was after a day and night of hard rain. The field was a marsh. Howell's first three pitches were balls. The next two pitches were out of the strike zone, but McReynolds swung and fouled them off.

On the ABC telecast, there was mention of a black spot on Howell's glove. Mets first-base coach Bill Robinson told manager Davey Johnson that Howell was tugging on the glove between pitches. Johnson waited another pitch, saw the same tugging, and approached home-plate umpire Joe West about what he saw.

Sportsmanship, indeed, was out.

West went to the crew chief, Harry Wendelstedt, and the two walked to the mound to see Howell's glove. Second baseman Steve Sax, first baseman Tracy Woodson, and catcher Rick Dempsey went to the mound to find out what was going on. The Dodgers' dugout was clueless. They thought maybe Howell went to his mouth, and a ball would be called, thereby leading to a McReynolds walk.

"When they came out to check, I walked to the mound," said Woodson, now the head coach at Valparaiso University. "I knew I wanted to coach and manage. I walked in a lot. If Perranoski came out to the mound, I would always go out there. I wanted to hear what was being said, and I wanted to learn. I wanted to be involved. [The pine tar] was on there. Wendelstedt was using his thumb to rub and see what was on there."

Wendelstedt and West ejected Howell for having a foreign substance on his glove. Howell offered no protest as he walked off the mound.

"The place went nuts," Woodson said. "I remember seeing Jay Howell's face. He was just shocked. I didn't know anything about it."

Sax added, "It was flagrant. It wasn't happenstance that a bunch of pine tar ended up on his glove."

In the 2001 book *True Blue*, Howell said the following: "Guys have been using it for a million years. Most hitters don't give a shit. They don't care about pine tar. They don't like spitballs. Anyway, I'm pitching to Kevin McReynolds. Then Davey Johnson comes walking out of their dugout. Davey says to Harry Wendelstedt, 'Take a look at his glove.' He turns around and throws me out of the game. I said, 'Harry, what the fuck are you doing? Why don't you just take the glove? I'll get another glove.' But it's too late. The fans are going bananas in New York. And I go into the dugout and I'm thinking, *This is bullshit. David Cone is using a black glove. Doc Gooden uses a black glove. Are you kidding me?* There's no mystery why guys use a black glove."

The rowdy crowd at Shea Stadium chanted "L-A Cheats! L-A Cheats!" Sitting next to owner Peter O'Malley and their wives, hearing the abuse from Mets fans, general manager Fred Claire steamed.

The *Philadelphia Inquirer* reported that, during the commotion after the ejection, one Mets relief pitcher hurried into the clubhouse and changed gloves.

Alejandro Pena was forced to enter the game cold, without properly warming up, which enraged the Dodgers even more. Pena's first pitch was a ball, so McReynolds was aboard. McReynolds was forced out on a bad bunt by Howard Johnson, who made up for it by stealing second base. Carter flew out for the second out—and maybe Pena could somehow escape trouble.

Backman had other ideas. The second baseman crushed a double to right-center and the game was tied. Pinch hitter Lenny Dykstra walked, and that was it for Pena.

Next came Orosco. Mookie Wilson singled home the go-ahead run. Orosco hit Jefferies with a pitch to load the bases, and he walked Hernandez to force home another run. Ricky Horton entered the game next, and Strawberry singled home two more runs. It was a five-run inning and an 8–4 Mets lead.

The Dodgers went quietly in the ninth—against David Cone, of all people—to end a 3-hour, 44-minute game that wasn't anything resembling a masterpiece, but a classic for sure.

The Dodgers kept the clubhouse closed for 25 minutes after the game, 15 minutes longer than the usual 10-minute cooling-off period. When the doors opened, Howell knew what was awaiting him. He answered every question. He admitted putting pine tar on his glove but denied it was to gain an unfair advantage by making the ball move.

"The resin [bag] doesn't help on a cold day like this, and the ball gets so slippery you can't even grip it," Howell said that day. "All the [pine tar] is there for is to help me grip the ball. I regret all this. But I wasn't doing it to make the ball move any funny way."

That's not what the Mets thought.

Remember, the Mets were convinced that Mike Scott was scuffing the baseball during the 1986 playoffs. They had what they thought was evidence, a bunch of balls with scuff marks, but Scott was never caught with any foreign substances.

Remember too, this was a time when players were getting caught cheating regularly. In 1987 alone, Twins pitcher Joe Niekro was caught with an emery board in his back pocket, Phillies pitcher Kevin Gross was found with a strip of sandpaper glued to the heel of his glove, cork was found in the broken bat of Astros outfielder Billy Hatcher (who claimed it was pitcher Dave Smith's bat), and Howard Johnson's bat was confiscated twice (but never found illegal) after public accusations by Cardinals manager Whitey Herzog.

The tip on Howell originated from a butcher shop in Covington, Tennessee. That's where Tucker Ashford, a former teammate of Howell in 1982 with Triple A Columbus in the Yankees organization, was working when he observed how dark Howell's cap was in Game 1.

Ashford, a former minor league coach in the Mets' organization, didn't remember Howell throwing a curveball that broke as much as it did in Game 1. Ashford suspected that Howell was using pine tar, or some foreign substance, so he called Mets director of minor league operations Steve Schryver, who relayed the information to Davey Johnson.

"Certain pitchers have certain reputations," Johnson said.

"We knew Howell had a great breaking ball, and this kind of confirms that he had a little help," Carter said.

Howell's best defense came from Keith Hernandez, an unlikely source. "I feel badly for him because I don't think he was trying to make the ball do anything. He was just trying to get a grip on it. If the Dodgers would lose their best reliever now, that just wouldn't be fair."

Fred Claire didn't care about Howell's intent. A rule was a rule. The commissioner's office once called Claire, annoyed that the Dodgers placed more calls than any other team in the league about rules, and was concerned that Claire was trying to find loopholes in the rules. In Claire's mind, you went right up to the edge of the rulebook and looked for every edge possible. But you didn't cross the line. Ever. Claire was livid in the stands but needed to hold his composure. Once the game was over, Claire stormed into Lasorda's office.

"You bet I was pissed," Claire said 25 years later. "I wasn't quite sure what happened. I went into the clubhouse and said, 'You get Jay in here. You get Perranoski in here. I don't know what the fuck happened, but whatever happened, I want it declared exactly what happened. We don't cheat. Whatever the fuck happened, nobody better say anything other than exactly what happened. Period.' I was pissed. I'm still pissed today."

◆ ◆ ◆ ◆

Sunday, October 9, 1988
New York
Dodgers vs. Mets
NLCS Game 4

This was why the Dodgers acquired John Tudor. This was why they traded Pedro Guerrero. They acquired John Tudor to face the big, bad New York Mets—who were more vulnerable against lefties—in playoff games like this.

In the regular season, Tudor did what he was supposed to do. In nine starts, he posted a 2.41 ERA down the stretch. He went 4–3, and the team went 6–3. Tudor didn't join his new teammates in the champagne celebration that night in San Diego. He'd only been there a little over a month. He thought it was their celebration, not his, because they were going to win the division no matter what he did.

The playoffs were different. Tudor knew that's why he was acquired—to take the place of Fernando Valenzuela in the rotation. If he did his job and there was another celebration, Tudor would partake.

Tudor was starting Game 4 on eight days of rest. His last outing was September 30, and he lasted 1⅓ innings until the spasms in his hip ended his night. The start before that, he pitched just four innings. He had no idea how his arm and hip would respond until he was out there.

But now the Dodgers needed Tudor more than ever. On their 24-man playoff roster, they carried nine pitchers. Jay Howell was suspended for three games, so now they were down to eight pitchers.

Howell talked to reporters in street clothes flanked by Lasorda, Perranoski, and Hershiser for moral support. Howell felt the suspension was too severe, again maintained that he wasn't trying to cheat, and then headed back to the team hotel to watch the game on TV.

Kirk Gibson, Tudor, and a few others wrote the initials "JH" on their jerseys. The Dodgers felt the suspension was too severe. National League president Bart Giamatti weighed the pros and cons and wanted to make sure Howell was available for a possible Game 7.

Lasorda gave one of his trademark fire-and-brimstone pregame speeches. Lasorda said they were a team of character, of strength. Their backs were against the wall, but they would bounce back just like they did all year. He told them they were going to play with heart, with determination.

"We're gonna win this ballgame," Lasorda exclaimed, his voice rising with each word, "with or without Jay Howell."

As the meeting ended, Hershiser went up to Lasorda and told him, "I'll be your Jay Howell tonight." Lasorda was so emotional, he was already on the verge of tears. Lasorda didn't know if he should hug Hershiser, or tell him to fuhgetaboutit.

Game 4 started at 8:20 PM in New York. The field had a full 24 hours to dry out. The rain was gone, but it was still cold.

In the first inning, Steve Sax went back to the script on how to beat the Mets and Dwight Gooden. His slow roller to third base took a bad hop on Gregg Jefferies, and Sax was safe on an infield single.

Runners were safe 56-of-67 times stealing bases off the Gooden-Carter combo. Gooden threw over to first repeatedly. Gooden tried a slidestep and missed for a ball. Gooden went back to his high leg kick, and Sax stole second base. After spending so much attention on Sax, Gooden walked Mickey Hatcher on four pitches.

Gibson hit a chopper to the right side. Both runners advanced 90'. Marshall struck out on three fastballs, chasing a couple out of the strike zone.

John Shelby was 1-for-10 in the series. Gooden threw a fastball that jammed him on the hands. Shelby fought it off just enough, dropping a soft looper into right field. It was another classic Shelby hit—one of those that was important but not so important that he'd get bombarded by reporters afterward. The Dodgers led 2–0.

Tudor looked good for three innings, even with a fastball in the 80–82 mph range. He allowed just two hits, both singles, and two over the minimum.

It all changed in the fourth inning. Hernandez sent a lazy curveball off the end of his bat into right field for a single. Tudor challenged Strawberry with an inside fastball. Strawberry extended his hands and hit a line shot over the right-field fence. Strawberry was given a curtain call by the fans at Shea Stadium. The sound of the ball leaving the bat was impressive. After the next pitch, ABC would have replayed the home run with the sound off the bat, but the network didn't have time.

On that next pitch, Tudor threw an inside fastball to McReynolds, who promptly hit a solo home run into the left-field pavilion. Glenn Frey's "The Heat Is On" blared from the stadium jukebox. It was 3–2 Mets.

Tudor survived the rest of that inning and the fifth inning. McReynolds opened the sixth with a double down the left-field line, a ball that took an awkward hop over the glove of Jeff Hamilton. Carter was up next, and he hit a drive over Shelby's head in center. Shelby took an awkward route to the ball, turning the wrong way. The ball sliced back to his left. Carter slid head-first into third base.

It was 4–2 Mets, and that was it for Tudor. Brian Holton was super nervous before his first playoff appearance. He sang, "You take the high road, and I'll take the low road" to calm himself down. It worked. Holton cleaned up the sixth without allowing a run.

Ricky Horton, who had otherwise been a disappointment since his trade from the Cardinals and who kept the popular Tim Crews off the playoff roster, pitched a scoreless seventh and eighth.

Meanwhile, Gooden was masterful. Entering the ninth, he'd allowed just one hit after the first inning and struck out eight. He was three outs from his first postseason victory, which would give the Mets a commanding 3–1 lead in the series.

The crowd restarted the "Beat L.A." chant. John Shelby fell behind the count 0–2. That's never a comfortable position against anybody, especially Doc Gooden. Shelby felt remarkably calm and relaxed. He thought Gooden would try to make him a chase a pitch out of the strike zone. He just wanted to make contact, do anything to get on base.

Shelby kept fouling pitches off to stay alive. On the eighth pitch, Gooden missed high, and Shelby was on base with a walk. Shelby walked 44 times that year, and that was a career-high. Lasorda once said, "You couldn't walk Shelby intentionally. I used to tell him they could throw a paper plate from the stands and he'd swing at it."

Gooden turned his head backward in dismay after issuing the walk to Shelby. Dodgers coach Joe Amalfitano looked at Gooden's face after the walk and will never forget what he saw. Gooden realized that he'd walked Shelby, that he'd put the tying run at the plate, and he was out of sorts for a few moments. Next up was Mike Scioscia.

"Doc is throwing hard," Scioscia remembered. "It's like he found that extra gear, much like [Justin] Verlander does now. He's really bringing it. I look and Keith Hernandez is holding John on. Wally Backman always shaded up the middle when Doc was pitching. I looked and said, 'Oh my God, look at that hole.' I know he's going to throw a fastball. I don't want to be late on it. I want to get the bat out. If I miss-hit it, that's got to be a base hit. I just looked fastball, got the head out, made sure I was trying to hit it through that hole, and got a little bit of extension on it."

Indeed, the first pitch—Gooden's 127th of the night—was a fastball. Scioscia took a mighty rip and hit a low line drive to right field. It had just enough backspin to keep rising and give it a chance. Off the bat, all Scioscia thought was, *If this hits the wall and I don't make it to second base, Tommy is going to chew my ass out.* "I was running as hard as I could."

Strawberry could only watch. The ball cleared the wall, just barely, and the game was tied.

"There were 50-plus-thousand people there; they were going crazy, screaming the whole inning," Scioscia said, on the 10-year anniversary. "And as the ball went out of the park, it got so quiet that I could hear my spikes digging through the dirt when I was running. That's how quiet it got. It was eerie—to just have 50,000 people get so quiet. That's something I'll never forget."

It was pandemonium in the Dodgers' dugout. Scioscia had three home runs that year, one since June 27, and 36 total over his nine-year career. But the game was only tied. Fitting for his personality and his future as a manager, Scioscia said, "It felt great. But now we need to play defense. We had to keep going."

The Dodgers would put two more runners on base, with one out, but Randy Myers retired Sax and Hatcher to end the threat.

Alejandro Pena pitched a scoreless ninth, 10th, and 11th inning without a hit. Pena walked Mookie Wilson in the 10th, but Scioscia threw him out trying to steal second base. Pena walked two more in the 11th, but he retired Howard Johnson to end that threat.

In the 12th, Franklin Stubbs was in the on-deck circle to pinch hit for Pena. Only two pitchers—Tim Leary and Jesse Orosco—remained because Game 5 starter Tim Belcher was back at the team hotel, getting ready for a noon start the next day.

Hershiser went to Perranoski and volunteered to pitch in relief.

"Are you kidding?" Perranoski said. "After seven innings in the cold yesterday?"

Hershiser reminded his pitching coach that his arm didn't get stiff until the second day after a start. He was used to starting and relieving, after all those years of doing both in the minors. He'd done it earlier in the year, at Chicago, when the team was also short on arms.

Perranoski didn't answer. He didn't want to think about hurting Hershiser, about asking him to do something like that. Hershiser said he was going to the bullpen. He'd be available if needed. Perranoski still didn't answer him.

Hershiser was wearing only a T-shirt and windbreaker. He went into the clubhouse and put on a uniform and a cup.

Orel III was in the visitor's clubhouse. He was so cold, he'd bought a Mets sweatshirt to stay warmer, which he concealed under his raincoat. When he saw his son entering the clubhouse, father asked the son, "What are you doing?"

"I'm going to the bullpen," Orel IV told Orel III.

"You're going *where*?!"

Dad wasn't happy. His younger son, Gordie, a Dodgers minor leaguer, had already undergone two elbow operations. He would give the minor leagues one more year before retiring. Dad was always worried about the number of innings his sons were throwing.

"Someone is going to hit a homer, and I might have to pitch," Orel said.

Sax grounded to third on the first pitch. Stubbs struck out looking. Gibson stepped in the batter's box, mired in a 1-for-16 slump in the series. He hadn't hit the ball out of the infield. Gibson knew he'd been terrible in the series. He was disappointed. His legs were killing him. His confidence was shaken. But it was another test, another opportunity to defeat The Beast.

Gibson swung and missed at a first-pitch sinker. The second pitch was another sinker, but this one was flat and over the plate. Gibson pounced on it, blasting the ball 430' to that giant scoreboard in right field. It clanked off a potato-chip sign with the tagline, "Simply Delicious."

At the Grand Hyatt in Manhattan, Belcher and his wife screamed so loud in celebration, hotel security called and requested they keep the noise down. Other guests on the floor had complained about the cheering.

Hatcher pumped his fist, going crazy in the dugout. Lasorda greeted Gibson with a big hug. It was the first home run Roger McDowell had given up since April 29—a stretch of 99 innings.

"Nice prediction," somebody said to Hershiser in the clubhouse. Hershiser barely reacted. He didn't watch the replay. The uniform was on. He hustled to the bullpen and went into Bulldog mode.

Bullpen coach Mark Cresse asked, "What are you doing here?" Hershiser told him he was getting ready. Cresse called to the dugout, asking Perranoski for permission. Hershiser started to loosen up his body, just to see how his arm felt, so he could give them a legitimate answer.

Tim Leary, a starter most of the year, was the first pitcher Lasorda would have used if Tudor broke down physically early in the game. Now, Leary was trying to close out the game in the 12th inning. Mackey Sasser started the inning with a single to right after a tense eight-pitch duel. Orosco was the only pitcher in the bullpen getting loose.

Lasorda paced the dugout. Ron Darling pinch ran for Sasser. Lee Mazzilli pinch hit for Roger McDowell, and he was asked to lay down a bunt. Maz hadn't laid down a successful sac bunt in three years. Mazzilli fouled two pitches off and then singled up the middle. Here come the Mets; it was *déjà vu* all over again.

And here came Gregg Jefferies again. Lasorda paced the dugout more. Inexplicably, Davey Johnson asked Jefferies to bunt again. He'd asked Jefferies to bunt in the 10th, and he popped out. Johnson asked the kid again, and Jefferies fouled it off. Johnson then came to his senses. When you bat .360 in the minors, nobody asks you to bunt. Johnson took off the bunt sign, and Jefferies flied out to Gibson in left field.

Two lefties were due up, Hernandez and Strawberry. Lasorda knew he needed to bring in Orosco to face the two lefties. This is why they acquired Orosco. This was his job. Perranoski reminded Lasorda that nobody was left after Orosco. Lasorda went to Orosco anyway.

It was 10 minutes before 1:00 AM.

Orosco entered the game, and the fans at Shea Stadium were all over him. They loved him in 1986, hated him in 1987, and now were ready for Orosco to implode. All of the Dodgers' infielders said something to Orosco after his eight warm-up pitches.

The first pitch was a slider that crossed up Dempsey and nearly went to the backstop. Ball one.

"Is that Hershiser in the bullpen?" a stunned Al Michaels said on ABC.

Dempsey went to the mound to make sure they were clear on the signs. During the delay, Hershiser threw a couple pitches, adjusted his cap, and gave a reassuring nod of his head.

Hernandez swung and missed at a fastball, evening the count at 1–1. Another fastball was fouled back. Then a fastball missed inside, and the count was even again at 2–2. Mickey Hatcher paced in the dugout, too nervous to sit. Lasorda was remarkably still, hands in his jacket.

Orosco missed with a curveball. The count was 3–2. With each ball that Orosco threw to Hernandez, the crowd screamed a little louder. Orosco went to another curveball and missed again. Ball four. The bases were loaded.

Now it was Strawberry. Ball one. Lasorda sprinted out of the dugout. Lasorda rarely visited the mound. Perranoski made almost all the pitching changes. This wasn't a pitching change. This was Lasorda delivering a message to Orosco—equal parts encouragement and four-letter threats. Lip readers noted the message began with, "What the fuck is wrong with you?"

Lasorda returned to the dugout and told Perranoski, "Do you think the Lord will make it possible for this guy to strike out or pop up? Because if he does, I'm bringin' in the Bulldog."

Orosco went back to his fastball, and Strawberry fouled it off. He dropped in a beauty of a curveball for a 1–2 count. Another curveball was popped up to Sax on the infield. Two outs.

Still though, the bases were loaded. McReynolds was at the plate. The hitter the Dodgers feared most entering the series. The hitter who was slumping until his home run and double earlier in the game.

"Go get the Bulldog," Lasorda said to Perranoski.

"Tommy!" Perranoski said. "The guy pitched seven innings last night! What if they tie the game? How long can he go? He's all we've got!"

"They're not gonna tie this game," Lasorda said. "I'm puttin' the pot of gold on the Bulldog. Go get him!"

Perranoski left the dugout, and Hershiser saw him walking toward the mound. This was what he'd volunteered to do. The adrenaline shot through his body. Hershiser threw two final warm-up pitches and came into the game. It was just like Wrigley Field back in May when Hershiser entered the game in extra innings after Gibson had homered for the lead.

For a brief moment, Hershiser thought to himself, *What have I gotten myself into?* Then he snapped out of it, telling himself, *Don't think like that. You have one job, and only one job, and that's the next pitch.*

From the ABC booth, Al Michaels noted the Dodgers' predicament. "This is the seventh man on what's now an eight-man pitching staff," Michaels said. "The eighth is back at the hotel." Tim McCarver declared, "This is truly all or nothing at all."

Sax, of course, was pumped. "I thought it was fantastic," Sax reflected. "This is exactly what our team needed. Our team needed to keep Orel on the field as much as we could. When you have a starting pitcher who comes out of the bullpen, you just love that. Not a lot of guys will do that. You love that kind of attitude. Our team was a fighting type of team. What a fucking team, you know? That's what we were about. Orel comes into a game like that. It picks people up."

Belcher watched from the hotel room, as stunned as anybody. He received a call earlier in the night from the traveling secretary and was told that he might be summoned from his hotel room to the ballpark if they were short on pitchers.

"I think at some point," Belcher recalled, "they said, 'Forget the idea of bringing him back to the stadium. We'll figure it out as we go. If we have to use a position player, we will.' I don't think there's any question in my mind that Orel would have pitched another 3–4–5 innings if he had to."

A fan held up a sign that said "Orel Who?" It sounded like the entire Shea Stadium crowd was chanting, "O-O-O-O-O-rel, O-O-O-O-O-rel." Hershiser loved it. He used the chant to get worked up. Hershiser looked into the Mets dugout. He wanted to see their faces as he entered the game on zero days rest. He rearranged the dirt for his landing foot. He paced on the grass a little, feeling the moment, thinking of the dangers, working himself into a frenzy.

"This is a scenario that you could not imagine," Al Michaels told ABC's audience. "You sorta had a feeling the Howell suspension would come into play, if the game was close. But never did you imagine in your wildest dreams that Hershiser would come in and pitch."

Michaels mentioned that McReynolds was 7-for-41—a .171 career average—against Hershiser. Jim Palmer quickly added, "Those numbers don't reflect Hershiser threw 110 pitches yesterday." Over the loudspeaker, U2's "I Still Haven't Found What I'm Looking For" was played.

Lasorda paced the dugout like crazy. He was a nervous wreck and scared to death. He was putting the entire game on this one at-bat. But it wasn't just this game. The series was at risk. Hell, Hershiser's career was at risk.

Lasorda prayed. *Lord, I'll tell ya somethin'. Let Bulldog get this guy out, and I'll never ask ya for anything again.*

In the clubhouse, Mike Scioscia couldn't watch. He'd been replaced in the 11th inning, and he was now watching on television. Sure, he was nervous about the game's outcome. But he was more concerned about Hershiser and didn't want to watch a teammate wreck his career.

If you thought Dad was concerned, just imagine how Mom felt. Back in Los Angeles, Mildred Hershiser watched the game on TV. When she saw her son entering the game, she could no longer contain her emotions.

"It's not fair!" she cried out, tears running down her face. "It's not fair! His arm is going to fall off!"

In the outfield, Gibson, Shelby, and Marshall talked to one another as Hershiser made his final eight warm-up pitches. They all agreed to move a few steps toward home plate. They'd rather have McReynolds hit one over their head than get beat by another blooper.

"Lasorda's worst nightmare is for this game to end up tied," Michaels said. "Well, that's his second worst nightmare. You know what I mean."

Hershiser knew his plan against McReynolds. He wouldn't throw a curveball. He wouldn't risk the wild pitch. He wouldn't throw a sinker. He was going back to schoolyard ball. He was going to throw every pitch as hard as he possibly could. He was going to be, as Howell liked to say, a "brain-dead heaver."

The first brain-dead fastball was fouled straight back. Hershiser rubbed up a new baseball then asked for another one.

"He worked seven innings yesterday on a brutally cold afternoon," Michaels said.

The second pitch was a brain-dead fastball that missed outside for a ball. Hershiser's adrenaline was flowing so hard, the ABC radar gun had his fastballs at 94 and 95 mph. Normally, he's between 90–92 mph. The crowd chanted, "Let's go Mets," over and over.

The third brain-dead fastball tailed inside on McReynolds' hands. McReynolds broke his bat. It was a little looper, shallow center field. It was just like Game 1.

Shelby charged as fast as he could. This time, the ball held up. Shelby didn't need to dive. He reached down, made a catch at his knees, and reached the glove back into the air for dramatic effect. Sax jumped into the air in celebration.

"I knew I had to come in, and I had a good bead on it," Shelby recalled. "I just had to catch the ball."

"When you write the story of this game, where in the world do you begin?" Michaels asked the TV audience.

Hershiser had done it. The series was tied 2–2. The Dodgers reacted like they'd just won the series. Hershiser thrust his fist in dramatic fashion. Lasorda hugged Hershiser. Lasorda ran out to the outfielders and hugged Gibson. Let's face it, everybody was hugging everybody.

On the way up the ramp from the dugout to the clubhouse, Lasorda pumped both arms over his head. He yelled as loud he could, for everyone to hear.

"What a fucking team! What a fucking team! What a fucking team! What a fucking team! What a fucking team!"

Game 5 would start in less than 11 hours.

◆ ◆ ◆ ◆

Monday, October 10, 1988
New York
Dodgers vs. Mets
NLCS Game 5

Jay Howell watched Game 4 from his hotel room with his wife, Alison. Crank callers found out his hotel room and called to heckle him, pour more salt in the wounds. Normally, they'd have taken the phone off the hook. But they were awaiting another phone call.

Late that night, the call arrived. Alison's father, Otto Quale, died of cancer. Otto knew he was going to die. He never let his daughter and son-in-law know how bad his condition was. He loved Jay Howell like his own son and lived vicariously through his major league career. In his will, Otto arranged for his own memorial service to take place in November, just in case the Dodgers were in the World Series. Otto didn't want his funeral affecting Howell or the team.

Jay and Alison Howell never got the chance to say goodbye to Otto Quale. The only people who knew about his death were Tommy Lasorda and Fred Claire.

Howell's name was all over the newspapers. He wanted to appeal his decision and wanted to explain his motivation to National League president Bart Giamatti. He didn't want people to think it was sandpaper, that he was a cheater for life. An informal hearing expedited the process. Giamatti cut a game off the suspension, making Howell eligible to pitch in Game 6.

Giamatti told Howell, "You'll be in the headlines for a couple more weeks, and somebody else is going to take over in a big way, let me tell you. You're not going to make headlines for long, I can assure you."

Howell didn't realize what that meant at the time. But a few months later, when Howell heard that Pete Rose was being investigated for betting on baseball, he knew what Giamatti meant.

Tim Belcher, after watching Game 4 from his hotel room, was one of the most rested players on the field for Game 5. It showed as he retired the first nine Mets hitters he faced.

"I think that they played late and I was back at the hotel gave me some of an advantage," Belcher recalled. "The other thing was, remember, I was still a rookie. Our bullpen was spent. In the back of my mind, I thought I need a heck of an effort. I needed to pitch late in the game to give us a chance. It was a pretty pressure-packed game. After Game 2 was under my belt, I was feeling pretty confident."

Sid Fernandez, another one of those former Dodgers who was traded away for a left-handed reliever to replace Steve Howe, started Game 5 for the Mets. Scoreless in the fourth inning, Gibson lined out, Marshall singled to center, Shelby drew another rare walk, and Rick Dempsey doubled down the left-field line—just inches fair—to score two runs. Alfredo Griffin doubled him home, and it was 3–0 Dodgers.

Sax started the fifth inning with a single. Mickey Hatcher also singled to right. Next up was Kirk Gibson.

It was 13 hours after his dramatic home run put the Dodgers ahead in the 12th inning of Game 4. Gibson was running on virtually no sleep. He returned to his hotel room about 4:00 AM and went to bed but couldn't sleep. He wanted to play Game 5 immediately. He got up, packed his suitcase, and tried to fall back asleep. He didn't sleep much before heading back to the ballpark.

Gibson was thinking home run again. He tried to jack the first pitch he saw from Sid Fernandez, took what he admitted was "a stupid swing," and fouled the ball off his foot. Gibson stepped out of the box, scolded himself for trying to hit a home run, and just tried to hit the ball hard somewhere.

On a 2–1 pitch, Gibson pounced on a Fernandez mistake and hit it hard somewhere. So hard, in fact, it went over the right-field fence for a home run. The score was 6–0 Dodgers.

This home run trot was more mellow, until he reached home plate. Gibson body-slammed with the equally excitable Sax and nearly separated Mike Marshall's shoulder with the force of his high five.

Of course the Mets would rally, and of course they wouldn't wait long. Johnson and Backman singled. Dykstra hit a three-run homer off Belcher. The lead was down to 6–3. Belcher regrouped. He retired the heart of the Mets lineup, in order, in the sixth inning. He shook off a leadoff single in the seventh.

In the eighth, Dykstra doubled to right, and Jefferies singled yet again. The lead was down to 6–4, and the Dodgers' bullpen would be tested again. This time, Lasorda went to the seldom-used Ricky Horton. Pena wasn't available after those three innings yesterday. Orosco was barely getting anybody out. Leary wasn't effective the night before, and he needed to start Game 6.

Horton faced the two lefties. This was why Claire traded for him in late August, this exact scenario. Horton did half his job. He struck out Hernandez, and then Strawberry singled, making it runners at first and second with one out.

Lasorda turned to Brian Holton, whose performances were so important and so rarely made headlines all year. But after Holton, who was left? Incredibly, Hershiser was warming up in the bullpen *again*.

Luck helped end the Mets' threat. McReynolds hit a slow roller that neither Hamilton nor Griffin could reach. Jefferies saw the ball rolling the same direction he was running and tried to jump over it. The ball hit the lip of the grass, took a higher bounce than Jefferies was expecting, and nicked his left cleat. Jefferies was out.

Instead of a possible one-run game, there was still a two-run cushion and now two outs. Carter followed with a deep drive to left field, but it was not deep enough. Gibson caught it at the warning track.

In the top of the ninth, Gibson singled with two outs. Gibson was looking for one more insurance run. Considering the status of his knees and hamstrings, and the score, it was probably not the time to push the envelope. Gibson only knew one way to play the game, though. Gibson took off for second base, looking to manufacture one more run.

The pitch from McDowell was in the dirt and got away from Carter. No throw was even attempted. Gibson didn't look back. He didn't know he could ease into the bag. As always, he slid hard into second base. The infield dirt was hard from all that rain. He actually felt a pain, a pop, in his final strides.

Gibson knew he was leaving the game right away. The 50,000 fans at Shea Stadium cheered his departure. It wasn't a classy move at Shea Stadium, but Gibson took it as a compliment. The injury was called an aggravated hamstring below his left knee.

In hindsight, the risk of stealing second base looked even worse. Marshall tripled to right-center. Pinch runner Jose Gonzalez scored easily. The score was 7–4.

Holton retired the Mets in order in the ninth inning. By far, that was Holton's No. 1 thrill of his baseball career. In the clubhouse, Hershiser thanked Holton for getting the final four outs and saving his arm.

The Dodgers were going back to L.A. leading 3–2, but the status of Gibson was unknown. He received a cortisone injection, said some prayers, and told reporters not to count him out. When it was suggested he took an unnecessary risk—something that even the Mets' Hernandez said wasn't smart—Gibson bristled.

"We were only two runs ahead, and it wasn't like the Mets were laying down," Gibson said that day. "They keep coming at you every inning. They weren't conceding the game, but they weren't paying attention to me. I had just beat out the infield hit, my leg felt fine. I didn't feel I was jeopardizing it by running. I wanted the other run and made up my mind to go. I'm sure they're sitting over there thinking I'm a dumb shit, but this injury is actually in a little different area than where I had felt it earlier. Besides, I can't change my style. I have to play aggressively."

Even through the lens of history, Gibson doesn't regret that stolen base.

"I didn't take it for granted that we had enough runs to win," Gibson said. "Shit happens. We were almost down 3–1. Now we're about to go up 3–2. You go. It's time to go. It's not time to say you've got enough runs. It's full go."

♦ ♦ ♦ ♦

Tuesday, October 11, 1988
Los Angeles
Mets vs. Dodgers
NLCS Game 6

David Cone was starting for the Mets. It seemed like an eternity since his newspaper career ended. He was glad the focus was just on baseball once again, called Game 6 the biggest start of his life, and was more worried about a suddenly potent Dodgers lineup than the bench jockeying he endured in Game 2. Davey Johnson gave him the option of traveling to Los Angeles ahead of the team to get more rest. Cone declined because he wanted to be with his teammates.

Tim Leary was starting for the Dodgers. An ineffective September pushed him to the bullpen at the start of the series. Leary understood. His arm was fatigued. He'd thrown a full Winter League season and then 228⅔ innings in the regular season. His brief relief appearance in Game 4 didn't go well. He was facing the team that originally drafted him. Ron Darling was his former roommate, and Wally Backman was his minor league teammate.

Orel Hershiser was not starting or relieving for the Dodgers. Hershiser started Game 1, started Game 3, pitched in relief in Game 4, and warmed up in Game 5. Hershiser volunteered to pitch Game 6 in relief. Lasorda said, "No chance." Hershiser was being saved for Game 7. "He's crazy, just crazy," Lasorda said. "No way he pitches. I'll tell Jamie [his wife] not to let him out of the house."

If it's possible for a game's tone to get set by the National Anthem, this was it. Saxophonist Kenny G played an over-styled National Anthem that clocked at more than two minutes—the over-under for Super Bowl National Anthems is usually 1:34—and at times didn't sound like the National Anthem.

Saxophone critic Steve Sax declared, "It was the worst I've ever heard, the absolute worst. It was terrible, fucking terrible."

Mike Marshall agreed, "It was a disgrace to America."

♦ ♦ ♦

Kirk Gibson, implausibly, was back in the starting lineup. The hamstring wasn't close to 100 percent, it was maybe 50 percent, but Gibson was going to play anyway. The decision was made about 30 minutes before first pitch.

In a season where Gibson could do little wrong, one of his biggest mistakes came in the first inning of Game 6.

David Cone told reporters before leaving for New York that he doesn't get nervous, he doesn't feel pressure. Then he started Game 6 by walking Steve Sax on four pitches. Then he threw two more balls to Mickey Hatcher.

Pitching coach Mel Stottlemyre, catcher Gary Carter, first baseman Keith Hernandez, and second baseman Wally Backman all came to the mound. "He was nervous," Stottlemyre said. "I could see it on his face. I could see he was tense and over-keyed up. He didn't say anything. I said, 'I know you're nervous. Try to relax, step off and throw to first twice, three times if necessary, to get loose.'"

Carter said he tried to settle Cone down.

Hernandez said he tried to pump Cone up.

Backman said he was trying to build Cone up, in a calming way.

After getting four different pieces of advice, Cone followed the advice of his pitching coach. He threw over to first base. In the process, he stumbled and almost fell down. Then he threw to first base without stumbling or almost falling down.

Cone threw home again and not only missed for ball three, it was a wild pitch that advanced Sax to second base. Cone was melting down in the Los Angeles heat. He finally threw a strike, then another ball, to put Hatcher on first base.

"Carter and Hernandez were telling me to sit back on my back leg, stop lunging," Cone said after the game. "But it's real hard to do when your heart is jumping, and at that point, all I wanted in the world was to throw a strike."

Cone got the world. He threw a strike to Gibson. Then Gibson did what Stottlemyre, Carter, Hernandez, and Backman couldn't do—he calmed down Cone.

Gibson, inexplicably, tried to bunt for a base hit on the next pitch. Cone was struggling to throw strikes. Gibson could barely run. Gibson had homered twice in his previous five at-bats. Yet, for some reason, Gibson tried to bunt. He bunted the ball right into Cone's arms.

"Oh my gosh," Carter said, "that was a bonus for us."

Marshall flew out to left field. Shelby struck out swinging. The threat was squashed. Including those two outs, Cone retired 13 of the next 14 batters.

By the time the Dodgers put a runner on second base in the fifth inning, the Mets took a 4–0 lead from Leary.

Mickey Hatcher got a run back in the fifth, an RBI single that scored relief pitcher Brian Holton (who got a rare at-bat and singled, after going 0-for-10 in the regular season). The lead was 4–1, but not for long. Dykstra doubled to chase Holton in the sixth, and Hernandez singled off Ricky Horton for a 5–1 lead.

That was all Cone needed. He allowed five hits, all singles. He walked one, after those two walks to start the game. He struck out six. He threw 120 pitches in the 5–1 complete-game victory.

"Gibson bunting probably turned the game around," Cone said. "I made a mistake, though. I should have let it drop. After I caught it, [Gibson] said, 'You should have let it drop.' And I probably should have."

If Cone had dropped the ball, it would have been an easy triple play. The runners held at their bases. Gibson stood at the batter's box.

Gibson patiently stood at his locker, answering wave after wave of questions about his health and about that fateful bunt. In his next three at-bats off Cone, he popped up to the infield each time. But that was a much different Cone than the nervous wreck in the first inning. Gibson took the blame for his decision to bunt.

"I screwed it up and should be held accountable," Gibson said. "I'm sure it gave Cone a breath of life, but I didn't second-guess myself then and I don't now. I'm a good bunter, but the results were terrible."

The best news for the Dodgers: Orel Hershiser didn't bother warming up in the bullpen in Game 6, and Orel Hershiser was starting Game 7.

♦ ♦ ♦ ♦

Wednesday, October 12, 1988

Los Angeles
Mets vs. Dodgers
NLCS Game 7

There was never a doubt that Orel Hershiser would start Game 7 for the Dodgers.

There was plenty of doubt—and questions remain 25 years later—about Ron Darling starting Game 7 for the Mets. Many question why Doc Gooden didn't start the game. Many believe the Mets thought they could win with Darling, and they were saving Gooden for Game 1 of the World Series.

But really, Darling was the Mets' only option because of the rainout. The rainout meant two off-days between Games 2 and 3 and no off-day between Games 5 and 6. Gooden started Game 1, then Game 4 on four days rest. With the travel day wiped out, Gooden would be starting Game 7 on two days rest. That just wasn't realistic. Gooden was available in relief, but he wouldn't start.

David Cone started Games 2 and 6 (on four days rest). Sid Fernandez started Game 5. That left Ron Darling, who started Game 3, to start Game 7 on three days rest.

How much did Hershiser have left in his arm? To review: he threw 100 pitches in 8⅓ innings in Game 1, 109 pitches in 7 innings in freezing cold weather on three days rest in Game 3, three pitches to one batter on zero days of rest in Game 4, warmed up in the bullpen in Game 5, and was now starting Game 7. It was three starts and four appearances in nine days.

"There's no telling what kind of condition The Bionic Man will be in," Mets manager Davey Johnson said in pregame. "I was amazed he was throwing [in the bullpen in Game 5]. He's going to have to be Superman. I don't expect him to have much stuff."

When told of Johnson's comments, Hershiser replied, "Tell him to grab a bat."

It wasn't the last time Hershiser would tell somebody to grab a bat in October.

◆ ◆ ◆ ◆

How big was Game 7? It was so big, Kirk Gibson shaved. And he started. Of course he started.

Johnson looked like a prophet in the first inning. Hershiser had no idea where the ball was going.

Lenny Dykstra flew out to left field, and Gibson hobbled over to make the catch. Wally Backman singled to left, and Gibson gingerly cut the ball off and threw it back to the infield. Keith Hernandez walked, and Lasorda looked noticeably nervous. He fidgeted with his hands. He paced more. All of the Bulldog's pitches were up in the zone, not down.

Remember, when Hershiser made a surprise relief appearance back in May, his next start didn't go well. In fact, it was Hershiser's second-worst start in 1988: seven runs on 12 hits in seven innings. Was history repeating itself?

"Let's go Bulldog," encouraged Lasorda, clapping his hands. "Come on, Bulldog."

Next up were the big boys. Strawberry grounded to Sax at second base, but it wasn't hit fast enough for Alfredo Griffin to turn the double play. Hershiser worked unusually slow—a sign he was struggling. Kevin McReynolds hit a line shot down the line…directly into the glove of third baseman Jeff Hamilton.

It took him 29 pitches, but Hershiser survived the first inning. Hershiser walked directly into the video room, pressed rewind on the machine, saw what was wrong with his mechanics, and made some adjustments. As he watched a video monitor, his teammates got him a lead.

Sax started it—again—with a single to right-center. With Sax running, Hatcher hit a liner off the glove of Jefferies at third base and down the left-field line. Sax stopped at third.

Gibson spent batting practice working with Manny Mota on a new swing. Because his legs were shot, he would swing with his upper body. Gibson spread out wide and took no stride toward the ball. In this game, he didn't try to bunt. He hit a fly ball to center, deep enough to score Sax. Darling struck out Marshall and Shelby to end the first inning, keeping the score 1–0.

Hershiser made the mechanical adjustment and pitched a cleaner second inning, allowing a deep fly ball by Jefferies that was caught at the warning track and a harmless two-out single to Kevin Elster.

In the bottom of the second inning, the Mets fell apart. Scioscia singled to right, and Hamilton singled to left. Alfredo Griffin, the No. 8 hitter, was due up. Hershiser was in the on-deck circle.

Johnson held up one finger in the Mets dugout, a signal for the type of defense he wanted. Johnson was expecting Griffin to bunt and even with the pitcher on deck. The call was for the corner infielders to charge. Jefferies nodded at the dugout and charged home. Hernandez nodded at the dugout but did not charge home.

Griffin squared to bunt and popped the ball into the air, directly right where Hernandez was supposed to be. Hernandez wasn't there. If he had charged he would have caught it easily. But he didn't. Darling had to field the ball, and now Hernandez couldn't get back to first base in time. Everybody was safe. Bases loaded.

"Aaaaaaaaaaaaaaaah," Hernandez yelled at himself. The best defensive first baseman of a generation screwed up a fairly simple bunt play. Hernandez didn't think Griffin was really going to bunt, not with Hershiser on deck, and out-thought himself.

Darling was rattled. He gestured with his glove toward where he expected Hernandez to be. Pitching coach Mel Stottlemyre visited the mount to calm down Darling, who stood there with his hands on his hips.

With Hershiser batting, the Mets brought the corner infielders in. On a 1–2 pitch, Hershiser hit a slow tapper to third base. Jefferies wanted to go home and peeked toward the plate. In the process, he didn't field the ball cleanly. He hesitated then realized it was too late to go home. He decided to throw to first, and in the process he dropped the ball. If Jefferies had caught the ball cleanly and thrown home immediately, Scioscia would have been out easily.

Everybody was safe, a run scored, and the bases were still loaded. There should have been two outs. Instead, there were no outs. Hershiser appeared to injure his leg sprinting down to first base. He was favoring one side.

222

Sax ripped a single up the middle, scoring Hamilton and Griffin. Hershiser cautiously went to second base and didn't think about trying for third base. The Dodgers led 4–0.

Darling was done. Johnson brought in Gooden to make his first relief appearance since high school. Broadcasting on ABC, Jim Palmer said that Johnson should have used submariner Terry Leach because he was used to entering in the middle of an inning, whereas this was all foreign to Gooden. Doc felt it was weird, unreal, unbelievable.

During the pitching change, the trainer visited Hershiser to check on the right leg—Hershiser's push-off leg when on the mound. But that wasn't going to stop Lasorda from pushing the action on the bases. He called for a hit-and-run, and Hatcher hit a slow roller to second base. The only play for Backman was to first base. Hershiser went to third, and Sax went to second base.

With first base open, Gibson was intentionally walked to load the bases. Even on one leg, Gibson struck fear in the Mets. They'd rather pitch to a healthy and dangerous Mike Marshall. The strategy worked.

Marshall hit a grounder to Backman, a tailor-made double play. Of course, no double play is assured if Kirk Gibson is running from first base. Backman's first mistake was playing the ball back, instead of charging the ball. That gave Gibson more time to reach second base. Even with a bad left knee, Gibson was breaking up the double play.

Gibson slid feet first at the bag and reached out with his hands to the right, trying to distract Elster. Backman's shovel to Elster was high and pulled him off the bag. Everybody was safe. Again. Those should have been the third and fourth outs of the inning. Instead, it was now 5–0, and there was still only one out.

"You would never know Gibson has the hamstring injury," Al Michaels said on ABC. "It was like he was cured in a second. He looked like he was 100 percent going into second base. Mind over matter."

Gibson was hurting, however, and bad. Real bad. He sprained the medial collateral ligament in his right knee on that slide. The right knee was the good leg. Gibson had two bad legs now.

Shelby hit a fly ball to left field, deep enough to score Sax. It was 6–0 Dodgers. Hamilton struck out looking to finally end the inning.

"That wasn't an inning," Hernandez would say later, sucking on a cigarette. "That was a nightmare."

The rest was academic. Hershiser wasn't going to blow a six-run lead. The only questions were whether he would need bullpen help, and how much was his leg hurting?

Before the third inning started, Lasorda urged Hershiser, "Don't let up! Go hard! Don't save anything! We've got somebody behind you, if you can't make it!"

It was his fourth appearance of the series, so Hershiser altered his usual game plan. He didn't think he could continue throwing sinkers low and away. He threw more fastballs. His curveball was working, so he threw that pitch more than usual, too.

Hershiser allowed four hits the rest of the game, two by Jefferies, who was 6-for-11 off Hershiser in the series. All the other Mets hitters were 12-for-77 (.156) against Hershiser during that series.

Gibson stayed in the game, but departed after three innings. Hatcher moved from first base to left field.

In the sixth inning, Hershiser's leg must have felt much better because he tried to bunt his way on base. He missed the bunt, then lined out. Sax singled up the middle, and Hershiser was shown on camera on the phone in the dugout.

"What's he doing, ordering champagne?" Michaels commented.

In the ninth, needing one more out to end the series, a fan ran onto the field. It was all smiles in the dugout. Even Gibson was back in the dugout. During the delay, the crowd worked itself into a frenzy, and Hershiser was so over-pumped by the moment, he forgot what pitch to throw against Lee Mazzilli. He was supposed to throw a sinker that starts inside and darts away from lefties. Instead, he forgot and threw a four-seam fastball that hit Mazzilli.

With two strikes against Howard Johnson, Hershiser stepped off the mound. Dodger Stadium was on its feet, roaring with delirium. Hershiser wanted to soak up the scene, feel the energy of the crowd. Hershiser was nearly on the verge of tears. It was the situation he had dreamt of as a kid.

On a 3–2 pitch, Hershiser struck out Johnson looking for the final out. Hershiser dropped to a knee, said a quick prayer, and was mobbed by teammates on the field.

Gibson remained in the dugout. So did Fernando Valenzuela. It was a strange contrast of images. The entire team was celebrating on the field like little kids, except the legendary Valenzuela and the aching Gibson. Valenzuela shook Gibson's hand, and assured him it was smarter to stay in the dugout and not risk further injury in the celebration.

"I wasn't feeling like hopping around," Gibson recalled. "All I was thinking about is, '*What am I going to do to get myself ready to play in a few days?*'"

In the visiting clubhouse, it was stunned silence.

"Seven months, gone like that," Hernandez said. "This is the most disappointed I've been in my career."

"We beat ourselves," Strawberry said. "Now we have to live with it."

In the home clubhouse, it was raucous and wet—very wet. Hershiser still couldn't believe what he'd done, what his teammates had done, and that they'd beaten the big bad New York Mets.

"That's why everyone in here is even happier than we would normally be," Hershiser, the MVP of the series, said that night. "We're not a team of destiny. We're not a dominant team. We're a team of balance that works hard and plays with its heart. When we're firing on all cylinders, when we're bunting and moving runners and doing all the little things, we can beat anyone. When even one of the cylinders breaks down, we can look like a high school team."

Amid the chaos, Tommy was in classic Tommy mode.

"We saved a lot of people all over the country a lot of money," Lasorda exclaimed. "A lot of people travel to the Lady of Lourdes to see miracles. Now they don't have to. They can come to Dodger Stadium to see the biggest miracle of all."

Ten years later, Marshall said, "Those games were the most fun I ever had in baseball."

Twenty-five years later, Hatcher said, "It was the most high that I've ever had in the game of baseball. I could not sleep. I just wanted to get to the ballpark the next day. I just wanted to play. Tommy was getting me in the lineup. I wasn't going to let him take me out of the lineup. It was the most adrenaline I've ever had in my life. When we played the Mets, we were playing the best team in baseball. Not taking anything away from Oakland. The Mets beat us up all year. When that final game was over, we all thought we'd beat the best team in baseball. That's why we went into Oakland thinking nobody can beat us now. That's how I felt. Talking to a lot of other guys, they felt the same way."

Chapter 16

World Series Game 1

Saturday, October 15, 1988

Los Angeles

Athletics vs. Dodgers

World Series Game 1

From the moment the A's arrived in Southern California, something wasn't quite right. They originally were going to stay at their usual hotel in Anaheim. The players didn't want to commute that far to Dodger Stadium, so director of team travel Mickey Morabito had to scramble for a different hotel in Los Angeles.

The Bonaventure, in downtown Los Angeles, was able to accommodate the A's traveling party at the last minute. The vibe wasn't right. Small rooms. Bad beds. Overall, not a good hotel. It wasn't a good omen. But nobody thought that at the time. These were the big, bad, forearm-bashing Oakland A's who had won 104 games and swept the Red Sox. Nothing could stop them.

Jay Howell's suspension was over. He was tired of seeing his name in the newspaper. Howell thought the worst of the controversy and attention was over and that he could slide back into the obscurity of the bullpen—until he was handed the ball late in another game. That's what made him even more blindsided by the latest headlines.

The Oakland A's completed their four-game sweep of Boston on October 9. They had six days to wait before Game 1 of the World Series, and there were six days where the media needed to fill newspaper space and airtime with reports. As the Dodgers and Mets dueled in their playoff series, the natural question was, "Which team would you rather face?"

Most players dodge these questions. Not Dave Stewart, however, who was born and raised in East Oakland, now played in Oakland, and maintained that Oakland chip on his shoulder. Stewart was the seventh of eight children. He was a fourth-generation Oakland resident.

Oakland is the city across the bay from—and always in the shadow of—San Francisco. Athletes from Oakland are notorious for being proud, stubborn, talking trash, and wanting to play the best to prove they are the best. Stewart said the A's wanted to play the Mets. The Mets won more games in the regular season than the Dodgers. That meant the Mets were the best team in the National League. The A's wanted to play the best team.

A's designated hitter Don Baylor made a similar statement. His direct quote: "I prefer to play the Mets for the world championship because they were the best team—based on their 100 wins during the regular season."

Baylor didn't stop there, though. Seemingly out of nowhere, Baylor went after the battered and beleaguered Jay Howell, too.

"What's he ever done?" Baylor told the *San Jose Mercury News*. "He couldn't save games over here [in Oakland], so they got rid of him. He was right where he wanted to be in Games 4 and 5 in New York. He didn't want to be pitching with all those people screaming at him. He can't handle that. He couldn't handle it when he was in New York with the Yankees. I know. I played with him."

A's manager Tony La Russa was livid at Baylor, calling the remarks total bull. La Russa defended Howell in the face of the pine tar controversy, respected Howell, believed in playing the game on the field, not ripping opponents to the press, and stressed that those comments didn't represent how the Oakland A's felt about Jay Howell.

Back at Dodger Stadium in 2012 as a coach with the Arizona Diamondbacks, Baylor sat at his locker in the visiting clubhouse, just like in 1988. When asked what triggered those comments, Baylor seemed to indicate it was more about the Dodgers' uniform than Jay Howell.

"I played for the Angels," said Baylor, who played more games with the Angels (1977–82) than any of his other six teams. "They hated us. They always called us the stepchild of Southern California baseball. That's ingrained in you. Back then, we hated the Dodgers, all those guys did, because they treated us like, you know. Maybe that had something to do with it."

Baylor didn't run from his comments and still doesn't regret his words about Howell. "We saw him enough. It was nothing I hadn't said about anybody else. It was more the time. They can hide behind Tweets now. That's the way I was brought up. Maybe that's when they started getting sensitive. There's been worse bulletin board stuff than that."

As for Howell, he was actually unfazed. He'd already been through so much, what was one more cheap shot?

"It sounds like, while doing the forearm bash, one of the A's caught Baylor in the head one too many times," Howell responded in 1988. "I think everybody has read my name enough. Everybody is as tired of reading it as I am. The only place I want to see it now is in the box score. If he was messing around, that's one thing. If not, who cares?"

Baylor vs. Howell wasn't supposed to be the top storyline going into the World Series. It was supposed to be all the former Athletics and Dodgers now on the other roster.

The Dodgers had Howell, Mike Davis, Tim Belcher, and Alfredo Griffin. The A's had Dave Stewart, Bob Welch, Rick Honeycutt, and Matt Young.

Even the coaching staffs had former ties. A's first-base coach Rene Lachemann was a Dodgers batboy when the team first moved from Brooklyn to Los Angeles.

A's third-base coach Jim Lefebvre, the 1965 Rookie of the Year with the Dodgers, punched Tommy Lasorda in the mouth in 1980 and left him with a bloody lip. This came in the KNBC studios in Burbank, after the two taped separate segments. Lefebvre had recently been fired as a Dodgers coach by Lasorda, and an argument led to thrown punches.

The Game 1 pitching matchup was Stewart vs. Belcher. Both had been traded, in separate exchanges, for Honeycutt. Both needed a change in scenery to get a new lease on their baseball lives.

For Stewart, it required a trade to Texas, a trade to Philadelphia, and then getting released in mid-summer of 1986. Stewart called the Dodgers after the Phillies released him. He met with Lasorda in his office. Lasorda was honest. There was a long list of pitchers already in the organization waiting their chance, and they would get that chance before Stewart did.

The news hurt. Lasorda had told Stewart, after he was traded three years earlier, to come see him if he ever needed a job in the future. Now a job wasn't there. Stewart's pain was mitigated when the Oakland A's signed him to come home.

The turning point in Stewart's career was July 7, 1986—his second start with the A's, on ABC's *Monday Night Baseball,* against the Red Sox at Fenway Park. It was Tony La Russa's first game as A's manager. Stewart faced Roger Clemens, who was 14–1 at the time, and out-dueled him. Jose Canseco homered. So did Dave Kingman. It was the first of many times that Stewart would beat Clemens—the Oakland kid beating the best, just as Oakland kids want—in head-to-head matchups.

Stewart toyed with a forkball earlier in his career. He was told to ditch the pitch in Texas. In Oakland, pitching coach Dave Duncan encouraged him to use it, and worked with him on two different grips—the first to throw for a strike; the second to throw in the dirt for hitters with two strikes to chase.

The forkball gave Stewart a new weapon and changed his career. Stewart won 20 games in 1987. He won 20 games again in 1988. He was returning to Dodger Stadium a much different man, a much different pitcher.

"I have a lot of fond memories about Dodger Stadium," Stewart said on the eve of Game 1. "And if I was going to come back here, I can't think of a better way than as the starting pitcher in the first game of the World Series."

Tim Belcher was feeling a lot of emotions on the eve of the World Series, too. He was starting Game 1 by default, he knew, because Hershiser wouldn't start on two days rest, and John Tudor's health was a question mark. The A's gave up on him, justifiably, because he couldn't throw strikes in the minors. Almost one-third of the A's roster contained his minor league teammates, including Jose Canseco and Terry Steinbach.

It was like a reunion for everybody. It's unreal how both A's-Dodgers trades helped both teams. Rick Honeycutt was the lefty the A's needed in their bullpen. Tim Belcher was the young starting pitcher the Dodgers needed. Bob Welch was the veteran starting pitcher the A's needed. Alfredo Griffin was the starting shortstop, and Jay Howell was the closer the Dodgers were looking for.

"Because Sandy and I ran together, we communicated," Dodgers general manager Fred Claire reflected on his relationship with A's general manager Sandy Alderson. "It wasn't something like, 'I'm trying to [swindle this guy].' It was total candor about making the deal. There was a comfort level. Whatever was happening with our player, I will tell you. It was very easy to deal with Sandy."

◆ ◆ ◆ ◆

Vin Scully and Joe Garagiola were the announcers for NBC. In those days, ABC and NBC rotated the rights to the postseason. In 1988, ABC broadcasted the two League Championship Series, and NBC had the World Series rights.

Scully began calling games for the Brooklyn Dodgers in 1950, so he was already in his 39th consecutive year working for the Dodgers. Six years earlier, in 1982, Scully was honored by the National Baseball Hall of Fame as the recipient of the Ford C. Frick Award.

In 1983, Scully began working for NBC as the lead play-by-play announcer for the *Game of the Week* and playoff games. He worked the NLCS for NBC in 1983, 1985, 1987, and 1989. Scully called the World Series in 1984, 1986, and 1988. In the years Scully wasn't on TV, he usually called the playoff games on CBS Radio.

Garagiola was an institution at NBC. He first called games for the network from 1961–64, returned in 1974, and shared the duties with Curt Gowdy for three years. Garagiola became the lead play-by-play announcer for NBC from 1976–82, teaming with analyst Tony Kubek. Upon the hiring of Scully, Garagiola was converted to analyst.

◆ ◆ ◆ ◆

In the two days since the Dodgers clinched a berth in the World Series, Kirk Gibson had received treatment, stayed off his two bad legs, and prayed a little. He hoped the combination of medicine and pain threshold and prayers would allow him to play against the A's.

During the on-field celebration after beating the Mets, Gibson had stayed in the dugout. He avoided most of the celebration in the clubhouse, as well. At one point, a media member with a mini-cam and some cables ran past him and clipped the back of his knee. Gibson wanted to kill the guy. Instead, he got the hell out of there before the celebration caused more damage.

On the morning of Game 1 of the World Series, the hamstring actually felt pretty good at 5:30 AM. That's when Gibson woke up. Then he walked around, and it didn't feel as good. Then he jogged a little, and he knew there was a problem. Gibson arrived at the ballpark early, and he was given an injection. In his heart, he knew he wouldn't play.

In the A's pregame meetings to go over the scouting reports, they didn't spend much time on Gibson. They didn't expect him to play. One of the coaches said if Gibson does get up, don't throw him anything soft. Dennis Eckersley thought to himself, *Yeah, but he's not playing.*

Tommy Lasorda thought Gibson would play. Sure, Gibson's body was hurting bad. But it was hurting bad against the Mets, and Gibson somehow played. Gibson found a way then. He would find a way again. Lasorda met with Scully and Garagiola about five hours before the game and mentioned how the trainers were really kidding around. The trainers told Lasorda that Gibson wouldn't start and couldn't play. Lasorda still thought Gibson would play.

So many injuries had piled up that it was tough for Gibson to pinpoint the exact source of the discomfort. For the most part, he could play through the hamstring injury but not the knee injury. He wished the series opened in Oakland, so he could be the designated hitter.

About an hour before the game, Gibson was in his underpants eating spaghetti in Lasorda's office. Bullpen coach Mark Cresse had to get Gibson a fork because he couldn't walk 10' to get one himself.

Just before the game started, Gibson called his wife down to the clubhouse. He told her, "I'm not gonna play tonight. Why don't you just go home?" They had a little baby at the time. Rather than deal with all that noise, Gibson's wife took her husband's advice and went home.

Gibson didn't even take part in pregame introductions, which floored one teammate. "If I had two broken legs and was on the roster, my ass would get out there," infielder Tracy Woodson said. "I'd figure out a way to be part of it. I was shocked. I don't know if he was getting treatment or if he didn't go out there because he thought, *These guys need to go on without me.* I would never miss introductions. I grew up watching the World Series. They go down the line and introduce guys, and they tip their cap. You get to the World Series, you get to do that. I always said I couldn't believe he wasn't out there, so I thought there was no way he was playing."

At least one Gibson was on the field during pregame. Debbie Gibson, who was 18 years old and enjoying a No. 1 hit song ("Foolish Beat") at the time, sang the National Anthem.

◆ ◆ ◆ ◆

The ideal person to start Game 1 for the Dodgers was Fernando Valenzuela. If he was on normal rest, Valenzuela started Game 1. In 1981, he started Game 1 of the division series (necessitated after the players' strike divided the season into halves) against the Astros. In 1985, Valenzuela started Game 1 of the NLCS against the Cardinals.

Valenzuela was the horse, the ace, the leader of the Dodgers' pitching staff through the 1980s. But his shoulder wasn't completely healed. He wasn't stretched out enough to be a starter. He wasn't accustomed to pitching in relief, and the bullpen was already so strong, Tim Crews was left off the playoff roster. It was too big a risk to put Fernando on the playoff roster.

So in the most amazing of seasons, the Dodgers were four games from a world championship, and the great Fernando Valenzuela was just another guy—there in uniform, but unable to help.

"It was a little bit frustrating," Valenzuela reflected. "There's nothing you can do. I knew my situation in the playoffs. The team goes to the playoffs and the World Series, so that's great. Of course I wanted to be on the roster. It didn't happen. But it's part of this business."

His teammates painted a more vivid picture. "It killed him," Hatcher recalled. "You could see it. It was probably tough for him to come to the ballpark. He was as down as I've ever seen him."

◆ ◆ ◆ ◆

The A's threatened in the top of the first inning. Carney Lansford struck out looking on a 95 mph fastball. That's all Belcher was throwing in the first inning, fastball after fastball. Dave Henderson singled up the middle, a liner over Belcher's head.

The scouting report prepared for the Dodgers was you had to jam Jose Canseco—pitch him up and inside with hard stuff. Canseco hit a ball completely out of Dodger Stadium in batting practice a day earlier. Belcher came inside and hit Canseco on the forearm. Dave Parker flew out to center for the second out.

The scouting report on Mark McGwire was the same as Canseco—hard stuff, up and inside. He was a low-ball hitter and crushed breaking stuff. Belcher was ahead in the count 0–2, but his minor league wildness returned and Belcher walked McGwire to load the bases.

Belcher fell behind 2–0 to Terry Steinbach, who had hit a home run off Dwight Gooden at the All-Star Game and won the MVP Award. Belcher was on the ropes in the first inning. Belcher threw another fastball and Steinbach hit a solid drive to deep center, but John Shelby tracked it down. Belcher survived the first inning—just barely.

In the bottom of the first, Stewart hit Sax with the first pitch near his neck. It was obvious that this was done intentionally. Stewart didn't look away or show frustration. Conventional wisdom back then was that Stewart was sending a message to the Dodgers after Canseco was hit in the wrist. Don't hit our star. That's what Garagiola said on NBC. That's why crew chief Doug Harvey warned both benches.

But that wasn't true. The familiarity of the players led to some trash-talking a day earlier. Sax and Stewart, teammates in the minors and majors, were among those jawing.

"I'm going to take you deep," Sax told Stewart.

"Oh yeah? I'm going to hit you in the neck," Stewart replied to Sax.

Stewart didn't miss the neck by much. Sax was reaching up on the bat, to either bunt or fake a bunt, and he just barely got out of the way. The ball hit Sax in his left shoulder. Sax never looked at Stewart. He dropped his bat and sprinted to first base.

"Yeah, if it wasn't for my cat-like reflexes, it would have hit me in the neck," Sax said, confirming Stewart's story. "I thought it was fantastic. Thank you. I'm either going to steal second, or what's going to happen? I'll take that every day in Game 1 of the World Series. He could try to hit me in the neck all he wants."

Franklin Stubbs flew out to center and Stewart was called for a balk. It was still the year of the balk. The final total of balks called in 1988 was 924 throughout the majors. The year before, 182 had been called.

Stewart was charged with 16 balks in the regular season, including 11 in his first six starts. The 16 balks remain a major league record. Rick Honeycutt was called for four balks in one game, a four-inning relief appearance on April 13. La Russa and pitching coach Dave Duncan were ejected after the fourth balk was called.

Stewart was stewing over the balk. But he wasn't worried. Mickey Hatcher was batting third, not Kirk Gibson. Stewart played with Hatcher in the minors. He knew Hatcher wasn't a long ball threat. Hatcher hit one home run in 202 plate appearances that year. Stewart would challenge Hatcher with fastballs and force him to put the ball in play.

Two pitches later, Stewart threw a fastball right down the middle. Hatcher hit it over the left-field fence. Hatcher sprinted around the bases like it was a race. It took him less than 16 seconds. By comparison, Dave Parker averaged a 26-second stroll around the bases. Hatcher returned to the dugout full of energy, high fives, and high tens, and the Dodgers led 2–0.

"I never had a game plan except to hit," Hatcher reflected. "Just play baseball. Some of these guys are so caught up on video. We just played the game. We knew what Dave had. You're in the locker room the day before. I even said, 'Hey Dave, I'm going to hit a home run off you,' and he said, 'Not if I throw it at your head.' We were just joking around. When I hit the home run, I didn't want to look at him. I just ran around the bases so fast."

Stewart wasn't worried. He knew two runs wouldn't beat the big, bad, forearm-bashing 1988 Oakland Athletics. The offense was too strong. Even without a designated hitter, it was a dangerous 1-through-6 lineup.

The A's No. 7 hitter, Glenn Hubbard, singled to start the second inning. Walt Weiss struck out looking, and Stewart came to the plate.

Dave Stewart hadn't batted in five years. But he wasn't bunting. Dave Stewart was an athlete. Dave Stewart stood in the batter's box like a man ready to tie the game himself. Stewart took a hellacious cut on two straight fastballs, fouling both back. Perhaps the swings got the attention of Tim Belcher because he showed remarkable respect for an American League pitcher.

Stewart laid off pitches outside the strike zone, worked the count full, and walked. Taking a cue from his childhood friend Rickey Henderson, Stewart flipped the bat toward the on-deck circle like it was his job to draw walks.

Lansford worked the count full, and he walked. The bases were loaded with one out. Now Belcher was really in trouble. This was why the A's had given up on Belcher. He couldn't throw strikes. Pitching coach Ron Perranoski visited the mound. Tim Leary warmed up in the Dodgers' bullpen.

Dave Henderson was ahead in the count 3–1. Lasorda bit his nails in the dugout. Belcher barely hit the outside corner for strike two. Lasorda folded his arms across his belly. Belcher threw another fastball, and Henderson missed it. There were two outs, but Canseco was next.

The first pitch was a high fastball. NBC put a graphic on the TV that Canseco had never hit a grand slam in his career. On the second pitch, Belcher threw another fastball, and this one wasn't close to inside. It was out over the plate. Canseco extended those mighty arms and swatted the ball into center field.

Center fielder John Shelby barely had time to turn around and see where the ball landed. It was a line drive that clanked off the camera in straight-away center field for a grand slam.

"Anytime the ball gets hit to me, I think I've got a chance to catch it," Shelby reflected. "When he hit that one, I broke back, and within seconds it was gone. I actually thought I had a chance at first. Next thing I know, it just kept going and I heard a big BOOM. If you see the highlight, I get back to the wall and it looks like I'm jumping to catch the ball. I actually flinched and dropped my head down after it hit the camera. I didn't know what it hit. It took me a few moments to realize it hit the camera."

Scully described it as a 2-iron shot. Garagiola said, "It didn't get up. It didn't get down. It just got out."

Canseco said he didn't get all of it. The A's bashed forearms and took a 4–2 lead.

Belcher wasn't done. He walked Parker, and he fell behind McGwire. "It's been quite a series already," Scully said. McGwire bounced to shortstop to finally end the inning. Belcher's night was done. He threw 71 pitches in two regrettable innings.

"I didn't pitch very well," Belcher said. "I was wild. I threw a pitch behind Carney Lansford's head. I hit Jose Canseco, and then he later hit me—that grand slam that knocked me out of the game. If there was one game that entire season that I reverted back to my 'wild-can't-throw-strike days' from the minor leagues, it's kind of ironic that it was against the team that traded me because I couldn't throw strikes. It was disheartening."

Tim Leary wasn't disheartened to pitch in relief, even after pitching so well as a starter that year and being in the Cy Young Award discussion in July and August. Leary faded in September, and he knows why.

"I was completely burned out," Leary recalled. "I'd thrown 500 straight innings without any rest, between '87 and winter ball and spring training [and '88]. It kinda made it a no-brainer. If you think about it, to start a rookie and have a veteran come in relief, it's much smarter than the other way around."

Leary started the third inning, and the A's were ready to put the game away. Steinbach ripped a smash off Jeff Hamilton's glove at third base for a single. Hubbard lined a single into left field. The A's just needed a knockout blow, another one of those forearm bashes, and this game was over. Hell, maybe this series would be over. The Sax beaning and the Hatcher sprint wouldn't matter.

Weiss flied out to left field for one out. Stewart, again, would not be bunting. Garagiola bemoaned the lack of bunting in baseball in the modern game. Stewart struck out on a checked swing for the second out.

The inning came down to Lansford, and he grounded out to shortstop to end the inning. The A's had sent 19 batters to the plate in three innings. But they'd only scored four runs and had stranded six base runners.

In the bottom of the third, the NBC cameras showed Gibson in the dugout. His hands were inside a Dodgers jacket as he talked to Jeff Hamilton. This was his first appearance in the dugout that night. Scully said, "His knee was injected with lidocaine and cortisone. His condition is day-to-day. Maybe he can play later in the series but not tonight."

Stewart settled down after the first inning—as usual—and was cruising. It was just a matter of time before the A's broke this game open and the forearms bashed again.

In the fourth inning, Henderson sliced a drive into the right-field corner that was touched by a fan for a ground-rule double. Leary fell behind 3–0 to Canseco, and La Russa gave his hitter the green light.

Canseco hit a chopper deep into the hole. Alfredo Griffin had no chance to throw out Canseco at first base. This is when Canseco still ran hard. It should have been runners at first and second with none out. Inexplicably, Henderson tried advancing to third. Henderson didn't think Griffin would even reach the ball and thought he would score on a single. Once Griffin caught the ball, Henderson thought Griffin would throw to third base, so he tried getting back to second base. The savvy Griffin threw to second base, where Sax was alert enough to cover the bag and apply the tag. One out.

"What are you thinking, Hendu?" Stewart wondered years later.

Parker hit a little nubber in front of the plate, close to the foul line. Parker is an enormous man. Leary didn't have an angle for a throw to first base. Leary's throw went down the right-field line. Canseco advanced to third, and Parker went to second base. Henderson should have scored for a 5–2 lead.

But the umpires ruled, correctly, that Parker wasn't in the running lane. He was out on interference. Parker didn't need to run out of the baseline. Even if Parker stayed in the baseline, Leary had no angle for a throw to first base. Canseco returned to first base, and there were two outs.

"I lucked out," Leary admitted.

The A's were killing themselves but were undaunted. Canseco showed off his 40–40 tools by stealing second base easily. Mike Scioscia dropped the ball in the exchange. With first base now open, McGwire was intentionally walked with a 2–1 count.

It was another chance for Steinbach. Leary got ahead with a 96 mph fastball and struck Steinbach out with the splitter that he learned commuting from Santa Monica to Tijuana in the off-season.

"I was confident and aggressive," Leary said. "Jay Howell and I threw every pitch harder than we possibly could. It just made sense. We weren't finesse pitchers. It was just pure stuff. Here it comes. To do it for nine innings is another story. For three innings, it was no problem."

The A's totals were four innings, six hits, five walks, 24 batters, four runs, and eight left on base.

◆ ◆ ◆ ◆

Steve Vucinich was the visiting clubhouse manager for the A's. He was helping with the A's clubhouse for the games in Los Angeles and preparing for whatever the Dodgers would need when they came up to Oakland. He walked down the hallway to the Dodgers' clubhouse to check on any last-minute details.

"I was talking to Gibby around the fourth or fifth inning," Vucinich said. "I went over there to say, 'How many guys are coming up, your staff,' that kind of stuff. Gibby, who I have known well from Detroit, is limping around. He was in his underwear and getting iced down. I thought there was no way this guy is playing in the game."

♦ ♦ ♦ ♦

All those wasted chances by the A's offense didn't figure to matter. Stewart had a 4–2 lead. Stewart didn't lose games that he led. From the second to the fifth inning, Stewart faced three over the minimum.

Trouble arrived in the sixth, as the Dodgers stopped trying to pull the ball. With one out, Stewart left a forkball up, and Mike Marshall went the other way for a single. John Shelby singled up the middle. Mike Scioscia lined a single to left where Parker was playing.

Parker had won the 1979 All-Star Game Most Valuable Player award based on two cannon-like throws. But that was a decade ago. Now, he had no arm. He was a designated hitter and only playing left field to keep his bat in the lineup in the National League ballpark. Marshall was waved around easily. Parker didn't bother throwing home.

The A's lead was down to 4–3. Tony La Russa warmed up Gene Nelson and the lefty Greg Cadaret in the bullpen. This was the year La Russa invented the modern bullpen. He used five or more pitchers 49 times or more that year, at a time when most managers' strategy was go to their best reliever whenever the starting pitcher left the game with the lead.

Stewart didn't know the bullpen was getting loose. Jeff Hamilton was at the plate. Stewart didn't even remember who Jeff Hamilton was. Stewart got Hamilton to bounce to third, and Lansford turned two to end the inning.

Lasorda went back into the clubhouse after that inning. He did that numerous times during the game. He'd seek out Gibson and ask how he was doing. Gibson didn't say a word. Gibson just put both thumbs down. Lasorda returned to the dugout disappointed each time.

The A's blew another chance in the seventh. Brian Holton, replacing Leary, walked Parker to start the inning. Before pinch runner Stan Javier had a chance to steal second, McGwire hit a tapper in front of the plate that advanced Javier to second. Steinbach hit a line smash, but directly into Hamilton's glove at third base. Hubbard flied out to right field to end the inning.

In the Dodgers' seventh, according to a Peter Gammons report in *Sports Illustrated*, Alfredo Griffin predicted to teammates Mike Sharperson and Fernando Valenzuela that Eckersley would enter the game in the ninth inning, look around, realize he was back in a National League park, "and the Chicago Cub will come out of him."

With two outs in the seventh, Sax singled and stole second base. On a 1–1 pitch, Stubbs hit a high fly ball deep to right field. The crowd rose to its feet in excitement. Stewart wasn't nervous. He knew it was off the end of Stubbs' bat. He knew the ball didn't carry at Dodger Stadium at night. Canseco caught it short of the warning track.

Still, at least one person thought he'd just missed history. Barely visible in the background of the NBC camera shot beyond the right-field pavilion, a car was seen leaving the parking lot and slamming on the brakes. At least one person was already leaving early.

The A's went quietly in the top of the eighth inning. During the commercial break, Scully told the producer inside the NBC Network truck to follow his lead as they returned to action. Normally, Scully would never say that to the truck. But he did it on purpose that inning because he wanted to preview the final two innings for the Dodgers. The inning started with a shot from the Goodyear blimp.

Hatcher led off the bottom of the eighth inning. Hatcher was hitting in Gibson's spot in the lineup. With the count 1–2, Scully said, "If you're in the ballpark with binoculars, your first thought would be, late in the game, *Is Gibson in the Dodgers' dugout?* The answer would appear to be no."

Wham, the camera showed the end of the Dodgers' dugout. Stewart struck out Hatcher on a checked swing. The camera panned the entire Dodgers dugout.

Scully said, "As you look, you see Fernando Valenzuela...you're looking for Kirk Gibson...and there is no Gibson...the man who was the spearhead of the Dodgers' offense all year...who saved them in the league championship series... will not see any action tonight, for sure...he is not even in the dugout."

Gibson was in the trainer's room. Bags of ice were on both legs. Gibson hated hearing other people tell him what he could do or couldn't do. After he heard Scully say he would not see any action, Gibson muttered, "Fuck it. I'll be there."

◆ ◆ ◆ ◆

In the spring of 1985, Mitch Poole was a student at Pasadena City College and played on the baseball team. One of his teammates worked in the Dodgers' clubhouse. Everybody on the team always asked if they could get a job. Everybody, except for Mitch Poole.

"One day," Poole said, "he came up to me and said, 'You've never asked me to do that. Why?' I said, 'Because I see what it does to you. I've known you for a long time.' My friend goes, 'Tomorrow is Opening Day at Dodger Stadium. The team is getting back from Houston late tonight. Do you want to unload the truck?' I said, 'Alright, I'll do that.'"

After unloading the truck, Poole was asked if he'd want to put on a uniform the next day and be a batboy. Of course, he said yes. Poole was hired shortly thereafter and never used his final year of college eligibility. He was part of the Dodgers family.

By 1988, it was Poole's fourth year working for the Dodgers. For most games, he was in uniform and perched down the left-field line. He routinely played catch with Kirk Gibson between innings. For Game 1 of the 1988 World Series, Poole was stationed inside the clubhouse. Poole was tending to business in the locker room when he heard Gibson yell, "Get my uniform!"

Poole brought Gibson's uniform into the training room. Gibson struggled to put it on. Hitting coach Ben Hines came up to the clubhouse. Gibson asked if he'd help him by putting balls on a tee. Hines needed to be in the dugout. Hines told Gibson to have Poole do it.

"He looked at me strange," Poole recalled. "Then he said, 'Let's do it.' I'm putting balls on the tee, and I was also tossing balls to him for location. You want movement. You're not going to get a ball just sitting there. It's funny. He was hitting. He was in pain. You could hear it in his voice, every time he swung."

Gibson whacked and grunted. Whacked and grunted.

"It's like he was fighting somebody back there in the cage," Griffin remembered. "I saw him go up there. I thought, *This guy is unbelievable*. He can't walk. He was swinging on one leg. It was amazing."

Poole didn't look Gibson in the eye. He focused on tossing the ball into the right location. Then Poole noticed that Gibson had stopped, and he wasn't ready for another pitch. Poole looked up at Gibson.

"Gibby said, 'Hey Mitch, this could be the script,'" Poole said. "I'm telling you, that is exactly what he said. 'This could be the script.' I told him, 'I wouldn't doubt you.' Then he goes, 'Go tell Tommy that I can hit.'"

Gibson's knees were numb. They'd been iced all day. He swung with all arms. Gibson brainwashed himself. He had the determination. He felt the emotion. He told himself that when he stepped on the field, 56,000 people would provide the adrenaline, and he would no longer hurt.

"I ran down to the dugout," said Poole, who was not in uniform, so he didn't want to walk across the dugout. "I was screaming at Tommy. I was down by the well area. Players and coaches were looking at me like, 'What are you doing?' I yell, 'Tommy!' Then I yell, 'Tommy, Get over here!'

"Everybody is still looking at me, like this guy is kinda strange. He came running over and said, 'What is it? What do you want?' I told him, 'Gibby just told me that he can hit. He wants to talk to you up there.' Tommy wallowed his way up the stairs. I followed Tommy. I heard their little conversation."

Gibson told Lasorda he could give him one at-bat. They agreed that Mike Davis would hit in the No. 8 spot for Griffin, and Gibson would bat in the pitcher's spot. Lasorda told Gibson to stay underneath and out of sight. He didn't want the A's to know he was available.

◆ ◆ ◆ ◆

As the bottom of the eighth inning continued, Marshall popped out to second base for the second out. Shelby flied to right, and Canseco made a nice sliding catch to end the inning. Canseco really did it all back then. Stewart was at 114 pitches, back when pitch counts weren't discussed on the air and weren't in the next day's box score.

"There was no way I thought he was going to take me out of this game," Stewart said during a MLB Network broadcast that ranked the game the 10th best in baseball history. "No way. This was a typical game for me. [La Russa] always said, 'As long as you get outs, you stay out there. You have the right to complete the game.' That's how I completed games."

Stewart completed 14 games that year, tied with Roger Clemens for most in the majors. He exceeded 120 pitches 11 times that year. He threw 149 and 142 pitches in consecutive starts, July 15 and 20, in complete-game losses. He was pitching on five days rest that night.

La Russa didn't say anything when Stewart entered the dugout. Stewart put his cap down. He put his glove down. He grabbed a towel. He grabbed his coat to stay warm. Stew was ready for the bottom of the ninth.

Henderson struck out to begin the top of the ninth inning. As Canseco walked to the batter's box, La Russa walked over to Stewart and told him that was it. He was done for the night.

Stewart looked at his manager puzzled. What do you mean? Stewart felt great. He didn't want to exit. With a stronger tone, La Russa said that Eckersley was coming in. Stewart asked a second time to stay in. Nope. Wasn't happening.

La Russa told Stewart that Eck needed the work. Eck pitched four times in five days, saving all four games in the ALCS. Now he'd gone five days without pitching. Eck probably wouldn't pitch the next day, if Hershiser kept shutting out everybody. Then with an off-day, it might be eight days until Game 3.

Canseco was ahead 3–1 in the count. Pena threw a fastball. Canseco, the strongest man in baseball at the time, swung as hard as humanly possible. If he had connected, the ball would have hit the San Gabriel Mountains on the fly.

But Canseco missed. He swung so hard, he nearly fell down. Canseco stepped out of the batter's box. It was almost like he needed to give himself a standing eight-count after that swing. He adjusted his back and body. He dug back in.

Pena threw another fastball. Canseco swung with about 90 percent of the authority of his previous swing, which was still harder than anybody else in baseball. He fouled the ball straight back. Canseco grimaced, knowing how close he'd come to hitting another home run.

Undaunted, Pena challenged Canseco with yet another fastball. Maybe Pena was crazy. This was a fastball on the hands, though, where the scouting report said you had to throw, and Canseco missed again. Pena's reaction was dramatic, pumping his glove in excitement.

Of Canseco, Scully said on NBC, "I wonder if he ever takes a half swing."

Stan Javier reached on an infield single. It was the Athletics' first hit since Henderson's double in the fourth. McGwire lifted a fly ball to right field, and it was caught by Marshall on the warning track to end the inning. As NBC went to commercial, Scully said, "And Dennis the Menace is on his way to the mound."

♦ ♦ ♦ ♦

Stewart grabbed his cap and walked into the clubhouse. Stew was stewing again. He iced his arm. The game wasn't on a TV in the clubhouse. He sat in the trainer's room, still pissed, and listened to the bottom of the ninth on the radio: 790 KABC, the Dodgers' flagship station.

Eckersley, initially reluctant to pitch in relief, warmed up to his new role in the bullpen quickly. Eckersley had saved 45 games in the regular season and four more in the ALCS against the Red Sox. He issued nine unintentional walks in 72⅔ innings, allowed five home runs, and the league hit just .198 against him.

243

One thing Eckersley didn't like facing was lefties. The numbers showed virtually no difference in 1988. Lefties hit .198 and righties hit .197 against him. Still, Eck didn't feel comfortable against lefties.

The first batter in the ninth was lefty Mike Scioscia. He took a ball then popped out to the shortstop Weiss—one out. Eck felt great. He got the lefty out. The game was in the bag. Scully reminded people, "Coming up next, except on the West Coast, local news and *Saturday Night Live*."

Scioscia returned to the dugout. "I was pissed because I always felt pretty comfortable hitting against Dennis Eckersley, even though he was really good. I always saw the ball good. I felt like I was going to start this rally off and we're going to get going. I pop up. I'm coming back and sitting there, like, damn. You feel that disappointment."

Hamilton fouled off the first pitch. The cameras spotted Gibson in the dugout. He was in uniform, helmet on, tightening his batting gloves, the bat resting between his legs. Scioscia sat next to him, right leg crossed over his left leg, his left arm on the bench behind Gibson.

"Gibby went on the bench a little prematurely," Poole recalled. "I think they wanted to hide him. But he was in a zone. You look at him, and he's like twitching all over the place."

Eckersley pumped another strike for an 0–2 count on Hamilton.

Harry Coyle, directing his 36th and final World Series for NBC, recognized the story was in the dugout. He cut back to Gibson in the dugout. Scully said, "You have a former Oakland A out on deck, Mike Davis. We'll see what all that means. I doubt he would hit for Davis. I think it would be up to Davis to extend the inning and give Gibson one last shot."

Coyle cut back to home plate. Scully said, "0-and-2...sidearm...mean...strike three called...that came from around the corner."

As planned, Mike Davis hit for Alfredo Griffin. This was a risk. What if Davis didn't get on base and Gibson never batted? The camera showed Gibson in the dugout with a bat in hand. It was clear he was ready to hit. But the Dodgers weren't thinking about a game-tying Gibson home run. Gibson could barely stand.

Davis had only 55 hits and 25 walks in the regular season, leading to an on-base percentage of a mere .260. He was nearly an All-Star 15 months earlier with the A's. He was nearly on his way to the Yankees 10 months earlier. He stepped in a pothole in Puerto Rico six months earlier that changed his season. He'd lost his starting job four months earlier. He had barely played the last three months. His career was on the ropes.

Eck went into his windup, and Davis asked for time. Hitters did this all the time against Eck. He threw so many strikes, and worked so quickly, that they tried to throw off his timing. Eck threw home anyway and pumped in a strike. But the umpire granted time. No pitch.

"The guy is hitting a buck ninety," Eck said later. "What the hell's he doing calling timeout?"

Davis dug back in. Eck shook off catcher Ron Hassey, who entered the game defensively for Steinbach, and pumped in a fastball that Davis fouled off. The count could be 0–2, but the umpire had granted time, so the count was just 0–1.

Scully said, "By the way, Gibson is not on deck. Dave Anderson is."

Eck missed with a fastball outside. The count was 1–1. Eck started his windup, and Davis asked for time again. This time, Eck didn't throw home. Eck was seething that Davis kept calling time. Coyle cut to another shot of Gibson in the dugout. His helmet was off.

Next came another fastball from Eck, again missing outside. The count was 2–1.

In the A's dugout, reliever Matt Young said, "It doesn't look like Eck's got it."

Mike Thalblum—an A's batboy then, and the visiting clubhouse manager now—couldn't believe what he was hearing. Thalblum thought to himself, *Don't say that!*

Over the years, a popular story is that the A's pitched Davis carefully because Anderson was on deck, unaware that Gibson was lurking in the dugout.

"I don't think that's an issue," Anderson reflected. "I don't think Eck even thought about that. He led the world in saves. He was the best closer in baseball. I don't think he was too concerned about who was coming on deck and wasn't able to play anyway."

Catcher Ron Hassey vehemently denied that the A's pitched around Davis because Anderson was in the on-deck circle.

"Why would we pitch around Davis when we have two outs?" Hassey said, 25 years later. "You don't pitch around a guy with two outs to face another hitter. That would never make sense. You have your closer out there. That's just not true. That's a good story. As far as I know, Gibson is on the roster. Is he not? You're not going to waste a guy that can't play. He's active. We knew what we were going to do. That was no surprise. It makes it sound good—like Lasorda made a miracle move, but it was no miracle move. We know of the possibilities."

The A's knew what Mike Davis was capable of doing. Eck saw what Davis had done a year earlier, when the outfielder had 20 home runs at the All-Star break. The A's were probably the only team in baseball that would give Davis that type of respect.

Eck threw another fastball away, which missed for ball three. Garagiola said, "If he gets on, we're going to hear some roar."

Davis wanted to make the crowd roar himself. In Davis' personal script, he was hitting the dramatic home run. One swing would make up for his entire season of frustration. In retrospect, Davis wondered if Eck had the read the box scores all year—because if he had, Eck would have thrown every pitch right down the middle.

Eck threw another fastball, which also missed off the outside part of the plate. Ball four.

Coyle quickly cut to Gibson, who had spent the last two batters sitting at the end of the bench and now emerged onto the field. Scully didn't miss a beat saying, "And look who's coming up."

Gibson walked to the on-deck circle. He put pine tar on his bat. He took a half-dozen swings with a donut on his bat. Eck wanted the at-bat to start right now. He hated waiting. He wanted to get this inning over with now.

"Gibby always talked about how you just think something is going to happen, and you visualize it," Poole reflected. "I had the same experience. I was at the end of the dugout. My hair was coming up on my arms. I just remember seeing this ball go out to right field. I got this picture in my head. It was a ball to right field. I don't know why it came over me. It wasn't like I was trying to wish it over the darn wall. This thing came over me. I thought, *Dang, that would be awesome. This place would go crazy if something like that happened.*"

Scully didn't say a word for 10 seconds, letting the images and crowd tell the story, before he finally spoke, "All year long, they looked to him to light the fire… and all year long, he answered the demands…until he was physically unable to start tonight—with two bad legs."

Gibson approached the batter's box. The entire crowd was on its feet. Eck was always antsy. Now he was extra antsy. When the hell was this at-bat going to start? *Let's go*, thought Eck. *Let's go.*

Scully added, "The bad left hamstring…and the swollen right knee…and with two outs, you talk about a roll of the dice, this is it."

Gibson dug into the batter's box, stepped out again, and took a few more practice swings. Coyle called for a graphic on the TV that Eckersley had not allowed a home run since August 24. Gibson looked Eckersley in the eye and thought to himself, *Bring it on. This is what I've been waiting for.*

Scully said, "So the Dodgers, trying to capture lightning, right now," and Eckersley came set at the waist. From the time the Davis at-bat ended, until this moment, one minute and 21 seconds had elapsed. It felt like 30 minutes to Eckersley.

"We knew what we would do," Hassey recalled. "We had meetings on all their hitters. Here he comes. Down and away or up and in. That's Eck. It wasn't like Eck had to trick anybody. He had great stuff."

The first pitch was a fastball right down the middle. Gibson fouled it back. It wasn't a pretty swing. Gibson looked helpless. He nearly fell down in pain. Scully said, "4–3 A's, two outs, ninth inning…not a bad opening act."

In the bullpen, Jay Howell saw Gibson almost fall down. Years later, he recalled thinking, *This is a joke. Why is he even up there? He's gonna strike out, and we're going to lose.*

Eck threw over to first base, trying to keep Davis close. Davis stole 7-of-10 bases he attempted on the year. Eck's leg kick was high, making his delivery one of the slowest in the league. Davis knew he could easily steal second base. Davis also knew, based on the season he had, if he somehow was thrown out, the city of Los Angeles would wring his neck.

Eck threw another fastball down the middle, and Gibson fouled it away. That one hurt. Now the count was 0–2. Lasorda sat down. Eck threw over to first base again. He wasn't close to picking off Davis. He just wanted to prevent him from getting too huge a lead.

Mike Marshall did the math in his head to see if he could bat in the inning. That's what he always did. He wanted to hit. Gibson was in the ninth spot. Marshall batted fourth. Marshall realized it was impossible to bat in the ninth—he would only get a chance if the game went into extra innings. After watching the first two swings, Marshall felt for Gibson. He hoped Gibson wasn't doing something that would permanently hurt his career.

In the A's clubhouse, this is what Stewart heard from Don Drysdale on Dodgers radio:

"Well, the crowd is on its feet, and if there was ever a preface to 'Casey at the Bat,' it would have to be the ninth inning. Two out. The tying run aboard, the winning run at the plate, and Kirk Gibson standing at the plate."

On TV, director Coyle cut to a wide shot of the Athletics' defense. Canseco was a few steps from the warning track. McGwire was holding Davis at first.

With two strikes Garagiola said that Davis was now a threat to run. Beyond the right-field pavilion, you could see the red lights of a few cars leaving the parking lot.

Gibson spread out as wide as he could. He was at full mercy, his emergency stance. He was just trying to make contact, just trying to survive. He was thinking, *Just a short stroke. Put the ball in play. Move Davis over. Let Sax drive him home to tie it.*

Another fastball. Gibson barely made contact. A little nubber up the line that just rolled foul. McGwire, Eckersley, and Gibson were all within steps of each other. Nobody made eye contact. Eck thought if the ball had rolled a couple feet to the left, it was fair, and the game would be over. Gibson gingerly walked back to home plate, hands on his hips.

Garagiola said, "He almost has to talk to his legs, like 'Hey, let's go, we gotta get out of here'" as the replay is shown. Scully added, "It's one thing to favor one leg, but you can't favor two."

Twenty-five years later, Scully reflected: "My only thought when he came up to hit was, 'Please God, don't let him strike out.' My thought only being this is the national stage. This guy has been absolutely inspirational all year long, spurring on the team. I know he can barely walk, so he can't run. All those agonizing pitches and the little squirted foul balls. If any of them stays fair, they throw him out easily. That was my only thought. 'Please don't let him strike out.'"

Coyle cut to a shot of the A's dugout. Pitching coach Dave Duncan gestured with his hands up and pushing back. He called for a fastball, up in the zone, out over the plate.

Eck pumped another fastball. This one missed outside. Hassey turned and snapped a throw to first base, using Gibson as a screen. Davis didn't see it initially and was nearly picked off. The count was 1–2.

Davis took off on Eck's next pitch. It was another fastball away, and Gibson fouled it off on the third-base side. Scully said Gibson was "shaking his left leg, making it quiver…like a horse, trying to get rid of a troublesome fly."

Eck threw another fastball away. It missed for a ball. It didn't miss by much. Eck sometimes got that call. Eck didn't get the call this time. That was 15 straight fastballs. Every pitch in the inning, so far, was a fastball. The count was 2–2. The crowd hadn't sat down the entire time. Another throw to first base. None of these pickoffs were close.

Davis took off again. Eck threw his first slider of the inning, which missed way outside for ball three. Gibson followed the flight of the ball, his concentration on full alert, and his momentum carried him over the plate. Hassey jumped out of his crouch to throw to second. Hassey's glove hit Gibson's left arm. Gibson jumped out of the way.

Hassey looked back at home-plate umpire Doug Harvey, looking for an interference call. Hassey didn't attempt a throw to second base. If he did throw, it would have been interference on Gibson. No question about it. Gibson would be out and the game would be over.

"I had to throw it," Hassey reflected. "I might have asked that question [to Harvey]. I don't recall. I'm not sure if that was the conversation."

Sitting on the Dodgers' bench, Scioscia knew how close the game came to ending right there. "If he had made the throw and hit Kirk, the game is over," Scioscia said. "The parameters of that call, you have to make an effort to make a throw. [Hassey] didn't put a good enough effort in the umpire's mind to warrant considering calling Kirk out."

The count was 3–2. Eckersley called Hassey out to the mound to make sure he knew what sign they were using with Davis now on second base.

In the dugout, Shelby thought to himself, "*I hope he hits it out or into a gap—because if he hits it anywhere on the ground, they would throw him out.* It wasn't the prettiest at-bat to watch. It looked like he hurt with each swing. Man, those were some terrible hacks. Then he fouled one off and tried to run, and there really wasn't much to his run. I just hoped he would hit it far enough that they couldn't throw him out at first base."

In the on-deck circle, Sax thought the A's might intentionally walk Gibson, and take their chances with the right-on-right matchup against him.

"The only reason I'm thinking they don't walk Gibby to get to me is they think he was hurt and there was no way that he could do anything with the bat," Sax reflected. "And it was pretty obvious as he was fouling the ball off. He had some really feeble swings. I don't think they thought he was much of a danger. I'm thinking about how I'm going to try and win the game."

When asked if they considered intentionally walking Gibson, Hassey said simply, "No."

Scully said, "Now the Dodgers don't need the muscle of Gibson as much as a base hit."

That's exactly what Eckersley thought. A home run never remotely entered his mind. Eck was worried about Gibson just flipping the ball into the outfield, dumping in a single, and tying the game.

Coyle cut to Lasorda in the dugout. Lasorda bent his right leg to the top step of the dugout. His right arm rested on his right leg. Orel Hershiser was a couple steps away.

"Three-and-two," said Scully, and just before Eckersley started his windup, Gibson called time.

Gibson thought back to the pre-series scouting report meeting. In Gibson's head, he heard Mel Didier's famous Texas drawl, "Paarrrtner, as sure as I'm standing here breathin', if Eckersley goes 3–2 on you, you're goin' to see a backdoor slider. I've seen him freeze George Brett with it. I've seen him freeze Wade Boggs. If you get him 3–2, get ready to step into it, because it will be that backdoor slider."

Didier had always liked Gibson. When Didier scouted for the Mariners in the late 1970s, he tried to persuade them to draft Gibson. The first five picks in that 1978 draft were Bob Horner, Lloyd Moseby, Hubie Brooks, Mike Morgan, and Andy Hawkins. The Mariners selected somebody named Tito Nanni with the sixth pick. Gibson went 12th to the Tigers.

Gibson trusted Didier. In his mind, it wasn't just a hunch. If Didier said it, it was an absolute, sure-fire guaranteed lock that Eck would throw the 3–2 slider. Gibson was ready for it.

Drysdale was on Dodgers radio: "So the battle of minds starts to work a little bit. Gibson a deep sigh. Re-gripping the bat. Shoulders just shrugged. Now goes to the top of the helmet, like he always does. Steps in with that left foot."

Hassey put down the sign for a slider away. A backdoor slider. Eck nodded in agreement. Eck was going to throw the nastiest backdoor slider he'd ever thrown in his life.

From the time Davis had drawn ball four until the time Eck started the fateful final pitch of the Gibson at-bat, six minutes and 41 seconds had elapsed. It was 8:37 PM Pacific Time.

Indeed, Eck threw that backdoor slider. Gibson's swing was awkward, all arms and no legs, and straight out of *The Natural* script.

♦ ♦ ♦ ♦

Vin Scully on NBC: "High fly ball into right field... she iii-is goneeeee!"

Scully didn't say a word for one minute and 14 seconds.

"In a year that has been so improbable, the impossible has happened!"

Scully didn't say a word for another minute. As the replay showed Gibson's entire trip around the bases, Scully spoke again: "And, now, the only question was, could he make it around the base paths unassisted?... And, look at Eckersley—shocked to his toes!... They are going wild at Dodger Stadium. Nobody wants to leave."

Upon reflection three decades later, Scully still shakes in head in astonishment. "When he hit the home run, of course, I was as shocked as everybody else," Scully said. "People ask me where I would put that home run. To me, considering the entire buildup, looking into the dugout, it was the most theatrical home run. That's like Hollywood staged that one."

That famous line Scully uttered, "In a year that has been so improbable, the impossible has happened." Where did that line come from?

"I have no idea," Scully said. "Never used it before. Nor again. I don't want to make it sound corny. But once in a blue moon, I gotta believe that I got a gift from the man upstairs."

After Scully wrapped it up from the broadcast booth, he sent it downstairs to Bob Costas and Marv Albert on the field for the NBC postgame show. Scully then experienced something that is highly unusual for him.

"After that home run, for maybe the only time in my life, I couldn't sit down," Scully recalled. "My wife was here. She was sitting in Peter O'Malley's booth. I walked down and had a drink in Peter's booth. You talk about electrifying? I couldn't sit down. I kept walking and walking, trying to burn off whatever energy this was, that was manufactured by the home run. That I remember very well. The only time. Usually, I'll call a game winner, close the [score] book, and get on the elevator. That night, no. That was really different. It had a totally different effect."

◆ ◆ ◆ ◆

Don Drysdale called the homer on KABC radio: "Eckersley working out of the stretch, here's the 3–2 pitch…and a drive hit to right field (voice cracking) WAY BACK! (voice screaming) IT'S BACK! IT'S GONE!"

Drysdale didn't say another word for one minute and 55 seconds. All you heard on Dodgers Radio was the crowd losing its mind in disbelief. "This crowd will not stop! They can't believe the ending! And this time, Mighty Casey did *not* strike out!!!!"

Drysdale waited another 52 seconds before saying another word. "The crowd still on their feet. The Dodgers, waiting for Gibson to lumber around the bases, were verrrry careful, as if they were touching a Rembrandt at home plate. And in the eyes of the Dodgers fans, that's what it was. And here he comes out on the field again. Listen …"

Drysdale went silent another 19 seconds.

"So Kirk Gibson, Trans America indeed salutes you. And at Trans America, the power of the pyramid is working for you. Final score in game number one, in dramatic fashion, a two-out home run by Kirk Gibson in the bottom of the ninth inning—the Dodgers defeat the A's 5 to 4."

◆ ◆ ◆ ◆

Jack Buck on CBS Radio, the national feed: "We have a big 3–2 pitch coming here from Eckersley…Gibson swings…a fly ball to deep right field…this is gonna be a home run! Unbelievable! A home run for Gibson, and the Dodgers have won the game 5–4…. I don't believe what I just saw! I don't believe what I just saw! Is this really happening Bill?"

Bill was analyst Bill White. Buck kept going.

"I don't believe what I just saw! One of the most remarkable finishes to any World Series game. A one handed home run by Kirk Gibson, and the Dodgers have won it 5–4. I'm stunned. I've seen a lot of dramatic finishes in a lot of sports. But this one might top almost every other one. How could he do it?"

"It was simply one of the most dramatic moments ever. Will you give me a slap alongside the head, so I can realize what I saw is the truth? Unbelievable!"

♦ ♦ ♦ ♦

Fred Wallin was the host of *Post Game Dodger Talk* on flagship station 790 KABC. Wallin grew up in Culver City, not far from the station's studios. The Dodgers were his life, and hosting *Dodger Talk* was his dream job.

Within minutes of the home run, KABC general manager George Green told Wallin, "You're going to take every phone call about the Dodgers the rest of the night. I don't care how long we're on the air. We're not going to any other programming until we've taken every single call from every single person who wants to call and talk about this game."

These were the days before 24–7 sports talk stations. Normally, *Dodger Talk* would air for about an hour after the game before returning to its news-talk format.

That night, Wallin fielded phone calls and talked about the game for well over three hours. The phone lines wouldn't stop ringing. Wallin finally signed off the air at 12:30 AM.

♦ ♦ ♦ ♦

Mitch Poole now believes in the power of visualizing something.

"When he got a hold of that ball, I swear to you, I saw the same path of what I saw earlier," Poole said. "It hit the exact same place in the stands. To this day, if I see it on TV, the same thing happens. My hair comes up on my arm. Let's put it this way, there aren't many times that I see that home run and my arms don't get those goose bumps. Very strange."

It was chaos in the Dodgers' clubhouse. The players couldn't sit down. Nobody could sit down. They were all high on adrenaline. The media was packed inside the clubhouse, getting reactions and answers to how it all unfolded.

Hitting coach Ben Hines walked by, and the reporters asked him how Gibson got ready. Hines said he didn't know and to ask Mitch Poole. The reporters swarmed around the 25-year-old Poole.

"That's unprecedented," Poole said. "You think a hitting coach would ever do that? But he did that. I got backed up against that mirror [in the clubhouse]. It was the first column of *Sports Illustrated*. You see Eckersley and Gibson going at it in a full-page spread, and then there's my name over there. It's so cool.

"Gibby has always made me feel part of it. He always has. He still does to this day. People can think what they want about Kirk Gibson. But that was my single most incredible moment in baseball that night."

◆ ◆ ◆ ◆

Eckersley was more shocked than anybody. Walking off the mound was the loneliest feeling. As he made his way into the clubhouse, nobody would make eye contact with him. The whole thing was like slow motion. He was still in shock when reporters entered the clubhouse, shock that can be seen on his face as he did interviews.

In the cramped visiting clubhouse at Dodger Stadium, Eckersley stood at his locker. Wave after wave of reporters approached him. Only a few could hear him at a time. They would get their quotes and leave. Another wave of reporters surrounded him. They'd get their quotes and leave. And then another wave engulfed him.

"It was a dumb pitch," Eck told one of those waves of reporters. "It was the one pitch he could pull for power. And he hit the dogmeat out of it. He didn't look good on any of his swings, and that's why we threw him so many fastballs away, and that's why it was stupid to throw him a breaking ball. If I throw him another fastball away and he hits it out to left center, I can almost live with that, but I can't throw him a pitch he can pull. I mean, I threw him the only pitch he could hit out."

Eckersley answered every question. He never complained about the same question getting asked. He never asked for a PR official to help give him some privacy, and he never lost his temper. *Sports Illustrated* reported that Eckersley answered questions for nearly 45 minutes that night.

The entire A's clubhouse was shocked and filled with disbelief. Few words were spoken. The looks on the faces told the story.

"No one said shit to me," Eckersley told *ESPN the Magazine* on the game's 20th anniversary. "No one would look at me, let alone talk to me. Everyone gave me my space. They're trying to process it themselves. I just wanted eye contact, for chrissakes. But I guess in those situations, no one knows what to say."

Don Baylor saw that look on his teammates' faces that night. He'd seen that look before—many times, in fact. He saw it on the faces of the Angels in 1986, when his Red Sox were down to their last strike and won Game 5 in Anaheim. He saw it on his own teammates' faces two weeks later, after the ball went through Bill Buckner's legs. He knew his team, the big, bad, forearm-bashing Oakland A's, were in deep trouble.

"I was not very confident," Baylor said. "For Eck to give up a Game 1 home run? We expected, every time he went out there, to get the save. For him to give up that, he wore everything on his sleeve anyway."

Ned Colletti, now the Dodgers' general manager, worked in the public relations office of the Chicago Cubs in 1988. He was helping out Major League Baseball for that Series with PR duties. Colletti was in the corner of the A's dugout in the ninth inning, ready to grab Canseco, Eckersley, or La Russa for an interview with NBC.

Colletti remembered stone silence, total shock, and not a word spoken in the A's dugout after the Gibson home run. About 45 minutes after the game, Colletti returned to the A's clubhouse to check on Eckersley, a friend from their years together in Chicago.

Seated at a table in the middle of the clubhouse, Eckersley knew the fate of his life was sealed. "As long as they play baseball," Eckersley told Colletti, "they're going to show that highlight. That's all they will ever remember about me."

♦ ♦ ♦ ♦

Then-Dodgers general manager Fred Claire normally went into the clubhouse after games. If there was an injured player, he wanted to find out the extent of the injury and show his concern. If he was unhappy about something from the game, he'd go down to ask questions. He'd walk through the clubhouse before every game. In case a player needed to talk about something, he wanted to be available. The same applied after games.

But after Gibson's home run, there was no need for the GM in the clubhouse.

"It was the most surreal thing I've ever seen at Dodger Stadium," Claire remembered. "When he hits the home run, I leave my box, and I walked along the club level. And nobody was on the club level. No one. I swear. No one was on the club level. I walked along the club level. I walked into my office. Picked up my briefcase. Walked out of Dodger Stadium. Nobody was in the parking lot. It was like I dreamt this. No one. Walked down to spot 15. Get in my car. Drive out of the parking lot. There's no cars moving."

♦ ♦ ♦ ♦

Joe McDonnell was covering the game for KFI Radio in Los Angeles and the Associated Press Radio Network. He was in the media workroom, where you watched the game on TVs, and was ready to file his reports. Just as the final pitch was delivered, the TV monitors went blank. McDonnell never saw the home run. He headed downstairs to the clubhouse.

Back then, the media had access everywhere—the trainer's room, the food room, everywhere. McDonnell was walking near the training room and heard a recognizable voice from the shower.

"Joe, get your fat ass over here," Gibson said, laughing. Gibson was in the shower, wearing a towel, taking a few moments before he would get bombarded with interviews. Gibson asked McDonnell if he wanted to get his interview done right there in the shower. McDonnell did.

"That was awesome," McDonnell said when the interview was complete.

"Yeah, it was pretty neat, wasn't it?" Gibson said.

◆ ◆ ◆ ◆

Where did Mel Didier's famed scouting report come from? Previous accounts tell us it was good old-fashioned scouting. But this is where the story gets interesting.

"This is the question I've been waiting for," Hassey said. "You go through the history of the year, how many times did Eck go to a 3–2 count?"

In the mid-1990s, while working at ESPN, Peter Gammons sent a research staff looking into how often Eckersley reached a 3–2 count against lefties in 1988. Gammons said the staff reported it never happened the entire year. Not once.

This author went through Eckersley's game log on Baseball-Reference.com to confirm the findings. The 1988 season is the first that pitch-count totals are available and the first when the count is listed when an at-bat ends.

This author found that Eckersley faced 131 left-handed batters in the 1988 regular season. Eck went to a 3–2 count eight times. Four of those times came in May, when it's doubtful the Dodgers were already scouting the A's for a World Series matchup.

After the All-Star break, Eckersley went to a 3–2 count against a lefty four times in the regular season and once in the playoffs:
- On July 29, Eck gave up a single to Seattle's Alvin Davis.
- On August 11, Eck struck out California's Thad Bosley swinging.
- On August 16, Eck struck out Baltimore's Eddie Murray swinging.

- On September 17, Eck walked Kansas City's Jim Eisenreich.
- On October 5, in Game 1 of the ALCS against Boston, Eck walked lefty Rich Gedman. Eck never went to a 3–2 count against a lefty in his next three appearances in that series.

What isn't known is how many times Eckersley threw a backdoor slider on those nine 3–2 counts to lefties in 1988. If nothing else, it wasn't a very big sample size for such a no-doubt prediction.

The scouting report for that entire series was compiled by Dodgers scouts Mel Didier, Steve Boros, and Jerry Stephenson. Didier delivered the famous line about Eckersley, so he's given the most credit.

It's possible the scouting report was based on Eckersley's three years in the National League with the Cubs from 1984–86. No data exists on 3–2 counts in those years. Even if it did exist, that's two years removed, and Eckersley was a starting pitcher with the Cubs in those years. He was a different pitcher as a ninth-inning closer.

Didier's famed quoted included the line, "I've seen him freeze George Brett with it. I've seen him freeze Wade Boggs with it."

In examining the pitch-by-pitch data in 1988, Eckersley never went to a 3–2 count against Brett or Boggs that year. Eckersley faced Brett just once. He struck him out swinging on a 1–2 pitch on September 17. Swinging indicates Brett wasn't frozen.

Eckersley faced Boggs twice in the regular season and twice in the ALCS. On May 16, Boggs grounded to short on a 0–1 pitch. On August 21, Boggs grounded out to second base on a 2–2 pitch. On October 5 in Game 1 of the ALCS, Boggs struck out swinging on a 0–2 pitch to end the game. On October 8 in Game 3 of the ALCS, Boggs lined out to deep left on a 2–2 pitch.

Even if the scouting report was shaky based on old reports or limited data, the bottom line is that Didier was right. Eck threw a backdoor slider. Gibson was waiting for it. Gibson whacked it.

Didier rushed down to the Dodgers' clubhouse afterward and told Gibson not to tell the press that he knew the 3–2 pitch was coming. If a similar situation came up later in the Series, the Dodgers didn't want Eck to know that they knew what was coming.

At his locker that night, Gibson said, "I was well prepared for him. You have to give him a lot of credit. He's the best reliever in the game this year. We've had our scouts scouting him well. You can call it lucky or whatever. I really do feel like I was lucky. You look at his record, nobody has hit a home run off him in 3–4 months. I hit a good pitch. I was lucky to hit it out."

The story about the scouting report didn't reach the press until after the World Series ended. The first time the *Los Angeles Times* reported on the scouting report, Didier's quote was, "If you're a left-handed hitter and you get in a tough, tough situation with Eckersley, he's going to throw you that backdoor slider."

Over the years, the more generic phrase "tough situation" has morphed into the very specific "3–2 count" when the story is told.

Tim Leary gave his copy of the scouting report to this author. The fifth sentence on Eckersley states, "Likes to 'backdoor' slider to LH hitters with 3–2 count."

In retrospect, Steve Sax can't help but chuckle. Even if Gibson knew what pitch was coming, Sax said, "Gibson was completely fooled on the pitch. He was way out in front of the pitch. But he got enough on the meat of the bat, and there she went."

Marshall spent almost the entire season watching Gibson hit from the on-deck circle. He knew Gibson's swing and was not surprised at how far the ball went. "If anybody knows the way Gibby hit, he was an upper body hitter," Marshall said. "With two strikes, he spread out. He was an early guy who didn't even stride. That he could hit a ball 400', it made sense. No stride. Widens out. Hits with upper body. He's a strong human being. Great hands. Great upper body. He didn't hit with his lower body. When he hit the ball out, it didn't surprise me as much as everybody else. The swing wasn't as affected as everybody thinks."

Hassey doesn't buy the scouting report legend. "It's a great story, ain't it?" Hassey said. "Mel Didier, another storyteller. Makes himself look good with that, 'We knew he would throw a 3–2 breaking ball.' It puzzles me. How many times did Eck ever get to 3–2?

"It was a good pitch. You tip your hat to Kirk Gibson. I don't think these other side stories mean anything. He hit a good pitch in a tough situation. He was able to do the job. All the rest of the stuff sounds good—Tommy Lasorda outsmarting the A's, Mel Didier coming up with the advance report. The player has to do it. The player did it."

Eckersley has always expressed doubt about the 3–2 backdoor slider story. "First of all, I didn't get to 3–2 on too many hitters," Eckersley said, in a 2008 interview in *USA Today*. "If [Gibson] wants to give the credit to the scout, that's okay. I'm the idiot who threw the crappy slider."

Hassey still doesn't regret calling the slider. "I thought that pitch [the backdoor slider] was a tougher pitch than his fastball," Hassey reflected. "If I had to do it all over again, I'd call the same pitch. You can say, 'With his physical ability, Eck should have thrown a fastball.' But if he hits a fastball out, you'd say, 'You should have thrown the breaking ball.' That's how it goes."

◆ ◆ ◆ ◆

Ken Levine was a writer on *Cheers*, the most popular TV show in America for most of the 1980s. But what he really wanted to do was become a baseball play-by-play announcer. Levine went to Dodger Stadium on a regular basis in 1986 and 1987, usually sat in the first row of the top deck, and practiced his play-by-play into a microphone.

That led to a minor league job with Triple A Syracuse. After the minor league season ended, Levine returned to Los Angeles to continue his TV writing career. He obtained World Series tickets from his father, a salesman for KABC Radio.

"I had finished my first year of minor league baseball with Syracuse and wanted to make a tape of a major league game. So what better than the World Series? My seat was in the Bob Uecker section—reserve level, right field. The crowd was so loud the two people sitting on either side of me said they never even heard me calling the game.

"It was tough to call from that angle, and I struggled. I did have a great view of Kirk Gibson's home run, though. It sailed right across my line of vision into the stands. My home run call was fine, but I knew it would be compared to Vinny's and Jack Buck's and it wasn't nearly at that level, so I didn't use that inning for a demo. I have the tape somewhere but God knows where. Since I determined it was not usable, I just tossed it into a box.

"Here's what I remember after the home run: We just stood, many on our chairs, and cheered…endlessly…for at least 10 minutes. It just didn't die down. I've never seen anything like it. I was in Dodger Stadium when they clinched the NLCS against the Phillies in '78 and Mets in '88, and although the place went nuts on both of those occasions, it paled in comparison to this celebration. It made no difference that it was only Game 1. The jubilation just fed on itself, and it was like perpetual motion."

♦ ♦ ♦ ♦

Bob Mercer is a longtime Dodgers season-ticket holder. He sat in the loge level (the second deck) on the third-deck side. Mercer had low expectations that year for the Dodgers, didn't think they'd beat the Mets, and thought his favorite team had no chance to beat the A's. Mercer took a friend and his son to the game. His memory:

"My buddy said, 'This will be a Hollywood ending if he hits a home run.' Damn if he didn't do it.

"I've never clapped so hard in my life. It was unbelievable. I've never been so excited. I've been to a million games and had season tickets for a long time. I've never experienced anything like that in my life. It was amazing. My hands never stopped. I'm going to say, I won't exaggerate this, it was 10–15 minutes as far as I was concerned of nonstop cheering.

"When we walked out of there, my buddy said, 'We're never going to forget this in our lifetime' and 'There's going to be a lot of people who said they were here and they weren't there.' First of all, you never thought they would compete with Oakland. But they did, and they won. It was amazing."

His son, Sean Mercer, has a memory that is unforgettable for a different reason:

"I was playing baseball at College of the Canyons in 1988. It was my freshman year. I was trying to make the team. It was a junior college but known for baseball. I was working my butt off to make the team. My coach nicknamed me Bulldog. He saw me like an Orel Hershiser–type of guy. I got his approval to not go to practice and attend the game. I drove separately. My dad was coming up from OC. I was coming down from Valencia. I ended up parking outside the stadium and was stoked to be going to the game. I was excited as could be. The Dodgers were always my team. I had blue in my blood.

"We got to the ninth inning. I remember Dennis Eckersley was coming in. I was saying to myself, *Eckersley was unhittable. I knew Kirk Gibson wasn't going to play.* I thought I had all the answers. I wanted to beat the traffic. I parked out in the boondocks. I wanted to get a head start. I was probably halfway through the parking lot, and I heard the roar of the crowd. It was nothing I ever heard before. I ran over to a guy who was watching the game on a transistor TV. I watched the replay. I couldn't believe it. I couldn't believe I missed one of the greatest moments in baseball history.

"Other people left early, too. We all couldn't believe it. We all ran over to the transistor TV. It was probably a 4" x 4", a tiny little TV. It was just somebody in the parking lot. He didn't have a ticket for the game. He sat in the parking lot in his car with the TV. That's as close as he could get. It was an amazing experience to not experience it. It was not something I recommend to any fan. I pretty much told everybody. I'm real ashamed of it, but I'm real honest. I didn't see it. That's something I will never let myself forget."

♦ ♦ ♦ ♦

The memories never fade, even 25 years later.

"It was chaotic in the locker room," John Shelby said. "Guys were jumping up and down and screaming. I wanted to see my wife. She was pregnant at the time. I wanted to see her and have her tell me what the excitement was like in the stands. Come to find out, my wife had to go to the bathroom. She missed it. She was pregnant. She couldn't hold it. She had to go. She heard all this noise from the bathroom and had no idea what happened. She missed the whole thing."

"I watch myself [on replays] and I look like an idiot jumping around," Tracy Woodson said. "I laugh when I see Hershiser jumping up and down, Sax pushing me out of the way. Gibby said, 'Easy, easy.' I remember everybody was hugging him and he said, 'Easy' because it hurt him when you squeezed him hard. I came outside [the clubhouse] 10–15 minutes later, and the fans hadn't moved. That place was still going nuts. My dad was up in the stands, too. He said it was unbelievable."

"I can't think of a worse game that I ever pitched in the big leagues, on the biggest stage—and that was the best game that I was ever part of," Tim Belcher said. "There was virtually no way he could give us anything that entire Series. Seeing him hobble out of the dugout in the ninth inning, to me, it was great theater. I didn't view it as great theater then. It was just a game—'Come on Gibby, do something here.' Looking back on it, watching years and years of postseason baseball, that's as dramatic as it gets right there."

"Worst moment of my life," said Steve Vucinich, the A's equipment manager. "I was happier when my first wife left me."

Shawn Green, who played five of his 15 years in the majors with the Dodgers, attended the game with his family. He was a few weeks from turning 16 years old. They lived in Tustin, down in Orange County. It's a long drive home. They left early. His family wasn't the car slamming on the brakes as the ball went over the fence. But they missed the whole thing, too.

Jon Garland, who pitched 12 years in the majors and had two different stints with the Dodgers, grew up in nearby Granada Hills. His grandfather was a season-ticket holder, and he went to many games. Garland attended Game 1, sitting in the reserve level that night. Garland didn't leave early.

Ryan Braun, the 2011 National League Most Valuable Player, was among the players asked by espn.com's Jim Caple for what game in baseball history he'd most want to travel in time to witness. Braun picked "the Gibson game." Braun was four years old at the time. Braun told Caple, "I've seen the highlight so many times, and having grown up a Dodgers fan, that was a pretty special moment and extremely dramatic. I would have liked to have caught the ball. That would have been cool. I would be in the right field bleachers, fourth row, fifth row."

Sparky Anderson with the Detroit Tigers was Kirk Gibson's first manager in the majors. Sparky loved Gibson like he was his son. Before his death, Sparky said the following: "I wasn't there, but I was there. I didn't think he had a chance. I told my wife. She was sitting behind the kitchen table. When he hit that home run, I don't think I ever wanted to cry harder than that moment. That moment to me is what all the years of baseball had all come together in one. To see somebody you had first, as a young kid, to do under those circumstances. That's my most marvelous moment of Gibby."

Kirk Gibson wrote the following in his book about rounding the bases: "A lot of things go through your mind really quickly. Obviously, you're happy. You're taking in the scene, the response to the game-winning home run. You're thinking about your parents and about the people who supported you and about what other people mother-fucked you. Baseball is a very humbling game. It's a game of failure. And it's one where a lot of expectations are laid upon people. I was the next Mickey Mantle. That was the label they gave me. And if you don't live up to that...so this was like vindication, when you tell all those people, 'Thanks for your support. And don't worry about those idiots all over me. I knew our day would come.' And now it has."

Jocelyn Becker was three years old in 1988, too young to watch the game or understand it. She grew up to become a huge Dodgers fan and decided one day to re-create the bottom of the ninth inning on Nintendo's *RBI Baseball*. It took 24 hours of her life to get it perfect: Scioscia's popup, Hamilton's strikeout, Davis' five-pitch walk, all of Gibson's foul balls, the little nubber that went foul up the line, all the throws to first base. She finally got it exact and laid Scully's words over the background. At last check, it had more than 69,000 views on YouTube. It's stunning to watch the accuracy and hear Scully's voice. It's worth a look at http://www.youtube.com/watch?v=InlRcSrSKk0

Former A's outfielder Jonny Gomes, now with the Boston Red Sox, was seven years old, living in Petaluma, California (48 miles north of Oakland, near Santa Rosa), and a die-hard A's fan. "When you're a kid, your baseball heroes are like Superman or Batman or the Hulk," Gomes said. "They don't die. It was my cartoon days. Cartoon heroes didn't die at the end of the thing. They rescued the chick. They put the fire out. They found Clifford the Big Red Dog. They never die. Then the fucking A's died. That was my first experience with real life. Life is not a fucking cartoon."

◆ ◆ ◆ ◆

On a random Monday afternoon in 2012, before the start of the fifth inning of a Dodgers-Giants game, the home run was replayed as a promo to an upcoming bobblehead promotion of Gibson. Scully watched it on his monitor and waxed nostalgic about that moment in baseball history for a minute or so.

Scully added, "It still gets to you, doesn't it?"

Chapter 17

World Series Games 2–5

Sunday, October 16, 1988

Los Angeles

Athletics vs. Dodgers

World Series Game 2

Jose Canseco walked onto the field for batting practice and was approached by an autograph seeker. But this was a unique request. It was Jimmy Mott, a cameraman from NBC, the one who operated the center-field camera, the one that Canseco dented with his grand slam in Game 1.

Canseco walked out to center field, climbed up the scaffolding, and signed the following onto the camera: "Jose Canseco, grand slam, '88 World Series."

In Kansas City, Bo Jackson made his season debut for the Los Angeles Raiders. He arrived at the team's training camp in El Segundo four days earlier, taking a week off after finishing the baseball year with the Royals.

Bo only knew a few plays and didn't start. On his first carry, Bo gained eight yards on a sweep. On the second, Bo gained three yards and a first down on a sweep left. Then Bo went six yards on a sweep left. Then Bo caught a pass for five yards and a first down. Marcus Allen returned and got one yard. Bo came back and gained five more. And so it went.

Bo averaged 5.5 yards a carry in the first half, as the Raiders took a 14–0 lead en route to a 27–17 win over the Chiefs.

◆ ◆ ◆ ◆

Bob Verdi, the longtime columnist from the *Chicago Tribune*, knew Dennis Eckersley well from his days with the Chicago Cubs. Verdi checked on Eckersley's psyche before Game 2. Eckersley provided a golf reference for him, "If you're going to take an 8, might as well do it on the first hole."

Both teams were loose before the game. They sat around the clubhouse, watching the Sunday NFL games and hollering at the televisions.

George Earl "Storm" Davis started Game 2 for the Athletics. He was cursed by the "next Jim Palmer" label when he reached the majors with Baltimore in 1982 at age 20. Davis tried to emulate Palmer, which was impossible to do. Davis spent five years with the Orioles, went 61–43 with a 3.63 ERA, and was traded to the Padres after the 1986 season.

It was a miserable five months in San Diego. Davis went 2–7 with a 6.18 ERA, lost his spot in the rotation, and clashed publicly with manager Larry Bowa. At the low point, Bowa said Davis thought the "SD" on the cap stood for Storm Davis.

"I don't think I learned anything from the man," Davis told reporters that October. "Larry said a lot of things about me out of frustration. But I know if he walked up to me now, he'd say he meant every one of them."

Davis was ecstatic to get traded to the A's in August 1987. The Padres received left-handed reliever Dave Leiper and first baseman Rob Nelson in return. Davis resurrected his career, going 16–7 with a 3.70 ERA in 1988 with the A's and started Game 2 of the ALCS.

Orel Hershiser started for the Dodgers on three days rest—again. It was the third straight time he was starting on short rest. Actually, you could no longer call it short rest. That was his normal rest. Hell, he might pitch again in relief any day. His arm didn't seem to ever need rest.

NBC led off its broadcast of Game 2 with a recap of the night before. Bob Costas called it "Echoes of a Miracle," and it included Kirk Gibson's home run interspersed with fictional character Roy Hobbs' home run in the movie *The Natural*.

The feature was created by David Neal, who had grown up in the L.A. suburb of Woodland Hills and attended USC. It was completed less than five minutes before NBC went on the air.

Gibson took early batting practice around 1:00 PM, a good four hours before the start of the game. Afterward, Gibson said he couldn't start. Unlike in Game 1, Gibson was in the dugout and in uniform during the game.

In the excitement of Gibson's home run, Hershiser forgot to bring home videotapes of the A's hitters to study. When he got to the ballpark for Game 2, he was cramming for a final exam and decided to make a cheat sheet. He wrote the scouting report on A's hitters on a piece of paper, had it laminated, and put it inside his back pocket.

As Hershiser took the field, he showed the cheat sheet to home plate umpire Durwood Merrill so there would be no confusion about sandpaper or pine tar or other foreign substances. He wouldn't need the notes very often, consulting it two to three times during the game.

Organist Nancy Hefley played the song "Master of the House" from *Les Miserables* when Hershiser took the mound. Hershisers were all over the field. His parents, Orel III and Millie, were selected "Parents of the Year" by Little League Baseball and threw out the ceremonial first pitches. Magic Johnson watched the game from the stands.

The first time through the A's lineup, Hershiser faced the minimum number of hitters. The only blemish was a second-inning single to Dave Parker, who was quickly erased on a Mark McGwire double play. The free-swinging A's were retired on 14 pitches through two innings.

In the top of the third, Hershiser felt something in one of his legs. Catcher Mike Scioscia came out to visit the mound. Hershiser appeared to be favoring the leg as he walked off the mound after the inning. Trainer Bill Buhler and Gibson checked on Hershiser between innings.

In Hershiser's mind, pitching was work, and he always felt pressure. Hitting was fun. Nobody expected him to hit, so there was no pressure. It brought out the kid in him.

With one out in the third, Hershiser felt like the happiest kid in Los Angeles. He squared around to bunt, pulled the bat back, and slapped a single up the middle off Storm Davis, who had retired seven of the first eight batters he faced.

Hershiser took his lead at first base and wanted to ignite a rally. He thought about stealing second base. He imagined breaking up a double play. Whatever he felt in his legs a half inning earlier wasn't too serious.

Steve Sax lined a single to right field, and Hershiser was determined to reach third base. He put his head down, never looked at third-base coach Joe Amalfitano, and challenged the arm of Jose Canseco in right field. Canseco still cared about defense back then, and he had a great throwing arm. But this throw was cut off, and Hershiser slid into third base safely.

Hershiser was either winded at third base, or his legs were still tight, or both. He went down to a knee on the base to gather himself. After a strike, Franklin Stubbs bounced a single into the hole to score Hershiser and move Sax to third. It was 1–0.

Lasorda kept the pressure on. He called for a hit-and-run with Mickey Hatcher up. Hatcher hit a chopper up the middle. The ball squirted past the dive of shortstop Walt Weiss in front of the bag and also past second baseman Glenn Hubbard behind the bag. Stubbs jumped over Weiss, landed on second base, and moved onto third base. It was 2–0 Dodgers.

"They had the bigger-name team, but for some reason, we felt we were the better team," Stubbs reflected. "We executed better, especially the little things that we did to win games. We felt our pitching could neutralize their hitting. Once we won Game 1, I actually thought we were going to sweep them. I just felt like after that game, with Hershiser able to pitch the second game, they were pretty much a done deal."

Mike Marshall was due up. Marshall was the only power threat in the Dodgers' lineup. John Shelby was on deck. An intentional walk would load the bases and set up the double play. But the A's didn't intentionally walk batters, not in the third inning. Marshall wasn't surprised. He knew that he was a strikeout threat. Kirk Gibson would get intentionally walked in that situation, but not Marshall.

The count was quickly 0–2, and Davis was looking to put Marshall away. Davis wanted to climb the ladder, throwing a fastball up and inside. The pitch missed the location. Marshall didn't miss the pitch, however, and he hit a high fly ball into left field.

Dave Parker was playing left field, since there was no designated hitter. Parker went back to the fence, ready to time his jump and make the catch. But just as he was about to jump, his back hit the wall. His glove couldn't reach high enough. It was gone.

"I know the book on me," Marshall reflected. "They're going to pound me inside, especially when they get ahead. As soon as I hit it, the game is over because

Hershiser is on the mound. It's over. I'm trying to get the one [run] in. I know he's coming inside. He came in, and I beat him 0–2. Again, it was all preparation."

It was 5–0 Dodgers. With Hershiser pitching, it might as well have been 50–0.

When Marshall homered in 1987 at Candlestick Park, after Giants manager Roger Craig had intentionally walked the previous hitter, Marshall had pointed at the Giants' dugout. Marshall regretted that display. After that, Marshall was always reserved after hitting home runs, never wanting to show up the opposition.

After this home run, the usually stoic Marshall showed little emotion rounding the bases, even as his teammates went wild and the stadium shook. Marshall did manage a wry smile as he returned to the dugout. Sax gave him a high ten. Lasorda hugged him.

Given the big lead, Hershiser altered his game plan. He started thinking about his Game 5 start, and didn't want to show the A's everything. He threw more changeups than usual, and altered his pattern of pitches.

Hershiser struck out the side in the fourth—Carney Lansford, Dave Henderson, and Canseco. Against Canseco, most pitchers were scared to throw their fastball. They tried to get him to chase sliders and hoped they didn't hang anything. The scouting report was hard inside, not to let Canseco extend his arms, and then soft stuff away. Hershiser didn't bother with off-speed pitches.

All he threw Canseco, except for one pitch, was fastballs. The only curveball Hershiser threw to Canseco went over Canseco's head. It was the first time Canseco had ever encountered a pitcher who threw him almost exclusively fastballs. Canseco couldn't believe he didn't hit even one pitch hard. Canseco mumbled to himself as he returned to the dugout each time.

Canseco was 0-for-4. Everybody was 0-for-something, except Parker. Hershiser allowed three hits, all singles to Parker, walked two, struck out eight, and needed just 108 pitches for the shutout.

Don Baylor was announced as a pinch hitter in the eighth inning. The L.A. fans unleashed their loudest round of jeers for Baylor. When Baylor struck out, chasing a curveball out of the strike zone, it was the loudest round of cheers for any whiff all night.

Hershiser collected as many hits as he gave up. After a Griffin infield single in the fourth, Hershiser showed bunt, then flipped a double down the right-field line, scoring a run and chasing Davis with the score 6–0.

While running the bases, Hershiser wore trainer Charlie Strasser's jacket, which had Strasser's name on the back. On NBC, Vin Scully said he guaranteed Hershiser did it to give Strasser some publicity.

Hershiser also doubled down the left-field line in the sixth inning, too hard for Carney Lansford to even react at third base. He was a one-man wrecking crew. Considering the hitting and base running—and yet another shutout, the ninth start in his last 12 without allowing a run—Hershiser considered it the most complete game of his career.

"It seems like you just give him the ball, and he pitches a shutout," Sax marveled.

Even then, people were questioning about the long-term effects these innings would have on Hershiser. The Bulldog was adamant that he wasn't taking a risk, and he had no second-thoughts.

"If I threw a screwball or a zillion pitches, it would be one thing," Hershiser said then. "I'm basic. I get a lot of quick innings. I don't go deep into many counts. I don't worry about what will happen down the road. I may never be through anything like this in my life, so I'm going to roll with it and enjoy it. I know my arm, and I feel great. If something happens, well, there's life after baseball. But I'm not sacrificing what we've got our hands on to think about how many years and how much money I've got left. I was raised to throw properly."

The A's remained defiant and confident, at least publicly.

Parker said that Hershiser "pitched a great game," but when asked about the best pitcher in baseball, Parker named Houston's Mike Scott.

"Nobody believed it was going to be easy," Parker said that night. "I haven't seen anything exceptional from the Dodgers.... We're still going to win. We're going to win the World Series. We're going to get back to Oakland and kick their ass."

♦ ♦ ♦ ♦

Monday, October 17, 1988
Los Angeles
World Series off-day

Kirk Gibson stepped into the batting cage to test how his knees and hamstrings and legs felt.

A sea of cameras followed his every move. Gibson would hit a slow roller to second and yell an expletive. He'd hit a home run into the right-field pavilion and feel better. Cameras were placed on the ground for low-angle shots. Gibson gave the photographers a laser death stare. He faked throwing his bat at the lens.

Another slow roller to second. Another grunt. Another expletive. Another home run. Another slow roller to second. It seemed like that's all he did, hit home runs and slow rollers to second and curse.

Gibson returned to the Dodgers' dugout trailed by a swarm of reporters. "Don't smother me," he yelled. Microphones moved toward his mouth. "Get those out of my face," he growled.

A reporter asked, tentatively, "How'd it go out there, Kirk?"

"Shitty," Gibson replied.

Another reporter, "How does the right knee feel?"

"It's sorer today than yesterday," Gibson said. "It's pretty obvious what my role is gonna be, if any."

Another reporter, "Is it frustrating that you're not able to start and might not be able to play the rest of the series?"

"The most frustrating thing is talking to you guys," Gibson replied. "You follow me around while I'm trying to work. I don't understand it. You've seen me loosen up 1,000 times."

Another reporter, "What about being the designated hitter?"

"I can't run," Gibson said. "You figure it out. How am I going to DH if I can't run? I tried to jog in the outfield. It was a fake jog. It was a joke."

Gibson looked at a fat reporter. "You could've beaten me in a race," Gibson told him.

In Detroit, Gibson wasn't getting any sympathy or any respect for his home run. Tigers owner Tom Monaghan was still pissed at the Dodgers. He still thought the Tigers were a better team without Gibson, especially in the clubhouse, even though the Tigers finished one game behind the Red Sox in the American League East.

"We weren't hurt by Gibson leaving," Monaghan told WJR radio in Detroit. "We were helped defensively."

The radio host replied, "You can't be mad at the Dodgers."

"Yes I am," Monaghan said. "I think it's unethical to sign other team's players. Every club in baseball is mad at Los Angeles."

"Gibson is probably the MVP in the National League," the radio host said.

Monaghan replied, "He's a liability in the field, and his numbers aren't that great. How many home runs did he hit? 24? 25? What'd he bat? How can anyone figure those are MVP numbers?"

Gibson batted .290 with 25 homers, 76 RBIs, and 31 stolen bases. The only number that mattered on the off-day was one. "If I play one game, it might be my last," Gibson said. "Ahead 2–0, this isn't the time to play."

Gibson had a sprained MCL in his right knee, plus injuries to his left knee and hamstring. He couldn't be the DH because he couldn't run. He might be available to pinch hit again but only in the perfect scenario.

They play organ music at Dodger Stadium. They play loud rock 'n' roll music at the Oakland Coliseum. A reporter from a music magazine asked Lasorda what he thought of the heavy metal that would be played in Oakland.

"You mean that hippie crap?" Lasorda answered. "Sometimes they play weird music at ballparks during batting practice. It sounds like ugly noise to me. Or somebody recovering from a bad meal. But hey, if the players can hit to that stuff, what do I care?"

John Tudor was starting Game 3 on eight days rest. He'd pitched twice in the last 17 days. He wasn't happy about it. He wasn't used to it. His hip injury was no longer an issue. Clearly, the Dodgers were concerned about something because the playoff hired-gun had been bypassed for rookie Tim Belcher.

Lasorda knew they'd done a disservice to Tudor. The bottom line, though, was that Belcher was pitching better and not a health risk. Besides, Lasorda thought the veteran Tudor could handle the long rest better. He thought the veteran would be better on the road.

Orel Hershiser was asked one word to describe Tommy Lasorda. Hershiser thought about it. "The first word is motivator. The second word is intensity. The third word that comes to mind is will to win. That's what I think of when I think of Tommy. His will to win."

Hershiser paused and thought about his answer. "How do you like that? I sound like a dumb jock," Hershiser said. "You ask for one word, I tell you I'll give you three words, and then I give you five."

◆ ◆ ◆ ◆

Tony La Russa held a brief team meeting after Game 2, telling his players to not get discouraged, to look forward to the next game. He made the team's off-day workout optional, and only one-third showed up. La Russa was happy. He wanted his players to relax and not spend all day answering questions about the 2–0 deficit.

When he arrived at the workout, a hand-written note was on his desk:

> *Skip—I was out here at 10 o'clock. I worked out till 12. My arm felt fine.*
>
> *—Stew.*

La Russa was already leaning toward starting Dave Stewart in Game 4 on three days rest. His other option was Curt Young, who had pitched 1⅓ innings of relief in the ALCS and hadn't started since September 29. "I know Stew," La Russa said, laughing. "He probably came in Sunday night and wrote the note so he didn't have to work out today."

It was suggested the A's had taken the Dodgers lightly. "Nobody's taking anyone lightly," Parker said. "That's Lasorda's bullshit. How can we take them lightly?"

◆ ◆ ◆ ◆

Tuesday, October 18, 1988
Oakland
Dodgers vs. Athletics
World Series Game 3

Marty Cohen was a disc jockey at the aptly named San Francisco radio station KFOG FM. At 8:00 AM, Cohen called the Dodgers' team hotel, requested John Tudor's room, and was patched through.

"Good morning, John, you're on the air," Cohen said.

"No, I'm not," said Tudor, hanging up.

Kirk Gibson still wasn't able to start, not even as the designated hitter in Oakland. When Vin Scully gave the Dodgers' starting lineup, he said Gibson was available to pinch hit.

Bob Welch started Game 3 for the A's. Welch was known for being hyper. He was hyper for spring training starts. Welch couldn't control those emotions in his only start against the Red Sox in the American League Championship Series.

Welch allowed five runs in less than two innings before the A's rallied for a 10–6 win in Game 3.

On the Steve Sax 1–10 scale of hyper, Mike Scioscia predicted Welch would be a nine as he faced his former teammates.

When they were teammates, Sax would stand at second base shaking his head in amazement at how Welch would hit the corners all day. Now he was facing his former teammate. He couldn't think about who it was. All he would think was that Welch was the enemy.

Sax started the game with a single to right. Welch threw to first base nine times in the first inning. Sax tried to run, but two pitches were fouled off when he was running. Welch got his emotions under control. Welch struck out Franklin Stubbs swinging, struck out Mickey Hatcher looking, and struck out Mike Marshall swinging. Welch struck out two more in the second inning.

La Russa stressed patience against Tudor. He wanted them to think up the middle. La Russa was willing to settle for 15 singles. That result wouldn't surprise Tudor—he was one of the most pessimistic people you'd ever meet. One longtime Dodgers employee said Tudor was his least-favorite player ever.

Tudor retired the side in order in the first inning, but he was grimacing in pain after each pitch he threw to Jose Canseco. A trainer visited the mound, yet Tudor convinced the staff he could remain in the game. Canseco hit a towering fly ball to left field for the final out in the inning.

Tudor struck out Mark McGwire to begin the second inning on a half swing, but he yelled out in pain in the process. Tudor walked off the mound, stopped at the first-base line, kicked the dirt, and turned back around to the mound.

After a discussion with trainer Bill Buhler and Lasorda, Tudor departed the game with a sore elbow. On a 24-man roster, Gibson's injury put it at 23, and now Tudor's injury dropped it to 22.

Tim Leary was summoned into the game. After pitching three important scoreless innings of relief in Game 1 to keep the game close and make Gibson's heroics possible, Leary was back on two days rest to replace Tudor.

In the third, the A's offense finally woke up. They hadn't scored since the second inning of Game 1, a stretch of 18 innings. Glenn Hubbard started the third inning with a drive off the left-field wall. Mickey Hatcher played it perfectly and held Hubbard to a 330' single. On a busted hit-and-run, Scioscia double-clutched because Alfredo Griffin was late covering the bag, then his throw bounced into center field. Hubbard advanced all the way to third base.

Ron Hassey served a single into left field, the A's led 1–0, and Scully said on NBC, "The drought is over for Oakland."

In the fourth inning, Mike Marshall's back flared up again, and he was forced to leave the game. The injury actually happened in Game 2. He gutted his way through that game and tried to play in Game 3. Now the Dodgers were down to 21 players. Danny Heep pinch hit for Marshall and was one of two strikeout victims in the fourth inning. Welch had eight strikeouts after four scoreless innings.

Heep stayed in the game in left field, and Hatcher moved to right field to start the fourth. The first batter was Canseco, and he hit a drive into right-center. Hatcher came charging in, after taking a weird angle, he stumbled and made a diving catch. The leader of the Stuntmen was playing like a leading man. McGwire crushed a ball to dead center, but in the cool air at the spacious Coliseum, it was caught by Shelby at the wall.

In the fifth, Jeff Hamilton singled to center. Griffin bunted him to second base but was clearly out of the base line. If the umpires had called Griffin out of the baseline, as they did Parker in Game 1, Hamilton would have been forced to return to first base.

The difference was evident when Franklin Stubbs hit a one-hopper off the wall in right-center. Hamilton scored easily from second base for a 1–1 tie. If Hamilton was at first base, he might not have scored—a point that Tony La Russa made to home-plate umpire Bruce Froemming for missing the call.

The Dodgers threatened in the sixth, loading the bases with nobody out. La Russa took out Welch and brought in lefty Greg Cadaret. Scioscia was jammed and fouled out to third. La Russa went to righty Gene Nelson, and he induced Hamilton to hit a grounder to third. Lansford went home for the force play and the second out.

Was it time for Gibson to come off the bench again? Gibson told Lasorda he was available. Hell yes, he was available. He practically came out of a wheel chair to hit three nights earlier. Gibson spent the entire game in the dugout, wearing a jacket and in uniform.

Two outs would be the ideal time. Gibson wouldn't have to worry about hitting into a double play. Griffin was the ideal hitter to remove. They still had

Dave Anderson to pinch run and stay in the game at shortstop. With the designated hitter rule in effect, you could use the bench earlier in the game without worrying about needing pinch-hitters later in the game.

But with Marshall already out, Lasorda didn't want to risk running out of players. He decided to save Gibson for later in the game. On the first pitch, Griffin hit a chopper to first, and McGwire caught it at the bag. Somehow, the A's escaped the bases-loaded, no-out jam. It took just five pitches. The Dodgers never got the ball out of the infield.

Jay Howell entered in the ninth with the game still tied 1–1. It was his first appearance in 10 days, since he was ejected from Game 3 of the NLCS with pine tar in his glove. Howell was back in Oakland, where the home fans had booed him at the 1987 All-Star Game, and they booed him worse afterward.

The A's fans were never so excited to see Howell enter a game. They chanted "pine tar, pine tar, pine tar" at him.

After all that time off, Howell was asked to face the Bash Brothers. The first batter was Canseco, and he wasted no time hacking. Canseco swung at the first pitch, shattered his bat, and popped out to Sax for the first out. In the dugout, La Russa told his players, "We're not going to win through the air. Line drives. Solid contact."

Mark McGwire had never faced Jay Howell in his life. McGwire had stood next to Howell during the All-Star Game introductions a year before, feeling the pain for his teammate getting booed, right after the crowd greeted McGwire with a lengthy standing ovation.

Howell jumped ahead 1–2 in the count on all fastballs. Howell missed with a fastball. McGwire, hitless so far in the series, fouled off three more fastballs. On the eighth pitch of the at-bat, Howell left a fastball up in the zone, right down the middle. McGwire bashed it over the left-center wall for the game-winning home run.

"The kid from Southern California breathes life into Northern California," Scully said on NBC.

Howell, who hadn't allowed a home run to a right-handed batter all year, was greeted by Hershiser between the first-base line and the dugout.

"Did you make a good pitch?" Hershiser asked.

Howell managed a brief nod, eyes down, lips closed.

"Then you gave it your best shot. We'll get 'em tomorrow." Hershiser said.

It took Howell a long time to emerge from the showers and the back of the clubhouse before he faced reporters. Howell wouldn't discuss pine tar, Don

Baylor's comments, David Cone's comments, his long layoff, or everything that he'd endured in the previous two weeks.

"No excuses," Howell said. "I just got a bad pitch up in the strike zone, and I didn't put enough on it to get it by him."

◆ ◆ ◆ ◆

Wednesday, October 19, 1988
Oakland
Dodgers vs. Athletics
World Series Game 4

Tim Belcher got lost on his way to the Oakland Coliseum for Game 3. He missed the team bus and got lost taking BART from the Dodgers' team hotel in San Francisco. Oh yeah, the Dodgers were staying in San Francisco, not Oakland. Think that rubbed some people in Oakland, the city with a perpetual chip on its shoulder, the wrong way?

Good thing for Belcher, he wasn't pitching Game 3. All he missed was a pregame press conference. Belcher took the team bus to the ballpark for Game 4.

Lasorda needed a lengthy talk with Dr. Frank Jobe before writing his Game 4 lineup. Kirk Gibson still wasn't available. Then Bill Russell came to Lasorda and said Mike Marshall couldn't start because he had a headache. Lasorda was furious.

"How the hell can a guy not play in the World Series with a headache?" Lasorda would say, years later. "So I got really mad and very demonstrative. For some reason, then I reached up and turned on the TV. And there's Bob Costas saying, 'This may be the worst team ever put on the field in World Series history.' I took it and ran with it. I mean, Bob was a very good friend. But I had to use it. I had to use it as a stimulator, right then and there."

The lineup Lasorda wrote out—Steve Sax, Franklin Stubbs, Mickey Hatcher, Mike Davis, John Shelby, Mike Scioscia, Danny Heep, Jeff Hamilton, Alfredo Griffin. They averaged four home runs and 34 RBIs in the regular season. They totaled 36 home runs. Jose Canseco hit 42 in the regular season and four more in the playoffs.

History would look back on the 1988 World Series as being over after Gibson's home run in Game 1. But this World Series would be decided by Game 4.

The pitching matchup was a rematch of Game 1—Belcher vs. Dave Stewart. If the A's won Game 4, they would not only tie the Series, they would be back in the driver's seat.

Even if Hershiser won Game 5, the Dodgers couldn't come back with John Tudor in Game 6. Tudor was done for the Series, probably needed surgery, and his career was in jeopardy. Tim Leary would need to start Game 6, on three days rest after 3⅔ innings of relief. If there was a Game 7, it was Belcher on three days rest again or Hershiser on two days rest.

Belcher never considered all those factors before Game 4, which was probably a good thing. He just wanted to redeem himself after his disappointing Game 1 performance. The jitters from Game 1 were now gone. He felt the same as he did in his two starts against the Mets.

Whether he realized it or not, the following subconscious thought came over him, *Hey, we're a huge underdog in this Series. There's no shame in pitching poorly against the Oakland A's. They had a tremendous lineup. Just relax and see what you can do. Go as deep as you can.*

Stewart didn't hit Sax in the neck to start this game. Instead, he walked him. Lasorda was going to hit-and-run and bunt whenever possible with this lineup. The hit-and-run would work in the first and seventh innings. It would fail in the third, fourth, and ninth innings. Trying five hit-and-runs in a game is an indication that Lasorda thought it was his only chance.

The Dodgers scratched out two runs on just one hit in the first inning. Stubbs lined out to right, and Hatcher slapped a hit-and-run single to right field that advanced Sax to third. Sax scored when a routine pitch deflected off catcher Terry Steinbach's glove for a passed ball.

It was 1–0 Dodgers. This was the third time in four games the Dodgers had scored first.

Mike Davis hit a grounder up the middle that bounced off Glenn Hubbard's bare hand for an error, putting runners at the corners with one out. Shelby hit a soft liner that deflected off Stewart's glove. If Stewart had caught it cleanly, it would have been a double play to end the inning. Instead, Hubbard's only play was first base. It was 2–0 Dodgers.

Shelby landed on first base awkwardly and limped into the dugout. The Dodgers couldn't afford another injury to an outfielder. Gibson and Marshall were already out. Danny Heep was the designated hitter. If Shelby couldn't continue, the center-field options were Mike Davis and the rarely used Jose Gonzalez.

"I hit the corner of the bag and turned my ankle," Shelby recalled. "The first thing I thought was I broke it. Then I realized I could walk on it. Once I realized I could walk on it, there was no way I was coming out of the game. I asked the trainers to tape me up. I went up into the clubhouse and got taped up."

Luis Polonia made his first start of the Series in the leadoff spot and ignited the A's in the bottom of the first inning. He dropped a soft single to left field, went to second on a passed ball, to third on a Dave Henderson tricky grounder to first, and scored on a Canseco grounder to second.

Canseco still didn't have a hit since his grand slam. But he had an RBI, as the forearm-bashing A's manufactured a run and trailed 2–1.

The A's defense self-destructed in the third inning again. Stubbs hit a one-out double to center, over the head of Henderson. Hatcher flew to left field for the second out. Davis hit a line drive right to shortstop Walt Weiss for an easy third out. However, Weiss played it too casual, took his eyes of the ball briefly, hopped a little when he didn't need to jump, and the ball deflected off his glove for an error. Weiss, who otherwise put on a defensive show in the Series, couldn't believe he missed the ball. The Dodgers led 3–1.

In the top of the fourth, the injuries continued to mount for the Dodgers. Scioscia started the inning with a single to right. On a 3–1 pitch, Lasorda called for another hit-and-run. Heep wasn't required to swing because he thought it was ball four. It wasn't. It was a strike.

"I'm out by 10', so I tried a pop-up slide," Scioscia recalled. "As soon as I popped up, I felt something in my knee. It was cartilage that tore and flipped over. As I tried to get up, my knee was locked because the cartilage had flipped over and locked in my knee. I couldn't even put pressure on it. I couldn't walk. I said, 'You've got to be kidding me.' I knew I couldn't catch."

Scioscia needed help coming off the field. If you're counting, the Dodgers 24-man roster was down to 20. Gibson, Marshall, Tudor, and now Scioscia were all out.

Rick Dempsey replaced Scioscia behind the plate, and coincidentally or not, Belcher's rhythm appeared to be disrupted. Henderson singled over Belcher's shoulder, and Canseco walked on four pitches. Pitching coach Ron Perranoski visited the mound, Tim Leary headed back to the bullpen, and Brian Holton started getting loose. Lasorda hollered encouragement.

Nobody was out, and the middle of the lineup was due up to the plate. The Coliseum faithful roared again, convinced this was the time the big, bad, Bash Brothers would finally bust out.

Belcher had other ideas, however. Parker struck out on a splitter. McGwire popped to center on a fastball. Lansford grounded to first on a checked swing. It was still 3–1 Dodgers. This wasn't the wild, nervous Belcher from Game 1. This was the focused Belcher from the regular season—and he was badly needed because the Dodgers' bullpen was on fumes.

In the fifth, Belcher worked around a leadoff single without allowing a run. In the sixth, Belcher had to do it again when Henderson singled to left. Ricky Horton and Brian Holton warmed up, just in case.

Canseco popped out into that huge foul territory, and Stubbs needed help from his teammates to avoid falling into the dugout. At any other ballpark, that's well into the stands and Canseco gets another swing. That happened a lot in Oakland. The A's averaged 2.21 foul-outs a game at the Coliseum in 1988, compared to 1.63 foul-outs on the road, a difference of about 50 foul-outs that year.

Belcher continued to challenge Parker with inside fastballs and retired him on a fly ball to left field. McGwire walked after a grueling eight-pitch duel to extend the inning. Lansford broke his own 0-for-12 drought with a soft single into right field to score Henderson. The Dodgers' lead was down to 3–2.

Still two on and two out and the A's needed another big hit. The crowd chanted "Beat L. A., Beat L. A." Belcher regrouped and got Steinbach on a grounder to first. The inning was over. Belcher had posted better statistical lines in the regular season, but this night was his finest moment of the season.

Stewart, working on three days rest, didn't throw as hard in Game 4 as he did in Game 1. He battled through six innings, the runs were the result of shaky defense, and then the Dodgers answered with another typical rally in the seventh inning.

Griffin walked with one out and took third on a chopper up the middle that eluded the dive of Hubbard. That ended the night for Stewart, and La Russa went back to lefty Greg Cadaret to face Stubbs.

Lasorda countered with righty Tracy Woodson, called for yet another hit-and-run on a 1–2 pitch, and Woodson hit a grounder to short. Weiss' throw to second base wasn't in time because Sax was running, so the A's only got one out. Griffin scored, and it was 4–2 Dodgers.

"Tommy was hot," Woodson said, upon reflection. "He made the right moves. The hit-and-runs were right on. Sax was running on the play. All I had to do was put the ball in play." To review, the Dodgers' four runs in the game scored on a passed ball, two on groundouts, and one on an error.

Another chance for the A's arrived in the seventh. Weiss reached on a one-out infield single and moved to second on a groundout. Henderson fell behind 0–2, but he pulled a hanging 2–2 curveball down the left-field line for a double that scored Weiss.

The Dodgers' lead was down to 4–3. At 119 pitches—and with Canseco, Parker, and McGwire due up—Belcher's night was over.

In the dugout, Belcher shook his head, pointed both index fingers at his temples, and mouthed the word "stupid" at his pitch selection to Henderson.

Lasorda needed seven outs from his bullpen for the victory. He'd all but given up on Jesse Orosco by this point. Alejandro Pena had given him three innings in Game 3, so he was unavailable. Brian Holton had been up earlier. But the game was in the balance right now, so Lasorda decided to go with Jay Howell early.

If ever there was an example of how bullpens were managed differently in 1988 than in the current era and how Tommy Lasorda managed with his gut, this was it. Forget the setup man. Howell was the stopper and closer. Howell would need to get seven outs—with the tying run at second base on the night after giving up a walk-off home run—to get the save.

The Coliseum cheered. The A's fans couldn't wait. This was the exact Dodgers relief pitcher they wanted in the game. At that point, Howell had faced seven batters in the playoffs, and he had retired only three of them.

♦ ♦ ♦ ♦

Jay Howell was heading down the path of Tom Niedenfuer in playoff infamy.

Niedenfuer wasn't just the pitcher who allowed Jack Clark's deciding home run in Game 6 of the 1985 NLCS. Niedenfuer also allowed Ozzie Smith's walk-off home run in Game 5 of that series. It was the home run that caused Jack Buck to tell Cardinals fans on the radio, "Go crazy, folks! Go crazy!"

Lasorda went right back to Niedenfuer in Game 6, in the seventh inning of a 4–3 game, with two outs and a runner at first, and Ozzie Smith at the plate again.

Smith tripled to tie the game. He walked Tommy Herr intentionally then struck out Clark and Andy Van Slyke. Niedenfuer pitched a scoreless eighth, and he was back out there in the ninth.

Two outs, runners at second and third, first base open, Van Slyke on deck, and Lasorda trusted Niedenfuer to get Clark out. It didn't work. Clark homered, and Lasorda was roasted.

Now, three years later, Lasorda would give Howell the same chance to redeem himself that he gave Niedenfuer. Just like in 1985, it was the seventh inning of a 4–3 game. Just like in 1985, it was less than 24 hours after giving up a walk-off homer. Just like in 1985, Howell would need to get seven outs to get the save and preserve the win.

◆ ◆ ◆ ◆

The first batter was Canseco. Howell worked carefully and walked Canseco on five pitches (three weren't close to the strike zone). Orosco and Holton were warmed up and ready to go. Lasorda stuck with Howell. Dave Parker hit a routine soft liner up the middle, and the sure-handed Griffin flat-out dropped the ball. Everybody was safe. The stage was set.

The bases were loaded, and it was time for the rematch: Howell vs. McGwire. The entire crowd was on its feet.

Howell had lost the duel the previous night with a high fastball. Unfazed, Howell went back to the fastball. On the first pitch, he threw a fastball right down the middle. McGwire took a mighty cut, but the pitch had just enough tail toward Big Mac's hands and he popped it straight up. Woodson made the catch at first base to end the seventh.

A long road still remained for Howell. In the eighth, Steinbach hit a deep drive to right-center, but the ballpark held it. Hassey came off the bench to single with two outs, ensuring that Canseco would get one more at-bat. Howell struck out Weiss to end the eighth inning. Just like Niedenfuer in '85.

Dennis Eckersley, in his first outing since Game 1, pitched a scoreless top of the ninth. Kirk Gibson was wearing his batting gloves in the eighth inning, and had a brief discussion with Lasorda in the dugout. But he didn't bat in the eighth, and there was no Eckersley vs. Gibson rematch in the ninth inning.

The stage was set for Jay Howell, once again, in the bottom of the ninth. Luis Polonia jumped ahead 2–0, worked the count to 3–2, and flew out to left field.

Dave Henderson singled to left, his fourth hit of the game. That brought Canseco to the plate.

In the ALCS, Canseco hit three home runs—all giving the A's the lead or tying the game. He hit that grand slam in Game 1 of the World Series and was hitless in 13 at-bats since. Canseco was due.

Howell got ahead with a fastball. Then he hung a curveball—a big, fat, hanging curveball. Canseco would remember that pitch for years. His eyes lit up. He took a mighty swing, a hellacious swing, and fouled the pitch straight back. Canseco couldn't believe it. He was stunned. He shook his head, incredulously. He thought for sure he'd win the game with a walk-off home run. How could Jose miss that pitch?

Dempsey and Sax came out to the mound. On an 0–2 pitch, Howell threw another curveball. This one had better bite and made Canseco flinch, but it missed low and inside. Then a fastball missed up and inside, nearly hitting him. Another hanging curveball missed up and inside.

The count was full. Dempsey put down two fingers. Howell nodded. The crowd was on its feet. Howell threw the curveball of his life, sharp tilt, down and inside, and Canseco whiffed. Two outs.

Perranoski and the whole infield met on the mound. Stan Javier ran for Henderson. Parker was up. Jesse Orosco was warmed up and ready for a lefty-on-lefty matchup, but even Scully said on NBC there was "no way" Lasorda would bring in Orosco.

McGwire was in the on-deck circle, or was that Jack Clark in the on-deck circle?

Niedenfuer looked in for the sign—no, it was Howell who looked in for the sign. Parker swung at a first-pitch fastball, popped it up into that vast foul territory in Oakland, and Jeff Hamilton squeezed the final out.

Howell did it. He avenged his own defeat the night before. He avenged his pine-tar stained reputation. He got the seven biggest outs of his life. In some ways, Jay Howell avenged Tom Niedenfuer and Tommy Lasorda that night, too.

Lasorda gave Howell a hug as if he'd just saved his life. Maybe not literally, but Howell had done just that.

"In my career," Howell said that night, "this game was the biggest."

It would be easy to gloat. It would be understandable to gloat. Howell didn't gloat. He smiled a little. He sipped on a Coca-Cola while talking to reporters.

"I know stuff has been said about me that has been negative or nasty," Howell said that night. "But I don't think I have to come back and say anything in the same way. I had a good year I'm proud of, and I'm proud of this win tonight."

Reminded of the details 25 years later, Scioscia shook his head. "Jay got seven outs in that game? That's incredible."

On the field, Marv Albert interviewed Lasorda on the NBC postgame show.

"You should give the MVP to Bob Costas," Lasorda said. "We were in the clubhouse and he said, 'This is the worst-hitting team ever to play in a World Series.'"

"There was a roar in the clubhouse?" Albert asked.

"It was something like, 'Kill Costas, Kill Costas.'" Lasorda replied.

Costas heard all of this in his earpiece. He walked across the Coliseum infield to where the interview was taking place.

"Just happy to help out Tom," Costas said.

"I'll call you when I need you again," Lasorda said.

Costas laughed. Lasorda laughed. Albert laughed. The Dodgers laughed.

The A's were not laughing. La Russa wondered if it was all a setup. The A's players were shell-shocked. "I couldn't tell you what's going on right now," Canseco said that night. "I wouldn't even try to analyze it. What people have seen here is not the real Oakland A's. We're not advancing runners or getting the big two-out hit. We're not hitting the ball hard, and I really don't understand why."

The "kill Costas" line was an exaggeration. "That's made up," Sax said. "We did use it as fuel. Maybe he wasn't on his third phone book reading a teleprompter. We didn't feel like [Costas] was that important."

What was important—Orel Hershiser was starting Game 5.

♦ ♦ ♦ ♦

Thursday, October 20, 1988
Oakland
Dodgers vs. Athletics
World Series Game 5

Fred Claire called the Dominican Republic and tried to find Gilberto Reyes, a catcher who had nine at-bats in the majors in 1988 with the Dodgers and 46 in his career. Reyes was needed because Mike Scioscia might not be able to play the rest of the Series.

"I met with Dr. Jobe," Scioscia recalled. "They said, 'Can you play?' I said, 'You better believe I can play. I can play.' They said, 'Squat for us.' I squatted, and it hurt like hell. I said, 'I'm good.' I didn't start the game. Rick Dempsey started, but I was available for Game 5."

Claire wasn't as convinced. He asked Commissioner Peter Ueberroth to make a roster move in the middle of the Series, which was not allowed at the time. Reyes got on a plane, and he arrived at the Oakland Coliseum in the first inning. Scully said before first pitch that Scioscia was available "in absolute desperation."

Down in Los Angeles, Mayor Tom Bradley's office began planning the World Series parade hours before the clinching game started.

Orel Hershiser kept having the same nightmare. He heard Vin Scully say that he gave up a run, that he didn't really break the record. Then he would wake up.

Going into Game 5, Hershiser felt the pressure. He knew it was Game 5 or bust. He knew the injuries were taking a toll, the pitching staff was on fumes, and they'd be in trouble if the Series returned to Los Angeles. He knew some felt he was on a magic carpet ride that was due to end and resented the opinion.

Bobby McFerrin sang the National Anthem before Game 5. His hit song, "Don't Worry Be Happy" was recently No. 1 on the *Billboard* chart.

Hershiser spent the morning before Game 5 killing some time in San Francisco. He came upon a store that made personalized shirts. Hershiser waited until the media left the clubhouse, then reached into his bag and put on the shirt that he had made.

The shirt read: "Don't Worry I'm Pitching."

"I do remember wearing that," Hershiser recalled. "It was a way to break the ice of the team. I just walked around. I'll make this a little bit of a joke to ease the pressure. I didn't wear it during the game. I just put it on, walked around for about five minutes, and let everybody get a good chuckle. Then I get back into my regimen."

Hershiser had allowed three earned runs in his last 92⅔ innings. What was the A's strategy against Hershiser? "Hope he's not sharp," La Russa said.

Storm Davis had allowed six runs in his 3⅓ innings in Game 2. He would start Game 5 on three days rest. He was an uninspiring choice for the Oakland faithful, especially after his performance in Game 2. Some thought it would be better to try Curt Young, even if he was rusty. Maybe he would be fresher. Anything to give a new look and change things up.

The A's brought out Gene Tenace, Reggie Jackson, and Rollie Fingers—the MVPs of the World Series in 1972, 1973, and 1974, respectively—to throw out the ceremonial first pitches.

Mike Marshall's back responded to treatment and an injection, so he was back in the Dodgers' lineup.

Davis took the mound with the theme from "Rocky" playing. Three batters into the game, the A's were already on the canvas. With one out, Franklin Stubbs singled to right field on a big curveball. On a 1–1 pitch, Mickey Hatcher did it again, hitting a two-run home run to left field. He sprinted around the bases—in 16 seconds flat, just like in Game 1—looking like the awkward star from 1980s TV show, *The Greatest American Hero*.

When he returned to the dugout, Hatcher knocked off Ron Perranoski's cap during the high fives. Hatcher attempted a forearm bash with trainer Charlie Strasser that didn't go so well. Strasser hit the funny bone on Hatcher's right hand, and it went numb for a couple innings.

With Hershiser on the mound, it felt like the game, and the Series, were over.

Hershiser retired the first six batters he faced, including a strikeout of Jose Canseco on one of those rare ¾-angle curveballs that pitching coach Ron Perranoski hated, even when they worked.

In the third, Carney Lansford ripped a single up the middle. On a hit-and-run, Tony Phillips (starting in place of Glenn Hubbard at second base) hit a ball in the hole, and all Griffin could do was keep the ball in the infield. Walt Weiss bunted them 90' ahead. Stan Javier (the fourth different player to start in left field) lined out to left field, scoring Lansford on a sacrifice fly.

It was Hershiser's first run allowed in his last 21 playoff innings. Maybe he was human. The lead was 2–1. Hershiser was a little wild. He didn't look as comfortable on the mound and paced frequently.

Hershiser nearly hit Henderson in the head, then nearly hit him in the waist, and walked him on four pitches. Perranoski visited the mound to settle him down. Here came Canseco again, and the Coliseum was alive again.

After throwing all fastballs to Canseco in Game 2, Hershiser went to the sinker this time. Canseco grounded sharply to Griffin for a fielder's choice to end the inning.

Hatcher opened the fourth inning with a high chopper to Lansford. Hatcher's head-first dive looked like more of a belly flop, as he crash-landed safely into first base. Davis struck out Marshall and struck out Shelby. With two outs, Mike Davis came up.

◆ ◆ ◆ ◆

Remember Mike Davis, the $1 million free-agent bust?

In May, his slump was so bad that general manager Fred Claire offered him batting advice. Claire was a former sportswriter who never played the game. Davis considered that rock bottom.

In June, Marshall told Lasorda he couldn't play first base anymore because it aggravated his back. Lasorda moved him to right field and benched Davis almost permanently. Davis complained that players were running the team, not the manager.

In August, Davis declared, "There's no way I'm going to have the same thing happen to me next year. I'd play in Egypt first."

Davis wasn't happy. But when he put his ego aside and thought about it objectively, he didn't blame Lasorda. He was from the other league. Lasorda didn't know what he could do.

"I'll take all the blame," Davis said, "because I stunk the league up."

In a three-year stretch from 1985–87, Davis averaged 22 home runs, 23 stolen bases, 31 doubles, and 79 runs. It all went downhill on that March day in Puerto Rico when Davis stepped in a pothole and sprained his ankle. He batted .196 on the year. He hit two home runs. After one of them, Rick Dempsey feigned a heart attack. Davis drove in 17 runs.

Poor performance limited Davis to 281 at-bats and 108 games. But he played his own unofficial games every night. Around the third inning, he went into the tunnel at Dodger Stadium and got into the batting cage. He'd set up the pitching machine and started swinging. He was the manager, deciding when to bunt, hit-and-run, and grip-and-rip. It was his summer in a batting cage.

◆ ◆ ◆ ◆

Before the fourth inning began, Steve Sax told Mike Davis, "It's been a tough year, but I got a feeling you are going to go deep one more time and finish it off right."

Sax said that stuff all the time. Sax loved making predictions like that. Maybe it was the Lasorda in Sax. That's just the way Sax was wired. Sax loved his teammates and looked for anything possible to fill a teammate with positive energy before an at-bat.

Davis vs. Davis. The pitcher fell behind in the count 3–0. Lasorda decided to give Davis the green light. Why not?

Storm Davis grooved a fastball right down the middle, never expecting Mike Davis would swing. Oh did Mike Davis swing, taking out seven months of frustration with a towering blast into the right-field bleachers. It was 4–1 Dodgers.

Davis knew it was gone. He watched it all the way. He pointed back to the dugout before touching first base. He took his time rounding the bases (25 seconds, nine longer than Hatcher). He wanted to soak up the feeling. He wanted that feeling to last forever.

The homer by Davis gave Hershiser some breathing room, and the Bulldog settled into a groove by throwing way more changeups and slow sweeping curveballs than usual. Hershiser issued a harmless two-out walk to Hassey in the fourth, but it irked Hershiser. He displayed rare emotion after the inning, throwing his glove and hat onto the dugout bench.

During the top of the fifth inning, the NBC cameras showed Hershiser in the dugout with his eyes closed. He wasn't sleeping. He was reminding himself to think one pitch at a time. He took deep breaths that looked like yawns. He didn't want his skeptics to think he couldn't handle the pressure of closing out a World Series game. To relax, Hershiser sang hymns to himself.

The A's tried to get under Hershiser's skin by asking for time as late as possible before a pitch, similar to what teams did to Dennis Eckersley. Tony Phillips did it in the bottom of the fifth, prompting Hershiser to walk toward home plate.

"How late can they step out on me before it's a problem?" Hershiser yelled to umpire Jerry Crawford, wanting Phillips to hear.

"You know they can step out for a lot of reasons," Crawford replied.

"You can tell them it only makes me more aggressive. I only want to get them out even more," Hershiser said.

Professional fan "Crazy" George, who invented "the wave" during the A's 1981 playoff series against the Yankees, stood on top of the A's dugout and fired up the Coliseum.

It didn't rattle Hershiser. He took great satisfaction striking out Phillips, he got Weiss on a routine grounder to second, and he consulted the cheat sheet in his back pocket before striking out Javier looking. From the fourth to seventh innings, Hershiser faced one batter over the minimum.

In the sixth inning, the Fat Lady warmed up her voice a little more. Reliever Gene Nelson walked Davis with two outs. Lasorda put on yet another hit-and-run, Rick Dempsey doubled over Canseco's head in right field, and it was 5–1 Dodgers.

Hershiser finally started to run out of gas in the eighth inning. The A's mounted a last-gasp rally, giving the Coliseum faithful one more hope that they could salvage this game and their season. It started with a walk to Phillips, then a hit-and-run grounder by Weiss moved him to second base.

Javier lined a single up the middle, his second RBI of the night, to score Phillips. The score was 5–2, Perranoski visited the mound, and Hershiser was pacing on the mound again.

Henderson walked on four pitches, the crowd chanted "Ohhhhhhh-rel," and now the tying run was at the plate. It was Jose Canseco—the future MVP, the 40–40 man, the best player in baseball. Dempsey started to make his way to the mound for a visit. Hershiser waved him off, as if to say, "I got this." Dempsey came out anyway. The dugout looked down to the bullpen, asking if Jay Howell and Alejandro Pena were ready.

Hershiser didn't want Lasorda to think he was tired, so he had to act confident. But he couldn't act too confident, or else Lasorda would know he was faking it. Hershiser didn't want to come out. He wanted to go the distance. He had to go the distance and finish it himself.

"That was a driving force in the last game for me," Hershiser reflected. "I wanted to be on the mound. I visualized myself throwing the last pitch. I did not want to get taken out of that game. That was really important to me. After the 59 scoreless, and us getting to the World Series, and looking like we're going to beat the Oakland A's, and I'm on the mound.

"Everything that could have been accomplished that year was now resting on a pitcher's arm that supposedly has been able to do everything. If I let them down then, it's not good. I felt a lot of pressure in that game. I wanted to be the guy who stood on the mound at the end."

From the dugout, Lasorda told his coaches, "Let him go." Lasorda was trusting the Bulldog.

Canseco vs. Hershiser: the best hitter in the game against the best pitcher in the game. On the first pitch, Canseco ripped a fastball down the third-base line, just foul. Hershiser missed away with a fastball, and Canseco lined another fastball foul into the Dodgers' bullpen.

"You know what?" Scully said on NBC. "This is the way it should be."

Canseco fought off a tough sidearm curveball, staying alive at 1–2. It wasn't mentioned at the time, probably because Canseco wore batting gloves on both hands, but Canseco's right hand was heavily taped. Getting hit by the Belcher fastball in Game 1 was possibly a factor in Canseco going hitless since his grand slam.

Hershiser shook off Dempsey twice. Actually, he snarled his nose. Hershiser decided to come back inside with another fastball. If Hershiser missed his spot, Canseco would turn on the pitch and tie the game with one swing of the bat. Such a pitch was risky. So risky, Hershiser figured, Canseco would never be expecting it.

The fastball was right on target. Running inside on Canseco's hands, it jammed him, and he popped weakly to first base. Two outs.

Next was Parker, the man who singled three times off Hershiser in Game 2. After a wild pitch advanced the runners, if Parker singled, it would be a one-run game. Hershiser threw a strike, then Parker chased a 55' curveball, and Dempsey blocked it masterfully. Hershiser threw another curveball in the dirt, Parker chased it again, and the inning was over. It was still 5–2.

In the stands, Orel Hershiser III was miked up for the game. "That's pitching," said the proud father, extending his arm in a thumbs-up gesture. "That's a Bulldog!"

Back in the dugout, an NBC camera was fixated on Hershiser, and he knew it. Hershiser smiled. A yawn turned into a deep breath. He leaned back against the dugout bench. He looked into the camera, held up three fingers, and mouthed, "Three more outs."

In the ninth, McGwire crushed a ball to deep left-center. It was the third time McGwire hit a drive deep to the outfield that night. But that's where homers go to die in night games in Oakland, and Shelby caught it at the wall. Hassey struck out looking on a big curveball. One out remained.

Lansford hit a roller deep into the hole. Griffin somehow gloved it and was close to the foul line as he winged a throw across the diamond. Lansford was barely safe. Lansford took second, and he took third as Hershiser worked from the windup against Tony Phillips and fell behind 3–0.

At 8:31 PM Pacific Time, on his 117th pitch of the night, Hershiser threw a 3–2 fastball to Phillips. Scully described it this way:

"Got him! They've done it! Like the 1969 Mets, it's the impossible dream revisited."

The Coliseum DJ cued the Andrew Gold song, "Thank You for Being A Friend."

The Dodgers' celebration was on. Dempsey picked up Hershiser and held him above the scrum of bodies. Hershiser pumped his fist into the air.

"I love that memory," Hershiser recalled. "It gives you a lot of confidence the rest of your life. Even in tough situations, you can look back and go, 'Look, I can rise to the occasion. I can deal with pressure. I can put the work in that it takes. I can be successful.' It gives you a lot of confidence and some stability. Not in an egotistical way, just in a realistic way."

♦ ♦ ♦ ♦

In the A's clubhouse, it was disbelief. "My heart is broken right now," La Russa said after the game. "I felt like we let a lot of people down. Fans. The league. Ourselves. Yeah, we let a lot of people down."

"I'm ticked off," Parker said that night. "I don't want to cry on camera or punch anybody in the face, but it hurts. It hurts inside to lose. We never played up to our potential offensively, and that bothers me."

Twenty-five years later, Don Baylor and Ron Hassey reflected on that night. "It was David vs. Goliath," Baylor said. "You look at our club, and you go, 'No way.' How could you not think that club would win?"

"[Gibson's home run] was a great moment for the Dodgers," Hassey said. "It gave them momentum. That shouldn't have bothered us—with the team we had and the hitters we had and our pitching staff. It just wasn't our Series. People can look at it like it's a downer. It wasn't. Yeah, you want to win the World Series. You go through spring training and six months to get there, that's a lot of work and grinding as a team. Unfortunately, we didn't win it. But it's not a downer."

♦ ♦ ♦ ♦

In the raucous clubhouse, Mike Scioscia's destroyed knee didn't prevent him from celebrating. Kirk Gibson's two bad legs didn't prevent him from celebrating. Hell, they could have covered Gibson's body in eye black and he wouldn't have cared.

The players gathered in the middle of the clubhouse. Gibson led the chant as players gathered in a circle. They counted down: three…two…one…and all yelled in unison, "What a fucking team!"

"We just grew together and had so much fun together," Gibson reminisced. "It was a different group of guys that all understood and made a commitment to each other to win against all odds. Tommy was very masterful. He challenged us to not believe what others were saying about us."

It was the crowning moment of Lasorda's career to date. He used every slight (real and imagined), every hit-and-run, every ounce of Hershiser's arm, and every corny piece of motivation he could summon. As the party raged, Lasorda stepped onto a small stool and tried to get his team's attention. It took a while before he had command of the room.

"Nobody thought we could win the division!" Lasorda screamed. "Nobody thought we could beat the mighty Mets! Nobody thought we could beat the team that won 104 games! But we believed it!"

With that, Lasorda lifted both hands above his head. Gibson drenched Lasorda's body in champagne. Gibson's teammates followed his lead, once again. It looked like Lasorda might drown in alcohol, before he ducked for air and cover.

All that happened before reporters were allowed in the clubhouse. John Tudor and Gibson had struck a deal with Major League Baseball. Dozens and dozens of autographed baseballs were expected from each team. Tudor and Gibson said the team would do it, but only if they got 15 minutes alone without the press inside.

"I can still see it; it was pretty wild," said Steve Vucinich, the A's visiting clubhouse manager at the time. "MLB gave in to them. I thought it was kinda neat. It was just the players, and it's a small clubhouse anyway. Now, they try to do most of it on the field, which is pretty cool."

It was one of the rare clubhouse champagne celebrations in which plastic didn't cover the lockers.

"It was a getaway day," Vucinich explained. "They were leaving after the game anyway. The bags were packed. I laid plastic across the top of it. I had a garbage can liner working as a suit bag over their dress clothes, so nothing got in there. I remember Danny Heep was on the team. He said, 'Why don't you cover the lockers?' I said, 'What's to cover? Everything is in the bag, except for your dress clothes.' It was a pretty wild celebration."

The Game 5 celebration had the usual spraying of champagne and guzzling of beer, but the euphoria was greater after Game 1.

Gibson's home run was so unexpected, so stunning, it was one of those life-defining moments where you never forget exactly where you were. Since it was at home and on a Saturday night, Dodgers fans could revel in that miracle together with the team all night long. By Game 5, with Hershiser on the mound in Oakland, victory was a foregone conclusion.

"In some ways," Hershiser reflected, "the '88 World Championship is a footnote to Gibson's home run. People remember that home run more than they remember [anything else]."

♦ ♦ ♦ ♦

Mickey Hatcher was told he was named the Most Valuable Player.

It was well-deserved. Hatcher started all five games, went 7-for-19 (.368) with five runs scored, five RBIs, a double, he hit that big home run early in Game 1, and he hit that big home run in Game 5. There was the diving catch in Game 3. Twice, he turned doubles into singles with his play in the outfield.

The smile was wide across Hatcher's face. He had been released two springs earlier, was back home in Arizona, thinking his career was over and begging his agent to call the Dodgers one more time, to see if the new GM would sign him after the injury to Bill Madlock.

Now he was the MVP of the World Series. Hatcher was escorted to a stage for the MVP presentation. Then an executive came over to him.

"Sorry, Mickey, there's been a mistake."

Orel Hershiser was named MVP. The person who told Hershiser was Ned Colletti, the Chicago Cubs' public relations man helping out Major League Baseball for the playoffs.

Hatcher was disappointed, but he didn't care. He was a world champion. The chairman of the Stuntmen was a world champion. "I got to the stage, but I couldn't get on the stage," Hatcher said, that smile still on his face 25 years later. "I was honored they even thought of me. At least I got a ring."

When Hershiser was presented the MVP trophy, the first teammate he mentioned was Mickey Hatcher. What more could you say about Hershiser?

The Bulldog went 3–0 with a save and a 1.05 ERA in 42⅔ playoff innings. In the last 101 innings of his season—from the 59 scoreless in the regular season amidst the pressure of a pennant race and against the two best teams in baseball in the playoffs—Hershiser allowed five earned runs and seven overall for a 0.45 ERA.

"After the Series, the league above the major leagues will draft Orel No. 1," declared Marshall that night. "Then he'll be the top pitcher in the Ultra League."

Chapter 18

After the Champagne

October 21, 1988–October 2012

The Dodgers flew back to Los Angeles early the morning of Friday, October 21. The airplane was packed. It was probably illegal how many people were on the plane. People were standing in the aisles. It didn't matter. The Dodgers were the world champions of baseball.

"When the season was over and it was all said and done, it was a huge relief because I'd put all this time and effort and energy into baseball," reflected pitcher Tim Leary. "It took nine years since I was in college to actually come through with a big season. I remember telling myself, 'My career could be over right now, and it would be okay.'"

The charter plane landed at LAX well after midnight. Depending on who you ask, the crowd waiting for them at the airport was between 7,000 and 30,000 fans.

"That was the greatest feeling in the world," first baseman Franklin Stubbs recalled. "I wish I could put you in my body so you could feel what that was like. It was hard to explain. I'm waving a towel around my head. My wife thought I was crazy. We're getting in at 1:00 or 2:00 or 3:00 in the morning, whatever it was, and they're sitting there roaring. Unbelievable. I will never forget that. That memory has never wavered. It will never leave my mind as long as I live."

Mitch Poole, who had given up his junior college baseball career four years earlier to work the Dodgers' clubhouse, carried the world championship trophy and Orel Hershiser's MVP trophy through the masses.

"We were told a plan of getting ourselves to a car or a van that was waiting for us at LAX," Poole said. "This guy took us to the wrong door. He opened it up to about 7,000 people. I was literally beating people away with this trophy and trying to get to Orel's wife. She broke her shoe and lost her shoe. She was trying to get through. I got lost. They got farther and farther away from me."

Eventually, Poole made it through all the people and shoved the trophies underneath the bus that transported the players back to Dodger Stadium.

◆ ◆ ◆ ◆

The day after beating the Oakland Athletics, Orel Hershiser appeared on *The Tonight Show*. Johnny Carson asked him about singing to himself in the dugout between innings. Hershiser explained it was just a way of relaxing, keeping his adrenaline down, so he wouldn't get too excited.

"Do you just hum, or what?" Carson asked.

"I sing," Hershiser said.

The audience started clapping, wanting Hershiser to sing.

"I'm not gonna sing," Hershiser said.

"Yes, you are. Oh, yes you are," Carson replied.

Hershiser sang four notes of a praise hymn. It was more nerve-racking than anything he'd done on the mound the last two months.

◆ ◆ ◆ ◆

On October 26, the Dodgers were the guest of president Ronald Reagan in the White House. Fred Claire, trying to right a wrong from August, made sure that Don Sutton and his wife were invited. Claire hoped that all was forgiven for the way Sutton was released. "They said yes, and enjoyed the trip," Claire said. "I was happy that happened."

On the flight home to Los Angeles, Tommy Lasorda learned he was named Manager of the Year by the Baseball Writers' Association of America. Vin Scully made the announcement over the plane's intercom to inform everybody of the news.

From the plane, Lasorda told BBWAA secretary-treasurer Jack Lang, "This completes my day—one of the greatest days of my life."

Later that off-season, the awards continued to roll in. Fred Claire was named Executive of the Year. Tim Leary was the pitcher named to the Silver Slugger team, and he was also named Comeback Player of the Year. Tim Belcher finished third behind Chris Sabo and Mark Grace for National League Rookie of the Year but won the less-prestigious Rookie Pitcher of the Year Award handed out by *The Sporting News*.

"For me personally," Belcher reflected, "to be Rookie Pitcher of the Year, and win three games in the playoffs, and win a championship in my first year in the big leagues, and be on the losing end of a perfect game, it was a magical year."

Orel Hershiser was the unanimous winner of the Cy Young Award. Danny Jackson finished second, David Cone third, and nobody else received a vote.

On November 15, having just returned from a hunting trip in Iowa, Gibson was named the National League's Most Valuable Player. Clearly, the word "valuable" meant more than overall stats. Gibson's 76 RBIs were the fewest by an MVP–winning position player since Pete Rose drove in 64 runs in 1973.

Since 1988, only four National League MVP winners had less than 100 RBIs. The only MVP winner in the National League with fewer RBIs since 1988 was Barry Larkin in 1995 with 66.

Gibson received 13 out of 24 first-place votes. The two hitting stars of the Mets, who had overall better numbers than Gibson, split the other 11 first-place votes. Darryl Strawberry received seven, while Kevin McReynolds received four. Gibson's 272 points in balloting were 36 more than Strawberry. Orel Hershiser finished sixth in the voting.

"We went to a restaurant in Michigan, there were 50 people there, the media was there and everything," Gibson recalled. "I remember sitting there thinking how much I hated it because it was all about me. Now, the parade? That was fun. There were a million people and all my teammates. That was a party. The individual things are just not how I'm made up. That parade was different. That was some kind of party—just the opportunity for my teammates and I, and everybody who supported us, to come together and celebrate."

Tom Monaghan, the Detroit Tigers owner who had blasted Gibson on his way out of town, called Gibson's business associate to apologize for his comments.

Gibson called Monaghan back and was invited to the Domino's Pizza headquarters for a lunch to make amends.

Gibson thought about it briefly and offered a classic Gibson response.

"You're a year late with your phone call," Gibson began. "I question your motivation for calling me. We have nothing in common. We have no reason to have lunch together. From the little bit that I know you, I would say that you're trying to put together a little public relations event here, where I come in and have lunch, and you have them snap a few shots of us, smiling, and then everything's fine. But it's not. It won't be. Good luck with your team. Good-bye."

◆ ◆ ◆ ◆

In November, Orel Hershiser went to Japan for an exhibition tour with other American ballplayers. As if he hadn't pitched enough innings already that year—309⅔ total innings, including the playoffs—Hershiser pitched again in Japan.

It was during this trip that Hershiser finally allowed a home run—his first since Giants catcher Bob Melvin took him deep on August 14. It was a solo home run, the only run he allowed in four innings.

Hershiser appeared on a television show in Fukuoka. The host started the interview by noting Hershiser's lack of intimidating presence. It led to a hilarious exchange:

Host: "You don't look like a great pitcher. You look like a ..."
Hershiser: "A librarian?"
Host: "No."
Hershiser: "An accountant?"
Host: "No."
Hershiser: "A nerd?"
Host: "No."
Hershiser: "Ronnie Howard? You know, Richie Cunningham from *Happy Days*?"
Host: "No."
Hershiser and the host finally agreed he looked like a lawyer.

A couple days into the exhibition tour, Hershiser returned home to Los Angeles because of an illness to his son, Jordan, who had been born between the third and fourth starts of his scoreless streak.

♦ ♦ ♦ ♦

Orel Hershiser was used to a certain level of notoriety. But after his magical, amazing, mind-boggling 1988 season, life changed instantly. Going into public was difficult. The doors that opened, literally and figuratively, were flattering. The people he met were beyond his wildest dreams. The attention was appreciated. But it was also scary.

Hershiser went to a L.A. Kings hockey game at the Forum and needed six security guards to help him navigate the crowd. When he attended a Clippers basketball game, he was on the late local news.

Another night, he attended a Michael Jackson concert at the Sports Arena. The show couldn't begin because there was so much commotion surrounding the impromptu autograph session. Hershiser was told to either stop signing or watch the show from backstage.

The supermarket tabloids called Hershiser's old friends from high school and college, looking for dirt. Wade Boggs had his affair with Margo Adams that went public. Steve Garvey went from a clean-cut family man to disgrace with paternity suits. Hershiser told his old buddies to tell the truth. There's nothing to hide. There is no dirt.

One time, Jamie Hershiser asked her husband to get a few items at the grocery store. Orel brought along the boys for a brief father-son outing.

"By the time we got out of the car, and walked through the parking lot, people knew already," Hershiser recalled. "By the time we'd get to the milk station and get up to the counter, it was 15–20 people just to get out. It was very hard to function at times. The boys paid a price. The family paid a price from all the attention that is pulling at you."

Hershiser changed his home telephone number once. Then a second time. Then Jamie went shopping one day, returned a mere three hours later, and there were 40 messages. Finally, he just hired an answering service.

They went to the White House three times.

On November 16, Orel and Jamie were guests at a state dinner hosted by president Ronald Reagan. Jamie sat with Henry Kissinger, Chief Justice William Rehnquist, and publisher Malcolm Forbes. Orel sat with British prime minister Margaret Thatcher, Nancy Kissinger, publisher Walter Annenberg, and president Reagan. Also at the dinner were Mikhail Baryshnikov, Tom Selleck, and president-elect George Bush.

The next day, the Hershisers were in New York to meet with a lawyer about endorsement deals. The following day, they were in Orlando. Orel played golf with Payne Stewart and Bob Hope, and he cut a quick promo for Hope's *Jolly Christmas Show*. That night, he chatted with Ron Darling and Frank Viola at the Grand Cypress Resort for a charity event benefiting Florida Hospital.

The whole family went to Disney World the day after that. Security guards used walkie-talkies to plot each move and avoid chaos. Orel and Quinton goofed off with Goofy, took pictures with Mickey, and ate lunch at Cinderella's Castle.

As they ate, Orel's brother, Gordie, went into an impression of Bill Murray's character from *Caddyshack*. "There he is, the Cinderella pitcher, coming from out of nowhere. Nobody can believe it. Fifty-nine scoreless innings, MVP of the World Series."

Just then, Cinderella appeared at their table. Cinderella was told the best pitcher in baseball was sitting there, but she didn't know it was the skinny guy with glasses at the end of the table.

In December, Hershiser was named *Sports Illustrated*'s Sportsman of the Year. Out of all his career accomplishments, that one meant the most to him, because it involves every sport.

Later that month, Orel and Jamie were buying Christmas presents at a store in Pasadena. Orel was spotted immediately. Shoppers bought balls, bats, and any other baseball item they could find in the store and rushed over to get Hershiser's autograph. It was such a mob scene, the Hershisers found the store manager and asked when the store was most empty. They were told Tuesdays at 10:00 AM. That's when they returned, in more peace, to finish shopping.

The family took a weekend trip up the California coast to Monterey. Orel and Jamie went to the last showing of the movie *Rain Man*. When they exited the movie theater at 12:30 AM, there was a TV camera. Orel said to Jamie, "Wouldn't it be a crack-up if this guy is here to interview me?"

A crack-up indeed. The cameraman heard Orel was in the movie theatre, and asked him for an interview.

"I never sat around and thought, 'Oh wow, I'm famous, this is great,'" Hershiser reflected. "I felt like it was my duty and my role to do the right thing: to smile and shake somebody's hand and listen to their story, and sign their autograph, and then move on. When an autograph request comes, it might be the 200th priority on my list of things to do today, but it's No. 1 on that person's list. That's what happens with athletes and autographs. If you don't rework your priority list in that 1–2 seconds when that request comes, you're not going to have a very good reaction sometimes. You're going to brush people off. You immediately have to re-work your priorities."

The final two months of the 1988 season were such a blur, Hershiser didn't have time to reflect on what he'd accomplished. He didn't have time to reflect while it was still going on because there was more to accomplish.

The quietest moments of his off-season came in the middle of the night, when Orel would feed Jordan. Hershiser put VHS tapes into his VCR, and that's when he finally realized what he'd accomplished. He watched games from The Streak, from the demoralizing Game 1 defeat to the Mets (which he blamed on himself), his dramatic save in Game 4, the clincher in Game 7, and his two victories over the A's in the World Series.

Even though he knew the result, Hershiser was nervous watching the games. A runner would get into scoring position, and he'd think, *Oh, my God, this guy's going to score.*

◆ ◆ ◆ ◆

Hershiser's extraordinary season earned him a three-year, $7.9 million contract, making him the highest-paid player in baseball history at the time. He was given a $1.1 million signing bonus, a salary of $2.4 million in 1989, $1.6 million in 1990, and $2.8 million in 1991.

Two years earlier, when Orel became a millionaire, a man approached his father on a golf course. "What's it like having a son make more money than you?" the man asked.

"He's not there yet," said Orel III, who owned a Detroit-based business printing newspaper inserts and retired before he turned 50.

Now the son was finally outearning his father.

Longtime Dodgers traveling secretary Billy DeLury passed out paychecks in the spring training clubhouse on March 1, 1989. DeLury gave two checks to Hershiser—one for the signing bonus and the other for the first two months of 1989. The two checks added up to $1,093,998.10 after taxes.

Hershiser didn't know whether to laugh or cry. Rookies Chris Gwynn and Mike Devereaux looked at the checks in amazement. Even veteran Rick Dempsey gasped at the quantity.

"Hi honey, I'm home," Hershiser said, later that day, returning to his spring training residence. He asked Jamie if she wouldn't mind depositing a couple of checks. He tried to contain his giggling as he waited for her to look at the amount.

Those weren't the only checks for Jamie to deposit. Hershiser signed endorsement contracts with Pepsi, Mitsubishi cars, Toshiba copiers and office equipment, Ebel watches, baby shampoo, athletic shoes, baseball gloves, and underwear. Those would total more than $1 million, as well.

Offers from beer and cigarette commercials were rejected. They didn't fit his image. Hershiser was wary of projecting an otherworldly squeaky-clean image. He knew he wasn't perfect. But he didn't have to take every offer, and he just wanted to be consistent with people.

Hershiser vowed the money wouldn't change him. He recalled the early days of his marriage when he was a minor leaguer in San Antonio and he and his wife both worked at banks to get by on his paltry minor league salary.

They didn't move from Pasadena to Beverly Hills. They didn't buy fancy sports cars. They did buy a beach house on John Island, off the coast of Florida. They also bought a house in Orlando, closer to his family, and made that his legal residence because there are no taxes in Florida. That would save him $400,000 per year.

Orel IV had been a business major at Bowling Green. He rejected offers to invest in golf courses, restaurants, and radio stations. Instead, he opted for commercial real estate, bonds, treasury bills, and certificates of deposit.

◆ ◆ ◆ ◆

Hershiser knew how fleeting fame can be. All he had to do was look at teammate Fernando Valenzuela. Orel-mania was still nothing compared to the height of Fernando-mania, which was just as much cultural phenomenon as baseball. Eight years later, the wear-and-tear of pitching in the majors had taken a toll on Fernando, reducing him to a statistically average pitcher. Only a few kids would ask for his autograph each day.

Everywhere Hershiser went in DodgerTown in 1989, he was mobbed for autographs. He couldn't leave the clubhouse like his teammates. The crowds were too big. He went through the laundry room, out a back entrance, and climbed inside a van that was waiting for him.

Hershiser was nervous about jealousy in the clubhouse. When Quinton left bubble gum wrappers scattered on the ground, Orel insisted that he pick them up and put them in the trash. After Orel's first exhibition start in 1989—three innings in Vero Beach—Quinton was in the clubhouse and eager to go home. But the kid would have to wait. Thirty-three reporters were waiting to interview his dad.

Hershiser told the reporters he was, "set up for the biggest fall of my life.... If I don't win 20 games, I'll be considered a failure.... The only way I can avoid criticism for that is if I have another unbelievable year. If I have an average year or if I win 20 games and lose 12, people will say, 'Oh, you're supposed to win the one-run games when you get paid that much money.' But all I can do is just be the same person. Just because I went to the World Series and had a streak doesn't mean that I became a different person."

♦ ♦ ♦ ♦

All the magic and miracles were gone for the Dodgers in 1989. The team finished 77–83, in fourth place and 14 games behind the first-place Giants. The A's and Giants met in a Bay Bridge World Series that was interrupted by a 7.1-magnitude earthquake before Game 3. The A's swept the Giants in four games.

Hershiser's scoreless streak carried over to 1989, even though in his mind it was over. Hershiser gave up runs in the playoffs, runs in Japan, and 10 runs in a single spring training game, so it didn't feel like the continuation of a streak. Hershiser started the second game of the season—Tim Belcher started the opener, after Hershiser was stricken with the flu in the final week of spring training—and the Reds scored a run in the first inning. Todd Benzinger singled with two outs to score Barry Larkin.

The streak ended at 59 innings.

The entire 1989 season was a nightmare for Kirk Gibson. Early in the year, after eating dinner with his family in Santa Monica, a car followed him home. When the family pulled into the driveway, a kid about 20 years old put a handgun in Kirk's chest.

The assailant ordered Gibson into the car, pointed the gun at his temple, and told him to start the car. The assailant knew Gibson had money. He demanded all his cash, which was $800, then jumped into the car and tore off. Gibson didn't sleep for two nights. He sent his family back to Detroit, checked into a hotel, and stayed there the rest of the season.

It wasn't much of a season. Gibson had laid it all on the line to win the 1988 World Series. He sacrificed his body, played through pain, and made base running decisions that would have long-term consequences. Despite rest and rehab, Gibson was not close to 100 percent.

As always, Gibson tried to play. He was a fraction of his usual self. His legs ached every day. He kept playing. Tests were conducted. Nothing was conclusive. He went on the disabled list and missed 21 games. He came back and tried again. His numbers were awful—a slash line of .213/.312/.368 in 71 games.

In mid-August, Gibson underwent surgery. Gibson described it the following way in his 1997 book, *Bottom of the Ninth*:

"They opened up my leg, saw nothing obvious, then decided to invade the sheath surrounding my hamstring tendon. The moment they cut into it, a mess of tissue and debris burst from the sheath.

"There, at long last, was the answer. Fully 50 percent of my hamstring had torn, had frayed like strands of a cable. Dead, degenerative tissue had knotted up and bulged, sliding up and down within the sheath each time I took a step. Small wonder the thing had been killing me."

Gibson's nightmare 1989 season was over. He played six more years. Most were uneventful and injury-marred. He never had the luxury of turning down an All-Star Game appearance. Gibson was limited to 89 games with the Dodgers in 1990, the final year of his three-year contract.

The Dodgers never offered Gibson a new contact, but general manager Fred Claire told Gibson's agent they would offer him arbitration for a one-year deal. Gibson received offers from the Montreal Expos and Milwaukee Brewers. He signed a two-year contract the Kansas City Royals.

Gibson enjoyed a relatively healthy 1991 season. He played in 132 games and got 462 at-bats, but his slash line was still .236/.341/.403 with 16 home runs and 55 RBIs.

Midway through spring training in 1992, the Royals traded Gibson to the Pirates for pitcher Neal Heaton. On May 5, with a slash line of .196/.237/.304 after 56 at-bats, the Pirates released Gibson.

That wouldn't be the end of Gibson's career, though. He mended fences and launched a comeback with the Tigers in 1993. At age 36, Gibson played in 116 games, hit 13 home runs, drove in 62 runs, stole 15 bases in 21 attempts, and batted a respectable .261.

The long-awaited rematch between Gibson and Eckersley came on Opening Day 1993 at the Oakland Coliseum. The A's led 5–4 in the eighth inning. Runners were at second and third base. There were two outs. Tony La Russa ordered that Eckersley intentionally walk Gibson. Eckersley seethed inside but did as he was told. Eckersley struck out Rob Deer, and finished off the save in the ninth.

The two finally squared off, for real, on August 20, 1993, at Tiger Stadium. The A's led 7–2. Eckersley entered with the bases loaded and nobody out. Eckersley struck out Cecil Fielder then Gibson hit a run-scoring single off him. Eckersley held on for the save.

Gibson's power finally returned in the strike-shortened 1994 season. At age 37 he hit 23 home runs in 330 at-bats, good for a career-high .548 slugging percentage. Gibson's final year with the Tigers was 1995.

Simply put, Kirk Gibson was never the same player after 1988. Not even close.

"But I'd do it all over again," Gibson reflected. "I really would. It's a no-brainer for me. I don't expect everybody would do it or should do it that way. That's just the way I am, and the way I will always be."

After his playing career, Gibson was a coach for the Tigers and later the Arizona Diamondbacks. He was named D'backs manager midway through the 2010 season and led them to the 2011 National League West title.

In November 2010, the bat Gibson used for his Game 1 home run off Dennis Eckersley fetched $575,912 in an auction. Gibson's jersey went for $303,277. The entire collection of items that Gibson put up for auction netted $1.2 million.

For as long as Kirk Gibson lives, the first thing that will come to people's mind when they hear his name is that impossible World Series home run off Dennis Eckersley.

"I personally named the seat [where it landed] Seat 88," Gibson said in 2009. "Whenever I walk into Dodger Stadium I immediately look out there. Damn right it's been good. There was a perception of me, and I earned it because I was really intense, really gruff. I treated certain people poorly at times. It was because of who I was. It was almost my strength. I came in all business. I tried to find ways to fit in with that demeanor, but it's not easy.

"Now here I am almost 52 years old, it's really easy. I'm way more at peace. But when you're a competitor, and you're as intent on becoming the best in the world as I was, it comes with consequences."

◆ ◆ ◆ ◆

Hershiser didn't win 20 games in 1989. He won 15 and lost 15. He led the league in innings pitched for a third straight year with 256⅔. His ERA was 2.31, just a tick higher than a year before. He went the distance eight times, threw four shutouts, and finished fourth in the Cy Young race behind Padres reliever Mark Davis, the Astros' Mike Scott, and the Cubs' Greg Maddux.

"I thought he pitched even better in 1989," said Dave Anderson. He wasn't trying to be cute. He was being honest. Hershiser lost four 1–0 games. He was 14–8 in early August, then went 0–7 over his next nine starts, despite a 2.32 ERA, and took a losing record into the final day of the season. Back then, won-lost records still mattered. Hershiser didn't want to finish with a losing record. So he pitched and pitched and pitched—11 innings total—before winning 3–1 to finish 15–15.

As usual, Hershiser pushed the limits on what an arm could handle. He threw 130 pitches on April 10 and 141 pitches on May 20.

When the Dodgers went into extra innings on June 3, Hershiser threw 87 pitches over seven scoreless innings (the 14th inning to the 20th inning) on two days rest. In his next start, he gave up four runs and only lasted six innings. Four days later, he went the distance and threw 122 pitches. Through a 10-day period he threw 20 innings and 249 pitches.

On June 25, Hershiser threw 139 pitches. On September 8, he threw 125 pitches. On September 13, he threw 134 more pitches. On the final start of the season, with nothing on the line except Hershiser's desire to end the season with a .500 record, he threw a whopping 169 pitches during 11 innings.

Four starts into the 1990 season, all those innings and pitches finally caught up with Hershiser. He was supposed to go undergo a somewhat routine arthroscopic surgery by Dr. Frank Jobe. However, the damage to the shoulder was far more than what Jobe expected, and he felt it mandatory to reconstruct Hershiser's shoulder. The rim of the shoulder was torn and rolled back in front of the joint. Reconstruction was needed on the anterior capsule, plus a tightening of ligaments.

The tears in tissue looked, Jobe said, "like they had been pounded with a hammer."

Dr. Jobe had pioneered the so-called Tommy John surgery on elbows. He pioneered shoulder surgery that day with Hershiser on the operating table. Jobe used a technique never previously attempted. Instead of detaching the muscle in the shoulder to repair the joint, which would have jeopardized his range of motion, the doctor split the muscle and made the repair.

In news articles immediately after the surgery Jobe said, "I think that the number of innings he threw had something to do with the injury. We have to learn more about how much a man can throw before trauma sets in."

Hershiser missed the rest of the 1990 season and two months of the 1991 season. He wasn't the same pitcher when he returned, and he didn't throw more than 94 pitches in any of his 21 starts. Still, he compiled a pretty good 3.46 ERA and was named Comeback Player of the Year.

After the surgery, Hershiser pitched for 10 more years, where he made 275 appearances, including 271 starts, 1,648 total innings, and won 105 more games.

In 1995, he signed a three-year contract with the Cleveland Indians. Hershiser pitched in the playoffs all three years for the Tribe, including eight innings of two-run ball in Game 5 of the 1995 World Series to keep the series alive. The Braves won the Series in Game 6.

Late in his career, he needed to pitch with more guts and guile. In 1998, at age 39, Hershiser looked awfully strange pitching for the San Francisco Giants, but he didn't miss a start and actually won over skeptical Giants fans with his trademark down-to-earth personality. He made 32 more starts for the Mets in 1999 and pitched in relief in the playoffs that year.

Hershiser returned to the Dodgers in 2000 for one last season. The end wasn't pretty. His record was 1–5. His ERA was 13.14 after 10 games. His final four appearances resulted in a blown save and three losses. In his final appearance, he allowed eight runs in 1⅔ innings against the Padres.

Davey Johnson, who had been the enemy in 1988 and the Dodgers' manager in 2000, told reporters after that game, "I've had some sad days. Today really tugged at your heartstrings, to see Orel struggle like that. It's been hard on him, and it's been just as tough on me. It was not fun."

The next day, the Dodgers released Hershiser. Just like with Don Drysdale in 1969 and Don Sutton in 1988, the Dodgers hoped Hershiser would retire. If he did, the Dodgers wouldn't have to pay him. Hershiser wasn't ready to retire. At least not right away, and not with a $2 million guaranteed salary. Hershiser asked for his release. No team signed him.

Hershiser never pitched again.

♦ ♦ ♦ ♦

In the euphoria of the champagne-soaked visitors' clubhouse in Oakland in 1988, catcher Rick Dempsey approached general manager Fred Claire, reached into his back pocket, handed him the baseball from the final out, and said, "This belongs to you."

Claire isn't a big memorabilia collector. This was before any baseball—especially the final out of a World Series game—was viewed as a big souvenir that might bring big money in an auction. Claire took the baseball home and put it on his shelf.

In 2004 after the Red Sox won the World Series, Doug Mientkiewicz made the final putout and put the ball in his back pocket. He initially refused to give the ball to the Red Sox and engaged in a temporary standoff with the team over the baseball.

The New York Times wrote a lengthy article about famous baseballs in early 2005. Claire read that only one ball from the final out of a World Series was in the Hall of Fame—and that was from the early 1900s.

"I called the Hall of Fame," Claire said. "I told them, 'I have a baseball.' They said, 'We know you do.' I said, 'I want to give it to you.' They said, 'You have any idea what that ball is worth?' I said, 'Well, there isn't enough money to buy it.' They said, 'We'll be on an airplane tomorrow.' They came out, picked up the ball, and I gave it to the Hall of Fame. It's now on display. I told them there's only one stipulation in giving it to them—anytime the Dodgers want to show it or use it, they get it. The 25th anniversary might be the perfect time. But that ball resides in the Hall of Fame."

♦ ♦ ♦ ♦

As great as Dennis Eckersley was in 1988, he was greater in 1989. His ERA dropped from 2.35 to 1.56, and the A's won the World Series in a four-game sweep of their Bay Area rival San Francisco Giants.

Then Eckersley was even greater in 1990. Eck posted a 0.61 ERA, had the mind-boggling statistic of more saves (48) than hits (41) and walks (4) combined (45), and he won the Cy Young Award.

Eckersley pitched until age 43. Despite not becoming a full-time closer until the season he turned 33 years old, he finished his career with 390 saves. Eckersley's last year in the majors was 1998 with Boston.

The first year Eckersley was eligible for the National Baseball Hall of Fame, he was inducted with 83.2 percent of the vote. The press never forgot that Eckersley answered every question after giving up the home run to Gibson in 1988. It has been discussed often during the last 25 years, especially if a closer blows a save in a regular season game and hides from the media.

This book's author, who covered the A's for the *Oakland Tribune* at the time Eckersley was inducted into Cooperstown, asked Eckersley if answering every question that fateful night in 1988 was therapeutic.

"I couldn't see it any other way," Eckersley responded. "That's what I thought I had to do. As far as the importance of that game, the pain was immense. Maybe it is a little therapeutic, taking it like a man. I had to. If I could accept all the accolades before then—I was the MVP of the ALCS—who am I to hide in the trainer's room? I felt like it had to be done."

Eckersley might not enjoy talking about the home run Gibson hit off him. But through the years, he's been a good sport and recognizes how special the moment has become for baseball.

"I get numb to [the video]," Eckersley said, at the 20th anniversary. "It's like that's not even me. Time heals everything. When I look back and all is said and done, I saved more than 300 games since that moment. And we won it the next year. If that had been my only chance to win the World Series, I'd kick myself in the ass.

"All I can say is Kirk Gibson will have fond memories of that dinger, but I'm in the Hall of Fame. I'll take the Hall. He can replay that home run until the cows come home."

◆ ◆ ◆ ◆

The Dodgers haven't won a World Series since the Miracle Men of 1988.

They were eliminated from a playoff spot in the final weekend of the 1991 season by the Giants. The Dodgers returned the favor in 1993, eliminating the Giants on the final day of the season. In 1995 and 1996, the Dodgers won the National League West, but they were swept in the first round of the playoffs by the Reds and Braves, respectively.

Tommy Lasorda was forced to retire due to health problems in 1996. Peter O'Malley sold the Dodgers in 1998 to News Corp.

The Dodgers didn't return to the playoffs until 2004, under first year owner Frank McCourt. They finally won a playoff game—behind a spine-chilling, complete-game performance by Jose Lima at Dodger Stadium in Game 3—but lost the series to the Cardinals in four games. Another playoff berth in 2006 ended with a three-game sweep in the division series, this time by the Mets.

The playoff drought ended in 2008 when the Dodgers swept the Cubs in three games. It was reminiscent of 1988, when the Mets were 10–1 against the Dodgers in the regular season, because the Cubs had beaten the Dodgers 5-of-7 games in the regular season. The Dodgers lost to the Phillies in five games in the NLCS.

A similar thing happened in 2009. The Dodgers lost 5-of-7 regular season games to the Cardinals, swept them in the first round of the playoffs, and lost in five games to the Phillies in the NLCS.

In 2011, when Frank McCourt put the Dodgers up for sale, Orel Hershiser joined a group that was bidding to take over control of the storied franchise.

"I wanted to be part of it just because I was embarrassed at what the Dodgers had become," Hershiser said. "I couldn't say that in that time because we're trying to court Frank McCourt. I couldn't give the gut-wrenching truth of how embarrassing it had become for a lot of us."

Hershiser's group was outbid dramatically when a group named Guggenheim Baseball—with Earvin "Magic" Johnson as the public face of the ownership group—bought the Dodgers from Frank McCourt for $2 billion. The Dodgers held a 7½-game lead on May 27. Injuries to key players began taking a toll. The new ownership group acquired players and took on enormous contracts during the season, but the Dodgers failed to make the playoffs.

The 2013 season is the 25th anniversary of the improbable, impossible, miraculous Dodgers of 1988.

◆ ◆ ◆ ◆

In 1995, the Los Angeles Sports Council polled more than 5,000 media and sports enthusiasts and ranked the 100 greatest moments in Los Angeles sports history.

Gibson's home run in Game 1 of the 1988 World Series was ranked first.

Vin Scully and Kirk Gibson got together on a stage at UCLA to celebrate the ranking, rehash the details from that memorable night, and tell the story of how Scully's words made Gibson get off the training table.

With a mischievous grin, Scully told this author, "When I look back on my career, the single greatest accomplishment I ever did for the Dodgers was get Gibson off his ass."

Chapter 19

Where Are They Now?

Where are the 1988 Dodgers?

"Without a doubt, it was one of the most intelligent teams that have ever played the game. You look on down the line, every player is either managing or coaching or involved in baseball, or had the highest IQ level. We had high intelligence on the field, which I think is overlooked."

—1988 Dodgers outfielder Mike Marshall

Infielder Dave Anderson is a coach for the Texas Rangers.

Pitcher Tim Belcher is a special assistant to the GM with the Cleveland Indians. He was previously the pitching coach of the Indians.

General manager Fred Claire was part of a group that tried purchasing the Dodgers in 2012 from Frank McCourt. Claire is the executive vice president for Sports Management Entertainment, Inc., a partner in the baseball analytical company AriBall.com, and he serves on the board of the Rose Bowl operating company and the Special Olympics of Southern California.

Pitcher Tim Crews was killed along with Cleveland teammate Steve Olin in a 1993 boating accident near the Cleveland Indians' training camp in Winter

Haven, Florida. Among the members of the 1988 Dodgers at the funeral were Kirk Gibson and Orel Hershiser. At the funeral, Jay Howell said, "We all know what Tim's accomplishments on the field were. But the quality of his life and his love, dedication, and commitment to his family and friends were of Cy Young status. That's how we will remember you."

Catcher Rick Dempsey is a member of the Orioles' broadcasting team, working on the *O's Xtra* pre- and postgame shows on MASN, and working as the analyst on select games. He was previously a coach for the Orioles. He started his post-playing career as a minor league manager with the Dodgers, winning the 1994 Pacific Coast League championship with Triple A Albuquerque.

Mel Didier, the scout who assured the Dodgers that Eckersley would throw a backdoor slider to lefties if the count reached 3–2, was the advance scout for the Cincinnati Reds two years later in 1990. Didier knew the A's well. The Reds swept the A's in the 1990 World Series. Didier is now a senior advisor/professional scout for the Toronto Blue Jays.

Bob Engel, the second-base umpire who called Brett Butler out for interference to preserve Orel Hershiser's scoreless streak in San Francisco, continued on the job for two more years for an even 20. His career ended when he entered a plea of no contest to charges of stealing 4,180 baseball cards from a Target store in Bakersfield, California. A security officer told police he saw Engel put seven boxes of Score brand baseball cards, valued at $143.98, into a brown paper bag he pulled from the waist of his pants.

Left fielder Kirk Gibson is the manager of the Arizona Diamondbacks. The Dodgers honored his historic World Series home run with a bobblehead in 2012, as part of their 50th anniversary celebration of Dodger Stadium and asked him to throw out the first pitch. Gibson called it "stupid" because he's the manager of a division rival. Gibson requested Mitch Poole throw out the first pitch instead.

Shortstop Alfredo Griffin started his 14th season in the Angels' organization in 2013, serving as a first-base coach and infielders coach. He was on the Angels' coaching staff for the World Series title in 2002.

Infielder/outfielder Pedro Guerrero played four more seasons with the Cardinals, including a bounce-back 1989 season that saw him finish third in the MVP voting. Guerrero was acquitted of drug conspiracy charges in 2000 when his attorney successfully argued, "My client is too stupid" to commit the crime. Guerrero quit drinking in the early part of this decade and wanted to get back into coaching baseball. His only coaching was a brief experience in 2011 in the independent Arizona Winter League, when he re-united with Mike Marshall.

Utility man Mickey Hatcher works for the Dodgers as a special assignment to the general manager. He spent 12 years as a coach with the Angels, winning another World Series in 2002. Before that, he was a minor league manager and coach in the Dodgers' organization from 1991–98.

Outfielder Danny Heep is the head coach for the University of the Incarnate Word, a Division II school located in San Antonio that competes in the Lone Star Conference.

Pitcher Orel Hershiser is an analyst for ESPN on *Sunday Night Baseball*, and *Baseball Tonight*, and appears across various ESPN platforms. He was previously the pitching coach for the Texas Rangers.

Pitcher Ricky Horton is a broadcaster for the St. Louis Cardinals. He's also active in the Greater St. Louis Area Fellowship of Christian Athletes, assists with the Baseball Chapel for the Cardinals, and also works with the St. Louis Rams football team in leading chapel and Bible studies.

Pitcher Jay Howell was the pitching coach for Cal State Northridge from 1998–2005. Among the players he coached was Dodgers relief pitcher Kameron Loe.

Jaime Jarrin, the Spanish language radio announcer, begins his 54th consecutive season with the Dodgers in 2013. Jarrin was honored by the National Baseball Hall of Fame in 1998 as the recipient of the Ford C. Frick Award. In the 2005 book, *Voices of Summer,* Jarrin was named baseball's all-time best Spanish-language broadcaster based on "longevity, continuity, network coverage, kudos, language, popularity, persona, voice knowledge, and miscellany." His son, Jorge Jarrin, broadcasts Dodgers games on Spanish-language television.

Manager Tommy Lasorda is a Special Advisor to the Chairman with the Dodgers. He was forced to retire from managing due to health concerns in 1996, was briefly the Dodgers interim general manager in 1998, and led Team USA to the Gold Medal in the 2000 Olympics. The 2013 season is his 64th consecutive season working for the Dodgers.

Pitcher Tim Leary still lives in Santa Monica. He's worked as the pitching coach at UCLA, Loyola Marymount, and Cal State Northridge. Now he does private pitching lessons, is part of the Dodgers' speakers bureau, and works for Humana as an insurance sales agent.

Right fielder Mike Marshall is the manager of the San Rafael Pacifics, an independent minor league team that competes in the North American Baseball League.

Pitcher Ramon Martinez is the senior advisor of Latin America for the Dodgers.

Pitcher Jesse Orosco is retired and living in San Diego. He follows closely the career of his son, Jesse Jr., a minor league pitcher.

Reggie Otero, the scout who recommended the Dodgers trade Welch to get Alfredo Griffin, went to bed after the 1988 World Series a happy man. He never woke up, dying of natural causes.

Pitcher Alejandro Pena is the pitching coach for the Dodgers' rookie league team in Santo Domingo, Dominican Republic.

Catcher Mike Scioscia retired in 1992 and became a minor league coach in the Dodgers' minor league system. Prior to the 1999 season, then-GM Kevin Malone hired the more experienced Davey Johnson as manager of the Dodgers, instead of Scioscia. Malone now admits that was a mistake. The Angels hired Scioscia as their manager prior to the start of the 2000 season. Scioscia led the Angels to their first World Series title in 2002 and remains their manager. He's the longest-tenured manager in baseball and is signed through the 2018 season.

Second baseman Steve Sax wrote a book in 2011 that included candid reflections on his throwing problems in 1983. He briefly ran for a seat in the California State Assembly 5th district. He was also a partner in the Sax/Hinman Sports Professional Group. He begins the 2013 season as a coach with the Arizona Diamondbacks.

Play-by-play announcer Vin Scully is starting an unprecedented 64th consecutive season as a Dodgers broadcaster. He was honored by the National Baseball Hall of Fame in 1982 as a Ford C. Frick Award winner.

Center fielder John Shelby is a coach for the Milwaukee Brewers. His coaching career began in 1998 with the Dodgers, where he spent eight years as the first-base coach.

First baseman Franklin Stubbs is currently the hitting coach for the Dodgers Triple A affiliate at Albuquerque, New Mexico.

Pitcher Don Sutton was inducted into the National Baseball Hall of Fame in 1998. His broadcasting career began in 1989 with a brief stint doing select

Dodgers games on TV. He's been an analyst for TBS and NBC, for the Washington Nationals in 2008–09, and he returned to the Braves in 2010 as a broadcaster.

Pitcher John Tudor retired after the 1990 season, and he played first base briefly in the Boston-area Intercity League for fun. He worked in the minor leagues as a pitching coach or roving instructor for the Cardinals, Phillies, and Rangers from 1992–96.

Pitcher Fernando Valenzuela pitched two more years with the Dodgers after 1988, including a no-hitter in 1990 when the last batter was Pedro Guerrero. He later played for the Angels, Orioles, Phillies, and Padres and finished his career with the Cardinals in 1997. In a 17-year career, Valenzuela finished with a 173–153 record, 3.54 ERA, and 2,930 innings. He's now an analyst for the Dodgers Spanish-language radio broadcasts.

Infielder Tracy Woodson has been the head baseball coach at Valparaiso University since 2006. He also referees college basketball games in the SEC and Atlanta-10 Conference.

♦ ♦ ♦ ♦

Where is The Streak?

The closest any pitcher has come to breaking Orel Hershiser's 59-inning scoreless streak was Brandon Webb of the Arizona Diamondbacks. Webb pitched 42 consecutive scoreless innings before Prince Fielder ended it with a first-inning RBI single on August 23, 2007.

The oddest threat to Hershiser's record came from Oakland Athletics relief pitcher Brad Zeigler in 2008. Not only did Zeigler pitch 39 consecutive scoreless innings, it was the first 39 innings of his major league career, and they all came in relief. Zeigler tied a 101-year record for most scoreless innings by a reliever.

The "longest" scoreless streak—in terms of months without giving up a run—belongs to Zack Greinke. He put together a 38-inning scoreless streak that began on September 18, 2008. His streak sat at 14 innings through the off-season and ended on May 5, 2009. The streak ended on an unearned run.

Mets pitcher R.A. Dickey pitched 32⅔ scoreless innings from May 22 to June 13 in 2012. That streak also ended on an unearned run. Dickey went another 12 innings before he allowed an earned run. When the unearned run streak ended at 44⅔, Orel Hershiser was in the booth broadcasting the game for ESPN.

◆ ◆ ◆ ◆

Where is The Ball? What happened to the baseball hit by Kirk Gibson on that fateful night in Los Angeles has long been one of the great mysteries in collecting circles.

In October 2010, Gibson auctioned off the jersey, bat, and batting helmet used when he hit the home run in Game 1 of the 1988 World Series. When asked the fate of the home run ball, Gibson didn't know.

"A lady sent me a picture of her leg," Gibson said at the news conference. "It hit her like in the inner thigh, kind of high on her skirt, so to say. She was all black and blue. But I've never, ever seen the ball. I just have the picture of where it landed, which was on a young lady's leg."

Dodgers team historian Mark Langill didn't know who claimed ownership of the ball, so sports business reporter Darren Rovell put out an All-Points Bulletin to find it.

Rovell received 31 emails from people who claimed to have the ball or knew who had the ball. Most of the stories sounded dubious and provided no concrete evidence to support the claim.

The strongest evidence came from a man named Ed Moran. He created a website—http://gatherspot.com/kirkgibson/—with a video that follows the flight of the ball as it clears the fence, rolls on the bleacher seats, and into what he says is the hands of his uncle Carlos. The website shows a photo of Carlos Moran and Jasmine Moran holding a baseball with the World Series logo evident and dated the night of Game 1.

According to Ed Moran, his uncle Carlos was attending his first baseball game when he retrieved the ball. Since he wasn't a baseball fan, Ed Moran gave the baseball to a girlfriend a few years later. At the 20-year anniversary in 2008, Carlos asked the woman about the ball, and she said it was in her garage. The ball has still never surfaced.

Numerous attempts were made to contact multiple members of the Moran family. All were unsuccessful.

In all likelihood, the ball is forever lost.

Sources

Books

Claire, Fred with Steve Springer. *My 30 Years in Dodger Blue*. Champaign, Illinois: Sports Publishing LLC, 2004.

Delsohn, Steve. *True Blue: The Dramatic History of the Los Angeles Dodgers, Told by the Men Who Lived It*. Perennial, 2001.

Gibson, Kirk with Lynn Henning. *Bottom of the Ninth*. Sleeping Bear Press, 1997.

Hershiser, Orel with Jerry B. Jenkins. *Out of the Blue*. Wolgemuth & Hyatt Publishers, 1989.

McNeil, William F. *Miracle in Chavez Ravine*. McFarland & Company, 2009.

Weisman, Jon. *100 Things Dodgers Fans Should Know & Do Before They Die*. Chicago, Illinois: Triumph Books, 2009.

Newspapers/Magazines/Websites

Dodgers.com/mlb.com

Los Angeles Times/latimes.com

New York Daily News/nydailynews.com

New York Times/nytimes.com

Orlando Sentinel/orlandosentinel.com

Philadelphia Daily News/philly.com

Sports Illustrated/sportsillustrated.cnn.com

The Sporting News

Washington Post/washingtonpost.com

Index

B

Babe Ruth League, 50
Backman, Wally, 201, 203, 207, 216, 218-19, 221, 223
Bailor, Bob, 2
Baldwin, Doug, 14
Baltimore, 104
Barber, Red, 188
Barker, Len, 37
Barkley, Iran, 83
Bartley, Boyd, 73
Baseball Chapel, 313
(National) Baseball Hall of Fame, xiii, 231, 308, 313-14
Baseball Tonight, 313
Baseball Winter Meetings, 6
Baseball Writers Association of America, 296
Bash Brothers, 276, 280
Bass, Kevin, 34, 90, 125, 130-31
Bay Bridge World Series, 303
Baylor, Don, xiii, xiv, 228-29, 254-55, 269, 276-77, 291
Bean, Billy, 78
Beane, Billy, 78
Becker, Jocelyn, 263
Beckwith, Joe, 93
Bedell, Howie, 156
Bedrosian, Steve, 128
Behenna, Rick, 37
Belcher, Tim, xiv, 12, 36, 60, 75, 84, 87-89, 104, 118, 139, 141, 168-74, 180, 186, 196-97, 208-9, 212, 215-16, 229-30, 233-36, 261, 272, 277, 281, 297, 303, 311
Bell, Buddy, 125, 130-31
Bell, Juan, 166
Bene, Bill, 78
Benes, Andy, 78
Bengals, 107
Beniquez, Juan, 14
Bentsen, Lloyd, 196
Benzinger, Todd, 303
Berenger, Tom, 105
Big Red Machine, 72
Biggio, Craig, 90
Birtsas, Tim, 8, 44, 81, 173
Black, Bud, 64
Blass, Steve, 67
Blauser, Jeff, 51-53, 91, 94-95
Blocker, Terry, 51-52, 91, 95
Blue Jays, 7-8, 78, 139, 164, 312

Blyleven, Bert, 40
Boggs, Wade, 250, 257, 299
Bonds, Barry, 58, 110, 116
Bonilla, Bobby, 58, 116
Bonin, Greg, 119-20
Boros, Steve, 144, 257
Bosley, Thad, 256
Boston, 101, 228, 257, 308
Boston Garden, 6
Boston-area Intercity League, 315
Boswell, Thomas, 148
Bowa, Larry, 41-42, 184, 266
Bowling Green State University, 50
Bradley, Mark, 93
Bradley, Tom, 285
Braun, Ryan, 262
Braves, 5, 37, 41, 51, 78, 86-87, 91, 94, 96, 127, 307, 309, 315
Breeden, Louis, 107
Brenly, Bob, 136
Brennan, William, 113, 139
Brett, George, 250, 257
Brewers, 11-12, 44, 63, 65, 78, 304, 314
Bristol, xx
British, 299
Brito, Mike, 3
Brock, Greg, 4, 11, 45, 63-64, 106-7
Bronx, 10, 49
Brookens, Tom, 14
Brooks, Hubie, 126, 250
Brown, Chris, 80
Browning, Tom, 34, 129, 169-71, 174
Buck, Jack, 252, 259, 281
Buckner, Bill, 254
Buffalo, New York, 49
Buhler, Bill, 141, 267, 274
Bumbry, Al, 100
Burns, Todd, 173
Burrell, Louis, 10
Bush, George, 59, 191, 196
Butler, Brett, xiv, 36-37, 101, 117, 119, 136, 153-55, 161, 312

C

Cadaret, Greg, 239, 275, 280
Cal State Los Angeles, 78
Cal State Northridge, 313
California, xvii, 10, 13, 31, 33, 43-44, 156, 171, 183, 227, 229, 256, 263, 276, 300, 311-12
California State Assembly, 314

Q

Quale, Otto, 214
Quayle, Dan, 196
Queens, 50
Quick, Jim, 39, 170
Quick, Mike, 107
Quinton, 300, 302-3

R

Raiders, 1, 77, 86, 265-66
Raines, Tim, 15, 45, 152
Ramirez, Rafael, 97, 121, 130, 166
Rams, 313
Ramsey, Mike, 2, 36, 100
Rangers, 2, 63, 93, 311, 313, 315
Rarmirez, Rafael, 125
Rasmussen, Dennis, 80-81
Rawitch, Josh, xv
Rawley, Shane, 69
Ready, Randy, 175, 179, 182, 184, 187
Reagan, Ronald, 296, 299
Reardon, Jeff, 128
Red Sox, xviii, 3, 144, 200, 227, 230, 243, 254, 263, 271, 273, 308
Reds, 312
Reed, Jeff, 71, 73
Rehnquist, Chief Justice William, 299
Reuschel, Rick, 34, 128
Reuss, Jerry, 79-80, 93, 126
Reyes, Gilberto, 284-85
Reynolds, Craig, 86
Reynolds, R.J., 110
Rickey, Branch, 2
Righetti, Dave, 16
Rijo, Jose, 8, 34, 44, 81, 173
Riles, Ernest, 118-19, 153, 155, 157-59
Ripken, Cal Jr., 115-16
Rivera, Luis, 148
Riverfront Stadium, 71, 169
Roberto Clemente Sports City, 30
Roberts, Thomas, 13-15
Robinson, Bill, 202
Robinson, Brooks, 19
Robinson, Don, 34, 118
Rose Bowl, 311
Rose, Pete, 34, 61, 73-74, 76, 80-83, 88, 135, 215, 297
Rosen, Al, 34, 120
Rotary Club, 4
Rovell, Darren, 316

Royals, 34, 63-64, 265, 304
Rozema, Dave, 24
Runge, Paul, 51-53, 138, 160
Russell, Bill, 4, 22, 165, 277
Ryan, Nolan, 34, 84-85, 90, 125, 129-30, 171

S

Sabo, Chris, 34, 71, 73, 82, 168, 170, 297
Salem, 50
San Antonio, Texas, 66, 92, 136, 302, 313
San Diego, California, 10, 14, 41, 106, 169, 175, 179, 183, 185, 189, 205, 266, 314
San Francisco, California, 1, 9, 43-45, 68, 116-20, 135, 153-54, 160, 228, 273, 277, 285, 312
Santa Monica, California, 64-65, 238, 303, 313
Santa Rosa, California, xx, 263
Santa Rosa Press Democrat, xx
Santana, Rafael, 8
Santiago, Benito, 179, 182-84, 187
Santo Domingo, 17, 314
Santovenia, Nelson, 149
Sasser, Mackey, 67, 210
Savage, Jack, 6-9
Sax Hinman Sports Professional Group, 314
Schroder, Ellen, 25
Schryver, Steve, 204
Scioscia, Mike, xiv, 30, 35, 40-41, 47, 51, 54, 57, 61, 66, 82, 85, 87, 91, 103, 105, 117, 125, 131, 136, 142, 148, 174, 179, 184-87, 192, 194, 201, 207-8, 213, 222, 224, 238-39, 244, 249, 263, 267, 274-75, 277, 279, 284-85, 291, 314
Scott, Mike, 34, 65, 84, 166-67, 203, 270, 306
Scully, Vin, x, xiv, 131, 156, 163, 181-82, 184, 187-88, 231-32, 236-37, 240, 243-51, 263, 270, 273, 275-76, 283, 285, 290, 296, 310, 314
Searcy, Steve, 140
Seattle, Washington, 173, 256
SEC, 315
Sharperson, Mike, 18, 27, 89, 201, 239
Shea Stadium, 102, 200, 203, 206, 210, 212, 217
Sheen, Charlie, 104
Shelby, John, xiv, 16, 19, 35, 37, 40, 51, 53, 71, 85, 88-89, 91, 99-105, 110, 125, 130, 138, 142, 145, 148, 153, 166, 170, 175, 179, 183, 185, 194, 201, 206-7, 213, 215, 219, 222-23, 234, 236, 239, 242, 249, 261, 268, 275, 277-79, 287, 290, 314
Shipley, Craig, 18
Silver Slugger, 73, 296